2/9

Animal thought

8⁰⁰

International Library of Psychology

General editor: Max Coltheart
Professor of Psychology, University of London

Animal thought

Stephen Walker
Department of Psychology,
Birkbeck College, University of London

Routledge & Kegan Paul
London, Boston, Melbourne and Henley

First published in 1983
First published as a paperback in 1985
by Routledge & Kegan Paul plc
14 Leicester Square, London WC2H 7PH
9 Park Street, Boston, Mass. 02108, USA,
464 St Kilda Road, Melbourne,
Victoria 3004, Australia and
Broadway House, Newtown Road,
Henley-on-Thames, Oxon RG9 1EN
Set in Baskerville by
Thomson Press (India) Ltd, New Delhi
and printed in Great Britain by
Unwin Brothers Ltd
Old Woking, Surrey
© Stephen Walker 1983

Library of Congress Cataloging in Publication Data

Walker, Stephen F.
Animal thought.
(International library of psychology)
Bibliography: p.
Includes index.
1. Animal intelligence. I. Title.
II. Series. [DNLM: 1. Animals, 2. Psychology,
Comparative.   QL 785 W184a]
QL785.W144   156   825210

ISBN 0-7100-9037-4(c)   AACR2
ISBN 0-7102-0707-7(p)

For my parents

Contents

Figures

Preface

My argument in this book is as follows: human thought is intimately connected with the activities of the human brain; other vertebrate animals apart from ourselves have very complicated brains, and in some cases brains which appear to be physically very much like our own; this suggests that what goes on in animal brains has a good deal in common with what goes on in human brains; and laboratory experiments on animal behaviour provide some measure of support for this suggestion. In presenting this argument I deal with philosophical opinion about animal psychology, anatomical and physiological studies of the brain, evolutionary theory and the natural life of vertebrate species, and experimental tests of the psychological capacities of animals. I am very much aware that I have given an incomplete account of all these specialised areas, but I have tried to include enough material to give the intelligent layman, or the intelligent undergraduate, a general impression of what kinds of information are available. Some gaps now seem particularly glaring: I have deliberately avoided the question of how theories of animal psychology might impinge on opinions about our moral responsibilities towards animals, but in evolutionary biology and brain physiology many new findings and hypotheses have simply been missed out.

I conclude that it makes sense to suppose that awareness and mental organisation occur in animals, without the involvement of language, but I do not deny that human speech and writing constitute an exceptional influence on mental activity. In the following pages I have attempted to minimise the use of technical terms, in the hope that there may be some underlying ideas which are more accessible without them.

Acknowledgments

I am grateful to W. H. Freeman and Company for permission to reproduce the drawing in Figure 4, and to Professor Harry J. Jerison and Academic Press for permission to reproduce the graph in Figure 2. My thanks are due to Max Coltheart both for his encouragement and for his detailed reading of the manuscript, and to Valerie Hogg and Carol Machen for their typing, although all errors and omissions are of course my own. Lastly, my special thanks go to Lynne Walker.

1   Descartes's dichotomy

'*Animal thought*' could be an extremely short book. I could define thought as something which never occurs in animals, and spare myself and the reader any further efforts. There are certainly precedents for this—the weight of opinion is that animals don't think, but people do. In this century, few psychologists have been disposed to argue the point: in fact, the main psychological movement which has concerned itself with animals, behaviourism, can be said to be founded on the proposition that neither animals, nor people, think.

The last ten or fifteen years have seen a turning away from the restrictions of behaviourism and a freer attitude to the study of mental life even within the bastions of academic respectability. It is appropriate therefore to exhume certain long-buried problems in the field of animal psychology, and to address new questions which have arisen from the application of modern behavioural and biological techniques.

That there are problems, both old and new, can be seen by examining a little more closely the assumption that thought is a uniquely human activity. There is such a long list of human attributes—speech and writing, art and science, savagery and civilisation—that it would seem at first sight sensible to conclude that every aspect of human mentality is unique. There is something to be said in favour of this conclusion, but difficulties appear when the characteristics of human knowledge are analysed into component parts. Thought can be defined as any form of mental activity, but the study of thought must always begin by the separating out of different kinds or modes of mental experience. Traditional categories include perception, memory, feeling, reasoning, awareness, reflection, foresight and intuition. Are all these things equally excluded to animals?

This is where subtle differences of opinion begin to blur the initial unanimity of view. Are all animals to be denied all of the various faculties of the human mind, or may we allow that certain of the most favoured members of the bestiary have feeling, but not reason, perception but not memory, or intuition with no reflection? There is at least room for argument. Before examining some of the arguments, it is worth pointing out that the questions are put in a form which asks about some, rather than all, members of the animal kingdom. The possibility of differences between animal species, aside from differences between animals generally and man particularly, will have to be taken seriously in later chapters. Strictly speaking, all forms of life not considered plants or fungi may count as animals, from single-celled organisms to primates. But clearly some species, such as the chimpanzee, are very much more like ourselves than others, such as tapeworms, and for that reason questions about human-like thought in chimpanzees are more important than similar questions about the tapeworm. I shall follow a technically improper, but common, usage, of usually meaning vertebrates, from fish to man, when I say animal, and in many cases the interest will mainly be in mammals.

I intend in this chapter to canvass the views of philosophers on the nature and extent of thought in animals. The limits of human knowledge, and in particular its relationship to perception via the senses, and to intuition, reason and language, are topics that philosophers have opinions about. The ways in which human thought and knowledge depend on the human brain—the mind-body problem—is, like the other matters, the subject of highly technical philosophical considerations. However, I shall attempt to use the mind-body problem as an avenue by which the area of animal thought can be approached. Briefly, there is a considerable body of work which attempts to show that the human mind can be conceived of entirely in terms of states of the human brain. Since there is a large amount of scientific evidence available concerning the similarity of human and animal brain function, tying human thought to brain function automatically implies a continuity between human and animal thought.

Any survey of views on the status of the animal mind should, however, begin with Descartes (1595–1650), who denied its existence. Descartes is considered to be the father of modern philosophy, since he believed that the application of a scientific method could supply new and better answers to all questions about the physical nature of the universe. He is in many ways a paradoxical figure, a reductionist who wished to discuss geometry in terms of numbers, and physiology in terms of geometry, but yet a supporter of theological orthodoxy. Whether his religious orthodoxy was a product of conviction or convenience is uncertain, but it was strong enough to make him suppress the publication of his major work *Le Monde* when he heard of Galileo's run in with the Vatican in 1633. Only fragments of *Le Monde* were ever published (after his death) and possibly in this or other unpublished work Descartes experimented with out-and-out materialism, doing away with souls in either animals or men. It is certain that he shared Galileo's heretical views about the rotation of the earth, and the infinity of the universe, and there are points where his analysis of human physiology begins to make the soul seem superfluous. But his positive and published statements about the separation of the soul from the body are clear enough. In a craven and slavish dedication of his *Meditations* to 'the very sage and illustrious Dean and Doctors of the Sacred Faculty of Theology in Paris', Descartes avows the goal of his work to be to convince infidels and atheists of the reality of God. In the *Discourse on Method*, for which he is largely remembered as a philosopher, he says that, as theological errors go, 'there is none more powerful in leading feeble minds astray from the straight path of virtue than the supposition that the soul of brutes is of the same nature with our own.' (Feeble-minded readers, beware!)

The dangers of the assumption that animals have souls like our own are not now particularly obvious. At the time the worry was apparently that the hopes and fears about life after death, which were held responsible for keeping feeble minds to the straight and narrow during their earthly sojourn, would somehow be diminished by the proposition that flies and ants would also be present on the Day of Judgment. But as aids to conscience other religions have made use of a supposed interchangeability of souls by threatening miscreants with a future life as a fly or an ant. An alternative tactic would be to allow animals inferior and temporary souls, which did not survive after death, or to allow animals immortal souls, but diminished moral responsibilities. St Thomas Aquinas, for instance, was considerably more charitable towards animals in terms of their mental capacities and possible after-life than Descartes (see Aquinas's *Philosophical Texts*, 1951).

Because Aquinas accepted both an Aristotelian scale of being, and the Platonic version of souls which can be present even in vegetables and inanimate objects, his estimation of animal intelligence matches or exceeds that of the most anthropomorphic post-Darwinians. In Aquinas's view there is a fairly continuous grading of souls between plants and God, with animals distinguished from plants by having sensitive souls—animals perceive external objects through their senses, and this data is held in the imagination before entering the deeper store of memory. The sensitive powers of animals are 'conscious within themselves' and consequently 'what begins from without is worked up from within'—a very sophisticated kind of information processing. Men are superior to animals in having intellective souls which can reason, deliberate, and reflect on themselves. However, animals, especially the higher ones, retain and preserve their perceptions, exhibit anticipatory actions, can adapt means to ends, and can perceive purposes not immediately apparent to the external senses. As far as the purely sensitive or perceiving soul goes:

> Man's superiority to beasts in animal shrewdness and memory does not result from anything proper to the sensitive part, but from an affinity and closeness to intelligence which, so to speak, flows into them. These powers in man are not so very different from those in animals, only they are heightened. (Aquinas, 1951, p. 230)

Because the role assigned to the animal soul in sensing and feeling is very much the same as that for the human soul performing similar functions, Aquinas is able to speak of the souls of horses and the souls of men in the same breath, and to entertain the idea that the souls of animals are immortal. He thinks that this would be improbable, but notes that it would not conflict with Plato (see 1951, p. 199 and also pp. 182, 195, 198, 201, 203, 228–30, and 256).

Although Aquinas wrote in the thirteenth century, he was the major theological authority of the fifteenth, and one to whom Descartes might have appealed—Aquinas having been a member of the Faculty of Theology which Descartes tried to placate. Descartes was not being particularly conventional in denying the existence of an animal soul; on the contrary, the mechanistic interpretation of animal behaviour could be seen as a suspicious change in the tradition of having souls with everything—and this may explain Descartes's protestations of virtue and orthodoxy in the case of man. Descartes was not original in being a dualist, but innovative in abandoning dualism for animals other than man.

Descartes's dualism

When Descartes moved from Paris to Holland, where he was to live for twenty years, he took with him very few books, but among them were the works of Aquinas. His own theories stripped away most of Aquinas's dualism, substituting systematic materialism and determinism. All life with the exception of the human soul became, in Descartes's hands, reducible to the laws of physics. In his view, animals are unthinking machines, or automata, lacking conscious perception of even the immediate world about them. There is thus a fixed and unbridgeable dichotomy, with animals, as machines, on the one side, and men, possessing rational souls, on the other.

There are three parts to Descartes's argument that animals are automata. The first is the argument by analogy with the clockwork models popular at the time. The most long-lived example of these toys is the cage of mechanical canaries. If such things can be fabricated by human industry, says Descartes in the *Discourse on Method*, how much better might be machines put together by the hand of God? The second theme, by which more substance is added to this analogy, is the detailed description of mammalian sensory physiology and anatomy—the divine biological machinery. Descartes was most concerned with the sense of vision (dioptrics), but he was also a fervent admirer of Harvey's experiments which demonstrated the circulatory function of the heart, and gives a comprehensive account of emotion and perception of the sort one would nowadays find in a textbook of physiological psychology (see *Principles of Philosophy* (1978a), part IV, and *Passions of the Soul* (1952)). Although his physiology was rather primitive by modern standards, if one interprets 'movements' passing through nerves as their electrical activity, and 'animal spirits' as brain chemicals, some of what Descartes said would not be out of place in an up-to-date text. His own experiments included the dissection of an ox's eye with observation of the inverted visual image formed on the retina. His discussion of why the inversion of the image does not matter, because features of the information contained in the image, not pictures themselves, are transmitted down the optic nerve, is fascinating, and the account of the roles of binocular disparity and eye

movements in the perception of distance, and the automatic adjustments of pupil size and focal length in the eyeball, are hard to fault.
There may have been much that Descartes did not know about the
neurophysiology of the visual system, but his description of how the
perceived qualities of brightness and colour (the only qualities peculiar
to sight) and position, distance, size and shape are 'determined by the
strength of disturbance' at the eventual termination of the 'optic nerve
fibres in the brain' is remarkably consistent with recent theories, as is
also his discussion of the after-images and visual persistence experienced when we close our eyes after looking at bright objects.

Ironically, the strength of Descartes's theories was largely due to his
general idea that perception and feeling should be interpreted in terms
of a one-to-one correspondence with neural states of the brain. In his
view, of course, there was a further one-to-one correspondence
between states of the brain and experiences of the soul, but the rigour
with which he developed the first correspondence was original and
exceptional (especially bearing in mind the naivity of some of his
contemporaries, such as the English philosopher Hobbes, who still
believed emotions were experienced in the heart). Descartes analysed
taste, smell and hearing, as well as vision, in terms of the motions
existing in the relevant sensory nerves, but the general flavour of his
theory is given here:

> We must know, therefore, that although the human soul is
> united to the whole body, it has, nevertheless, its principle seat
> in the brain, where alone it not only understands and imagines,
> but also perceives; and this by the medium of the nerves, which
> are extended like threads from the brain to all the other
> members, with which they are so connected that we can hardly
> touch one of them without moving the extremities of some of the
> nerves spread over it; and this motion passes to the other
> extremities of those nerves which are collected in the brain . . . .
> the movements which are thus exited in the brain by the nerves,
> variously affect the soul or mind, which is intimately conjoined
> with the brain. (*Principles*, 1978a, part IV, §II, pp. 214–15)

The arguments with which Descartes supported his thesis that
perception and feeling take place in the brain, and are to some extent
isolated from other parts of the body, and from external objects, are
instructive, and some of them have been repeated ever since. The most

familiar to readers of present-day psychological texts is probably the argument from the 'phantom-limb' phenomenon. In the *Principles*, Descartes quotes the case of a girl with an ulcerated hand, who had her eyes covered whenever the surgeon changed the dressings as she could not bear the sight of the sores. Amputation at the elbow became necessary, and in Descartes's story linen cloths were substituted to give the impression of a remaining forearm. After the operation the girl continued to complain of pain in the now absent hand—sometimes in one finger and sometimes in another. Descartes gives the now standard explanation that neural messages reaching the brain mimicked those which occurred with the limb intact. Retained subjective feeling 'in' the removed limb is a common phenomenon after amputations, even without subterfuges to disguise the limb's absence, and the fact is still used to support physiological theories of sensation (e.g. Hebb, 1966). Similarly, 'seeing stars' after a blow on the head, or after relatively minor distortions of the eyeball, suggested to Descartes that it is activity in the optic nerve which gives rise to the subjective sensation of light. But the sensory nerves for the various modalities look sufficiently similar to one another to imply that they all convey information to the brain in the same form. Therefore we should assume that nothing at all reaches the brain besides 'the local motion of the nerves themselves' (*Principles*, 1978a, part IV, §XI).

The observations on nerves, and on the structure of the eye, applied to animals; but by working out in such detail the way in which sensory and nervous apparatus functioned, Descartes was painting himself into a corner, with his soul uneasily surrounded by mechanisms. Others, such as La Mettrie (1709–51), completed the job, and became pure mechanists or materialists, supposing that the conscious perceptions of both animals and men can be explained by a sufficiently detailed account of brain functioning. What were Descartes's grounds for resisting this extension of his own physical determinism? Apart from extraneous theological motives, there was an aspect of Descartes's systematic method which approached the problem of sensation from another direction—the method of doubt concerning all subjective knowledge.

Descartes is remembered not so much for his neurophysiology as for his proposition that while one can doubt the existence of sensory mechanisms, or the existence of the body itself, one cannot doubt the subjective experience of perception, or if one does, one cannot then doubt the subjective experience of doubting. Because of this, 'I think, therefore I am' is given a higher value than studies of mechanism, and the soul is assigned the role of doing the thinking, doubting and feeling. It is important to emphasise that Descartes takes thinking in this context to be *anything* we are subjectively conscious of, including sense-impressions and emotions—he does not draw the distinction between reasoning and perceiving that others do, and this eventually determines the reduced status of animals in his system (see Descartes, 1970, translator's note, and 'By the word thought, I understand all that which so takes place in us that we of ourselves are immediately conscious of it'; *Principles*, 1978a, part I, §IX). In other words, 'cogito, ergo sum' is in the first place an existential appeal to the primacy of all subjective consciousness.

Since Descartes makes it abundantly clear that, in man, subjective consciousness is very intimately connected with brain mechanisms, why is it not so that animals, in so far as they have similar brain mechanisms, have similar subjective consciousness? This remains a problem. Undoubtedly a motive for denying animals any subjective consciousness arose because, in stressing the unity of conscious experience, Descartes had conflated Aquinas's sensitive and intellective souls, and was thus faced with giving animals all or nothing. The main argument for giving them nothing, rather than all, repeats the grounds for denying animals intellective faculties, which, since these have become closely bound up with perceptual and emotional awareness, means than when animals fail the intellectual tests, they lose the limited but appreciable spiritual status that Aquinas had been prepared to allow them.

These tests supply the third part of Descartes's proof that animals are automata: they are means by which men with souls can be distinguished from animals or cunningly constructed mechanical devices. The difference between a man and an ape is that a machine constructed to look and act exactly like an ape would be indistinguishable from the real thing but, if a similar machine were made to mimic a man 'as far as is morally possible', then we should be able to apply two tests to this robot, which it would fail (*Discourse*, 1978a, pp. 44–7).

The first test is creative language. It is supposed that the robot might be able to cry out that it is hurt, or ask what the next question is, 'and such like', when appropriate buttons are pushed. But it could never, according to Descartes, be made to speak well enough 'so as appositely to reply to what is said in its presence, as men of the lowest grade of intellect can do'. This was an argument developed by Turing, the English mathematician whose ideas did much to foster interest in computers, but Turing was not so sure that a robot, or a computer, would necessarily fail the test. Already there are computers which can recognise simple spoken instructions, and there are computer programs which can play the part of a psychotherapist in interchanges with real patients (Holden, 1977), so the inability of machines to conduct low-grade conversations is no longer such a strong point.

By the conversation test 'we may likewise know the difference' between men and brutes. Since animals refuse to converse with us at all, even though parrots and magpies are quite capable of producing the requisite sounds, and even though human idiots, and the deaf and dumb, can make their thoughts understood: 'this proves not only that the brutes have less reason than man, but that they have none at all' (*Discourse*, 1978a, p. 45). This argument has had a considerable influence on research in linguistics and comparative psychology over the last twenty years. Chomsky tends to appeal to Descartes as an authority to support the view that something very profound is lacking in animals, while much effort has been spent on trying to show that Descartes was empirically wrong, by persuading chimpanzees to 'make their thoughts understood'. The whole question of the communication of ideas by animals will need to be addressed in a later chapter. But we may note here that, accepting for the time being the empirical correctness of Descartes's supposition that animals will not converse with us, it is still a rather unjustly stringent test on which to base the conclusion that animals have no reason *at all*, unless we define reason in terms of human language: some capacity for inference and problem-solving might be allowed for in the complete absence of communicative expression.

More strongly, it is obvious that as it stands, the conversation test is unsuitable for eliminating perception and feeling in animals, except in forms that are intimately concerned with language. Descartes is extremely unusual, though not alone, in lumping together understanding, willing, imagining, perceiving and feeling, as all equally restricted to the human mind. He goes so far as to say that 'I walk, therefore I am', or 'I see, therefore I am', are equivalent to 'I think, therefore I am' (*Principles*, 1978a §§I, IX). 'Consciousness of seeing or walking' is 'referred to the mind, which alone perceives or is conscious that it sees or walks'. As walking or seeing are made just as special as thinking in their relationship to the mind, this means that if it appears that animals do not think as we do, one has to conclude that their seeing and walking are just as different from our own, despite other evidence to the contrary. According to Descartes, the difference is of course that animals are purely and only automata, lacking not only reason and choice but any form of conscious sensitivity; man shares with animals the biological machinery necessary for perceiving and acting, but conscious perception and action, as well as speech and rational choice, only become possible because the machinery interacts with, and is directed by, the human soul.

What of Descartes's second test? This is somewhat more obscure, and seems rather more applicable to the question of the limits of man-made machines than to the investigation of the capabilities of animals. It is that 'although such machines might execute many things with equal or perhaps greater perfection than any of us, they would, without doubt, fail in certain others from which it could be discovered that they did not act from knowledge': they could act only for specific purposes, in accordance with the prior organisation of the constituent bits of their working parts; we on the other hand can use reason in a creative fashion, to apply to every possible set of circumstances. Our reason is flexible, inventive and universal, whereas machines can only accomplish tasks they have been built to perform. This seems to be a clear foreshadowing of Lady Lovelace's objection to her friend Charles Babbage's nineteenth century brass calculating machines. No matter how elaborate the brass gears and differentials, such apparatus can only ever do what it is designed to do in the first place. This certainly applies to the typical way in which we tend to use electronic computers—they can be very fast at calculating bank balances, but are not programmed to show the same degree of judgment and initiative in response to overdrafts as we would hope for from our bank manager. Whether it is theoretically impossible ever to build electronic devices which are capable of matching human judgment and initiative is another matter—there are many who think so, for reasons similar to Descartes's, but others, working in the field known as 'artificial intelligence', believe that, given sufficient time and money, it could be done. Pocket-sized computers are now available that can play chess at a typical, if not outstanding, human level, accompanied by a rudimentary attempt at conversation about the game, but these are grist to the mill of Descartes's second test, since they have particular internal arrangements to control particular actions. In the face of modern electronic technology, though, it is less obvious that it is impossible for physical devices to achieve human flexibility than it was in the seventeenth century.

However, the question of consciousness and thought in machines is still rather different from the same question applied to animals, at least in this, that we know how the machinery works in physical devices, and we know that it is different from our own machinery, while although we know less about the biological machinery contained in human and animal nervous systems, its method of operation, in terms of neural transmission, brain chemistry and so on, is sufficiently similar in man and animals to make it difficult to draw a clear line between man and animals on the grounds of internal physical design.

But Descartes did draw the line, and might claim today that animals can be considered as having the same moral and intellectual status, more or less, as a collection of microchips, while the human species is distinguished by the privileged intercommunication of its internal computing processes with conscious and rational souls. If there are those to whom such a dichotomy would now seem ridiculous, it may be pointed out that Sherrington, a pioneer in the modern study of neural mechanisms, put forward a view like this in the 1930s, and Eccles, an equally eminent neurophysiologist, has maintained a pure Cartesian dualism of this kind, most recently in a version developed with the collaboration of the philosopher Karl Popper (Eccles, 1965; Popper and Eccles, 1977; Sherrington, 1940). On the other hand, those to whom Descartes's theory seems in accord with their own intuitions and convictions should be aware of the numerous logical difficulties, inconsistencies and incongruities which have plagued Cartesian dualism since its inception. I am most concerned here with the dichotomy between man and animals, but problems on either side of the line—is it correct to consign animals to the oblivion of the mechanical? is it possible to interpret man as a conjunction of the mechanical and the ethereal?—both have a bearing on the plausibility of the dichotomy, even though most attention is naturally given to the human condition.

The main objection expressly put to Descartes concerning his treatment of the animal world was in fact emotional, rather than logical. Henry More, a Cambridge don, wrote to Descartes:

But there is nothing in your opinions that so much disgusts me, so far as I have any kindness or gentleness, as the internecine and murderous view which you bring forward in the *Method*,

which snatches away life and sensibility from all the animals.
(Williams, 1978, p. 282)

Bernard Williams (1978) comments that this seems to give vent to a
particularly English spirit of outrage—whatever it is about English
culture that produces a concern for animal welfare, it was clearly
evident in the seventeenth century. (And no doubt before: in Thomas
More's *Utopia* written a century earlier, only bondmen were allowed to
kill the animals kept for food.)

Technical difficulties of logic were put to Descartes by the English
philosopher Hobbes, who as a Royalist extremist and suspected atheist
fled to Paris in 1640 at the beginning of the Long Parliament, just
when Descartes was preparing the *Meditations*. Hobbes saw these
before they were published, and Descartes printed his objections to
them, along with his own replies. Hobbes's comments were biting, if
good-humoured. Descartes rested a good deal of his subjectivism on
the difficulty of knowing whether one is awake or dreaming—if waking
life is just another dream, this is a ground for doubting everything but
our own awareness. Says Hobbes: 'it is a common observation how
hard it is to tell waking life from dreams. So I am sorry that so excellent
an author of new speculations should publish this old stuff'. Replies
Descartes: 'such doubts seem to me to be quite indispensable, and I did
not use them to hawk them about as novelties' (Descartes, 1970,
p. 127). This is an introductory knockabout; Hobbes's Second
Objection points out what has become a hardy perennial (Ryle, 1949;
Williams, 1978)—there ought to be a distinction between an experience itself and the existence of the experiencer. Hobbes does not
agree that 'I think, therefore I am' implies the existence of a soul:

> It seems not to be a valid argument to say 'I am conscious,
> therefore I am consciousness', or 'I am intelligent, therefore I
> am an intellect'. For I might as well say 'I am walking,
> therefore I am a walk'. (Descartes, 1970, p. 128)

This is the first, though not the last, indication that resting a
philosophical system on immediate subjective awareness may not be as
conclusive as it appeared to Descartes. Hobbes puts forward as an
alternative to the necessity for a reasoning soul a materialist account of

verbal inference. He proposes that we learn the names of things, and then learn to combine the names according to certain conventions:

> If so, reasoning will depend on names, names on imagination, and imagination perhaps (and this is my opinion) on the motions of the bodily organs; and thus the mind is nothing but motions in certain parts of an organic body. (Descartes, 1970, p. 133)

This is a useful example of a 'nothing but' concept of mind which does without anything immaterial. The superiority of the human over the animal mind would for Hobbes depend not on non-corporeal essences, but on the development of names, conventions for using them and also on covenants allowing for social institutions. Without these artificial conventions and covenants, human life would be literally brutish, as well as nasty and short (Watkins, 1973).

It is ironic that Descartes, the dualist, had such a clear idea of the importance of the brain, whereas Hobbes spoke of motions in the bodily organs generally. However, Descartes's attempt to pin down the crucial organ of consciousness is hardly any better than leaving reason to the heart or liver. He did not, in the first instance, describe in any detail the interaction of the soul with the body, beyond saying that one's soul is united to the body as a whole, but has its principal seat in the brain (*Principles*, 1978a). He was led to make various elaborations primarily by the intervention of the young Princess Elizabeth of Palatine. Although she was not the only reader to be dissatisfied by the *Principles*, Descartes had dedicated the book to her, and in the dedication rather touchingly congratulated her on her intellectual powers, which were evident to him, he says, partly because she had understood his previous work better than anybody else. She had been his pupil, and their relationship was apparently one of affection as well as mutual scientific interest. There seems little doubt that Descartes took her criticisms seriously—*Passions of the Soul*, which was to be his final work, was written partly in response to them. Although Elizabeth wished her letters to Descartes to be destroyed, and it was not until 200 years later that some of them turned up, those which survive suggest that she was a worthy adversary. She was the aunt of George I, but also a Stuart, her cousin, Charles II, being founder of the Royal Society. (It may be the case that royal females held a special fascination for

Descartes, or vice versa. At the height of his success, he took up an appointment as tutor to Queen Christiana of Sweden. For someone who had done his best thinking while sitting in a large oven, this was unwise, and a chill attributed to early morning discussions with the Queen in the middle of winter proved fatal.)

Elizabeth of Palatine's criticisms were succinctly put, go directly to the heart of Descartes's system, and may be applied to any subsequent version of dualism. If an immaterial and purely mental structure is assumed (a) to receive information from the physical body, and (b) in turn, to react back and control the sequence of physical events in the body, the interface between the mental and the material presents a number of problems. First, how can real matter (whether atoms and molecules, or animal spirits) be pushed and pulled about by something which is by definition not part of the physical world? Second, how does the immaterial mind gain information from the physical world, while remaining separate from it? Third, if one can allow that the mind may extract useful messages from the body, why is it also necessary for mental states to be enslaved by all sorts of bodily conditions?

Elizabeth, and generally other critics as well, were ready to accept that an immaterial mind could observe the material world, and choose to be influenced by it. But she felt that there were contradictions in the idea that the soul, with no extension in space, and no physical properties or dimensions, could instruct the body in voluntary actions. Descartes's first attempt at an answer was to say that the soul moves the body in the same way that gravity moves lifeless objects. Today he might still refer to gravity, or to electromagnetic fields: theoretical physicists are notoriously seducible by the psychic and the paranormal. Elizabeth, however, pointed out that gravity was surely part of the physical world, that Descartes had said in discussions of physics that it was an aspect of matter, and that gravity could hardly have the same relation to God as a soul, and that the idea of gravity as something that carried objects to the centre of the earth might in any case be theoretically unsound. Descartes had to write back that gravity was rather a lame simile, and that perhaps the best idea was to think that the soul *did* have matter and extension, since this is more or less what he had meant by his repeated assertion that a soul is united to its body, in order to be able to act and suffer along with it (Descartes, 1970, pp. 274–82).

The principle of intimate conjunction between soul and body must also be applied to the third problem, the unseemly dependence of the soul on bodily conditions. If the soul possesses all 'the power and the habit of correct reasoning', why are these powers so disturbed by an attack of the vapours, asked Princess Elizabeth. Why is the soul 'so much governed by the body, when it can subsist separately, and has nothing in common with it'? Descartes's answer is that the soul must pay a high price for being so entangled with the body as it is. Although it is present and conscious in the foetus, it cannot do much reasoning there because of the novelty of its new sensations, and in adulthood, the intermingling of mind and matter means that brain fatigue, sickness or bodily distractions may interfere with mental functions, and consciousness is of course suspended while the brain sleeps.

This is still rather vague, and Descartes prided himself on not leaving anything out of his system. In *Passions of the Soul* we are given a more detailed, though also, it must be said, a more confused and contradictory, account of the relations between body and mind. Again it is central that though the body does many things, it does not think (*Passions*, 1952, Article 4). It is still stated that 'the soul is united to all parts of the body conjointly' (Article 30), until it withdraws itself from the body in its entirety, as a consequence of the body's cooling after death (Article 5). However, most of the mind's business is conducted through a small part of the brain—the pineal gland. This was an unfortunate choice in terms of later anatomical plausibility, since it is hard to think of a structure in the central nervous system which is now thought to have less connection with human reason than this gland. In terms of size, it seems to have had most importance in certain extinct reptiles, and in general the pineal gland is thought to have the function of modulating hormonal secretions in accordance with light cycles. In man it is exceedingly small but, according to Descartes, especially mobile. His main reason for choosing it was the fact that it is positioned in the centre of the brain, and is not duplicated (Article 32).

The way in which Descartes thought that the pineal gland worked went like this. First, it was the point at which the soul received sensations. For instance, visual images from the two eyes travel down the optic nerves, and eventually fuse at the same place on the pineal, and this causes the soul to see a single image (the strictures against little pictures in the brain seem to have been suspended). Next, the pineal gland initiates voluntary action. While Descartes supposed that sensory nerves transmitted information to the brain as if they were strings being pulled, he thought that motor nerves worked by a sort of pneumatic pushing, with liquids or gases (the 'animal spirits') travelling down, through the motor nerves, from the ventricles of the brain to muscles; the idea being that when we wish to make a particular movement, the wish in the mind causes the pineal gland to pump animal spirits to the appropiate muscles (Article 7). When we wish to remember something the gland is caused to bend, 'now to one side and now to another', impelling animal spirits towards this and that region of the brain, until they come upon pores of the brain that have been expanded by use in a way that matches the particular movements of the animal spirits. When this has happened, a special movement is exited, back at the gland, which enables the soul to 'know what it wished to remember' (Article 42). This takes care of memory, but with memories stored in the body. Attention is explained somewhat more simply since 'when we wish to hold our attention fixed for some little time on some object, this volition keeps the gland bent in this direction' (Article 43). Conflict between body and mind takes place when the soul tries to move the gland to one side, but the animal spirits push it in the opposite direction (Article 47). Language learning occurs as the soul learns habits which allow the meanings of words to be put into a code of pineal gland movements that produce appropriate activities in the tongue and lips (Article 44).

With the hindsight of more recent knowledge of brain function, this may appear to be an extremely strange and fantastic theory. However, we should try to ignore the physiological details. Would the theory be improved by saying that, instead of the pineal gland, a network of cells in the cerebral cortex of the human brain, which all now agree is very much concerned with cognition and language, serves as the interface between an immaterial conscious mind, and the physical activity of the brain? For movements of the pineal gland, we could substitute the activation of certain patterns of cells in the cortex. This is more or less the modification of Descartes's theory proposed by Eccles (1965 and see Popper and Eccles, 1977), who provides the convenient metaphor of the brain containing a radio transmitter-receiver unit, which acts as the liaison between mind and body. We would thus view animals as robots acting mechanically, controlled by mechanisms confined to the brain, with ourselves having the same internal connections plus two-way communication with an immensely more powerful conscious and immortal control centre.

Would this account have satisfied the critical judgment of Princess Elizabeth of Palatine? The analogy of radio waves might well have proved more convincing that the analogy of gravity, though one suspects that the Princess, as a Calvinist, would not have been entirely happy with the idea of the soul as a sort of personal telephone call-in programme. However, even if we granted that some as yet undetected limited liaison may be available to interrelate brain function with personal consciousness, some of the problems remain. If consciousness is independent of the brain, but in communication with it, why is consciousness disturbed by brain malfunctioning? Because subjective states are at the mercy of the vapours, or, if you like, Valium, it is much clearer that consciousness is determined by physical states of the brain than it is that a separate mind perceives and acts through the brain. If there is a reasoning process which is independent of the body, how is it that reasoning can be substantially altered by a few glasses of wine? It is precisely because of these peculiarities that Descartes rejected the notion of a soul which was only in liaison with the body (the rejected Platonic metaphor being that of a pilot steering a ship) in favour of a mind which is united and conjoined with the body. If the mind only interacts with the brain as a pilot steers his ship, or as a driver controls his car, the everyday interdependence of mind and body is left out. Malfunctions of the car might prevent the driver steering, but they should not incapacitate the driver himself, whereas malfunctions of the brain can directly affect every subjective experience, and alter every mental capacity.

Materialist theories of mind

Descartes's dualism of mind and body, which gives rise to the dichotomy between man and animals, is far from being satisfactory, and other versions of dualism, such as those of McDougall (1911), Broad (1937), Sherrington (1940) and Eccles (1965) suffer from many of the same difficulties, even though they lack the absurdities of the pineal gland theory. Armstrong (1968) reviews yet more varieties of dualism, including those where the problems of mind/body interaction are sidestepped by saying that there is no interaction. This tactic is referred to as epiphenomenalism or parallelism, and, though the problems of interaction are disguised, the explanatory force of dualism is thereby diminished. Other watered-down versions of dualism are the 'double aspect' or 'attribute' theories, where brain and mind are said to be alternative facets of the same thing. However, few subsequent theorists have made as plain a stand as Descartes on the issue of animal minds, which is our main concern here. Even Eccles is argued into 'agnosticism' on the question of animal consciousness by Popper, who believes that animals have subjective experiences without a fully developed consciousness of self, or other human attributes (Popper and Eccles, 1977, p. 518).

We should now examine the materialist alternatives to dualist theories of mind. We have seen that Hobbes was content to define mind as 'nothing but' forms of bodily activity. A number of more sophisticated modern versions of this materialist strategy are available, under the names of identity theory, physicalism, materialism, or central state theory (e.g. Armstrong, 1968; Levin, 1979; Quinton, 1973; Russell, 1959; Wilkes, 1978). The essential theme is that mind, in all its glory, is physical, material, identical with states of the brain, and nothing else. Epigrammatically, 'the mind is simply the brain' (Armstrong, 1968, p. 73). I shall, for convenience, refer to these accounts generically as brain-state theories. There are many subtle differences between them in argument and conclusions, but the implications of the main point for the status of thought in animals are fairly crude. If all aspects of human thought, and of human mental states, are interpreted as forms of brain activity, and nothing else, then the only grounds for placing any limitations on animal thought are that brain anatomy, brain chemistry, or brain organisation, are different and inferior in animals. We could thus perhaps dispense with philosophical and psychological analysis altogether, and answer all questions about animal minds by a sufficiently detailed neuro-physiological survey. However, there are obvious practical reasons why this would not be enough. For one thing, information about neural organisation, even as far as it can be observed in dead animals, is limited. Scientific knowledge of exactly how brain activity mediates mental processes in either animals or man is even more rudimentary. Few would claim to be able to predict what an awake animal was doing, by studying records of its brain activity obtainable by current techniques; still less what, or if, the animal was thinking.

A second reason for not abandoning all investigation, apart from the scrutiny of brain activities, is that brain-state theories may be wrong, or if not wrong, incomplete. They could be wrong because Descartes was right, or wrong because Popper and Eccles are right, and something else as well as brain activity is necessary for thought. For both practical and theoretical reasons therefore, it is premature to expect that mental states in man or in any other species can be satisfactorily studied in physiological terms. However, there are few, and they certainly do not include Descartes or Eccles, who would claim that mental states can be accounted for without any reference at all to their physical concomitants.

The possible incompleteness of brain-state theories, even if they are right as far as they go, can be illustrated by the familiar hardware/software distinction in computing. There is certainly a sense in which what computers do is 'nothing but' activity in electronic circuits, but the theory of computing and the writing of computer programs are not the same as theories about the electronics. Similarly, how brains work in producing thought may need to be discussed in more abstract terms than brain-state theories immediately suggest. In particular, once we begin to discuss the content of thought or mentation, instead of its general qualities, it may be impractical if not erroneous to enquire too closely as to its physical substrate. To take a very simple example, if we say 'that dog wants to go for a walk' we will be more likely to judge the truth of this assertion on the basis of whether or not the dog appeared carrying its leash than on the basis of the state of its brain. Two different dogs may both want to go for walks, we might suppose, without having brains which are in all respects in identical states. More generally, it may be necessary to talk about ideas, or memories, or expectancies, without knowing very much about the relations of these things to particular brains or particular brain states. Popper makes a strong case for a world of ideas in human thought which are in some sense outside brains altogether. In his terms, World 1 is the brain, World 2 is subjective consciousness, and World 3 contains logical relationships in books, musical scores and other physical products of human societies. The suggestion is that ideas in books ought to be allowed to exist even when no one is reading the books, so that no brains contain the ideas (Popper and Eccles, 1977). This world of ideas is denied to animals, although Popper believes them to have subjective awareness of simpler mental events. However it might be as well to leave open the possibility that logical relationships contained in external reality provide a domain of mental events which may take place in the brains of animals, but which can be considered in isolation from their instances in particular brains, rather as the ideas in Popper's World 3 provide a psychological category of things outside the human brain. Since, in the external world, bananas grow on trees, we may wish to ask whether chimpanzees have mental representations of bananas and trees. Although it is mainly because the chimpanzee brain has a great deal in common with the human brain that this question is entertained, we look to behavioural experiments, rather than measurements of brain activity, to answer it.

Perception, memory, abstraction and reason

Descartes has it that animals have no thought, whereas Armstrong (1968), the materialist, suggests that animals may have beliefs, intentions, conscious perceptions and even introspections about their intentions. Thus on one side we have the theory that animals are automata which cannot be said to perceive or remember in the same way that we do, and, on the other, a brain-state theory which implies that there are few limitations on the capacity of animal brains. It is worth pointing out that the relation between animal status and mind-body theories does not have to take this form : it is perfectly possible to be a dualist who believes that animals have immortal souls, or to be a materialist who is convinced that the physical superiority of the human brain is so great as to place an unbridgeable gulf between human and animal capacities. However, Descartes provided the historically important extreme of a dualism which excludes animals, and Armstrong's brain-state theory gives a clear opposing view. Other opinions are both chronologically and logically stretched out between them. Middling views will of course take the general form of saying that animals can do this, but they can't do that. By and large, one can keep an ordered scale of perception, memory, abstraction, and reason, and place a theory in terms of how far up this scale animals are put, but there are some exceptions. I shall therefore take philosophical developments in chronological order after Descartes.

Locke (1632–1704) : animals have perception, memory
and reason but no abstraction

Philosophers after Descartes paid very much less attention to physiology, and concentrated on the mental almost exclusively. This is partly a consequence of Descartes's assertion that mental states and subjective awareness are primary, even though he himself always insisted that they were intimately intertwined with bodily mechanisms. Assuming the primacy of subjective apprehension of knowledge, irrespective of physical realities, also meant that the status of animals ceased to be a central concern after Descartes, although, as we shall see, philosophers such as Locke peppered their accounts of the bases of human thought with asides on the extent to which these were shared with other animals.

The main themes of Locke's psychology are the dependence of knowledge on the accumulation of subjective experiences over time, an emphasis on the interrelating of mental events in the human mind, and an extraordinarily thoroughgoing rejection of the possibility that any aspect of thought depends on preformed innate ideas or inherited determinants of mental states. The theory that knowledge is determined by the accumulation of experience, rather than by innately determined rules, intuitions or revelations, is empiricism. The metaphors used by Locke to illustrate his kind of empiricism include the allusion to the mind's starting off as a blank tablet (*tabula rasa*) on which subsequent mental experiences can be written, or as an empty cabinet into which ideas can be placed as they are acquired. One might assume that the cabinet was equipped with shelves or hooks so as better to receive certain sorts of idea if they presented themselves, but it is supposed to remain empty unless anything is actively put in it. The rigour with which Locke adhered to the assumption of the initial emptiness of the mind can be seen by his assertion that the ideas of hunger and warmth come to children only as a result of prenatal experiences in the womb, and his claim that early mental development proceeds 'according to the divers circumstances of children's first entertainment in the world'. He supposes that the order in which children acquire ideas will be very variable, depending on the diverse circumstances, and is in any case irrelevant (*An Essay Concerning Human Understanding*, 1959, p. 185). Modern theories of cognitive development assume a great deal more by way of predetermined sequences of intellectual achievement, and reactions to hunger and warmth at birth are innate if anything is, but this need not detain us.

Perception

Perception for Locke is rather a passive process, but involves mental awareness of impressions received from the senses. Animals perceive; indeed, 'perception puts the difference between animals and vegetables', although animals with limited sensory apparatus will obviously have dull and obscure perceptions. In fact Locke has perception as such entirely dependent on the quality of the available sense organs.

Cockles and oysters do not need to perceive very much, and do not appear to have much by way of sensory apparatus; we can therefore conclude that, although they are not insensible, their perceptions are exceedingly dull (1959, p. 190). But there is no perceptual gulf between cockles and men, except that due to the effectiveness of peripheral sense organs. Rather pessimistically, Locke suggests that if one becomes sufficiently decrepit in old age as to lose one's memory, and to be blind and deaf, and to retain little sense of taste and smell, then one's superiority to a cockle will be a matter of some doubt: 'How far such a one (notwithstanding all that is boasted of innate principles) is in his knowledge and intellectual faculties above the condition of a cockle or an oyster, I leave to be considered'. And if anyone had the misfortune to have dull senses from birth, 'I wonder what difference there would be, in any intellectual perfections, between him and the lowest degree of animals' (1959, pp. 190–1).

Memory
Given some conscious perceptions, the next step towards making intelligent use of them requires the retention of sensory information after it has first been received. Locke considers two aspects of retention: first, keeping a simple perception or idea 'in view' for some time after it has been initiated, and second, reviving or retrieving a perception from the storehouse or repository of ideas. This distinction, between continuation in a short-term memory or 'working memory' as opposed to the retrieval of items from a long-term store is very little altered in current theories (e.g. Gregg, 1975; Baddeley, 1976). Even the hypothesis that we cannot keep 'in view' many things at once, and that this is what determines exchanges between the long-term repository and immediate contemplation, appears little changed in the modern concept of limited capacity in short-term memory. As has been rediscovered in the last few years, it is not difficult to find evidence that similar mechanisms operate in animals. 'Brutes have memory', says Locke, giving as his example birds which can be seen on one day getting closer and closer to imitating a tune which they heard the day before. This is not a wholly convincing example, but, as Locke says, there are many others, and I shall examine some of them in a later chapter.

Discernment, comparison and compounding
Locke next considers what he calls discerning—there is not much point in having and remembering perceptions if we cannot tell any two of

them apart. It is on improvements in the accuracy of telling perceptions and ideas apart, and on the analysis of clear relations and distinctions between them that human understanding rests, rather than on innate principles: 'On this faculty of distinguishing one thing from another depends the evidence and certainty of several, even very general, propositions, which have passed for innate truths' (1959, p. 202). Locke's theory of knowledge thus rests on something rather like the processes studied under the heading of 'discrimination learning' in animals (see chapter 3). However, Locke supposed that the capabilities of animals for the various methods by which improvements in discernment are brought about are limited. One method is the comparison of ideas with respect to such features as time and place, and 'Brutes compare but imperfectly' since they probably limit their comparisons to ideas about tangible objects, whereas men compare more abstract and general ideas.

A second quite separate and fundamental operation of the mind is constructing, enlarging and elaborating ideas by the 'compounding' and adding together of simpler notions. Again, brutes come far short of man, since, although a dog may use a collection of simple ideas for a single purpose, such as recognising his master by his shape, smell and voice (together or apart), in Locke's view these elements are not properly compounded by the dog into a single complex idea of his master. In modern terms, the dog might be said to lack adequate facilities for cross-modal comparisons.

Abstraction

The 'perfect distinction' between man and beast in Locke's theory lies in the faculty of abstraction, which is tied to the use of words to represent ideas. Children, once they have some ideas fixed in their memories, 'begin by degrees to learn the use of signs' (1959, p. 206). Next, when they have acquired the skill of framing articulate sounds, they begin to use spoken words to communicate their ideas to others. Some of the words they borrow from those already in use, while others the children make up for themselves, 'as one may observe among the new and unusual names children often give to things in their first use of language'. However, for Locke, the crucial process was not so much in naming itself, as in the subsequent consequences of naming. In order to prevent the growth of an endless list of names for all particular ideas, the mind extracts general features from specific ideas, which serve to identify mental representations of things independently of real existence. The mind then gives general names to these general features—'and thus universals, whether ideas or terms, are made'. This sounds rather grand, but the example given is a simple one, the possession of the idea of whiteness, independently of its connections with milk, chalk, or snow (1959, p. 207). No animals are thought by Locke to have any capacity for this sort of abstraction, 'since they have no use of words or any other general signs'. Although the use of words is difficult to assess, it should be pointed out that many animals could easily be trained to push one button whenever they saw anything white, but another button whenever they saw anything that was not white, irrespective of shape of the objects inspected. If detecting whiteness is the paradigm of abstraction, then Locke's contention, 'Brutes abstract not', may be empirically false.

Reason

Having established a line between men and animals for abstraction, Locke was quick to disavow a distance of Cartesian proportions between men and beasts. The distance resulting from human abstraction was itself vast, but having already allowed animals perception and memory, Locke specifically adds to these a modicum of reason. Animals have reason, 'as they have sense' but can reason only about ideas directly received from their senses, and thus 'they are the best of them tied up within these narrow bounds' (1959, p. 208).

We ought at this point to acknowledge that Locke was being notably idiosyncratic in assigning any degree of reasoning to animals at all. The Aristotelian and medieval scholastic tradition was to take reason as the Rubicon uncrossed by animal species, and the convention is retained by most subsequent authorities. Leibniz (1646–1716) picks out Locke's departure from the norm in his *New Essays Concerning Human Understanding*, written as a commentary on Locke's essay, with the main purpose of resisting Locke's attack on innate ideas, but including agreements and disagreements paragraph by paragraph. Leibniz agrees that there may be connections between one and another 'imaginations' in animals, and refers to the case of a dog fearing a whipping when his master takes up a stick. But Leibniz wishes to preserve 'received usage' and restrict the term reasoning specifically to human inference. (The apprehensions of dogs reappear intermittently in philosophical texts—recently in Wittgenstein's characteristically pungent dictum that 'We say a dog is afraid his master will beat him; but not, he is afraid his master will beat him tomorrow. Why not?', *Philosophical Investigations*, para. 650.)

Leibniz concurs with Locke that animals do not form abstract thoughts, but wants to go a lot further than Locke in distinguishing between human perceptions and animal sensations. However, a Germanic hankering for unity in nature seems to persuade Leibniz of a currently obscured organic potential: 'the animals even, having attained a condition of stupidity, ought some day to return to perceptions more elevated; and, since simple substances always endure, we must not judge eternity by a few years' (1896, p. 142). Descartes was prepared to consider non-human intelligence within infinite space, rather than eternal time — 'I do not on that account infer that there are intelligent creatures in the stars or elsewhere; but I do not see that there are any grounds on which one could prove that there are not' (Descartes, 1970, p. 295).

Association of ideas

Locke introduced the association of ideas into his system as an afterthought, adding it to the fourth edition of his *Essay*. He used it to explain mental aberrations, and 'A degree of madness, found in most men', not the natural correspondences and connections between ideas which should give rise to true understanding, if a proper use of words is kept to by correct definitions of terms. Locke should not therefore be classed, as he sometimes is, as a supporter of the doctrine of associations as the basis of thought. Hobbes, slightly earlier, and Hume and Hartley, later, made the association of ideas, however their conjunction might occur, a fundamental mechanism; but Locke reserved it for unreasonable connections of ideas 'not allied by nature'. Conceivably, he was reacting against Hobbes. They were on opposite sides of the seventeenth-century political divide, Hobbes being a Cavalier Royalist, who returned to England with Charles II at the Restoration, while Locke was a Roundhead Parliamentarian, who was eventually forced to take his turn in exile not long after Hobbes came back. Hobbes was also an atheist, while Locke was a Calvinist who spent his last years in biblical scholarship. At any rate, although Locke suggests that the influence of association is generally pervasive, he thought its results were invariably perverse. The supposition that accidental pairings of events cause irrational antipathies, such as aversions to certain foods whose ingestion has accidentally preceded illness, or a dislike of books following painful experiences at school, is congenial to present-day behaviourists, but Locke did go on to discuss the possibility of irrational associations explaining animal learning.

Leibniz, however, did. He seized on the principle of association with great glee, revealing that Hobbes was said to have a phobia for dark places because of their associations with ghosts in stories told to him as a child, even though he did not believe in ghosts. Moreover, the example of the dog afraid of punishment, and all other so-called examples of animal reasoning, as well as irrational human behaviour, could be satisfactorily put down to learned associations (Leibniz, 1896, p. 283). This, written in 1704, must be one of the earliest versions of the associationist view of animal behaviour, taken to its limits in this century by Hull (1943; see chapter 3).

Hume (1711–76) : animal inferiority is a matter of degree

Locke had taken Descartes as his model in trying to account for our awareness of knowing by beginning from subjective first principles, and applying a method of doubt. Unlike Descartes he had ignored the question of mind/body interaction ('I shall not meddle with the physical condition of the mind'), and what he doubted was mainly the possibility of innate ideas. Berkeley (1685–1753) is usually coupled with Locke as a believer in accumulations of subjective experience, and he solved the mind/body problem at a stroke by denying the material existence of the body, or any other physical object: as he thought that the brain, and animals, existed only in the human mind, the question of the function of the animal brain did not arise (1965, p. 172). Hume was in many ways more of a sceptic and a doubter than either Locke or Berkeley, but he did have a good deal to say about animals. Hume did not deny the existence of the material world, but assumed that the method by which our mental intentions acted on the body was 'unknown and inconceivable' (1902, p. 67).

In Hume's work, all human knowledge is divided into two categories, 'Relations of Ideas' and 'Matters of Fact'. Relations of ideas can be made intuitively or demonstrably certain by purely subjective mental activity, without interaction with the external world being necessary, as in the cases of Euclidean geometry and arithmetic—'Propositions of this kind are discoverable by the mere operation of thought, without dependence on what is anywhere in the universe' (1902, p. 25). Everything else is based on what Hume calls cause and effect, which applies to all cases of deducing one thing from another perceptual experience and to all 'Matters of Fact' (1902, pp. 26–7). All knowledge of this kind of cause and effect depends on experience, and the principle controlling our utilisation of experience is 'custom', or 'habit'. 'All inferences from experience, therefore, are effects of custom, not of reasoning', and 'Without the influence of custom, we should be entirely ignorant of every matter of fact beyond what is immediately present to the memory and senses' (1902, p. 43 and p. 45). Hume's scepticism lies in his assertion that we can know no more than our habitual experiences, when it comes to matters of fact. We can say that we have experienced heat and flame together but we cannot thereby assume that one causes the other—we cannot be sure of a 'necessary connection' between them. This is a rejection of Locke's distinction between natural connections and arbitrary associations. Especially if one has forgone any assistance from innate cognitive organisation, all connections must be equally arbitrary, depending entirely on what past experience happens to have been. This conclusion applies even to apparent certainties, such as the movements of billiard balls. We expect one billiard ball to move when it is struck by another, but our expectation is suspect, if it is induced from prior experience (cf. Popper, 1959).

The implications of this account for human/animal differences may not seem very direct. But it is clear that if, like Leibniz, we have assumed that animal reasoning takes place via arbitrary associations, and then we accept that any distinction between arbitrary and rational associations is invalid, the gap between human and animal inferences from experience will have been considerably narrowed. That there is, in fact, a difference between sorts of association is a current tenet of comparative animal psychology: No associations are arbitrary in practice; particular species are sensitive to particular conjunctions of events; and the human species, apart from having its own preferences, is probably the best species at being arbitrary and unnatural (Hinde and Stevenson-Hinde, 1973). But Hume followed his scepticism about inferences from perception to a consistent conclusion, and we can find his treatment of animal cognition in 'Of the Reason of Animals' (*Enquiries*) and 'On the Immortality of the Soul' (*Essays*).

Although Hume's description 'Of the Reason of Animals' is brief, it is extremely clear, and is worth considering in some detail. First, he reiterates his conviction that all our own reasonings are founded on a kind of analogy, or assessment of similarities—we expect a piece of iron to have certain properties in so far as we have previously observed other pieces of iron to have them. It follows as a principle of method that the more cases and analogies we can accumulate, the better. In particular, Hume proposes that the comparison of different species of animal is useful in studies of anatomy and physiology, giving the example of the circulation of the blood—we can understand the principle of circulation more thoroughly if it can be observed in fishes and frogs. The same proposal is then stated for psychology: Hume suggests that his theory of human understanding and his theory of the origin of the human passions 'will acquire additional authority, if we find that the same theory is requisite to explain the same phenomena in all other animals' (1902, p. 104). This is a surprisingly strong claim for the value of animal psychology, especially as it comes a hundred years before Darwin.

As we might expect, after this claim, Hume finds that his knowledge of animal behaviour requires him to adopt the same principles of explanation which he has previously applied to human cognition, namely the mechanisms of experience and custom. The evidence is drawn both from natural behavioural development in animals, and from the results of training procedures imposed by human intervention:

> First, it seems evident that animals as well as men learn many things from experience, and infer that the same events will always follow from the same causes. By this principle they become acquainted with the more obvious properties of external objects . . . . The ignorance and inexperience of the young are here plainly distinguishable from the cunning and sagacity of the old. . . . This is still more evident from the effects of discipline and education on animals, who, by the proper application of rewards and punishments, may be taught any course of action, and most contrary to their natural instincts and propensities. . . . the animal infers some fact beyond what immediately strikes his senses, and this inference is altogether founded on past experience. (1902, p. 104)

On the basis of past experience, animals make inferences, and construct expectations, going beyond the information which is immediately given to them by their senses; but they do not do this because they have reasoned that 'the course of nature will always be regular in its operations'. Animals are not guided by reasoning, as philosophers construe it, but then neither are children, neither are most people, in their everyday life, and neither indeed are the philosophers themselves, in their everyday life. Custom, in the form of accumulated experiences and habits, controls the beliefs and imagination of animals and men alike (1902, p. 106).

By discovering a common mechanism, Hume has, to his own satisfaction, strengthened his theory. But if there are common mechanisms underlying human and animal knowledge, what is the source of human superiority? Hume is remarkable for minimising the differences between animals and men, and although he recognises the problem, his solution to it differs from that of almost everyone else, including modern behaviourists such as Skinner, in that he avoids any clear-cut dividing line such as language, abstraction, or imagination, which does not apply as much to individuals within species as to differences between species. His tactic at the end of 'Of the Reason of Animals' is to list nine ways in which men can differ from each other, with the implication that exaggerations of these account for the inferiorities of animals. Attention, memory, powers of observation, accuracy of reasoning, the formation of general maxims, the perception of analogies, and 'many other circumstances' may affect the understandings of men: similar factors serve to differentiate men from animals. It is also true that animals derive many parts of their knowledge 'from the original hand of nature' in the form of instincts, but experimental reasoning, 'which we possess in common with beasts', is itself a kind of instinct, and whatever it is that teaches a man to avoid the fire is as much an instinct as the more exact forms which teach a bird 'the art of incubation, and the whole economy and order of its nursery'.

Hume could hardly have been more definite about the relation between human and animal thought: they are based on the same mechanisms, and human superiorities are a matter of degree. This is a direct contradiction of Descartes, and Hume's disagreement extended to the question of mind/body interaction, in so far as this entails a consideration of immortality. Hume attempted to demolish logical arguments in favour of the immortality of the soul, although he kept the theological escape route of Divine Revelation. If one has concluded that the mental capacities of animals differ from man's in only quantitative ways, one of the grounds for drawing moral and eschatological distinctions between men and beasts is removed, and it becomes less obvious that immortality should be reserved for the human species. One solution, which Aquinas was prepared to consider, but which Descartes was against because of the supposed consequences for public order, is to allow that any arrangements made for the continued existence of human souls may include accommodation for those of animals. These could be simpler that those provided for us, and presumably would not need to be divided between different extremes of comfort, but would not necessarily have to be less durable. However, the tack taken by Hume was that we should assume animals to be mortal, and should therefore have difficulty in establishing anything better for ourselves. 'The souls of animals are allowed to be mortal; and these bear so near a resemblance to the souls of men, that the analogy from one to the other forms a very strong argument' (1906, p. 427). Not everyone would agree that this is a strong case, but the use of the argument is a further demonstration, if any is needed, of the lack of distinction between animals and men in Hume's writing. In even clearer detail, 'Animals undoubtedly feel, think, love, hate, will and even reason, though in a more imperfect manner than men: are their souls also immaterial and immortal?' (1906, p. 424).

Hume left his views on immortality to be published after his own death, but the operation of mental and emotional mechanisms in animals was a preoccupation revealed in his earliest work, the *Treatise on Human Nature*, which he later revised and condensed into the *Enquiries*. The argument concerning reason is the one most at odds with previous authorities, and the one most likely to be resisted, but it is asserted forcefully, if not crudely, in the *Treatise*: 'no truth appears to me more evident, than that beasts are endowed with thought and reason as well as men. The arguments in this case are so obvious, that they never escape even the most stupid and ignorant' (1888, p. 176). Also included in the *Treatise*, but omitted from the subsequent condensations, were sections covering 'Pride and Humility of Animals' and 'Love and Hatred of Animals'. The gist is simply that pride and humility, love and hatred, and also fear, anger, courage, grief, envy and malice 'and other affections' all exist in animals, and 'the causes of these passions are likewise much the same in the beast as in us' (1888, p. 326). The causes are physiological, psychological, and social but 'these causes operate after the same *manner* thro' the whole animal creation'. This is of course an exceptionally strong claim for a common biological base governing human and animal behaviour, matched only by the excesses of current sociobiology (Wilson, 1975). However, Hume was not oblivious to human peculiarities. Pity, for instance, is not supposed to occur as often in animals as envy and malice, as it requires a greater effort of thought and imagination. And although beasts are susceptible to vices and virtues to the extent of their sense, appetite and will, our superior cognition and understanding immeasurably expand the possibilities of moral distinctions, especially those requiring knowledge of consanguinity and the right of property (1888, p. 326).

A minor theme of the *Treatise* is thus that human nature is in many ways not to be distinguished from animal nature. Apart from the sections expressly devoted to establishing that the mechanisms governing human psychology are also found in animals, there are places where briefer assertions are made in passing. It seems clear enough from this internal evidence that Hume was deliberate about the disagreement with Descartes, while attempting to build an equally comprehensive account of the human condition. It may not be merely a coincidence that Hume chose to write the *Treatise* at La Flèche, near Angers, where Descartes had received his Jesuit education. In any event, Hume's arguments provide an unmissable and vigorous opposition to the Cartesian split between animal automatism and human thought. At the time, Hume's continuity was at least as agreeable to other writers as Descartes's dichotomy (see for instance Diderot's comments made in 1749, ten years after the *Treatise* and one after the first *Enquiry*: Diderot, 1916, p. 76), and Hume's contributions might reasonably be taken as early pioneering along the route taken by Darwinians such as Thomas Huxley; but it is rare to find Hume's disagreement with Descartes's dichotomy between men and animals given much weight by later philosophers.

Kant (1724–1804) and Hegel (1770–1831):
disappearance of the issue

A retreat from the whole problem of the relation between the human and animal mind was begun by Kant, a towering influence who said virtually nothing on the subject in the course of several monumental books. Kant's importance for psychology in general is supposed to reside partly in the authority he gave to a preoccupation with the purely mental and spiritual, considered to a large extent as separate from real and physical nature, and partly in his systematic and powerful reassertion of the existence of innate ideas (e.g. Boring, 1950).

Kant claimed that Hume's first *Enquiry* awoke him from 'dogmatic slumbers': the unpalatability of the conclusions which resulted from Hume's scepticism was sufficiently stirring to require Kant's *Critiques*, but in bringing back nativism, in the form of innate or 'a priori' concepts, Kant was also in direct opposition to Locke. There was of course no science of genetics in the eighteenth century, and although Kant wrote on astronomy, meteorology and physical geography, he did not have Hume's interest in comparative anatomy. The source of 'a priori' concepts, as far as Kant was concerned, was thus a matter of spiritual intuition rather than natural inheritance or biological predetermination. But the tradition established by Kant of internal predetermined dimensions of cognition may be seen in both the 'Gestalt' psychology of human perception (Kohler, 1929; Koffka, 1935; see Boring, 1950 and Hilgard and Bower, 1975), and in the approach to animal psychology taken by ethologists such as Tinbergen (1951) and Lorenz (1966), who stress the importance of instinctual drives, inherited mechanisms of perception and biologically fixed patterns of movement, in the context of genetic inheritance and evolution.

Kant's proposal was that human knowledge, and in particular the perception of objects in time and space, depends on inevitable and universal intuitions or concepts, and is not, as the British empiricists held, a product of 'Pure Reason' in the sense of associations, rearrangements and inferences which take place partly as a consequence of the circumstances of perception within an individual's lifetime. Intuition, inspiration and inner feeling are the basis of perceptual and logical categories, including our ideas of relation, existence and cause—and they also ought to be relied on in the course of philosophical speculation. But whether we should assume that similar natural feelings and intuitions occur in animals is another question. Kant was interested in human moral responsibilities towards animals, but apparently on the grounds that an act of cruelty directed at an animal damages the human agent, rather than because of the possible feelings of the victim ('Duties towards animals and spirits' in *Lectures on Ethics*; see Midgley, 1980).

Kant had a teleological view of nature as being organised from the top down, expressing the design and purposes of a Supreme Being. The origin of animals was classed with the secrets of Providence and the mystical number 666 as 'one of the topics on which ingenuity and thought are occasionally wasted'. And 'It is indeed quite certain that we cannot adequately cognise, much less explain, organised beings and their internal possibility, according to mere mechanical principles of nature. . . . We must absolutely deny this insight to men' (1914, pp. 312–13). It is therefore not surprising that Kant himself spent little time on the details of animal behaviour. However in a footnote to Appendix 90 of the *Critique of Judgement*, Kant lets slip the conclusion that Descartes was wrong to say that animals are machines. This comes in the course of a discussion of 'Analogy' with the example of the construction of dams and nests by beavers, one which may have suggested itself to Kant because of his interest in the inner purposes of rivers. From the similarity of the artificial constructions of beavers to those of men 'we can quite rightly conclude *according to analogy*, that beasts too act in accordance with *representations*'. But we are not allowed to conclude that because man uses reason to design his buildings, so does the beaver, because the beaver uses instinct instead. The analogy between beast and man in this case is said to work in the same way as the analogy between the works of men and 'the causality of the supreme World-Cause': both are doomed to failure (1914, pp. 398–400).

Kant does not doubt that there are 'things in themselves' which may be causes of perceptions, even though the qualities and forms of perception are determined by native intuitions. Natural laws and mere mechanisms may be discussed, even though they are subsidiary to subjective reality. 'Universal principles of the nature of things' are all right as far as they go, but 'those principles are simply valid for nature, as an object of sense' and are not much use when it comes to more important matters, such as 'the particular concept of a Supersensible Being'. Others after Kant did away with external reality altogether—things need only exist as ideas in a self-conscious mind, if that is going to be the starting point. Hegel begins with self-consciousness and ends with Absolute Knowledge, with physical reality vaguely in between (*Phenomenology of Mind*). However Hegel is as a rule taken seriously, and a recent commentary suggests that 'Had Hegel lived in the present age we should now have had a long treatment of the Behaviourisms of Watson and Tolman and Skinner' (Hegel, 1977). The Hegelian approach can thus be set against behavioural treatments of animal psychology, but also against any strategy which identifies consciousness with physical reality. The Hegelian antidote to brain-state theories, and any form of physiological evidence, ought therefore to be mentioned: 'Brain fibres and the like, looked at as forms of the being of the mind, are already, an imagined, a merely hypothetical actuality of the mind' (1949, p. 371).

Schopenhauer (1788–1860) : animals have understanding and will without language

Kant believed that the predetermined constitution of our cognitive faculties means that we can only subjectively understand nature, if we stick to the highest kinds of reasoning, in terms of the designs of a supreme cause, but that subjective understanding is not the same as objective truth. The distinction between subjective understanding and physical reality becomes blurred in Hegel, since reason *is* reality, and the substance of the universe; and absolute knowledge, or infinite form, sets in motion the infinite material 'underlying all the natural and spiritual life which it originates'. Organic nature thus conforms to the absolute idea. In Schopenhauer's adaptation of Kant, however, the idea is subordinate to the will, and the world and all its phenomena can thus be interpreted as objectifications of will. This might not in itself be expected to have immediate implications for animal psychology. It does mean that Schopenhauer has to deal extensively with motives and volitions, and the workings of motivation in animals are somewhat more accessible than the processes of reason. (Schopenhauer himself coined the term 'motivation' in referring generally to motives: e.g. 'The action of motives (motivation) is causality seen from within'-1915, p. 171). The fact that Schopenhauer had a lot to say about animals may, however, be partly incidental. He was fond of animals, and had a poodle called 'World-Soul' of whose intelligence he was particularly proud, and he was well read in the comparative anatomy and theoretical biology of his day. He was an admirer of 'the excellent Locke', and therefore addressed the issues of animal capabilities in the same way as Locke and Hume, as well as delivering himself of Kantian metaphysical obscurities.

The most succinct statement of Schopenhauer's analysis of animal thought appears in 'On the Irrational Intellect', in the second volume of his magnum opus, *The World as Will and Idea*, and his biological theories are contained in the long essay *On the Will in Nature*. But, like Locke and Hume, Schopenhauer interrupted his discussions of human knowledge with comments on the approximations to such knowledge achieved by domestic pets and lesser organisms in general. He was more concerned than Hume with the details of the differences between human and animal minds, and few pre-Darwinian writers seem to have had as many things so say about relations between consciousness, memory, comprehension, deliberation and so on, although it must be admitted that consistency and accuracy were not among Schopenhauer's strong points.

Very explicitly, Schopenhauer claims that we can arrive at 'a complete knowledge of the consciousness of brutes', by selecting a limited set of the properties of our own consciousness. This was the view adopted by the later generation of introspective psychologists such as Wundt (1832–1920) and Kulpe (1862–1915), who supposed that some of the information obtained by the new introspective methods used with human subjects could be generalised back to animals, but who differed from earlier philosophers in wishing to conduct quantitative and experimental investigations of human subjective awareness in the first place. For Schopenhauer, the distinction between animals and men does not therefore lie in subjective awareness, but in the traditional mark of reason—'The brute feels and perceives; man, in addition to this *thinks* and *knows*: both *will*' (1883 vol. 1, p. 47). Animals live in the present, and have intuitive representations, which allow what Schopenhauer calls understanding, to the extent of understanding proper names (1915, p. 117), but are incapable of reflecting on past and future events (in particular their own death), and cannot form 'abstract conceptions'. Schopenhauer thus follows Locke in making abstraction a specifically human power of thought: the mental states of animals can be characterised as 'representations' (perceptions related to objects) but these do not allow human-like thought or knowledge. Schopenhauer accuses even Locke of losing sight of the primary aspect of abstraction, and falling into a wavering account of 'mangled and derivative manifestations' of its real inner nature, while Kant 'confused and falsified' the true conception of reason and abstraction, and the pitiable Hegel scribbled nonsense and tom-foolery—'three-fourths cash and one-fourth crazy fancies'—under the heading of an examination of reason.

What is the single essence of reason and abstraction, which others had distorted and mangled? Schopenhauer's candidate is not original, but his argument is unambiguous and as clear as a bell. 'It is by the help of language alone that reason accomplishes its most important achievements'. These include social co-operation, civilisation, the political state, and science and literature, in addition to memory and abstractions (1883, vol. 1, p. 48). All aspects of human reason can "be reduced to what is only possible for abstract, discursive, reflective, mediate knowledge, conditioned by words, and not for mere intuitive, immediate, sensuous knowledge, which belongs to animals also" (1915, p. 130). What distinguishes human thought from animal intelligence is thus language and words, which enable deliberation and reflection, and this classical distinction is only confused by the invention of a 'completely fictitious' faculty for metaphysical understanding. Schopenhauer prefers to reserve the term understanding for knowledge of causal laws which are discoverable by perception alone. Animals, even down to the very lowest, use some degree of this sort of understanding, which arises 'from the habit of seeing one thing follow another' (1915, p. 89). Clearly, this is a version of Hume, but Schopenhauer suggests that higher animals (mammals) not only have an understanding of learned perceptual associations, but also have a certain amount of a priori knowledge of causality. A young puppy, he says, is reluctant to jump off a table, because it foresees the consequences. Not everyone would accept this, since it tends now to be assumed that young mammals simply have an innate fear of depth, rather than a knowledge of the consequences of falling into depths, but the innate avoidance can reasonably be put down as a predetermined disposition and it may well be the case that the mammalian nervous system is extremely amenable to the formation of rules by which locomotion is linked with being in different places, even if such linkages are normally activated by experience—and this would certainly count as a Kantian a priori.

The other example of innate knowledge of causality in mammals quoted by Schopenhauer refers to the perplexity exhibited by World-Soul (his poodle) when new curtains were put up in his (Schopenhauer's) bedroom, of the kind that are drawn apart by a cord. On seeing the curtains open for the first time in the apparent absence of a human agent, the dog spent some time looking for an alternative cause. This is taken to indicate that there is a degree of animal intelligence even in the absence of language. Brutes, however, have only a single intellect, based on direct knowledge, whereas we have a double intellect, verbal reasoning providing the addition of thought, memory, deliberation, and the rest. Only faint traces of these latter faculties, including memory, can according to Schopenhauer be observed in animals, and then only in favoured individuals of the highest species. Schopenhauer had a special regard for elephants, along with dogs and monkeys representative of the highest species, partly due to his erroneous belief that they have a life-span of 200 years, and therefore a greater opportunity to exercise their inferior form of memory. His interest in animal intelligence was enhanced by his habit of reading English newspapers, and his best elephant story is taken from a report in the *Spectator* of a coroner's inquest held in Morpeth on 27 August 1830, at which it was concluded that a keeper, Baptist Bernhard, had been seized and crushed by an elephant in revenge for an offence suffered by the animal two years previously (1883, vol. 2, p. 233).

Resting memory and reasoning mainly on language acknowledges the most obvious separation of man and beast, but also has implications for restrictions on human thinking; and Schopenhauer did not ignore these. He deduced that it is only by learning language that the whole apparatus of human reason is made available. It follows that even badly educated children, as long as they acquire the subtleties of language, possess a form of concrete logic, but the deaf and dumb, unless they receive special training adapted to their condition, should have almost as little of the normal richness of human thought as animals (1915, p. 118). It must also be the case that the properties of human thought and reason depend on precisely what language or languages are available to the individual. This contention is familiar as the Sapir-Whorf hypothesis, which is now in disfavour because of the Chomskyan tenet that all languages have an identical underlying structure. Schopenhauer, although he had to contend with the nativist underlying absolutes and universals of Kant and Hegel, was firmly of the opinion that thought depends upon linguistic skills and preconceptions that are acquired by experience. The supposed limitations on knowledge and reasoning in the untutored deaf and dumb are matched by the enhancement of thought in those with a mastery of several (preferably ancient) languages (1883, vol. 2, pp. 238–40, and 'On language and words' in *Parerga and Paralipomena*—'When one knows many languages, just as many times one is more a man'). The superior structure of Sanskrit, and of Greek and Latin, allows a 'more perfect construction of thoughts and their connection', and Schopenhauer was aghast at the contemporary language reforms which involved simplifications in German grammar. He considered a general tendency for languages to become simpler and worse to be powerful evidence against the doctrine of human progress. The dependency of concepts on words was illustrated by difficulties in the translation of poems and deep or significant prose, Schopenhauer being especially taken by the claim that it was impossible to translate the book of Genesis into Chinese, because of the lack of Chinese terms with which to express the Judeo-Christian concept of a divine creator (1915, p. 367).

If human thought is so much governed by language, then the absence of language in animals should place crushing restrictions on the kinds of thinking that can be attributed to them. Schopenhauer provides a fairly plain alternative to both the dualism of Descartes and the extreme reaction against it by Hume: there is a dichotomy between man and beast, and the differences are not just a matter of degree, but the limitations on thought in otherwise intelligent mammals such as the orang-utang and elephant do not arise from the absence of an immaterial and invisible essence; the limitations may all be put down to a single factor, their comparatively tangible and visible lack of speech.

2 Darwinian continuity

The problem of the relation between human and animal minds clearly did not begin with the advent of the Darwinian theory of evolution, but all attempted answers to the problem after Darwin must be coloured by the existence of a theory which presupposes a common origin for human and animal existence. In one sense, Darwinian theory did remarkably little to alter the nature of the problem, since the concept of a scale of animal intelligence had been introduced by Aristotle. But Darwin's account of how human peculiarities could be reconciled with his general theory of species development and descent, and the boost which this theory gave to the thesis of continuity between the human and animal worlds, can hardly be ignored. In many ways, Darwinian theory was the culmination of two centuries of investigation of comparative anatomy and physiology, which began with Descartes; the French tradition of natural history, represented by Buffon (1701–88), Lamarck (1744–1829) and Cuvier (1769–1832) was a powerful influence, not so much on Darwin himself, but on his immediate precursors and contemporaries. But one of the reasons for the central position of Darwin in the growth of modern biology was the intense and public controversy surrounding evolutionary theory in Victorian England. And perhaps not so much the controversy, but the fact that Darwin, with the help of Huxley, won.

Buffon, in Hume's day, a century earlier, had produced a ten-volume *Natural History*, in which, Darwin admitted, 'whole pages are laughably like mine' (Himmelfarb, 1959, p. 143). Buffon held that species progressed and degenerated very gradually according to ecological pressures, and that thus, by descent, new species developed from old ones. In particular, all the component parts of the orang-utang, including the brain and the vocal organs, closely resemble those of man, and man and ape, like horse and ass, must therefore share a common ancestor. But Buffon was eventually obliged by the religious authorities to make a formal denial that there was any evidence in his work that would contradict the biblical story of creation. Darwin and Huxley, however, stood firm against theological pressures (although Darwin made many concessions to ill-advised scientific criticism), and succeeded, where previous protagonists had failed, in getting the evolutionary account accepted, if still sometimes uneasily, by most subsequent professional and intellectual opinion.

The factors which led to the eventual triumph of Darwin's evidence over traditional prejudices are many, and include most clearly the accumulation of fossil findings and the early Victorian concern with theories of geology, as well as the wild and undisciplined speculations of Herbert Spencer. As an influence on the popular imagination, pride of place should probably go to *Vestiges of Creation*, an unequivocal and provocative pot-boiler which promoted a theory of progress in organic life under natural laws of development, with very small and modest changes allowing one species to develop into another. This was published in 1844, went through four editions in seven months, and became a *cause célèbre*, parodied in Disraeli's *Tancred* as '*Revelations of Chaos*'. Its anonymous author was not one of the widely touted candidates such as Prince Albert or Thackeray, but Robert Chambers, a shrewd Edinburgh publisher whose firm still puts out the worthy Chambers Dictionary. Darwin later paid tribute to the excellent service performed by the *Vestiges* in calling attention to the subject and preparing the ground, in spite of its unsound zoology. And it was Chambers who persuaded Huxley to stay on at the British Association meeting at Oxford in 1860 to defend the Darwinian cause against the onslaught expected from Bishop Wilberforce, son of the anti-slavery Wilberforce and an extremely influential figure. The fact that Huxley was felt to have successfully countered Wilberforce's attack—by saying that he would rather be descended from an ape on either his father's or his mother's side as an alternative to being related to someone who posed such a frivolous question—is held to have been an enormous public relations coup for the Darwinian side (e.g. Himmelfarb, 1959, pp. 236–41).

However, a more enduring reason for the success of Darwinian theory is the evidence in its favour, and the persuasiveness of Darwin's argument. The *Origin of Species*, published in 1859, is remarkable for its detail, even though Darwin referred to it as an abstract, presented prematurely because ill-health might prevent his completing it. Two points are especially relevant to the question of mental abilities. First, it was one of Darwin's conclusions that his theory would eventually provide a new basis for psychology—'the necessary acquirement of each mental power and capacity by gradation' (1968, p. 458). Second, a chapter of the *Origin* is devoted to 'Instinct', a term which Darwin used synonymously with 'mental powers', 'mental qualities', or 'mental actions'. It is made explicit that these mental qualities are a product of evolution—they arise 'as small consequences of one general law, leading to the advancement of all organic beings, namely, multiply, vary, let the strongest live and the weakest die' (1968, p. 263).

This last is perhaps the briefest encapsulation of the theory of evolution given by Darwin, and it is in some ways not very representative of the more general argument. The facts which Darwin wished to explain were not enormously different from those known to Aristotle, and certainly not at variance with those collected by Buffon. But Darwin put forward a new and powerful analogy: the process of breeding and change in domesticated species of animals became the model for change in the natural world. And Darwin stressed, for instincts and for anatomical features, an aspect of natural history previously ignored—anomalies and accidents in the adaptations of wild species to their environments.

The analogy between domestic breeding and the natural origins of species is the core of Darwin's case, and it includes the consideration of instinctive mental tendencies: anomalous adaptations provide the support and ought to be remembered in the context of mental evolution. That particular species of animal are apparently designed for their own style of life is a starting point for all accounts of the origin of species alike, including those which appeal to a creator who designs species as a watchmaker designs a watch, those like Lamarck's which assume that species design themselves, and Darwin's theory which appears, as Dewey put it, to offer 'design on the installment plan'. Lamarck had supposed that animal forms were slowly changed by their needs, and this was interpreted by both Darwin and Schopenhauer as requiring a succession of acts of will on the part of individual animals (and plants). Schopenhauer, revising *The Will in Nature* only five years before the publication of Darwin's *Origin*, took the apparent 'universal fitness for ends' as evidence for a universal process of design, and was familiar with the popular examples of webbed feet in swimming birds, the teeth and claws of carnivores, and the long tongue of the anteater. But Schopenhauer was impatient with the slow and gradual willings proposed by Lamarck—if there was to have been any willing he would rather assume that a primary animal willed itself into existence in the form of the various species, fully equipped with all necessary organs, which would thus not have to go through aesthetically unsatisfying intermediary stages!

Darwin was equally dissatisfied with Lamarck's explanation, but sought for natural laws which would explain gradual adaptations to needs. Although unable to specify genetic mechanisms, he said simply that whatever causes gradual change in artificial selection which produces the strains and varieties of domesticated species, this also caused the development of natural species. Deliberate selection of animals to produce for instance, better breeds of sheep, is an extremely ancient art, but Darwin was able to draw on systematic work catalogued by nineteenth century specialists in horticulture and husbandry. A great many examples of selective breeding were thus provided, but many of Darwin's favourite cases were taken from the less utilitarian science of pigeon-fancying. Pigeon breeding was something he was able to take up himself and he was 'permitted to join two of the London Pigeon Clubs'. A skilful breeder could claim that 'he would produce any given feather in three years, but it would take him six years to obtain head and beak' (1968, p. 90). It was clear that all domestic breeds were descended from the same ancestor, the Indian rock-pigeon (*Columba livia*). But according to Darwin, the established varieties such as the English carrier, the short-faced tumbler, the pouter and the fan-tail, were so different in form and habit that an ornithologist judging them as wild birds would probably not even put them in the same genus, and as wild birds the domestic varieties would certainly be counted as separate species.

If deliberate selection by the intervention of human agency could bring about such changes in the humble rock-pigeon, in so short a time compared with the new geological scales, why could not a similar process account for gradual changes which result in the origin of new natural species? All that was required was an unseen hand, operating in nature as a substitute for human judgment, as a procedure of 'natural selection'. Such an unseen hand had already begun to be suspiciously visible in the Malthusian struggle for existence. The processes of reproduction would allow for geometric increases in the populations of all forms of life—only a small proportion of each species needs to survive in any generation for the species to keep up its numbers. One need look no further for a natural filter; indeed the struggle for survival is much more efficient than any human selection, since there can be a continuous assessment of minute differences in internal structure and the organisation of behaviour. The final piece in the puzzle is the presence of sufficient inherited variation in structure and function to provide something worth filtering for. The *Origin* has three chapters on variation—there is a good deal of wavering over the possible contributions of Lamarckian sorts of use and disuse and individual habits as sources of gradual change, but it is natural selection acting on inherited variation which is the distinctive Darwinian doctrine.

In the chapter on instinct, it is acknowledged that the first appearance of some peculiar mental habits can only be due to accidents. But a range of inherited individual differences can be seen between and within different breeds of domesticated species, as for instance in retrievers, pointers and sheep-dogs. Pronounced variations in the observed expression of nest-building and migratory instincts occur in wild birds, partly but not wholly dependent on climate and other environmental circumstances. There is generally plenty of diversity in instinctive behaviours in individuals of the same species, and within the same individual there are 'different instincts at different periods of life, or at different seasons of the year'. Any of these sources could provide a range of variation wide enough that 'one or the other instinct might be preserved by natural selection'.

Natural selection is blind to all considerations of fitness for function except those of survival and reproduction. The fact that instincts are 'liable to mistakes' is used by Darwin, like cases of anomalous bodily structures and vestigial organs, to counter theories of unique creation, and to support the contention that aesthetically unfit and partially adapted species can survive. The American ostrich (the emu) wastes 'a surprising number of eggs...strewed over the plains'; on the same plains of La Plata there is a woodpecker very like the European species which survives in the absence of trees; in nearby uplands there are geese with webbed feet which never go near water—while aquatic coots and grebes make do with only membrane-bordered toes, and the water-ouzel, whose body looks like that of any other thrush, subsists by diving into streams, grasping stones with its feet, and using its wings under water. Form does not always predict function, and function may belie form.

The *Origin* thus explained more of the facts than its predecessors, but does not in itself contain much by way of exciting speculations about human ancestry. *The Descent of Man*, first published in 1871, certainly did. It was immediately followed by *The Expression of the Emotions in Man and Animals* (1872), which was equally blunt about human evolution; after this Darwin concerned himself almost exclusively with plant life.

It is a measure of Darwin's genius that he not only cut the Gordian knot of contemporary evolutionary theories, by giving, in natural selection, a simple and elegant account of how and why gradations and radiations of species could result in the observed diversity of organic life, but also, in the concept of sexual selection, he elaborated his theory by discussing factors whose importance was not fully appreciated until the 1960s (see O'Donald, 1980). The term natural selection was used by Darwin to refer to the filtering action of the 'conditions of life'—the effect of climate, disease, predation, food supply etc. on the health and survival of individuals. But the successful negotiation of these trials, though necessary, is not a sufficient condition for Darwinian survival, since it is the inheritance of adaptations, and not their effects on individual longevity, which is crucial. The reproductive process is at the heart of natural selection, and in all but a handful of animal species this requires sexual interactions. The modern term 'inclusive fitness' emphasises the degree to which an individual's genes are included in the next generation—from one point of view coping with the conditions of life is merely an incidental preliminary to genetic reduplication—but Darwin's term 'sexual selection' is retained to cover aspects of structure and behaviour whose importance depends solely or mainly on their role in sexual reproduction. The simplest examples are the elaborate vocalisations and bodily decorations of male birds. These may be of no use in negotiating the conditions of life, but are 'essential to individuals if they are to attract females. It goes without saying that special-purpose instincts are as necessary as bodily accoutrements for competition, courtship, mating and parental care. Darwin's own treatment of sexual selection is exhaustive and complex, and the subject is now part of the domain of mathematical models in theoretical genetics.

One aspect of Darwin's discussion of sexual selection is the bizarre and surprising conclusion that human language first began, not as an aid to abstract reasoning, but as a technique of courtship. He assumes, of course, that speech very soon became a vehicle for thought, and indeed that the intelligent use of language promoted the large size of the human brain (1901, p. 134), but suggests that the initial emphasis on vocalisation might have arisen from its utility in charming and impressing sexual partners and rivals — 'some early progenitor of man, probably first used his voice in producing true musical cadences, that is in singing, . . . this power would have been especially exerted during the courtship of the sexes' (1901, p. 133). One may wonder if Darwin was led into strangely unsound speculation by the musical evenings and protracted engagements of middle-class Victorians, but his arguments are based on a characteristically thorough examination of the biological evidence. Sounds are used throughout the animal kingdom for emotional expression and social communication and 'a strong case can be made out that the vocal organs were primarily used and perfected in relation to the propagation of the species'. The case applies pre-eminently to bird song, but there are many exceedingly vocal species of monkey, and several types of gibbon ('lesser apes') have a social organisation based on neighbouring nuclear families, and are strong singers. According to Darwin's information some gibbons sing in semi-tones organised into octaves (but see Tenaza and Marler, 1977; Tenaza and Tilson, 1977).

Some sort of prelinguistic use of the voice in human ancestry can hardly be doubted, although whether at one stage 'the males or females or both sexes, before acquiring the power of expressing their mutual love in articulate language, endeavoured to charm each other with musical notes and rhythm' is another matter. It must be admitted that the breaking of the male voice at puberty is unlikely to be related to the intellectual uses of language, and singing and dancing, at least in their less refined forms, seem to have retained some connection with sexual display and attraction.

Darwin's concern with the emotional and sexual functions of human language, and its biological continuity with animal vocalisation, is perhaps a sufficient indication of his general position on differences between the mental activities of man and beast: although these differences are immense, they developed by imperceptible degrees, by the processes of natural selection, sexual selection, and in some cases as a consequence of civilisation. Higher animals possess attention, memory and association, and a certain amount of reason and imagination. More complex faculties, such as self-consciousness and rational abstraction, could have evolved via the elaboration and combination of simpler ones (1901, p. 128). The scale of the differences between man and ape should be compared to the difference between apes and lower vertebrates like fish.

Quantitative and qualitative intellectual differentiation

The 1901 edition of the *Descent of Man* is over 1,000 pages long, and remains an invaluable compendium of evidence and argument concerning the application of the doctrine of evolution to the human species. Moral, economic and linguistic development as factors over and above biological evolution are given their due. The question of animal mental abilities is covered mainly in the two chapters headed 'Comparison of the mental powers of man and the lower animals', and a concise and convenient summary of these is given at the end of Chapter 4, Chapter 21 being an overall summary of the whole work. The central ideas are that 'the difference in mind between man and the higher animals, great as it is, certainly is one of degree and not of kind' (p. 193) and the dimension of the quantitative difference is the learning of associations: 'The lower animals differ from man solely in his almost infinitely larger power of associating together the most diversified sounds and ideas' (p. 131).

A large part of the human intellect is thus attributed to the 'half-art and half-instinct' of language, since the first and simplest use of this 'wonderful engine which affixes signs to all sorts of objects and qualities' would have acted as a spur to brain expansion, and made available otherwise impossible trains of thought (p. 932). However, 'the extremely complex and regular construction of many barbarous languages, is no proof that they owe their origin to a special act of creation' (p. 140) since there is a curious and interesting parallel between the gradual changes and blendings which may alter languages, and the evolution of species.

Anecdotal evidence of animal thought—Darwin and Romanes (1848–94)

Darwin's theorising about human evolution seems sophisticated and modern. A. R. Wallace, given credit for anticipating the idea of natural selection, held, by comparison, rather old-fashioned views. His heresy, as he called it, was that natural selection could not account for the size of the human brain, since savage human races have human-sized brains, but because of their primitive conditions of life they should have only ape-sized brains if the usual evolutionary forces were responsible. Darwin's knowledge of the social organisation, linguistic complexity and skilled craftsmanship observed in what were then called the lowest savages prevented him from making this sort of blunder.

However, the type of evidence on which Darwin based his theorising about animal behaviour has just as much of an old-fashioned flavour as the most jingoistic Victorian anthropology. He relied on travellers' tales and hunters' stories, culled from contemporary sources such as *The Naturalist in Nicaragua*, and on letters written to him by interested readers about their pets. For instance, the existence of reasoning in dogs is documented by the report of a Mr Colquhoun, in *The Moor and the Loch*, that his retriever, on an occasion when he had winged two wild ducks which fell on the far side of a stream, first tried to bring both back at once, but then: 'though never before known to ruffle a feather, deliberately killed one, brought over the other, and returned for the dead bird' (1901, p. 118). And the existence of a capacity for connecting specific sounds with definite ideas, in animals other than man, is assumed on the basis of the beliefs held by the owners of pet parrots. In particular, Admiral Sir B. J. Sullivan remembered that a parrot kept by his father invariably addressed members of the household by their names, and once said 'you naughty Polly' to another bird which had got out of its cage and was eating apples on the kitchen table (1901, p. 130).

The assembling of anecdotal reports in this way now seems quaint, if not slightly ridiculous, since we are used to elaborate statistical analysis of carefully controlled experiments and field observations, from which the subjective impressions of the observer ought to have been eliminated. Darwin's attitude to anecdotal reports of animal behaviour, and to the behaviour of his own dogs and cats, is one of amiable credulity. Although he is concerned that his correspondents are 'careful observers', he does not believe in doubting ostensibly reliable reports, and indeed felt that too much scepticism of this kind would hold back the progress of science. His acceptance of rather weak evidence in favour of human-like mental attributes in animals seems to be at least partly due to a desire to support his contention that human intellectual abilities do not provide an exception to the theory of evolution. When animal behaviour seemed to provide evidence of abilities in excess of those to be expected on the basis of natural selection, no one was better than Darwin at interpreting complexities in terms of simpler mechanisms — the analysis of the method by which bees construct architecturally elaborate honey combs by the action of simple and understandable behaviour patterns, in the 'instinct' chapter of the *Origin*, is a superb essay of this kind. Therefore the failure to consider whether the behaviour of domestic dogs and parrots might not be explained in terms of mental abilities of a very much simpler type than those involved in human thought can be counted as a flaw in the case made out in *The Descent of Man*. Certainly the conclusions reached by Darwin, that dogs exhibit a sense of humour, a sense of wonder, and beliefs in supernatural agencies, are difficult to defend on the basis of the anecdotal evidence that he quotes.

This does not mean that Darwin was necessarily wrong. Laboratory testing of animal behaviour was virtually unknown, and methodologically Darwin may be said to have made the best use he could of the only evidence available to him. Although we cannot possibly accept the anecdotal evidence as satisfactory indications of the nature of mammalian cognition and feeling, this does not mean that Darwin's conclusions can be rejected out of hand, merely that better tests are required. Undergraduates ever since Lloyd Morgan (1894) and Thorndike (1898) have been warned against the dangers of over-estimating the 'mental powers of the higher animals', but Darwin made the point that it is possible to err on the side of underestimating these powers, if we too quickly assume that simple instinctive or associative mechanisms must provide the explanation for all non-human behaviour. The statistical unreliability of anecdotal reports (was the 'intelligent' action a rare accident?) and the fact that they often depend on the subjective judgment of the observer (what does it mean to report an animal's action as 'deliberate'?) leave the question of the explanation of animal behaviour open, not closed. I shall go into this further shortly, in discussing Lloyd Morgan.

The apotheosis of the Darwinian anecdotal method was reached in Romanes's *Animal Intelligence*, first published in 1881. Romanes was Zoological Secretary of the Linnean Society, and a devoted disciple and friend of Darwin's; and he was entrusted with a much expanded version of the 'Instinct' chapter of the *Origin* (included in Romanes's *Mental Evolution in Animals*, 1883) and all of Darwin's notes and files on animal behaviour. *Animal Intelligence* was based on this material and written with Darwin's collaboration. The introduction includes a reasoned assessment of the virtues and pitfalls of the anecdotal method, and expresses a resolve to give more weight to the reports of reliable observers, and facts which receive numerous confirmations. But it does not seem as though Romanes's enthusiasm was often assailed by doubts during the compilation of the substance of the book. It would be churlish, indeed, to be suspicious of the abilities of the grey parrot kept by Venn, the Cambridge logician (p. 268), or even perhaps of those of Buffon's parrot which, having been trained to offer its claw in response to a human request, is said to have acquired the habit of saying 'Give me your claw' to itself, and then complying with the request by placing one of its claws in its own beak. But the fact that stories of blind rats being led about by their seeing companions were very numerous was not, with the best will in the world, a very good reason for asserting that rats are highly intelligent (p. 360).

Therefore, although Romanes is given the credit for founding comparative psychology (Boring, 1950), his gullibility in *Animal Intelligence* tended to obscure the Darwinian case, and the occasional sensible things Romanes said in his later books, *Mental Evolution in Animals* (1883) and *Mental Evolution in Man* (1888). These works share a remarkable frontispiece which presents a curious and elaborate scale, divided into 50 levels, in which the 'Psychogenesis of Man', from the spermatozoa at level one to a 15-month-old child at level 28, is correlated with 'Products of emotional development' and 'Products of intellectual development' in various animal taxa. Consciousness appears to develop very gradually, with chordates at the same level as the human newborn, and insect larvae and annelid worms matching a 2-week-old baby. Romanes suggested that one might get some idea of the evolutionary progression of states of consciousness by experiencing them backwards as one loses awareness gradually under anaesthetic. Reason is bracketed with the recognition of persons, and association by similarity, and is identified with the higher Crustacea (lobsters) and a child of 14 weeks. Communication of ideas is seen in the social insects (ants and bees); understanding of words and dreaming both appear in birds (parrots having been reported to talk in their sleep); and the distinctiveness of mammals starts at the understanding of mechanisms (cows being particularly adept at unlocking gates). The highest level of intellectual development is rather oddly 'indefinite morality', observed in anthropoid apes and dogs. Romanes says in *Mental Evolution in Animals* that he sees this as the first approximation to a conscience, and that he will return to the topic in later work, but there is not very much more on it in *Mental Evolution in Man*. In that book, the emphasis has shifted to the differences between man and animals, rather than the similarities. The similarities are not forgotten, since it is stressed that in terms of emotions, instincts, volition and reason, the differences are minor. A stand is taken on abstraction, however, and Romanes quotes long passages of Locke. According to the frontispiece diagram, abstraction begins in mammals, but Romanes adopts the Lockean view that there are things called abstract concepts which humans have but even the best of animals do not. Nothing is added to Locke in this, but Romanes goes on to give a more extensive and searching examination of the character of human language.

It is first stressed that animals possess the germ of language in their faculty of making signs. Typical 'gesture-signs' are seen in the pointing of gun-dogs (and pigs can be trained to do the same thing). These are intentional acts of communication, inasmuch as the dogs expect their behaviour to influence human observers, and the natural behaviours may be artificially extended by training, as was apparently the case in Sir John Lubbock's experiments on 'teaching animals to converse'. Lubbock (1884) wrote words such as 'bone', 'water', and 'pet me' on cards and believed that his dogs became able to select cards according to their wishes. Dogs have difficulty in mimicking human vocalisation, but Romanes suggested that this is a matter of limitations of vocal organ anatomy, rather than psychological deficiencies. (Alexander Graham Bell wrote to Romanes that he had succeeded in training an English terrier to say 'How are you grandmama' with great distinctness, but, in a rare outbreak of caution, Romanes refused to believe him.) Although the ability to make 'gesture-signs', and other aspects of animal intelligence, are taken as support for the theory that human mental abilities evolved gradually, Romanes is quite clear that human speech differs radically from animal sign-making. For one thing, 'gesture language has no grammar' (1888, p. 114). In the post-Chomskyan era, this is a familiar point. Romanes's discussion of the abstractions underlying grammar may now seem rather primitive, but he should be credited with the attempt to pin down exactly what it is about human speech which is significantly different from animal gestures. In Romanes's terms, speech is distinctive because it allows predication, and the making of propositions (1888, p. 163). The unique ability of man 'consists in his being able to *mean a proposition*' (p. 164, original italics).

In other words, the essential feature of human speech is the sentence, or ideas expressed as relations between words, most simply as connections between subjects, objects and verbs. In all of Romanes's anecdotes, there were none which suggested that dogs, apes, or parrots communicated in this way, although he quotes cases of dogs appearing to understand sentences such as 'the sheep are in the potatoes'. Placing the line between man and beast at grammar would therefore have been supported by the evidence at hand, but Romanes followed Locke in going further back, to something in the naming of concepts, and added on, gratuitously in view of what he had written under Darwin's supervision, self-consciousness and reflection.

Huxley's materialism: mind and brain in ape and man

'I wish to God there were more automata in the world like you', Darwin wrote to T. H. Huxley. This was in March 1882 when Darwin had only a month to live, having suffered the final blow in a lifetime of poor health in the form of a heart-attack when he was ringing the doorbell of Romanes's house near the Zoo. Darwin's quip was a reference to Huxley's latest irreverence, the extension of Cartesian automatism to man, given initially in the paper 'On the hypothesis that animals are automata and its history' (*Method and Results*, 1893). Huxley (1825–95) was a brilliant physiologist and anatomist, elected to the Royal Society before he was twenty-six for his work with the dissecting scalpel and microscope. He was important as an essayist, educator and public figure, and a formidable champion of the Darwinian cause. He invented the term agnosticism, which enabled high-minded Victorian scientists to sidestep religion; he used Pasteur's experiments to argue for the physical basis of life, and he put forward the doctrine of epiphenomenalism, in which mental experiences were dismissed as by-products of the physical operations of the brain. Human subjective experience was thus kept firmly within the confines of scientifically investigatable material reality. Conscious experience is merely the 'smell above the factory' — the real workings of the mind are the activities of the brain. Huxley was therefore about as much of a materialist, reductionist and determinist as it is possible to be, but somehow managed to succeed in always seeming to be more morally serious than his opponents. In 1878, Huxley wrote (in six weeks) a 300-page book on Hume, in which most of Hume's scepticism was retained, but the subjective empiricism updated so that sense impressions are interpreted as states of the brain. (A rather similar version of Hume is given by Ayer, 1980.)

Huxley took on the job of explicitly bringing the human species into the Darwinian theory of evolution before Darwin did this himself, and dealt in greater detail than Darwin did with man's position within the order Primates (a Linnean term which Huxley preferred to Darwin's 'Quadrumana'). His first essays on these topics were in *Evidence of Man's Place in Nature* (1863), and there is a short but forceful supplement by Huxley in Darwin's *Descent of Man* entitled 'Note on the resemblances and differences in the structure and development of the brain in man and apes'.

A good deal of Huxley's time was spent on refuting the assertion of Sir Richard Owen (the ranking comparative anatomist of the time, who fought a rearguard action against human evolution) that the human brain contains bits not to be found in those of apes ('the third lobe, the posterior horn of the lateral ventricle, and the hippocampus minor'). All these structures were thought to be found in the occipital (posterior) lobes of only the human cerebral hemispheres, which cover the cerebellum. In small mammals, such as the rat, the cerebral hemispheres of the brain do not cover the cerebellum. But the occipital lobes of the chimpanzee and the gorilla do cover the cerebellum, and are anatomically very similar to the corresponding parts of the human brain, as Huxley easily demonstrated. Ironically, the occipital lobes of the rhesus monkey brain, which, like the rear of the hemispheres in all mammals, receive projections from the visual pathways, are now taken as very useful approximations to the posterior lobes of man—it is the anterior (frontal) lobes, at the other end of the brain, that are now most often said to be the repository of especially human intellectual qualities. Huxley's conclusion was that there are no anatomically identifiable components of the human brain that are missing from the brain of other large primates:

> So far as cerebral structure goes therefore, it is clear that man differs less from the Chimpanzee or the Orang, than these do even from the monkeys, and that the difference between the brains of the Chimpanzee and of Man is almost insignificant, when compared with that between the Chimpanzee brain and that of a Lemur. (Darwin, 1901, p. 312)

Even the greater size of the human brain, though it 'doubtless will one day help to furnish an explanation of the great gulf which intervenes between the lowest man and the highest ape in intellectual power', was not to be regarded as crucial, since 'the difference in weight of brain between the highest and lowest men is far greater, both relatively and absolutely, than that between the lowest man and the highest ape'. Huxley went into other obvious possibilities. The gyri and sulci of the human cerebral hemispheres tend to be more complicated than those of the chimpanzee, but 'Every principal gyrus and sulcus of a chimpanzee's brain is clearly represented in that of a man'. Human gyri and sulci seem to be asymmetrical when the left hemisphere is compared to the right, but 'the degree of asymmetry of the convolutions of the two sides in the human brain is subject to much individual variation' and 'in some individuals of the chimpanzee, their complexity and asymmetry become notable' (Darwin, 1901, p. 312). And therefore:

> Regarded systematically the cerebral differences, of man and apes, are not of more than generic value—his Family distinction resting chiefly on his dentition, his pelvis and his lower limbs. (Huxley, 1906, p. 96)

If the mind is construed as brain activity, and the human and chimpanzee brains are so similar, whence arises the intellectual gulf? Huxley curtly gives the language argument in a footnote:

> A man born dumb, notwithstanding his great cerebral mass and his inheritance of strong intellectual instincts, would be capable of few higher intellectual manifestations than an Orang or Chimpanzee, if he were confined to the society of dumb associates. (Huxley, 1906, p. 26)

Marx (1818–83) and Engels (1820–95) as post-Darwinians

Darwin was much more interested in plants and beetles than in human societies, and the brief section on 'Natural Selection as affecting Civilized Nations' in the *Descent* is largely defensive, with the aim of rebutting suggestions such as that of Galton, to the effect that, in civilised societies, the poor and reckless members outbreed the provident and virtuous, thus preventing any improvements by natural selection. Darwin countered that a high rate of mortality among the poor and reckless might do something to check 'this downward tendency' and in general seems ready to envisage natural selection operating in civilised nations in a rather ruthless way. He is against intentionally neglecting the weak and helpless, but hopes that they will not marry so freely as the sound, since 'excepting in the case of man himself, hardly anyone is so ignorant as to allow his worst animals to breed' (1901, p. 206). Because of our social and sympathetic instincts, we must tolerate 'the undoubtedly bad effects of the weak surviving and propagating their kind', although 'as man suffers from the same physical evils as the lower animals, he has no right to expect an immunity from the evils consequent on the struggle for existence' (1901, p. 206 and p. 219). Darwin was not quite the kindly old liberal he is sometimes portrayed as. But he had very little to do with social Darwinism in any of its forms, and turned down the chance of having the English edition of *Das Kapital* dedicated to him.

This is just as well for our purposes, since the Marxist position on the relation between human and animal mental life is not an obvious extension of the writings of Darwin, still less of those of Romanes or Huxley. That Darwin influenced early Marxist thought, but also that Engels, at least, felt free to make extravagant alterations to the biologically based accounts of mental evolution, can be illustrated by Engels's paper 'The Part Played by Labour in the Transition from Ape to Man' (written about 1875; see Marx and Engels, 1968). In this, Darwin's name is used, but little of his outlook. 'Labour', first as the use of flint tools, and then as the social organisation entailed by tool-using, necessitated, according to Engels, the creation of language and, with language, instigated the growth in the size of the brain in ancestral human species. And it is labour and society which produce human consciousness. Consciousness as we now experience it is therefore a product of history, rather than of biological evolution. In a phrase of Marx's, 'Man confirms his real social life in his species-consciousness and in his thought he merely repeats his real existence' (1971, p. 151). The reality here is political, rather than physical. This is important because it gives rise to a split of almost Cartesian proportions between the mental qualities of ape and those of man. If the human mind consists of internal reflections of exterior economic conditions, perceived in the light of a sense of history, then any continuity with the mental activities of animals was lost with the division of labour. In part, this is a restatement of the uniqueness of human self-consciousness and reflection, but clearly there is included a distinct hypothesis that these depend upon a sequence of social and economic events, and a considerable degree of confusion results from the use of the term 'consciousness' to imply an all-embracing Hegelian absolute, as well as to denote a specific result of the place of individuals in human societies.

It would be possible to agree that the acceptance of current social norms, or a knowledge of history, or an ideological commitment, might influence the way people think, without going on to deduce that a dog or a chimpanzee, lacking any of these influences, has no mental life at all. But in practice, accepting Marxist economic determinism tends to result in a theological kind of division between animal and human consciousness, and indeed between the mental states of members of the human species exposed to different sets of social institutions. Distinctions of this kind are found, for instance, in Steven Rose's *The Conscious Brain* (1976). Rose suggests that there is a discontinuity between the consciousness of man and other mammals and that this is because of the greater size of the human brain; but political rather than physical variables are lurking in the background. 'With the emergence of consciousness a qualitative evolutionary leap forward has occurred, making for the critical distinction between humans and other species' (Rose, 1976, p. 179). Consciousness is then defined as an interaction between the individual and the social environment, so that 'as human relationships have become transformed during the evolution of human society, so human consciousness too has been transformed'. When forms of society change, we must expect consciousness to change also, and therefore modern human consciousness is a very different thing from that which occurred in earlier members of the same species, living under different social conditions (Rose, 1976, p. 179). Rose makes it clear that he is using the term consciousness in the Marxist sense, as something which occurs in a society rather than in a brain, and which depends on such factors as the mode of production of consumer goods. As he points out, although this encompasses the dependence of thought on culture, it gives rise to a number of paradoxes. In particular, the pre-emptive social definition of consciousness begs the questions of what sort of mental processes might occur in isolation from human social forces, whether in isolated human beings, or in groups of individuals of other species. There may be an important sense in which 'a Robinson Crusoe figure, would scarcely be conscious at all' (Rose, 1976, p. 34), but this does not mean that such an individual might not sleep and dream, and wake and wonder, even if the contents of his dreams and wonderings were as limited as his physical and social circumstances. Similarly, because a troop of chimpanzees has no sense of history, no mythology, and no novels, there are obvious limitations on the thoughts of its members. But they will also sleep and dream, and behave as if they have hopes and fears when awake. Deciding whether these activities imply the existence of mental states may be difficult, but there is surely more to the question than merely defining consciousness in terms of human social institutions.

Lloyd Morgan (1852–1936)—the beginnings of the behaviourist reaction

The amiable credulity which Darwin and Romanes applied to anecdotal evidence of mental ability in animals quickly came under fire. Morgan supplied a heavy, but inaccurate, piece of artillery, by bringing forward, in his *Introduction to Comparative Psychology* (1894), what is known as Lloyd Morgan's Canon. This runs:

> In no case may we interpret an action as the outcome of the exercise of a higher psychical faculty, if it can be interpreted as the exercise of one which stands lower on the psychological scale.

Whether or not one adopts such a rule of thumb, and how it is applied, determines the answers one will give to many of the questions that may be asked about the extent of mental organisation in animals. Subsequent writers on comparative psychology frequently assume that the virtue of Lloyd Morgan's Canon is self-evident, because it expresses a law of parsimony, which underlies the success of scientific method, and derives from a maxim of logic, 'Occam's razor', accepted since the fourteenth century. The razor says 'Entities are not to be multiplied without necessity', or 'It is vain to do with more what can be done with fewer' (Russell, 1946).

There is no doubt that parsimony is generally a good idea. But it is debatable whether Lloyd Morgan's Canon necessarily leads to parsimonious explanations, and also whether parsimonious explanations, especially of biological and psychological phenomena, are necessarily the best ones. Applied to human actions, the Canon would require us always to assume that people act from the most straightforward and least intellectually demanding motives. This might be a useful palliative against the urge to search for deep and dark explanations every time someone forgets a name, or misses a bus, but it would surely be unwise to assume that the simplest explanation of a politician's promise, or a child's tears, is always true. Similarly, because all animals feed, and move, and fight, it does not follow that the mechanisms which control these actions in the lowest and simplest species are the only ones at work in all the others. 'Nature is notoriously prodigal; why should we interpret it only parsimoniously?' (Boring, 1950, p. 474). Clearly, because sticklebacks and chimpanzees both build nests, we should not be obliged to believe that the psychological processes available to the chimpanzee are the same as those utilised by the stickleback. Still less should we want to deduce that because the stickleback's nest is more elaborate than that of the chimp, that the stickleback exercises a higher mental faculty. There is a very general, and a very difficult problem behind all this, which infects the roots of behaviourist systems of explanation of animal activities. It may be described as the 'same behaviour—same mechanism' fallacy.

If one makes any attempt at parsimony in the explanation of behaviours, it seems eminently reasonable to apply similar explanations to similar behaviours. If a cockroach lifts its leg away from the source of a painful electric shock, and we can draw a nice graph of the strength of the leg-withdrawal response, as a function of the intensity and number of previous shocks received, we may be able to construct an aesthetically pleasing set of mathematical equations which simulate very precisely the way that behaviour changes, and which may even predict what will happen when other factors, such as the interval between the shocks, are varied. Now suppose that the same kind of experiments are performed on dogs, and the dogs flex their legs away from the shocks in more or less the same way as the cockroaches. Perhaps the dogs will be a bit quicker (or a bit slower) than the cockroaches, and we can alter a couple of constants in the mathematical equations, neatly dealing with the slight differences of behaviour. Surely this would mean that we ought to say that the dogs and the cockroaches are controlled by the same mechanisms? It would certainly violate Lloyd Morgan's Canon if we did not. But is it really parsimonious to assume that the 100-gram brain of the dog, which will playfully fetch sticks, and obey his master's voice, is working in the same way as the microscopic ganglia of the cockroach? Nothing could be more absurd, yet this is precisely what the invocation of parsimony, Occam, and Lloyd Morgan invites us to do. Such invitations are sent out because the Canon contains a fallacy—the fallacy that similar actions must necessarily be given similar explanations.

Therefore Lloyd Morgan's Canon ought to be rejected, and spurious invitations to parsimony refused. We should interpret an action as the outcome of the most likely causes, not as the outcome of the most ridiculously simple mechanism we have ever come across which could accomplish that sort of thing. The most likely cause will be the one which takes into account the most evidence. Assembling the evidence may be difficult, but it is not hard to make informed guesses about the probable capacities of a given species, or about the dispositions and circumstances that may affect a given individual. Just because an action *can* be attributed to the exercise of minimal psychological capacities does not mean that such an attribution is necessarily correct, if there are good grounds for alternative conjectures. In general, it is possible that actions which have much in common at the level of behavioural description are the product of quite different psychological processes. The vast majority of theorists, before and after Lloyd Morgan, have been ready to assume, for instance, that insects and cold-blooded vertebrates are controlled by collections of prewired reflexes, whereas large and specialised mammals like the dog and the monkey have evolved additional kinds of psychological capacity. If someone were able to provide a description of a monkey eating a leaf, which could be applied without alteration to an insect eating a leaf, few would feel compelled to deduce that eating leaves in monkeys results from behaviour-controlling mechanisms which are shared with the insect, although some behaviourists have gone a considerable distance in that direction. Even if one is dealing with the same species, or with the same individual, similar actions may not always result from the same causes. It is not unusual for even the most hard-bitten observers of animal behaviour to say that scratching or grooming in a particular animal may be a product of fastidiousness on one occasion, but boredom, or nervousness, on another. (That is, grooming may be classified as 'displacement activity'; e.g. Hinde, 1970.)

To propose that isolated incidents of animal behaviour should always be given the simplest conceivable explanation is therefore quite bizarre and unrealistic. In fairness to Lloyd Morgan and to William of Occam, it should be pointed out that neither of them held views of animal psychology as fatuously oversimplified as those their names are used to defend. Occam has been credited with the opinion that animal thought is a partial and restricted form of human thought: 'Man thinks in two ways—first, in natural terms, which he shares with animals, and second, in conventional terms, which are peculiar to man alone' (quoted in McCulloch, 1965). Morgan wished to be more careful than Romanes in accepting the interpretations implied in anecdotal reports, but had studied under Huxley, and was committed to the concept of the gradual evolution of mental abilities. He preferred to rely on his own experimental observations, and took a fairly conservative view of the psychological capacities of animals, by the standards of his day, but his theoretical agreements with Romanes now stand out more clearly than his methodological differences.

Lloyd Morgan's concept of consciousness

One indication of Morgan's concern with consciousness is the cross-quotation between his writings and those of Wundt (1832–1920), the founding father of the scientific study of conscious sensation. In *Lectures on Human and Animal Psychology* (1894) Wundt expounded the principle that the mental processes of animals must be estimated by comparison with our own introspections. This principle was repeated by Kulpe (1862–1915) before it was disputed by Thorndike and Watson. Even in the light of such estimations, though, Wundt recommended that we always 'choose the simplest explanation possible', explicitly repudiated Romanes, and adopted the tack taken by Leibniz, that manifestations of animal intelligence should always be interpreted in terms of relatively simple mental associations and conditioned expectations (Wundt, 1894, pp. 345–6, 354 and 362). Wundt succeeded in training his pet poodle to shut the various doors to his study on command, but stressed that after being trained with the first door, the animal did not immediately respond to commands directed at the other doors. One of the doors opened outwards, so that after the dog had pushed it closed, it was left outside. It would usually then scratch at the door to be let in again, from which Wundt deduced that the poodle did not properly understand the final purpose behind the operation, which was to save Wundt from getting up.

Lloyd Morgan, in *Habit and Instinct* (1896) repeats the strictures against Romanes, but in chapters on 'The relation of consciousness to instinctive behaviour' and 'Intelligence and the acquisition of habits', he puts forward a carefully considered theory of the limits and functions of subjective awareness in animals. The essence of the theory is the assumption that instincts, and well-formed habits, are automatic, but the non-habitual utilisation of previous experience requires consciousness. This is a very old distinction, and Darwin had specifically disagreed with the emphasis placed on it by Cuvier, but Lloyd Morgan gave it a systematic restatement. Habits depend on previous experience, and amount to acquired automatisms, after sufficient repetition. But, rather as the drilling of raw recruits requires the direction of a drill-sergeant, the organisation of activities which may become habitual requires the intervention of consciousness, 'represented in the flesh by the cerebral cortex'. Consciousness may be defined as whatever it is that 'enables an animal to guide its actions in the light of previous experience', something which 'looks on and makes a memorandum of what is going forward': 'when we say that conduct is modified in the light of experience we mean that the consciousness of what happened yesterday helps us avoid similar consequences today' (Morgan, 1896, pp. 127, 131 and 145). In other words, in 'the higher grades of animal life' at least, even simple associations require mental awareness, rather than only unconscious and mechanical connections. As examples of this, Morgan quotes his own observations of the effects of prior experience on the behaviour of young birds. A chick when it first sees a cinnabar caterpillar will seize and eat it, but find it extremely unpalatable. The next time it sees such a caterpillar, it shrinks from it on sight. Morgan assumes that the first encounter with the caterpillar must have been conscious, for it to have any effect on future behaviour. This is the topic of another Canon, now forgotten, which states that present behaviour can only be guided by previous experiences which were conscious in the first place.

Similarly, when moorhen chicks, which Morgan fed by turning over soil with a spade to expose worms, learned to run towards him as soon as he picked up the spade, Morgan deduced that the chicks must have been conscious at some point of the conjunction of the spade with worms. When they ran to the man with the spade it was thus because they remembered the worms. If they did this often enough, running to the spade might become an automatic habit, but conscious direction of actions by remembered experience was an essential initial phase of habit formation in Lloyd Morgan's theory. This is certainly not the simplest possible explanation of habit formation (although perhaps it was the simplest explanation that occurred to Lloyd Morgan). In any event, it should be noted that Lloyd Morgan's own application of the rule of parsimony did not preclude the discussion of awareness and memory in chicks, as a reminder that there may be such a thing as an explanation of animal behaviour that is too simple to be sensible.

3 Thorndike (1874–1949), Pavlov (1849–1936) and twentieth-century theories of animal learning

Thorndike's stimulus-response connections

It was really Thorndike and Pavlov, rather than Lloyd Morgan, who established the trend towards minimalist explanations of animal learning within comparative psychology. Lloyd Morgan not only assumed that 'the higher grades of animal life' consciously adjusted their actions to serve their needs, but intended to provide an account of mental evolution of essentially the same kind as Darwin's and Romanes's. Thorndike was keen to sweep away all such theoretical frills, and took up a fiercely combative position against the 'anecdote school' of Romanes and his North American counterparts such as Wesley Mills (there is a remarkably vituperative exchange between Mills and Thorndike in the *Psychological Review* of 1899).

Thorndike's PhD thesis was published in 1898, under the title of *Animal Intelligence*, and is notable for its innovations in experimental technique. In a sense, Thorndike introduced the laboratory experiment into animal psychology. Lloyd Morgan's and Wesley Mills's experiments were naturalistic in so far as birds or other animals were observed in the open air under free-range conditions. Thorndike did not have a laboratory as such, since he kept chicks, cats and dogs in his own lodgings, and the restrictions on space enforced in themselves a different sort of data gathering from that which Mills, for instance, was able to make with semi-wild foxes. Just as important as the physical restrictions on space was Thorndike's theoretical attitude. Although he adopted the conventional title for his thesis, he pointed out that previous authors had paid much more attention to animal intelligence than to animal stupidity. Thorndike's tone throughout is that of a man who is going to remedy this omission.

The experimental technique with which Thorndike collected behavioural evidence to support his belief in animal stupidity was the use of 'puzzle boxes'. Both dogs and cats were tested in these, and there were maze experiments with chicks, but the data which had pride of place came from the performance of twelve cats, each of which was tested in several different puzzle boxes.

The puzzle-box experiments

The boxes were small crates, hammered together from wooden slats, and only 20 inches by 15 in plan, and 12 inches high (see Bitterman, 1969, for an illustration). Although the cats were young—mostly between 5 and 8 months old during the experiments—all except two struggled violently when confined in such a small space. They were tested in what is described as a state of 'utter hunger', with a piece of fish visible outside the box, but Thorndike was in no doubt that the struggles were directed at getting 'out of' the box rather than 'to' the food. One of the criticisms put forward by Mills (1899), which seems reasonable under the circumstances, was that the state of panic which Thorndike succeeded in inducing in the cats was not likely to be conducive to considered and insightful solutions to problems.

The problem which the cats were required to solve was the detection of the mechanism by which the door to the box they were in could be released. Each box had a different system of pulleys, strings, and catches, arranged so that pulling a certain loop of string, or pushing a button, or pressing a combination of levers, would allow a door to fall open. Romanes's emphasis on the understanding of such mechanical devices as a distinguishing capacity of mammals was thus put to the test. Thorndike was able to say with some confidence that his cats did not work out or understand the sequence of strings and catches, and indeed the solutions are not always obvious to the human observer (see the illustrations in Bitterman, 1969. However, if the cats had simply failed to get out of the box, the experiments would not have been worth reporting. What happened was that the cats did get out, and eventually became very good at getting out, but Thorndike claimed that automatic and crude psychological processes were responsible. No inference, insight, thought, or even any 'looking over the situation' was, in Thorndike's opinion, used by the animals. Rather, simple associations between the stimulus of being in the box, and the response necessary to get out, were 'stamped in' in the course of trial-and-error learning.

This argument is strongest when the animal's tactics change very slowly, and Thorndike liked to quote his most gradual 'learning curve'. Cat 12, during the testing sequence in Box A, showed few signs of intelligence. Box A was one of the easier puzzles, since clawing at a loop of string near the front released the door. The first time cat 12 was confined in this box it, like the others, scratched, clawed and thrust its paw through any openings it could find. After almost three minutes of this (160 seconds) it succeeded in pulling at the loop of string, and opened the door. Now, according to Lloyd Morgan, the discovery that the pulling of the loop was followed by the opening of the door ought to have impressed itself on the consciousness of the animal, so that the next time it wanted to get out, it should pull the loop immediately. What actually happened was that the second trial was a quick one—the cat got out in 30 seconds—but the third and fourth tests did not suggest that it had fully grasped the solution to the puzzle, since the third and fourth scores were 90 and 60 seconds. The full list of scores, over 22 successive trials in this box, was 160, 30, 90, 60, 15, 28, 20, 30, 22, 11, 15, 20, 12, 10, 14, 8, 8, 5, 10, 8, 6, 6, 7. What Thorndike deduced from this is that cat 12 never really understood what was going on, but that there was a gradual, unthinking, and automatic improvement in the efficiency of its escape response. The theory is that a mental connection is strengthened, but that the connection is a direct one between the stimulus of being in the box, and the response of pulling the string, rather than an association between pulling the string and getting out. The cat is not assumed to think ahead about getting out, but the pleasure and relief it feels when it does get out act backward to make an automatic link between preceding stimulus and response. This is a parsimonious theory, which explains the success of the animal in eventually 'solving' the puzzle, while leaving out any process of inference, reasoning, or mental anticipation.

It is interesting that Thorndike did not go all the way with this stimulus and response theory, since he quite clearly left in mental states which appear to be largely superfluous. Although he firmly rejected all 'reason, comparison or inference, perception of similarity, and imitation', Thorndike believed that animals had subjective sense impressions, evaluative feelings, and impulses to respond connected to prior sense impressions. In his theory, animals have no mental life that is not concerned with the mediation between stimulus and response, and in this they differ fundamentally from man, who can have purely mental connections and free ideas and impulses which need not be directly tied to reflex-like responses to stimuli. Thus any progression in mental evolution 'is not from little and simple to big and complicated but from direct connections to indirect connections'. Only in man, and possibly in other primates, should we expect discrimination, generalisations and abstractions (Thorndike, 1898, pp. 108–9). This is in line with the speculations of Wundt, and Thorndike's mentor William James (*Principles of Psychology*, 1891, vol. II, pp. 348–60), but is the theory supported by Thorndike's new evidence?

First, it should be noted that the performance of cat 12 in Box A is not altogether representative of that of the other eleven animals. The average escape times of all the cats tested in Box A shows that about 5 minutes were taken to escape on the first and second trial, but less than 30 seconds on the third trial, with slow improvements thereafter. There are plenty of individual cases when cats appear to get the idea after the first or second trial, and escape immediately on all subsequent tests. Thus the gradual modification of response is not universal, or even typical. In some cases, Thorndike admits, especially when a cat had been paying attention to what it was doing when the release device worked, 'a single experience stamps the association in so completely that ever after the act is done at once' (Thorndike, 1898, p. 27). But in these cases, is it more sensible to say that act is performed as a reflex response to stimuli, rather than saying that the act is performed because the animal remembers that this is the way to get out? This is not an easy question to answer, but it is obvious that the mere fact of the performance of the response does not exclude one or the other explanation. Additional information would help. For instance, do the animals appear to anticipate getting out once they have made the response? Would they refrain from making the releasing response if for some reason they did not wish to get out? The only variables available in Thorndike's results are how difficult the puzzle seemed to be, and how gradually the improvements in skill took place, and even these allow an interpretation in terms of a gradual realisation of the relation between a particular manipulation and the opening of the escape door. It is worth noting that the most gradual improvements in performance took place when, in Thorndike's words, there was least congruity between the act and the result, such as when cats were released if they licked or scratched themselves, or when chicks were freed for pecking their feathers.

Immediately after his postgraduate work on animal learning, Thorndike took a job at the Teachers College of Columbia University, and devoted himself to the psychology of education. Although he had stressed the differences between human and animal mental processes, this did not prevent him from recommending 'animal-like methods of learning' in education. As he was sceptical about the influence of imitation and understanding on his animal subjects, so he tended to emphasise the importance of practice and activity in human education. Although the routine and mechanical formation of stimulus-response connections was a rather inferior 'form of intellection', 'this hitherto unsuspected law of animal mind may prevail in human mind to an extent hitherto unknown' (Thorndike, 1898, p. 105). *Elements of Psychology* (1905) and the three-volume *Educational Psychology* (1913) were extremely influential in their day (see Joncich, 1968 and Hilgard and Bower, 1975). The essence of Thorndike's recommendations are contained in his 'Law of Practice' and 'Law of Effect'. The Law of Practice was simply the increase in habit formation due to repetition, which in Thorndike's hands meant that 'the only way to teach fractions in algebra, for example, is to get the pupil to do, do, do' (Thorndike, 1898, p. 105). But practice by itself is not enough, since it is the *effects* of actions, in terms of state of satisfaction or dissatisfaction which result from them, rather than merely the repetition of actions, which is crucial in determining whether the actions become stamped in or not.

Pavlov and conditioned reflexes

In spite of Thorndike's great influence in ensconcing practice and motivation, rather than understanding and insight, as key concepts in learning theory, Thorndike's thunder as the arch-mechanist in early twentieth-century psychology has been stolen by the more extended and systematic investigations of Pavlov (1849–1936). It is inevitable that Pavlov's experiments raise more questions about the necessity of conscious mental experience in the alteration of response, since the responses measured were such as to be almost by definition involuntary, unintentional, and not necessarily known to the responding animal.

The behaviour measured in Pavlov's early work was the behaviour of the stomach, or rather of certain glands in the stomach. Pavlov's hypothesis was that the secretion of gastric and pancreatic juices was under the control of the brain, and not simply a matter of reaction to local stimulation. In fact, local mechanical and chemical stimulation and reactions to internal hormones also influence gastric secretions, but what took Pavlov's interest was the effect of remote and psychological factors on these internal activities.

The experiments on digestion, for which Pavlov received the Nobel prize of 1904, involved a number of surgical operations, performed on dogs. A first step, developed by others in the 1840s, was the chronic implantation of a metal tube in the dog's stomach, through which gastric juices (consisting mainly of hydrochloric acid) could be collected. Reasonable amounts of gastric juice are normally only obtained when the animal eats, and this means that the fluids collected are contaminated by food. The refinement introduced by Pavlov was the anatomical separation of the mouth from the stomach: the oesophagus was cut and the two ends independently brought out to the throat. This meant food could be eaten by the dog without reaching the stomach, or food could be dropped into the stomach without the dog's having eaten it. Although this sounds horrendous, animals survived these procedures for some years.

The physical separation of eating and digestion allowed the demonstration of the psychological dependence of the latter on the former. Bread dropped into the stomach without the animal noticing it is not digested, but eating bread with relish induces gastric activity, even if nothing is present in the stomach. This is not a simple matter of taste stimuli driving internal secretions, since the mere sight of food produces gastric juices, if the dog takes an interest in it, and the effectiveness of food in the mouth depends on how far it 'suits the dog's taste' (Pavlov, 1955, p. 142).

These results in themselves suggest that the previous experience of animals may determine the reactions of their internal organs to external stimuli. This conclusion was established beyond doubt in the further experiments by Pavlov on the secretion of saliva rather than the secretion of gastric juices. Practically all of the experiments reported by Pavlov as examples of 'conditioned reflexes' (see Pavlov, 1927 and 1955) employ precise measurements of the amounts of saliva secreted by dogs in response to various external stimuli, surgical externalisation of the salivary glands being used to allow saliva to run off and be measured, usually in terms of number of drops. The standard Pavlovian experiment presents a restrained and hungry dog with an electric buzzer, which if sounded is followed 10 seconds later by a piece of meat dispensed in front of the dog by a remotely controlled delivery apparatus. Dogs do not normally salivate when they hear a buzzer, but even after one experience of the conjunction of the buzzer with food, a dog may salivate when the buzzer is sounded again a few minutes later (Pavlov, 1927, p. 27). To establish a reliable response, a dog might be given half a dozen pieces of meat, each preceded by the buzzer, at 5-minute intervals, every day for a week or so. After this a demonstration of the 'conditioned reflex' could be given by simply sounding the buzzer, for 30 seconds, without giving any meat. This should now produce the same effect as showing the dog real food—copious amounts of saliva will be secreted, and the dog will lick its lips, look at the food dispenser, and perhaps wag its tail.

Much has been deduced from this sort of simple experiment. The first point is that salivation is no more an intentional action than gastric secretion, and so the idea of the dog salivating as a reasoned and deliberate action does not really arise. There are plenty of instances when 'conditioned reflexes' seem extremely simple, rigid, automatic and unconscious. If both the stimulus and the response are confined to the digestive tract for instance, as in the experiments of Bykov (1957) one would be reluctant to appeal to higher mental activities as the intervening mechanisms. Similarly investigators subsequent to Pavlov have claimed to find conditioned reflexes mediated by the spinal cord in mammals (see Ince *et al.*, 1978 for recent evidence of a conditioned reflex in lower spinal cord of a human paraplegic) and it is possible to get fairly conventional Pavlovian conditioning in animals whose cerebral cortex has been removed (see Russell, 1971). The beginnings of this trend lie in the experiments by Twitmeyer (1902) which seemed to show classical conditioning of the human 'knee-jerk' reflex. This result was undoubtedly influential in establishing the conventional view of Pavlovian conditioning as a process requiring only very rudimentary 'stimulus-response' associations. In any case the interpretation of Pavlov's results given by learning theorists such as Guthrie (1930) and Hull (e.g. 1929, 1937, 1943) has meant that 'conditioning' has become a watchword for explanations of animal (and human) adaptations to experience which exclude thought, mental ideas or inference, or anything of the kind.

It is important to point out that these minimalist interpretations are in violation of much of Pavlov's evidence, and that Pavlov himself, although he attacked the vague mentalisms of contemporary intro-spectionism and 'Gestalt' psychology, held relatively subtle views on the relation between conditioning, brain function, and cognition. His intention, already evident in his Nobel speech of 1904, was to provide a scientific account of 'higher nervous activity'—the workings of the cortex of the mammalian cerebral hemispheres. 'The cerebral hemispheres stand out as the crowning achievement in the nervous development of the animal kingdom' is the first sentence of *Conditioned Reflexes* (1927) which is subtitled *An Investigation of the Physiological Activity of the Cerebral Cortex*. Pavlov was aiming at a theory of the crowning achievement, not a reduction to the lowest common denominator of neural adaptability. He hoped for 'a fusion of the psychological with the physiological, of the subjective with the objective' (1955, p. 455). In the case of man, evidence concerning the fusion can be obtained because 'distortion of the human subjective world is linked, obviously, with anatomical and physiological disturbances of the higher part of the brain' (ibid). In the case of other mammals, it is impossible to know how to define subjective understanding, but, by the use of tools such as the method of conditioning, the animal's adaptation to experience can be discussed in terms of the 'analysing and synthesising' activities of the cerebral cortex in their brains. Thus Pavlov's treatment of 'higher nervous activity' was somewhat more liberal and flexible than many of his followers. And, moreover, it is arguable that the evidence from Pavlovian conditioning is consistent with even more liberal and flexible theoretical interpretations than Pavlov ever put on it.

Pavlov's theorising became detailed and complex, but it is possible to give a summary in terms of two general mechanisms, as he did himself succinctly in 1909 in 'Natural Science and the Brain' (see *Selected Works*, 1955) and more discursively in 1927. The first mechanism is the formation of temporary connections; this explains how arbitrary stimuli are able to function as signals, as in the case of the buzzer signalling food in the standard experiment discussed above. Note that these connections are not quite so restricted as those proposed by Thorndike, since they are not necessarily just connections by which a stimulus forces a particular response out of the organism. Signals for food may direct animals to acquire it, rather than only eliciting salivation (Pavlov, 1955, p. 210). Exactly how this happens is never very clear, but it would be Pavlov's line to say that various parts of the brain are used to react to food itself, and signals for food are stimuli which, because of previous associations, get these parts of the brain going even when food isn't there.

The second mechanism, treated separately from the first sort of simple association, is related to traditional concerns about the methods by which the external world is perceived and classified. Pavlov discussed these methods in terms of 'analysers'. 'An analyser is a complex nervous mechanism which begins with an external receiving apparatus and ends in the brain' (1955, p. 215). This sounds like what might nowadays be called a sensory pathway, but naturally the emphasis is on the way in which sensory information is received in the brain so that 'the given analyser can decompose the external world' (Pavlov, 1955, p. 216).

The salivary conditioning technique was used (a) to establish how far the sensory analysers could become sensitive to subtle distinctions in the external world, and therefore make fine discriminations, and (b) to discover the extent to which the analysing apparatus can synthesise experiences, this mainly in the sense of responding selectively to combinations of individual stimuli, or to members of sets of stimuli. Some of the results are well known, but others have tended to be disregarded by subsequent commentators on Pavlov's work. The simplest result is that a large amount of association by similarity is the usual concomitant of conditioning with a single stimulus. Thus if a note of middle C is made a signal for food, almost as much salivation will also be obtained if B flat or D is sounded, with progressively diminished responses to notes further away from the original. This is called by Pavlov 'generalisation', which has now become a common term; but he also saw it as a form of synthesis. It is perhaps not quite the same thing as what Aristotle meant by association through similarity, but clearly similarity is involved. Sound frequencies are not perceived in isolation from one another, but are organised on an internal scale of pitch.

Fine discriminations

However, generalisation along the scale is not a fixed and invariant process, but depends on experience. In particular, there appears to be a process of comparison, or contrast, within particular dimensions. If a dog continues to be given food whenever middle C is sounded, but gets no food for interspersed B flats, it will very quickly cease to give the generalised response to these non-rewarded tones. This Pavlov called the method of contrasts, and it was used because it led so rapidly to dogs salivating only to very precisely defined sensations. Protracted experience of just middle C may mean conditioned responses for any variation in pitch are much reduced, but this is an unreliable and extremely lengthy procedure for obtaining fine discriminations.

Pitch was one of the sensory dimensions examined extensively in Pavlov's laboratory. Usually wind instruments were used to produce the various tones, but Galton's whistle was needed for high frequencies, inaudible to the human ear, and the results were replicated with pure tones from automatic resonators. Dogs became 100 per cent accurate even with notes only one-eighth of a tone apart, which was the limit of the available apparatus. They were sensitive to the timbre of the wind instruments (although the limits of this were not established) and could detect differences in the rhythm of repetitions of the same note (e.g. between 100 and 96 beats a minute) which were not apparent to the human observer. So much for Thorndike's contention that animals are not capable of fine discriminations.

Synthesis

The 'synthesising function of the nervous system' was seen by Pavlov as a rather general characteristic. But as usual its nature was illustrated, rather surprisingly, by particular techniques of salivary conditioning. The most obvious type of result, which was said by Pavlov to be easy to obtain, without much further discussion, is selective response to a simultaneous combination of stimuli. For instance, if the dog gets food when a whistle and a tuning fork sound together, but not when these events occur singly, it only salivates to the combination. Similarly, if a lamp and a tone turned on together precede food, but are experienced individually without the food, only the double stimulus is perceived as a food signal. This procedure works equally well in the other direction; that is, if either of the two stimuli individually signal food, and elicit salivation, but the two presented together are always unrewarded, and are therefore *not* responded to in combination. The effects of combined sensations on salivation is not perhaps what Locke had in mind in discussing the compounding of ideas, but the effectiveness of arbitrary combinations of sounds in functioning as a distinct signal should throw doubt on whether an inability to perceive compounds is a defining limitation on animal thought.

Much more detailed work was done on a different sort of compound stimulus, where individual components were presented successively, in various orders or rhythms. In this case, says Pavlov, 'the synthesizing function of the nervous system is still more obvious' (1927, p. 145). Using a single brief tone, a signal could be composed of three soundings of it, with a 2-second interval before the first repetition, and then a 1-second break. This particular rhythm could be made the signal for food, by comparison with the alternative pattern of a 1-second break between the first two tones, followed by the 2-second interval. This alternative would certainly be responded to the first time it was given, but if the original sequence continued to signal food whenever it was given, but the reversed sequence was never rewarded, then dogs came to salivate when they heard one rhythm, but not the other.

Another sort of compound discrimination tested was that of an ordered sequence of different events. For instance, a rising arpeggio of the notes C-D-E-F within one octave was used as a signal for food, the dogs differentiating this from the other 23 sequences of the same notes such as C-E-D-F, C-D-F-E, and so on to F-E-D-C. This indicates a considerable degree of integration over time, or sensitivity to stimulus order. The effect of order was apparent also over longer intervals, even when it was less obvious that a particular order was a necessary condition for getting food. When a dog was usually fed once every 10 minutes over a period of 80 minutes each day, but with a fixed order of 4 individual signals, repeated, which was a metronome the first time, an electric lamp the second, a whistle the third, and a touch on the body for the fourth, the dog was measurably disturbed when this accustomed sequence was changed. It was this result which led Pavlov to the view that what he was investigating was a 'complex dynamic system' rather than a collection of isolated reflexes (1927, p. 232).

Pavlov's evidence can therefore be used just as well to support a theory of animal psychology which supposes that the inner causes of behaviour arise from 'complex dynamics' as to deduce that the inner mechanisms are like simple clockwork. Indeed, the results just quoted can be read as a demonstration that what Locke regarded as the underlying elements of human thought—discernment, comparison, and composition—are general aspects of the operation of mammalian cerebral cortex.

It should be admitted that although Pavlov occasionally took an imaginative view of the psychological implications of his results, the main thrust of his theorising was rather cumbersome and mechanistic. The essential axiom of his theories was the existence of physiological processes of exitation and inhibition in the brain, whose ebbing and flowing determined behavioural responses, and it is discussion in terms of simple mechanisms of exitation and inhibition that has been the major legacy of Pavlovian theory in English-speaking psychology (see Gray, 1979). Thus although Pavlov expressed the hope, as a final conclusion to *Conditioned Reflexes*, that his experiments would throw light on the relation between conscious and unconscious thought, his influence has not been in this direction. As he himself tended to discuss individual results as evidence for simple physiological mechanisms, he encouraged the tendency to view animal behaviour as collections of knee-jerk-like responses to external stimuli. However, it has recently become more common to give explanations for classical conditioning results in terms of the existence of more complex perceptions and cognitions. Thus it may be said that the dog in the standard experiment 'expects food' or has an 'internal representation' of food, when it hears the buzzer (cf. Mackintosh, 1974; Rescorla, 1979). The usefulness of this type of explanation can be illustrated by a minor experiment mentioned by Pavlov in passing. A dog was initially touched on the side before being given a mixture of breadcrumbs and dried meat powder, and developed the conditioned tendency to salivate when touched. But, when an additional association was introduced to the same animal, of a visual signal followed by Dutch cheese, salivating to the touch was much reduced, even if just the signal for cheese came at the beginning of an hour in which the touch/dry-mixture sequence was tested. There are many ways of interpreting this phenomenon. Pavlov said it showed 'analysing activity of the cerebral part of the chemical analyser for taste' (1927, p. 139). It would be just as parsimonious to suggest that if the dog thinks it might get cheese, it is not going to be very interested in the possibility of breadcrumbs.

However, Pavlov was the archetypal brain-state theorist, and consistently advocated the view that the subjective world of the animal should be disregarded, in favour of descriptions of hypothetical brain activities. Even though the nature of his experimental techniques means that the Pavlovian view of animal behaviour is taken to be that their activities are usually reflexive and determined by external stimuli in a mechanical and unthinking manner, it should not be forgotten that Pavlov firmly asserted that the brains of man and dog work in fundamentally similar ways. This can be interpreted, and usually is, as a slight on human capacities, but can also be used to emphasise the potential of the animal brain. Pavlov himself oscillated between unifying human and animal mental phenomena under the banner of conditioning ('habits based on training, education and discipline of any sort are nothing but a long chain of conditioned reflexes') and setting them apart at the familiar dividing line of speech. Speech 'provides conditioned stimuli' (1927, p. 407) and so is an expression of the fundamental signalling characteristic of the cerebral cortex, but at the same time the 'second signalling system', which is language, is self-contained and is independent of the 'first signalling system' of non-verbal perceptions, which is shared by man and other mammals (1955, p. 537). Thus although Pavlov's techniques established that animals can make extremely fine sensory discriminations, of both individual and compound sensations, the net result of his work has been to reinforce the Cartesian opinion, that animals may be rather efficient machines, but lack anything corresponding to human awareness or imagination.

Watson (1878–1958) and Hull (1884–1952)

The mechanistic and minimalist treatment of animal abilities which began with Thorndike and Pavlov was firmly implanted into the mainstream of academic psychology by the behaviourist tradition begun by Watson and continued by Hull and Skinner. 'Behaviourism' as a term was coined by Watson in a paper in 1913, which was followed up by textbooks in 1914 and 1919. Oddly, the three Americans, Watson, Hull and Skinner, were influenced just as much by Pavlov as by Thorndike—it is 'conditioning' rather than 'trial and error learning' which is the dominant concept. Watson's research had been in maze learning and colour vision in animals, but the appearance of the conditioned reflex method, rather than his own work, seems to have been the inspiration for the idea of behaviourism. There has always been a number of separate themes within behaviourism: first, a denial that subjective or mental events should be appealed to as causes of overt acts; second, the substitution of simplified explanations, derived from Pavlovian conditioning; and third, a reluctance to admit into the explanatory system not only innate ideas, but innate influences of any kind, except in the form of innate reflexes.

Watson is important as the originator of the behaviourist movement, but his academic career was cut short when Johns Hopkins University fired him in 1920 because of an affair with his research assistant. After this he worked his way up to a prominent position on Madison Avenue as a partner in J. Walter Thompson. He is best known for his application of behaviourist principles to people rather than animals—his belief was that human behaviour is a result of 'millions of conditionings' during life, and not affected by inherited predispositions.

If Watson's presidential address to the American Psychological Association in 1915 sounded a behaviourist call to arms, Hull's, in 1936, announced a battle won: in the 1940s 70 per cent of the papers about animal learning or related subjects in the main journals referred to Hull's theories (Spence, 1952). After putting forward 'A functional interpretation of the conditioned reflex' in 1929, Hull went to Yale, and was a dominating figure there until he died in 1952. His domination was due almost entirely to theoretical systematisation, rather than the discovery of new facts—although enormous amounts of experimental work were done in the name of the theory, it is the theory itself, rather than major additions to the experimental findings of Thorndike and Pavlov, which one looks back to.

Hull's theory could be described as the apotheosis of the simplified explanation. The aim was to reduce all behaviour, and therefore all psychology, to a few underlying principles, common to rats and human subjects. Postulates of the theory (16 of them in Hull, 1943) were written using an elaborate system of mathematical symbols, in imitation of Newton's *Principia*, the intention being to construct a rigid account of psychology, in which the behaviour of rats in mazes could be related to underlying principles in the same way that the movements of the heavenly bodies can be predicted from Newton's laws of motion. Although it would probably be now agreed that this attempt was always doomed to fail, during its heyday it sustained the most mechanistic aspects of Pavlov's and Thorndike's beliefs.

The underlying assumption in Hullian theorising is that *all* behaviour can be construed as responses to stimuli. After Watson and Thorndike, this was not unusual—'Stimulus-response' or 'S-R' psychology became the conventional wisdom. In Hull's theory (although there are various minor qualifications) whether or not an animal makes a certain response, when for instance it is put in a puzzle box, or hears a buzzer in a salivary conditioning experiment, depends on two aspects of its current state: drive and habit. Drive is a function of need, but only in so far as needs create inner tensions, not because needs make animals desire future goals. Habit is simply an accumulation of previous experience, expressed as the tendency for a stimulus to evoke a response. The essence of this theory is that there is a deliberate exclusion of anything like a conscious awareness of perceived stimuli, or an expectation of future events. Hull had found he could make very rudimentary electrical circuits mimic a response to a conditioned stimulus (Hull and Kruger, 1931) and directed much of his theoretical efforts to interpreting more complex phenomena as outcomes of the simple mechanisms of habit and drive (e.g. Hull, 1937). As with Pavlov, it was not Hull's intention to inculcate the opinion that animal intelligence worked in a fundamentally different way from human thought; indeed, he wanted to apply his general theories to child psychology, and psychoanalysis (Hull, 1938, 1939). But it has been one of the legacies of his theory that many concerned with explaining human perception and action, although they may regard stimulus-response theories as self-evidently inadequate when it comes to human behaviour, suppose that stimulus-response theories work reasonably well for the simpler task of explaining perception and action in rats, cats and dogs.

In fact, the plain postulates of drive and habit work for only the crudest sorts of Pavlovian conditioning experiments, and do not get very far in explaining how or why a dog retrieves thrown sticks. Cumbersome elaborations are needed to account for orientation in space and for rapid reactions to changed rewards. The emphasis on these features in animal experiments, which began to undermine stimulus-response theory almost from its inception, was largely due to Tolman.

Tolman (1886–1959)

Unlike the stimulus-response theorists, Tolman assumed that even rats possess some generally accessible knowledge about where they are, and what is likely to happen next, their actions being based on this knowledge rather than driven by automatic habits. He called himself a behaviourist, and relied on experimental evidence, rarely worrying about the question of subjective awareness in animals in so many terms. However, he took the behavioural evidence to require the supposition of some inner purposes and cognitions, which 'intervened' between perception and action or, more strictly, between the objective environment and the observed behaviour (see Tolman, 1932, 1948, 1949). An important form of cognition is knowledge of local geography—the term adopted by Tolman, which has now passed into general use, was the 'cognitive map' which, he said, was used by both rats and men to guide their movements from place to place. The behaviour of most animals in their natural environment suggests some fairly sophisticated methods of navigation, the migrations of birds and the homing of pigeons in particular still posing puzzles as to exactly what the methods are. A mammal that has a nest and uses a water hole does not usually appear to learn every possible route between them by Thorndikean trial and error, but often gives every sign of 'knowing' its territory well enough to make the term 'map' seem plausible.

The demonstration of spatial knowledge in laboratory tests is not quite so straightforward, but Tolman conducted a number of experiments on the ability of rats to find their way about artificial mazes that were sufficiently convincing to require major additions to simple stimulus-response theory.

Place learning

An experimental test divised relatively late in the Hull–Tolman controversy used a cross-maze, with four end-points that can be labelled as North, South, East and West for convenience, though compass orientation as such has not been shown to influence rats. Rats were started at North and South on alternate trials, some of them getting food at one place—East, say—every time, so that they had to turn left or right depending on where they started. Food reward for the others was shifted from side to side so that to get it they had to turn left all the time, whether they started from North or South. When this experiment was done by Tolman (Tolman, Ritchie and Kalish, 1946), the rats that had to go to the same *place* every time learned to do this correctly very quickly, whereas most of the rats supposed to make the same *turning response*, to end up in different places, never managed to do this consistently. Tolman's conclusion was that the exact nature of the response was not particularly important and that it was much easier for the animals to learn that food was always in the same place, even if they had to do different things to get there, compared to having the food in different places, but always available after a left turn. Although clearly the ability to learn about places must depend on the availability of some landmarks or spatial cues, there is really no doubt at all that animals in general and laboratory rats in particular learn something about geographical locations which is not coded in terms of particular sequences of movements, and this rather ordinary fact has never been incorporated satisfactorily into strict stimulus-response theories.

Hull's attempt to deal with evidence such as this, which suggests the use of a 'cognitive map', was the elaborate idea of 'Habit Family Hierarchies'. A successful response, such as turning left coming from North, would not only increase the strength of that particular habit, but would also increase other habits, perhaps as yet unperformed, such as turning right from South. This is what is known as an *ad hoc* modification of a theory, since it is not clear why turning right from South should be such a close relation of turning left from North in the rat's family of habits. Here another elaborate idea of Hull's comes in—the 'fractional antedating goal response' (see Hull, 1934, 1937, 1952). The way this should work can be summarised as follows. After turning left from North, the rat runs along the 'going East' bit of the maze just before it gets its food. 'Going East' comes before food, and is thus like a conditioned stimulus in a salivary conditioning experiment. Something about going East might thus make the animal salivate, or produce some other internal response characteristic of the goal—hence the 'fractional goal response'. But the 'going East' part of the turning left from North is shared by the response of turning right from South, and thus this second turning response will share in the anticipatory goal response—and that is why rats turn right from South after being rewarded for turning left from North.

This makes it pretty obvious why Tolman's cognitive maps have proved to be more popular than Hull's little goal responses and families of habits—Hull's system seems to require more cognitive effort by both the human theorist and the rats. The important part of both theories is that they assume a large degree of *organisation* of knowledge (or of habits or behaviour determining processes of whatever kind) inside the animal's head. A labelling which corresponds to 'food at point X' is available to influence many kinds of movement towards X by a hungry animal, which may start from various other points of space, and which may make use of various muscular movements. A rat possessing the information 'food at X' will jump, climb, dig, gnaw and swim in the course of getting there (e.g. MacFarlane, 1930).

More complicated experiments (Tolman and Honzik, 1930a) involved the choice of different routes to get to 'food at X' when the most direct path from a starting place to 'X' was blocked. If there were three paths which all led to X, of different lengths, then rats very sensibly learned to choose the shortest one. But if the shortest route was blocked, they switched to the next longest one. However, if the shortest path was blocked at a point where the middle length route had already rejoined it, then, according to Tolman and Honzik (1930a) most rats did not bother to try out the middle-length path, but went the long way round, demonstrating, according to Tolman, 'insight'. Not everyone has agreed that this is a reliable result, but Deutsch and Clarkson (1959) were able to obtain something similar by having two short routes to 'food at X' and one very long path, beginning at the same point as the two short ones, which eventually led to 'food at Y'. If one of the short paths was blocked, then a significant majority of rats (after experiencing the block) took the alternative short route. But if the animals found 'X' empty of food, or were prevented from eating by wire netting, they went back and tried the long path to 'Y', the alternative goal. More recently, with a technique which has been easily replicated, it has been shown that, given several bits of food in the same maze, for instance at the end-points of radiating spokes, rats are very good at not retracing their steps, that is, not visiting again a place where they have already eaten the food (Olton, 1978, 1979). All these results mean that some kind of memory for places is being utilised. It may not involve anything like human conscious memory, but the evidence as it stands suggests that what rats do in mazes is determined more by internal organisation of spatial information than by the minimal Hullian habit.

Approach to objects in open space, and around barriers

The advantage of searching for the simplest possible mechanisms to explain orientation in space is that it demonstrates the complexity of some very ordinary achievements. If a bowl of food is put down in the middle of a room, we are not surprised if a cat turns towards it from various distances and directions or even if the cat detours around or over other objects placed in the way. It is convenient to appeal to an internal 'cognitive map' to account for this, but in some ways Hull's more tortuous explanations are more revealing (Hull, 1952, ch. 8). Even to deal with simple approach to objects, special assumptions about the 'generalisation' of locomotor responses have to be made, and similarly, perception of objects has to be assumed to generalise over a 'distance-reception continuum'. To account for detouring round barriers (the 'Umweg' problem) Hull has to bring in whole systems of habit-family hierarchies, in which the shortest routes to goals have highest priority, but if these are not available (strictly speaking, after these have been knocked out by trial and error experience), more circuitous movement habits are substituted. It is evident that a considerable amount of inner shifting of gears, selection among possibilities, and application of principles, would be needed to make such a system work. Certainly, it is more straightforward to say that a cognitive map is being used, but it should not be forgotten that utilisation of a cognitive map may involve internal computations of considerable complexity. Equally, cognitive maps are not always perfect. Animals can get lost, and there are many occasions when they do not do the intelligent thing, and detour around barriers, but persist with rigid attempts to push their way through. The lesson to be drawn from Tolman's emphasis on orientation in space, and Hull's attempts to deal with it, is that to explain overt moving about, it is necessary in some cases to assume that there are means of inner mental organisation of spatial knowledge.

Cognitive maps and 'latent learning'

The emphasis on purely spatial aspects of an animal's internal knowledge was a comparatively late development in Tolman's theorising. His early concern was to provide a behaviourist account of the facts of consciousness and imagery ('A new formula for behaviourism', 1922) and of emotional experience, and his main theme remained close to that of 'Purpose and cognition: the determiners of animal learning' (1925) throughout his career. As a general strategy, he recommended that ideas, intentions, beliefs and expectancies could best be studied by linking them with observable acts, rather than by examining them directly in subjective experience, and that the laboratory rat should serve as a 'furry white test tube' in which these sorts of cognition may be seen to take place. Tolman's explicit conclusion in 'A behaviouristic theory of ideas' (1926) is that the best way to find out about the private mental contents of thought is to look at 'a really good rat in a really good maze'.

Few would now wish to follow Tolman in attempting to derive a universal theory of cognition and thought from the behaviour of rats in mazes, but we are interested here in whether rats demonstrate any thought at all. (Tolman wrote occasionally about wider issues, as in *Drives towards war*, 1942; and he spent the first year of the war advising the OSS, which afterwards became the CIA; but one would not want to advance this as support of the general applicability of his theories.)

The crucial aspect of cognition that Tolman felt could be demonstrated in rats is some sort of awareness of the likely consequences of actions. There is an absolute distinction between Tolman's view that mammals perform responses because they expect them to bring about desirable ends and the more conventional behaviourist assumption that movements only occur as automatic reactions to stimuli. Evidence in favour of Tolman's view comes partly from experiments in which variation in the availability of goals seems to have a direct effect on the animal's actions. One type of experiment of this kind is said to demonstrate 'latent learning', but is now more important in indicating relationships between behaviour and purpose.

The original experiments in Tolman's laboratory at Berkeley (Blodgett, 1929; Tolman and Honzik, 1930b) employed mazes in which rats had to make a sequence of 6 or 14 choices (to turn left or right) in correct order. Hungry rats given food at the end of the maze each day seem gradually to learn the correct sequence, performing randomly on the first day, but almost perfectly after one or two weeks (depending on the length of the maze). This could be interpreted as a gradual 'stamping in' of correct habits. Also animals allowed to run through the maze for an equivalent number of days without food rewards apparently learn very little, since they continue to turn into many blind alleys. At first sight this supports the idea that no reward means no 'stamping in' of correct responses. But if, after this preliminary experience, food was put at the end of the maze on one day, the rats ran the mazes almost perfectly on the next day.

The first deduction is that by the time the food was introduced, the animals already knew what the quickest way to run the maze was, even though they did not bother to take it—hence 'latent learning'. Just as important, however, is the fact that having found food at the end of the maze, after an incorrect sequence of responses, the rats ran through by the quickest route the next time they had the chance. A possible interpretation is that (a) the rats knew the quickest way to get through the maze, but also, (b) they now expected that food might be at the end of the maze and (c) they wanted to get to the food as quickly as possible, and (d) putting together all these resulted in the action of running the maze correctly.

There have been various modifications of these original latent learning experiments. If rats are allowed to explore a simple 'T-maze' incorporating a single left/right choice, and then fed once in either the left or the right arm of the 'T', they turn towards the place where they were fed when next allowed to run the maze from the beginning (Seward, 1949). If on the other hand they are put in one side of a T-maze and given an electric shock, they avoid going to that side in a subsequent run (Tolman and Gleitman, 1949). If rats experience food on the right and water on the left when running through a one-choice maze when neither hungry or thirsty so that they do not actually eat or drink, then if half of them are tested when hungry, they will run to the right, and others tested when thirsty will go to the left (Spence and Lippitt, 1946). There are some variations in the degree of success of this kind of experiment: it is necessary, for instance, to make sure that the animals can tell one part of the maze from another by differences in visual or textural cues, but it is now accepted by authorities such as Mackintosh (1974) that the evidence for latent learning in rats is unassailable.

Expectancies, beliefs and means-ends readiness

Precisely what theoretical conclusions should be drawn from the empirical phenomena of latent learning, and other sorts of intelligence exhibited in maze running, is not so clear. Tolman himself used a bewildering variety of terms to describe the internal mental processes he felt were involved, from 'initial cognitive hunch' (1925) and 'Sign-Gestalt' (1927) to 'expectancies', 'representations' and 'means-end readiness' (1959). There is currently a consensus of using 'expectancy' rather loosely as an explanation, together with the assumption that associations between responses and their consequences is a typical form taken by learning in the rat (Bolles, 1972; Mackintosh, 1974; Roitblat *et al.* 1984). In all these cases it is obvious that some kind of mental activity is being attributed to the animals; that is, there is considered to be some internal sifting and selection of information rather than simply the release of responses by a certain set of environmental conditions. Knowledge of goals, knowledge of space and knowledge of actions that may lead to goals seem to be independent, but can be fitted together by animals when the need arises.

Tolman's theory of consciousness and habit

It may be necessary to dispel the impression that rats are all-knowing, and never perform automatic actions. It is not difficult to perform experiments in which rats are apparently oblivious to everything except laboriously acquired mechanical habits. Tolman described an occasion on which he trained rats to run from one end to the other of a long narrow box, pushing through a white curtain half way down, to get into a food compartment at the end. He then put them directly into the food compartment but gave them an electric shock instead of food. On the assumption that the animals knew that they would end up in the same food compartment if they ran through the box, he was confident that they would now refuse to run. But when he carried the first rat back to the starting point it 'immediately dashed off gaily and just as usual through the whole discrimination apparatus and bang whack into the very food compartment in which he had just been shocked' (1933, p. 250), and the others did the same. Only when they had been shocked after getting themselves into the food compartment did they refuse to run again. This is fair enough in any case but Tolman supposed that long practice had made running automatic and 'fixated', and more like a traditional conditioned response. Any theory of cognition must include the possibility that much practised actions, which may have initially required active thought, can eventually be made habitually and automatically.

The opposite of a habitual and automatic response should perhaps be an action performed with a conscious intention. Since Tolman supposed that the purposes of humans and rats were of the same type (e.g. Tolman, 1932), and that human thinking 'is in essence no more than an activated interplay among expectancies', it is reasonable to align him with theorists such as Lloyd Morgan who assumed that animal behaviour may be guided by conscious memories and expectations. However, he was enough of a behaviourist to neglect the question of whether mental activities deduced from the reponses of rats ought to be equated with what is available to human introspection. His early attempt to pin down the behavioural criteria for a moment of animal consciousness was not a success. It went like this: 'whenever an organism at a given moment of stimulation shifts then and there from being ready to respond in some relatively less differentiated way to being ready to respond in some relatively more differentiated way, there is consciousness' (Tolman, 1927, p. 435). This seems to say that any novel response is a product of conscious mental organisation (cf. Shallice, 1972), and such a view is implicit in much of Tolman's writing, but on the whole he preferred to talk of 'Sign-Gestalts' and 'beliefs', tying these down to observed behaviours rather than putative subjective experience.

Skinner's operant conditioning: doctrines and techniques

Since Hull's death in 1952, Skinner has been the leading light of behaviourism. He solved the theoretical disputes between Hull and Tolman by ignoring them entirely, and thus under his influence most of the problems of animal cognition were left in abeyance. Skinner's behaviourism is of the most radical kind, since all questions concerning inner mechanisms, whether these are in terms of neural machinery, or of learned habits, or of mental states, are held to be improper. Naturally such an extreme position has led to a degree of academic isolation for Skinnerians—investigations of neurophysiology, and of human cognition, have flourished quite independently, but the existence of a strong Skinnerian school built up during Skinner's time at Indiana from 1945–8 and at Harvard since 1948 has until fairly recently acted as a heavy counter weight against speculations along the lines pioneered by Tolman.

To a great extent, Skinner's influence rests on his development of new and powerful experimental techniques and the addition of new experimental findings to the corpus of data concerning the behaviour of laboratory animals. It is important to distinguish, therefore, between the reliability of these findings and the interpretation (or rather, lack of interpretation) which Skinner chose to put on them. Both the findings, and the theoretical positions, were published in *The Behaviour of Organisms* in 1938 and have changed very little—since 1948 Skinner has become known for his promulgation of contentious behaviourist recipes for human society, rather than for further analysis of the causes of animal behaviour.

A large part of Skinner's technical achievement was in designing an automated method for engendering and recording repetitive behaviour in animals. The 'Skinner box' is a version of Thorndike's puzzle box. When an animal presses a lever or a button in the box, it does not get out to receive food, but a small amount of food is delivered to it while it remains inside. It is then free to press the lever again, and get another pellet of food, and to go on like this for as long as it, or the experimenter, chooses. In essence, this is simply another way of doing Thorndike's experiment (see pp. 62–5). The experimenter is freed from the task of replacing the animal in the box, and if the response of the animal is recorded electrically (in Skinner's experiments, it was made to pull a pen a small distance over a steadily unrolling sheet of paper, thus plotting an automatic 'cumulative record' of the behaviour), the human experimenter does not need to stand by with a stop-watch. But the results of the experiment in the basic form do not differ in the slightest from those of Thorndike. The finding is that when a hungry rat is left in the box, it will eventually put its paws on the lever and press it down, in the course of natural exploration. If this press on the lever results in the delivery of a food pellet, and it has previously learned to recognise when this happens, it will go and eat the food, and come back and press the lever again almost immediately. I have pointed out that most of Thorndike's cats needed only one experience to exhibit virtually complete learning of a simple successful response, and Skinner (1938) made a great deal of the fact that his rats usually switched to a regular pattern of pressing the lever and eating at a steady rate, as soon as they had tried it once. This counted as a case of 'one-trial learning', and Skinner wrote to a friend at the time that 'it leaves the insight boys with their mouths open' (see Skinner, 1979, p. 90). It may be said that Skinner tended to exaggerate the instantaneity of the results, much as Thorndike exaggerated the gradualness of his—the rats often took several food pellets before they got into their stride (see Skinner, 1938, pp. 66–9).

The fact that rats will perform the simple yet apparently arbitrary movements required to manipulate an object, because this results in their getting food, is the most basic of Skinner's findings. It was not particularly novel, except that pushing down a horizontal metal rod about a centimetre had not attracted much attention previously. It is the assertions made by Skinner about why this happened that are novel. Few before (or since) Skinner have been quite so systematic in denying the necessity for appealing to events inside the animal as explanations for what it does. Skinner contended that following the response with food increased its *strength* as measured by its future performance. As a descriptive shorthand this is difficult to argue with. But Skinner's argument was that anything else except a descriptive shorthand is necessarily invalid. This is a defensible, if vacuous, methodological point. One may be pessimistic, and say that the evidence that the behaviour occurs will always be insufficient to decide why it occurs. In other words one might decide to leave the question of explanation open. But this is not the outcome of Skinner's deliberations. Instead, he takes an overtly minimalist view—the rat pressing the lever and then rushing over to retrieve its food pellet is said to be exhibiting a chain of reflexes which are like the reflexes used in swallowing, or in postural adjustment (Skinner, 1938, pp. 54–5) which are quoted precisely because they are distinguished as being 'purely mechanical'. Skinner makes the case that the rat performs the response without knowing why it does so, in any sense of the term 'knowing'. He has recently reiterated his position with the example of a cat chasing a mouse. The movements of the cat, according to Skinner, are exactly like inherited reflexes—we should not assume that there is anything in the cat's brain which corresponds to trying to catch the mouse, or even that the cat likes the chase (Skinner, 1977).

Despite Skinner's protestation to the contrary (Skinner, 1950) this *is* a theory, and not just a methodological strategy. It is a strong statement that rats and cats do not have any cognitions. It is instructive to contrast this theory, applied to very simple behaviours, with that of Tolman (1937). Tolman wrote about the manipulations performed by rats to get food, but the case in point was slightly more elaborate than the lever press in a Skinner box; it concerned the ability of rats to draw a metal tray of food towards them by pulling on a string. Although monkeys and chimpanzees need very little persuasion to pull towards them delicacies tied on the end of string, similar behaviour requires a certain amount of training in rats. The method used by Tolman was first to accustom a rat to eat from a metal pan, which could be slid through a gap under the front of the animal's testing cage. On the day of string-pull training, a string attached to the pan ran through the cage, but was not needed at the start, since the pan was still inside. The first step was to try and slide the pan out of the cage while the rat was eating. The usual reaction of the rats was to immediately clutch the pan and pull it back. Once this began, the superior strength of the experimenter was exerted to drag the pan first to the limit of the animal's reach, and then just beyond it. When the pan itself was beyond reach, some rats managed to get it back by vigorous scrabbling, which was sufficient to move the string, others would immediately pull the string with their forepaws, and occasionally one would seize the string in his teeth. After they had succeeded in pulling in the food several times, they were capable of pulling in the pan from about 50 cm away. But, in these early stages, Tolman found it necessary to induce string-pulling as such, instead of general scrabbling, by either jiggling the string, 'pulling the string away and evoking a contesting tug', or, as a last resort, smearing the string with something edible.

Tolman (1937), saw these tactics as aids to the formation of new ideas by the rat, rather than stimuli which elicited only overt responses. His analysis is in terms of 'Sign-Gestalt expectations' (used interchangeably with 'hypotheses'). In paraphrase, he assumes that before the rat learns to pull the string, the pan as an object is recognised as something from which food may be obtained, and that when the pan is pulled away the animals already have an expectation that if they clutch it or scrabble for it, they will get it back. The crucial learning consists in forming a new expectation that pulling the string, as a separate act, will also result in access to the pan.

Applying this sort of theory to rats in Skinner boxes is relatively straightforward (although Tolman was strangely reluctant to deal with other people's data). A rat which discovers, on one occasion, that the depression of the lever is followed by the delivery of a food pellet is induced to form the mental hypothesis (or expectancy, or belief) that doing things with the lever will produce food, and will thereafter manipulate the lever whenever it wants food. If it is extremely hungry to start with, and only small amounts of food are obtained each time, the lever will be operated with some regularity. Something along these lines seems to be implied by Mackintosh's recent conclusion that Skinner's basic experiment, as an example of instrumental learning, should be explained by 'the statement that an association was formed between the response and the reinforcement and that this association underlies the increase in the probability of that response' (Mackintosh, 1974, p. 222 — 'reinforcement' was Pavlov's and Skinner's term for the food).

However, any explanation of this kind would be anathema to Skinner. It is true that the bare fact that the animal makes a response does not provide grounds for deciding whether it is making it as a reflex with a certain strength, or whether it is making it because it has the idea that the response will get it something. The Skinnerian position, which has been maintained with some success, is simply to refuse to discuss anything except strengths of various responses under various stimulus conditions. Whereas Hull attempted cumbersome modifications of his system, such as the habit family hierarchy, to account for extra inconvenient information like latent learning and orientation in space, Skinner resolutely ignores inconvenient facts or includes them only as examples of changes in behavioural strengths due to reinforcement by food or something acting in the same way as food.

The intriguing empirical aspect of Skinner's work is the degree to which the activities of rats, pigeons, and most other experimental animals can be 'shaped' by the careful provision of external rewards. Skinner's own *tour de force* was to train a rat not only to pull a string, but to pull a string which released a marble from a rack, which the rat then picked up in its forepaws and carried to a tube projecting two inches above the floor of its cage. Dropping the marble down the tube was the response which finally led to the delivery of food (Skinner, 1938). This performance was achieved by first rewarding the animal for pushing a marble down a hole in the floor, then for manipulating it into the tube rising a fraction of an inch from the floor, and so on. Every step was trained by a series of approximations. Our deduction is supposed to be that gradual changes in response strength, caused by food rewards, can eventually be accumulated into a complex sequence of behaviour, and hence complex sequences of behaviour are 'nothing but' automatically produced bits of responding. It certainly seems unlikely that the rat begins with an internal belief that it must pull the string, carry the marble, and so on, if it is to get its food, although the demonstration does not prove that this sort of mental process in rats is impossible. However, it would remain open to Tolman to see the sequence as a succession of small beliefs about what to do next, held together, surely, by an overall expectation that food would be forthcoming in the end.

One factor in the success of Skinner's tactics is that such phenomena as latent learning and spatial intelligence are less apparent within the limited confines of the Skinner box than in other forms of experiment, or in naturalistic observation. However, there are a number of aspects of behaviour in Skinnerian experiments that, although they are susceptible to analyses in terms of the strengths of unseen categories of response, make the universal application of explanations based only on the strengths of reflexive responses somewhat less plausible.

These have been extensively reviewed by Mackintosh (1974), who came to the conclusion, mentioned above, that, at the very least, it must be assumed that the rat learns something about the relation between the act it performs, and the reward which comes afterwards. I will mention here some of the features of Skinner's results which, it seems to me, are at least as compatible with the view that the animal's behaviour results from mental states as with the Skinnerian opinion that only various strengths of peripheral reflex-like movements need to be considered

First, in the case of the few rats which Skinner actually watched, he noticed that the early stages of lever pressing were characterised by a tendency for the animals to fiddle about with the metal rod, without actually operating it, and then to rush to the food dispenser. Since they in theory should only have had successful pushing movements strengthened, it is not obvious why any other forms of behaviour should appear, although of course Skinner interprets the fiddling about as a partial or initial stage of the 'proper' response. However, it is conceivable that the rat is working on the hypothesis that doing something rather generally with the lever will be followed by reward, and consequently searches for food after inadequate manipulations. The fact that a rat goes and sniffs and scrabbles around in the tray where a food pellet is usually delivered might well be taken as an indication that the animal expects (or perhaps just hopes) to find a food pellet there, instead of being downgraded as a manifestation of reflex-like conditioned approach movements (as in Skinner, 1938, pp. 53–4). After repeated experience a standard method of depressing the lever may indeed become habitual—this is certainly the case with human actions, such as assembly-line work, or changing the gears of a car, but it does not mean then that associated mental states were never present. In the human case conscious mental states reappear if something goes wrong—if the gears stick, or the assembly line breaks down. Similarly if the rat's food magazine breaks down, or is disengaged by the experimenter in the procedure known as 'extinction', the behaviour of the animal indicates some change of inner mood. The lever is rattled, banged, pressed harder than usual (e. g. Notterman and Mintz, 1965) and rats under these conditions employ numerous shifts in posture, changes of paw, and so on. Hull would appeal to a related set of habits, but it makes a certain amount of sense to assume that the rat retains the belief that doing something with the lever ought to produce a food pellet, and tries everything that comes to mind. If nothing works, the rat will gradually give up trying, although the original belief is not forgotten, since it can be quickly re-instated by the resumption of food delivery.

Intermittent reward

Every undergraduate text (e.g. Walker, 1975) recounts the tale of how Skinner discovered that very interesting behaviours arise if the rewards are not given for every response, but according to various 'schedules of reinforcement'. The simplest of these were discussed by Skinner in 1938 and the standard work on this subject is still Ferster and Skinner (1957). The easiest schedule of reinforcement to understand, from the point of view of procedures if not from that of theoretical explanations, is referred to as a 'fixed ratio', since the rule is that there is a certain number of responses before each reward. If the fixed ratio is ten, for instance, the rats must make nine presses on the lever without anything happening, before the tenth press delivers a food pellet, then there will be a further nine uneventful presses, and so on. If an animal has just got used to the basic procedure of being rewarded for every push (continuous reinforcement) and the rule is suddenly changed to fixed ratio ten, it will spend most of its time vainly searching for accustomed rewards, and may very well cease pushing the lever altogether. However, with a sufficiently persistent animal, or, as in Skinner's 1938 report, animals with prior experience of some other kind (on fixed interval reinforcement: see below), there is a gradual adjustment to the new rule. The eventual outcome is that the rat rests briefly after receiving a food pellet (but rests much longer than when it could get another pellet by the next press) and then goes over to the lever and makes ten rapid presses in succession, causing the release of another bit of food. Skinner's explanation of this is that the animal 'discriminates' the period after a reward as being a bad time as far as getting another reward goes, and 'as a result of this discrimination the rat stops responding for a short period' (1938, p. 288), and that rapid responding is 'preferentially reinforced'. This latter is certainly descriptively true: if the rat responds slowly, on fixed ratio ten, it will get its rewards slowly, and the faster it responds, the more quickly its rewards will come.

But the reader may note that a capacity in the rat for making comparisons between these cases has been surreptitiously inserted in Skinner's account—a stricter application of the rule of blind reinforcement would say that if the rat responds slowly (as it does to begin with) it will get reinforced for responding slowly, and therefore it should continue to respond slowly. Achievement of the 'typical' fixed ratio performance demands at least that the rat takes notice of the fact that if it happens to respond more quickly than usual it gets its reward sooner than usual. A more Tolmanian version of this would have the rat noticing that a certain amount of responding is necessary for each reward, and deducing that it might as well get the responding over with at a reasonable speed. There is in fact a considerable amount of evidence that the rat is indeed sensitive to the rudimentary demands of the schedule. If for instance the food mechanism is suddenly disengaged the rat will stop after ten or twelve responses and look for the food (or, if you like, make a conditioned approach to the food pan). Something like this was systematically investigated with two pigeons by Ferster and Skinner (1957, pp. 616–19). The birds were trained to make exactly fifty pecks at a disc for each food reward, but then there were arbitrary periods of 20 minutes or more when no rewards were given. During these periods the pigeons showed a clear tendency toward rapid runs of not much more than fifty responses at a time. Mechner (1958) showed that the judgment of the number of responses required in a fixed ratio is rather approximate, that is if rats are supposed to make eight responses before going somewhere else to get their reward, they often make seven or nine instead, but if it is not judgment at all, then response-strength explanations must rely on extremely *ad hoc* inner discriminations. The organisation and patterning of responding produced by fixed ratio schedules of reinforcement are thus quite compatible with the existence of inner purposes and beliefs in the behaving animals, although the usual deduction is that the performances observed in Skinner boxes require, at most, inner organisation of responses.

According to the behaviourist tradition, one might suppose that a belief *is* an 'inner organisation of responses', and nothing else. But the argument is whether the organisation of responses observed when rats (or chimpanzees) react to schedules of reinforcement is, as Skinner claimed, just like the sequences of muscular reflexes in swallowing, or leg co-ordination, which in man we know to be unconscious and automatic; or, alternatively, whether the actions of the animals are more like walking to a bus stop or ringing a door bell, which in ourselves we interpret as the result of mental intentions and expectations. Skinner, like Pavlov before him, sometimes appears to claim that both the learned activities of animals and the intentional actions of men are determined, like spinal reflexes, without the intervention of thought or deliberation, and this may be the origin of some of the confusion and obfuscation which has surrounded the problem of animal cognition in the behaviourist era.

Time-based schedules of reinforcement

Apart from ratios requiring a certain number of responses, Skinner (1938) also investigated the case where rewards are only available to the rat with a certain minimum interval between them. This is known as a 'fixed-interval schedule'. If, for instance, the fixed interval is one minute, the rat is allowed to get a reward by just one press on the lever, but must then wait for a minute or more before another press on the lever will result in the delivery of food. The most economical thing for the rat to do under these conditions would be to get a food pellet, and rest for at least a minute before going to manipulate the obtruding response-device again. This sort of thing will happen, with a not very enthusiastic animal, or very small (or satisfyingly large) rewards, but is usually avoided by experimenters concerned to get decent amounts of behaviour to measure. The textbook example of fixed-interval behaviour is an animal that usually gives no attention at all to the lever for the first fifteen seconds after a reward, begins to press it now and then about half-way through the minute, and gradually accelerates to a more vigorous and rapid working of the instrument just before the first recording of a response after the interval has passed delivers a reward.

The most obvious way in which this may be explained, in terms of response-strengths mechanically stamped in by food rewards, is to say that there is a 'biological clock' which provides an internal stimulus corresponding to the passage of time, and that responses made at about the right time are thus strongly conditioned while responses made too early become relatively weak (Roberts and Church, 1978). This interpretation of a 'temporal discrimination' underlying the distribution of behaviour is the one put forward by Skinner (1938, pp. 270–7), although there is also the additional claim that slow, or spaced-out, responses are 'preferentially reinforced' on interval schedules, in contrast to the automatic selection of rapid responding in the ratio procedure.

However, in an acknowledged lapse into the vernacular, Skinner expands this account by referring to what a person reacting to the conditions might be aware of, for instance the question of 'whether it was time for a reinforcement to occur' and the knowledge that 'he only has to wait long enough and a response will be effective' and the subjective factor that 'having tested the lever once unsuccessfully, he soon feels that it is time to try again' (Skinner, 1938, p. 277). It is arguable that the same sorts of mental processes have some influence on the development of the temporal discrimination in animals. Certainly the theory that rats develop expectancies as to the likelihood that a lever response will be effective can be easily mapped on to the way that responses are actually timed. After many hours of practice on a fixed-interval, or any other, schedule of reinforcement, it would not be surprising if some sequences of responding became fixed and habitual, but the many fluctuations in the pattern of respond-ing on fixed-interval schedules, which were remarked on by Skinner, and may go on for weeks in rats, could as well be due to interactions between hope and experience, and the development of expectations of reward, as to oscillations in response strength. The main sort of fluctuation in behaviour, apart from the timing of responses between rewards, is that animals will make rather a lot of responses between the rewards, for two or three reinforcements in a row, and then go on to make only a few lever presses in the periods between rewards for some time, before returning to the pattern of making numerous ineffective lever presses. According to Skinner's doctrine of reinforcement, a consistent and rigid pattern of behaving should emerge; he therefore went to some lengths to explain these fluctuations as a strain on response strength during the phases with lots of responses, followed by a compensatory decline during which response strength recovers (1938, p. 123 and pp. 302–3). As he says (p. 303), this is not very convincing, and it seems just as plausible that making many ineffective responses leads to a degree of despondency, whereas a sequence of 'cheap' reinforcements engenders a sense of optimism about the utility of responding, which in turn proves false.

Variable schedules of reinforcement
The single most popular Skinnerian technique is one which, it may be claimed, inculcates the most consistent and sustained expectancies of reward in the animals exposed to it, and thus gives the most reliable and persistent behaviours for the experimenter to record. This is the 'variable-interval schedule' introduced, among many other schedules, by Ferster and Skinner (1957). The procedure is the same as the fixed interval, described above, in that only one response, made at the right

time, is necessary for the production of a reward, but differs in that the time when a successful response can be made is unpredictable, and must remain unknown to the animal. A random sequence of intervals between rewards is provided by mechanical or electrical machinery, and thus a reward may sometimes be obtained by responding immediately after another one has just been given, but at other times rewards remain unavailable for long periods. As rewards *may* be obtainable at any time, it is reasonable to suppose that if the animal forms expectancies at all, it expects reward at any time, and is thus led to respond persistently until a reward is given, although there is some evidence that the longer the animal goes without reward, the greater is its tendency to make the required response (Catania and Reynolds, 1968). The alternative formulation, of course, is that the strength of the response is conditioned equally to all values of the internal sense of time passed since the last experience of food.

One of the most notable results of this variable-interval schedule of reinforcement is that, to an even greater extent than with the other Skinnerian schedules, exposure to the procedure means that if the experimenter disengages the food-reward mechanism at some point, the animal continues to respond in the normal way for an extremely long time. Although it can be said that this is due to the nature of the response, it having been conditioned very strongly to occur during long periods when reinforcement is absent, the data supports equally the contention that this is due to the nature of the expectancies held by the animal.

The final permutation of the rudimentary possibilities presented by the basic Skinnerian experiment is the 'variable ratio' schedule of reinforcements (see Ferster and Skinner, 1957). This is like the 'fixed ratio' discussed above, in that a certain number of responses (rather than just one response as in the interval schedules) is necessary to produce a reward, but the exact number of responses necessary for each successive reward is made to vary at random. This is a more difficult procedure for the animal, and for the experimenter, since if, at random, a number comes that is too large, the animal will give up. (On a variable interval, if the subject of the procedure stops bothering to respond for a while, the relevant time period will continue to elapse, and a subsequent single response will be rewarded, giving further encouragement; but with the ratio version, discontinuation of the animal's attempts will leave it as far from its eventual goal as ever.) But provided the animal is persuaded gradually, by small increases in the average requirement, to make more and more responses per reward, the effect is to generate the most intense devotion to the business at hand that is ever observed in the Skinnerian experimental apparatus. What is made clear in Ferster and Skinner's reports, however, is that the pattern of this responding is not sustained, but is often composed of bursts, or runs of responses, with pauses in between. The general Skinnerian tack is that this is due to a 'correlation between behaviour and reinforcement', and in particular to a preferential reinforcement of very rapid responding. But the brief bursts of responding observed during variable-ratio schedules, or after such schedules in 'extinction' when actual rewards are no longer given, would support the view that the animal is operating according to hypotheses that certain amounts of responding are necessary to produce the chance of reward (cf. Ferster and Skinner, 1957, pp. 397–411).

Skinner's operant conditioning versus theories of animal cognition

Although there has been much opposition to the Skinnerian thesis—that the experimental success of schedules of reinforcement in generating predictable and reliable behaviour in laboratory animals means that all explanatory theories of animal and human behaviour should be abandoned (Skinner, 1950)—the thesis has always carried a certain amount of weight. I have argued here that, on the contrary, the phenomena produced by Skinnerian techniques, rather than serving as a substitute for theories of animal cognition, themselves stand in need of a satisfactory explanation, and that, in some cases, such an explanation should be supplied in terms of the mental states of animals undergoing Skinnerian conditioning.

Since the heyday of Hull and Skinner, there has been a halting and tentative return to questions about animal cognition that were posed by Romanes and Lloyd Morgan, and others before them, and kept alive during the behaviourist interregnum by Tolman. I shall review briefly some of the recent developments in theory, but must begin by mentioning a writer who is not strictly speaking recent, nor strictly speaking concerned with animal behaviour. This is Piaget (1896–1980), a Swiss psychologist whose account of the development of knowledge in children has had a profound influence on educational theories in the English-speaking world over the last two decades.

Cognition without language in Piagetian theory

There are two reasons why Piaget's theories can be applied to the study of cognition in animals. First, he himself began academic life as a zoologist, and has provided a unified, if somewhat impenetrable, account of how human thought should be integrated with natural science, in his book *Biology and Knowledge* (1971). Second, and perhaps because of this, he is unusual among major thinkers in human psychology in denying that language is prior to cognition.

The interpretation of Piaget's writings is notoriously difficult, and I shall not attempt to discuss in detail what he says about children. The reader is referred to the assessment of this by Boden (1979). The most basic concept seems to be that of 'schemata'. These are mental entities, cognitive structures, things in the mind—the units of knowledge. According to Piaget animals have schemata, and therefore the question of animal cognition can be put in terms of the qualities of their schemata. Instincts are fixed and inherited schemata, so that a bird building a nest is using inherited *knowledge* about nest building—as opposed to only inherited *reflexes*. This seems reasonable enough: the difficulty with Piaget's style is that he says things like 'the assimilation of the pieces of straw into the forms of nest making activity is at that stage only functional, and so we speak of it as assimilation into a schema' (1971, p. 178). Instinctive schemata are not, however, so fixed as to prevent internal interplay between them, which would amount to a simple form of inference. As an extreme case, Piaget entertains the notion that inference occurs in certain species of land snail, which (a) lay eggs and (b) bury themselves in the ground to avoid predators and extremes of climate. Some species bury their eggs, and Piaget says that 'The tendency to lay eggs below the ground could be seen as the result of coordination and assimilation of the laying schema into the schema of self-protection or sheltering in the ground' (1971, p. 240). This perhaps should not be taken too seriously—Piaget has a soft spot for snails, since they were the subject of his Ph.D. thesis, and laying eggs in the ground is undoubtedly a separate and inherited behaviour pattern. But the variations observed in the location, shape, and composition of nests within the same species of bird, remarked on by Darwin, might well be best explained by the inheritance of mental concepts or schemata, which are susceptible to a certain degree of creative interpretation by individual animals.

Instinctive schemata are certainly subject to alteration and elaboration by accumulated experiences in the life of individuals: in Piaget's system Pavlovian conditioning is the passive assimilation of a new stimulus into the schemata of the original reflex, whereas in the sort of learning demonstrated by Skinner (pulling strings or pressing levers) new schemata are formed. The latter 'is no longer a matter of assimilation into previous schemata, but of construction in the sense of utilization of new relationships' (Piaget, 1971, p. 255 and p. 180).

Cognition in child and man is discussed in terms of progressive elaboration and construction of schemata (and new and sudden combinations among them), which proceeds in certain inevitable sequences, but depends on the activities and experience of the individual, and tends to occur before, rather than after, linguistic expression, especially in children. There are some stages of intelligence which only humans reach, but 'the line of demarcation between "intelligent" and "non-intelligent" is entirely a matter of convention': there is 'continuity of the learning processes from the most elementary upward' and this 'demonstrates the permanent part played by these assimilatory activities which seem to be common not only to animals and men, but also to all levels of cognitive function' (Piaget, 1971, p. 260).

Piaget thus clearly states a strong theoretical conviction that animal thought is continuous with human thought, and shares many of its properties. However, this should not be taken merely as a dogma; it is supported to some extent by the methodology by which Piaget investigates thought in the child. As an illustration, consider the perception of objects. This may seem to be a given, in so far as we tend to assume that everyone perceives objects in the same way, but it will be remembered that there have always been philosophical disputes about this, and there are obvious questions to be asked about whether a 6-month-old infant perceives objects differently from a 3-year-old, and so on. Piaget uses several practical behavioural tests. When does a baby first reach out to grab something? How successful is it at this? When does the baby begin to follow a falling object with its eyes? If a toy or rattle is hidden under a cloth while the infant watches, does it pull the cloth away to retrieve the toy? To the extent that a child passes tests such as these, it can be said to be developing 'sensory motor intelligence', and a particular form of this is 'object constancy' exhibited by remembering that things are under cloths, anticipating the reappearance of toys passed behind screens, and so on. Clearly, similar tests can be performed on kittens (Gruber *et al.*, 1971) and infant monkeys (Vaughter *et al.*, 1972) and gorillas (Redshaw, 1978). Equally clearly, infant mammals will be able to pass at least the simpler versions of the tests, but the Piagetian hypothesis is that the sequence of successive tests passed will be roughly similar to the sequence observed in human infants. This appears to be the case: kittens obviously become capable of following the trajectory of a ball of paper, and retrieving it from behind a chair, after fewer days of existence than a human baby, but the time course of perceptual development in young gorillas is roughly similar to that observed in humans over the first 12 months (Redshaw, 1978; see Chapter 9, this volume).

This may seem unremarkable, but the advantage of Piaget's discussions is that they emphasise that distinguishing between one's own body and the outside world, memory for the disposition of objects in the world, and elementary forms of interaction with objects, are cognitive achievements of some complexity, even though they may pale into insignificance by comparison with the eventual manifestations of fully human intelligence. Very roughly, the latter are divided by Piaget into 'concrete' and 'formal' cognitive 'operations'.

Concrete operations have to do mainly with logical relationships concerning objects, developing over the first 8 or 10 years of age, while formal operations are what most people would call verbal and symbolic, and seem to correspond to what a bright and educated 11 to 14-year-old knows about physics and mathematics. Formal operations are therefore specifically human. In so far as concrete operations concern knowledge of quantitative and qualitative aspects of objects, and the understanding of number, volume and mass, they may also be uniquely human. But elements of these achievements, such as understanding that a large predator (or conspecific) does not become smaller when it is seen further away, or at a less flattering angle (size and shape constancy) may be built in to animals' perceptual systems, or may be attainable with experience.

Further comparisons between the performance of monkeys and apes and human children on some of the more sophisticated Piagetian tests of cognitive understanding will be discussed in a later chapter. It is sufficient here to stress that many of the less spectacular abilities of children (and in some cases of adults as well), which are routinely taken to indicate thought and mental processing when they are studied in man, are abilities which are shared with animals.

The Question of Animal Awareness (Griffin, 1976)

Subjective awareness is not necessarily the same thing as cognitive complexity. Many who have had low opinions of the capability of animals for inference or abstract perception (for example, Locke) never doubted that their subjective experience of sufficiently simple things (pain, heat and cold, colour, sound) was as intense as our own. Since no one has yet discovered a completely watertight way to test whether this is so or not, the behaviourist tactic of ignoring the question still has something to be said for it. Griffin (1976) has however made a plea for more serious consideration of the possibility that the subjective feelings of animals should be granted a status close to that which we afford to other people's. He does not put forward a theory of cognition as such, but rather argues that the behaviour of animals should be discussed in terms of their awareness of mental events, irrespective of degrees of abstraction or cognitive complexity that may be inferred in various animal species. Consciousness is equated with the presence of mental images, and the existence of mental images in animals is indicated by orientation and navigation in space (the 'cognitive map' argument), and apparent seeking after goals. Griffin's short essay is thus a convenient and lucid restatement of what he acknowledges as Tolmanian theses, directed at the recent biological tradition of accounting for observed natural sequences of animal behaviour in terms of 'fixed action patterns' and 'innate releasing mechanisms' without discussion of possible intervening mental events (e.g. Hinde, 1970).

Griffin may have been rather over-optimistic, however, in supposing that 'a possible window on the minds of animals' is available in 'participatory investigation of animal communication'. In view of the difficulties in interpreting attempts to communicate directly with chimpanzees by means of imposed systems such as gestural sign language (see Chapter 9) one may doubt if there is very much to be gained by dialogues between a participating scientist and an electric fish (Griffin, 1976, p. 91). It is a weakness in Griffin's case that he ignores differences between species, and the factor of biological closeness to man, giving equal weight to the gestures of chimpanzees and the signals exchanged by honey bees, as prototypes for human language (e.g. pp. 59–60). A related gap is the connection between mental states and brain-states. If one ignores the dependence of subjective awareness on neuronal mechanisms, one is more likely to assume that the feelings of bees, or even plants, ought not to be distinguished from those of species more closely related to ourselves. This is the opposite tack from the one I am taking here.

The brain-state theories of Hebb (1949), Konorski (1967) and Bindra (1976)

Although, oddly, there is a biological tradition, followed by Griffin, of discussing animal behaviour in isolation, without any consideration of the role of the brain, which is exemplified by 'ethologists' such as Lorenz (1966) and by the recent vogue for 'sociobiology' (Dawkins, 1976a; Wilson, 1975), there has of course been no shortage, since Descartes, of theories as to how animal behaviour is determined by animal brains. What is relatively rare, however, is a theory which discusses animal *cognition* as a function of brain activity. It might be supposed that, if we adopt the materialist assumption that cognition *is* brain activity, then there is little need to go any further. But the assumption can only be justified if we know how it is that brains enable animals to do apparently intelligent things. Bindra's *A Theory of Intelligent Behaviour* (1976) attempts a comprehensive theoretical explanation of how goal-directed, voluntary, foresightful and conscious actions get produced by mammalian brains, with human cognitive faculties interpreted as special cases of more general aspects of brain function. In part, this serves as a compilation of support from the 'neural and behavioural sciences' for the contention that the mental processes we call cognition can be interpreted as certain forms of brain activity, but Bindra also puts forward specific suggestions as to what these fundamental processes are (or, at least, what they should be called).

Very broadly, Bindra belongs to the category of brain-state theorists who say that whenever we need to assume that a thought, as an internal act of knowing, takes place, there is a specific set of physical things in the brain which corresponds to this mental event. His particular assumptions and terminology are derived from the earlier explanations of Hebb (1949) and Konorski (1967). Hebb's idea was an elaboration of the widely accepted hypothesis that the brain works by developing links between individual neurons, or nerve-cells. The crucial concept was the 'cell-assembly'—groups of nerve-cells linked together (mainly, according to Hebb, because of a history of synchronous firing in the experience of the individual), are able to act as independent units. Thus inner sensations such as visual images or vivid hallucinations are explained as the activation of cell-assemblies derived from more real visual experience (Hebb, 1968). The organisation of mental states is thus reduced to the organisation of neuronal circuits. There are many rather similar versions of the hypothesis that connections between individual neurons underlie brain function (e.g. Barlow, 1972). There are also alternatives which follow Lashley (1929, 1950) in supposing there is something more vague and emphemeral about the location of information in the nervous system, and that something analogous to electromagnetic fields, or the coding of information in radio waves, means that specific nerve-cells, or groups of cells, are not so important.

However the other theory, apart from Hebb's, that Bindra draws on, is that of Konorski (1967), which goes to the extreme of assigning extensive cognitive functions to *particular* neurons. The simplest version of this sort of hypothesis suggests that there could be a single neuron corresponding to a single mental concept. A very large variety of visual patterns, verbal associations and emotional contexts may be related to particular mental ideas such as 'grandmother', but, as a limiting case, one may suppose that there is just one brain cell that fires when and only when 'grandmother' is being thought of. This is not to be taken too seriously, except as an illustration that a step-by-step sequence of links between neurons may allow some cells to map more closely on to mental categories than others. In Konorski's terms, there are 'gnostic neurons' whose knowledge is derived from their position in brain circuits. Konorski was the head of a Polish research laboratory working very much on Pavlovian lines, using dogs in conditioning experiments, and this can be seen as a development of Pavlov's theory of brain function, with 'gnostic neurons' as individual pieces in Pavlov's cortical mosaic.

Bindra retains the notion of the mosaic by concentrating on assemblies of brain cells, rather than individual neurons—his unit of brain function is the 'gnostic-assembly'. As he points out (p. 91), this is more or less the same thing as Hebb's 'cell-assembly', the main change of emphasis being that there is *not* supposed to be an exact correspondence between particular mental states and particular gnostic-assemblies. The gnostic-assembly for 'apple' represents combinations of features or dimensions of real apples, not all of which may be needed for any individual apple (Bindra, 1976, p. 360). The momentary experience of eating or seeing a particular apple is influenced by the existence of a gnostic-assembly about apples, but each bite of each apple is a unique mental state, and a unique brain-state. Bindra coins a new word for a particular mental experience in a particular brain: the 'pexgo'. While this neologism may not be very attractive, it is useful to make a distinction between relatively permanent aspects of neural organisation, and the precise form of moment-to-moment events in the nervous system. 'Pexgo' is a contraction of 'presently excited, distinctive neural (gnostic) organisation' (Bindra, 1976, p. 87), which serves as the unit of immediate perceptual knowledge. In a similar way, knowledge about actions is supposed to be contained in neural 'act-assemblies' so that the mental intention to act can be described as the activation of this sort of brain-state, which may then engage assemblies lower down in a neural hierarchy, which will deal with the sequencing and timing of movements. The meaning of words is defined in terms of gnostic organisations activated by words, remembering words depends on activating similar assemblies of neurons, and solving problems depends on exciting new gnostic organisations by 'progressive narrowing of the determining set' (Bindra, 1976, p. 344).

Whether this strategy of translating psychological terms into their hypothetical neural equivalents has any merit is of course open to dispute. I cite it here since in my view tying down the processes of human cognition to brain processes establishes a clear relationship between human and animal thought. If human thought is to be conceived of as patterns of neural excitation in the cerebral cortex, then it becomes reasonable to wonder about the cognitive functions of the cerebral cortex in other species. As it happens, Bindra himself does not seem to share this view, since his accounts of animal behaviour include very little reference to neural processes which would amount to memories or expectancies. Pavlov's dogs, fed after the sound of a bell, are assumed to acquire gnostic organisations which lead them to go and lick the food receptacle when the bell is sounded, but are not allowed an internal expectancy or image of the food (Bindra, 1976, p. 215). Skinner's rats, pressing a lever which gains them their food reward, are specifically denied an idea (or excited gnostic-assembly) of their own response (Bindra, 1976, p. 242), let alone the idea that the response causes the reward (pp. 278–9). Activating brain-states in a way that corresponds to the process of remembering is discussed only in the context of human memory.

Bindra's own explanation for why the animals in Pavlov's or

Skinner's experiments learn the things that they do is rather peculiar. Responses which appear to be voluntary are said to be made because there is conditioned excitation of inner stimuli which elicit the response (Bindra, 1976, p. 242). This is called an 'incentive-motivational view', harking back to a term of Hull's, and animals appear to be left with a compulsion to act, without memories of the results of previous actions, or anticipations of what might happen next.

Goals and expectancies in Mackintosh's *The Psychology of Animal Learning*

In 1974, Mackintosh published a comprehensive and authoritative review of 'the main areas of research that have developed from the pioneering work of Pavlov and Thorndike'. The question of how learning is produced by brain processes is excluded, but theoretical issues such as the degree to which animals are capable of anticipating future events are assessed on the basis of the enormous body of evidence about how laboratory animals behave in standard experimental tests. The arguments, and the experiments, are sometimes extremely detailed, and are not always conclusive. In general, however, it seems fair to say that the conclusions which Mackintosh derives from research initiated by Pavlov and Thorndike support not the 'conditioned response' theories which these pioneers began with, but rather the 'expectancy' theories of Tolman (see above).

As an example, theories like Bindra's, just mentioned, that animals act because compelled to do so by inner motivational states, irrespective of retained information concerning the consequences of actions, are weakened by several experiments which suggest that, even for laboratory rats, external stimuli, such as buzzers and lights, which were used as signals for food, did not promote diffuse states of enthusiasm, but rather, 'specific expectations of the reinforcer with which they had been paired' (Mackintosh, 1974, p. 227). It may be wondered what sort of experiment could demonstrate the existence of such inner mental events in rats. Suppose that hungry monkeys are tested in an elaborate version of a Skinner box, in which there is a raisin dispenser, and a peanut dispenser. When a buzzer is sounded, they can pull a chain which will deliver raisins, and, if they hear a whistle, pushing a button will operate the peanut dispenser. If they get this right, they can supply themselves with both peanuts and raisins, but if they get things the wrong way round, and go for the chain when they hear the whistle, or the button when they hear the buzzer, neither peanuts nor raisins are forthcoming. Monkeys should usually get it right, and a very simple incentive conditioning theory would say that they feel enthusiastic about chain-pulling as a conditioned reaction to the buzzer, and are motivated to push the button by the sound of the whistle, without knowing why they are drawn to these actions. The twist to the experiment is in giving the animals preliminary free trials, *before* they are required to learn to operate the dispensers for themselves. Suppose, in those preliminary experiences, raisins come preceded by whistles, and peanuts preceded by buzzers, and that is the opposite way round to what is going to happen in training, should this make any difference? If what is required is just a motivation to respond, without any expectations as to whether a peanut or a raisin is coming next, it should not. On the other hand, if we were exposed to such preliminaries ourselves, we should surely acquire mental associations that whistles go with raisins and buzzers go with peanuts, which would prove very confusing when the signals were reversed. It is because such reversals of the 'meaning' of experimental signals appear to be confusing for laboratory rats, in versions of the experiment just sketched out (e.g. Trapold, 1970), that Mackintosh suggests that specific information about what should happen next is somehow available to them, at least in the case of something as interesting as food.

An alternative phrase is that, in the Pavlovian kind of experiment, where one event follows another, the first can call up a 'rich encoding' of the second (Rescorla, 1980). Although sometimes disguised as 'the formation of an association between stimuli', Pavlov's result is increasingly being interpreted, because of more elaborate experiments, as due to 'central representations' (Mackintosh, 1974, p. 90; Rescorla, 1979). In other words Pavlov's result has to be explained by a brain process that is to all intents and purposes a mental association, so that the sound of the bell calls up an image, a representation, or a thought, of the previously experienced meat powder.

The utility of being able to think ahead in this way must lie in being able to take action on the basis of anticipated events. This may not always be obvious within the confines of the usual sort of Pavlovian experiment, but in the other kind of laboratory test, where animals are allowed to find their way through mazes, to discover methods of escaping from confinement, or to manipulate moveable objects which work food dispensers, the advantages of internalising experienced relationships between actions and pay-offs are made more transparent. Starting with Thorndike, the preferred assumption was that such an internal storing of prior experience could only take the form of rigid tendencies to make particular bodily movements. Mackintosh's conclusion, however, is that this assumption is inadequate: the experimental evidence is such as to 'suggest very strongly that animals are capable of learning that their behaviour has certain consequences' (Mackintosh, 1974, p. 211). The reason why animals make apparently intentional actions 'is precisely the expectation of an increase in incentive' (p. 269). The expectations are typically established on the basis of experience, so that 'disconfirmation of previously established expectancies' may in turn lead to changed actions (p. 417 and p. 346).

Thus, purely as a means of accounting for the accumulation of evidence from laboratory experiments in animal training, Mackintosh is led to adopt a significant fraction of Tolman's cognitive theory: animals have expectancies in so far as they are able to anticipate, on the basis of prior experience, specific and general properties of incipient yet absent events, and also have 'if-then' expectancies in so far as they anticipate the results of their own actions. This counts as a recent theory only because Mackintosh's text carries rather more weight than the protestations of Tolman a few decades ago; and it is two hundred years since we were told by Hume that animals 'learn many things from experience, and infer that the same events will always follow from the same causes'.

Conclusions: consciousness, abstraction, memory and brain processes in animals

What may be concluded from the astonishing variety of opinions concerning animal thought which have been reviewed in the last three chapters? It is clear that no single view is likely to command universal assent, but it ought to be possible to map out areas of dispute, to suggest borders that remain to be fought over, and ideally to indicate decisive sources of evidence. I must confess, however, that no such mapping out has suggested itself to me, and I propose instead to list cases where I am now going to take sides.

Human thought and consciousness

Evaluating the status of mental events in animals, except by comparison with what is assumed to exist in people, seems to be rarely attempted, and perhaps it is impossible. It may therefore be profitable to rephrase all questions about thought in animals in the form 'To what extent are animals like us?' and this is what I intend to do here. We can thus ask a number of separate questions, such as: 'Do animals have visual systems which work like ours?' 'Do animals have mental imagery like ours?' 'Do animals have hopes and fears like ours?' Such questions may be useful, even if we do not know very much about what is being used for comparison in ourselves. For instance, the function of sleep, and in particular of dreaming, remains shrouded in mystery, but the question 'Do animals dream like us?' is one to which, though there may be no definitive answers, plenty of relevant evidence can be addressed (see Chapter 6).

Although it is perhaps the most difficult of all, consider first the question 'Do animals have consciousness like ours?' Clearly we first have to say something about what features of human consciousness we are referring to. If we mean consciousness as in being awake, as opposed to being asleep or under anaesthetic, then the answer is a qualified yes. Sleep and anaesthetics seem to have all the effects in other mammals, and probably birds, that they do in us. Here we can point out what is probably a general rule, that the animals which are biologically more like us, that is mammals and especially monkeys and apes, are also more like us psychologically.

However, suppose we mean by 'conscious' being able to *say* that we are aware of something in particular, in ordinary human conversation. Then the answer is obviously no, since there are no animals that can tell us that they are aware of something in the same way that another person can. The uniqueness of human speech is the most commonly agreed boundary line between us and all other species, and the best strategy seems to be simply to conclude that anything that is verbal, and dependent on speech or language in some significant way, is not available to other species. This excludes a lot, it is true. Thought in the sense of 'eighteenth-century thought', 'Greek thought', or 'what Fleet Street is thinking today' just does not arise in any other species we know about. But this does not exclude everything, and it does not necessarily exclude everything that we happen to apply verbal labels to. If we say 'I feel hungry' or 'I think I am going to be sick' (and are telling the truth), then although verbal expression may add a considerable extra gloss to what we are conscious of, there is no reason to suppose that some of the feelings we are experiencing at the time might not be shared by individuals from other species, to the extent that they share the physical states that are responsible for our own hunger, or nausea.

The same argument applies to members of our own species, to the extent that someone who is retching, pale, and clearly suffering from seasickness, is probably feeling sick, even if he assures us that he is not. In particular we would suspect that he *was* feeling sick if he finally threw up.

Here we come to an important general point, and that is the relation of subjective awareness to physical states, and in particular to physical states of the brain. If it is accepted that all human subjective awareness arises as a result of brain processes (cf. Armstrong, 1968 and Chapter 1, p. 17), decisions as to the consciousness of other persons, and of members of other species, are considerably simplified, in theory if not in practice. The simplification is limited, since it could be claimed that the most important brain-states are those which mediate speech, in which case we would not be very much better off. But suppose that we want to decide whether someone who has been born deaf and dumb is enjoying his soup as much as we are. If we could know that (a) that soup is the same, (b) his taste-buds, olfactory apparatus and so on are the same, and (c) all his brain-states except those involved in speech are the same, we ought to be confident that his conscious appreciation of the soup has a good deal in common with our own. Knowing the name of the soup may make a difference, and someone who is convinced that he likes chicken soups may be more inclined to relish one made with rabbit if he accepts verbal assurances that it is chicken, but such niceties do not require us to abandon a general rule of identifying mental experiences with their physical causes.

If we grant that there is a physical basis to sensations, and that our own subjective awareness of perceiving things is due to particular sorts of reactions in our brains, we would be led to believe that our consciousness of certain well-defined sensations such as stomach-ache, pressure on the fingers, or bright lights flashing in our eyes, is roughly similar to the subjective sensations of animals which possess roughly similar bodies and brains to ours, and are exposed to roughly similar sets of events. There is some empirical support for this idea, in that, for instance, electrical stimulation of certain parts of the brain of patients who are awake, but have had their brain exposed for surgery, leads them to report feelings of touch or movement in particular places on the body surface; actual touching of the skin at these places causes measurable electrical changes in the appropriate locations in the brain; and similar relationships, apart from the absence of verbal reports of feeling, are observed in other mammals (e.g. Penfield and Rasmussen, 1950; Penfield and Roberts, 1959; Woolsey, 1965).

The proposition that states of the human brain have something critical to do with the conscious aspects of human perception has the clear implication that one of the criteria for whether the same kind of consciousness should be expected in animals is whether they have the same kind of brains. This means that the comparative anatomy and physiology of human and animal brains assumes the role of a decisive source of evidence concerning animal consciousness, and as such will be examined more closely in the next chapter. There is nothing very new in assigning importance to comparative brain anatomy—it is a view that was already being satirised by Charles Kingsley in 1886, in the course of digs at a thinly disguised Professor Huxley, who declares that apes have 'hippopotamus majors' in their brains, just as men have:

> You may think that there are other more important differences
> between you and an ape, such as being able to speak, and make
> machines, and know right from wrong, and say your prayers,
> and other little matters of that kind; but that is a child's fancy,
> my dear. Nothing is to be depended on but the great
> hippopotamus test. (*The Water Babies*, p. 172)

What is new, since 1886, is a good deal more information about how brains work, and a rather greater readiness to accept that this is pertinent to consciousness and thought.

It may be objected that an ape being consciously aware of a stomach-ache, because it has a similar brain, and a similar stomach, to ours, does not take us very far towards an assessment of animal thought. This is so: apart from Descartes and the behaviourists, most people, from Aristotle and Aquinas to Thorndike and Wundt, have in any case taken it for granted that mammals at least have an awareness of immediately perceived sensations. But it is important to confirm this to get over the barrier represented by the view that animals cannot possibly think because they are incapable of being aware of anything. The real concern is of course not whether an ape thinks that it has a stomach-ache, but whether it is capable of entertaining the possibility that another ape might have a stomach-ache, or whether it can remember that it itself had a stomach-ache the last time it ate unripe fruit.

If it were possible to make the large jump, and say that, because the ape's brain closely resembles ours, it must be capable of the complete range of cognitions available to a human being isolated from normal culture and education, in other words to assume that the imagination and inference available to apes is not violently different from those faculties that would be observed in the human species at an equivalently brutish stage of existence, this might save a considerable amount of further speculation. But even the most convinced materialist cannot make such a large jump, not only because what he knows as imagination and inference may be inseparable from culture, education and social traditions, but also because the advent of language, or some subtle change in brain utilisation prior to language, and conceivably prior to the development of social traditions and so on in *Homo sapiens*, may mean that human brains, while undoubtedly sharing a great many properties with other mammalian brains, are able to do some new and different things.

Descartes's contention that human brains have access to a superior controlling agency has been caricatured as a claim that our brains are only the instruments of thought, as a piano is an instrument for a piano-player. The separate existence of the piano-player, or the 'ghost in the machine', presents problems, especially if one accepts Darwinian theories of evolution. However, if we view brains as pianolas, rather than pianos, operated by sets of instructions within themselves, it is easy to see that as physically similar pianolas may be capable of playing different kinds of tunes, so physically similar brains may have different capacities for the sequences of operations we call thought. We would have to test pianolas by listening to them play, and we must also examine animals' brains by the tunes they generate, that is by assessing the kinds of behaviours they are capable of sustaining.

In other words, a form of behaviourism remains essential for the evaluation of cognition. What animals do will have to be the final test for what they think.

Abstraction and perception

We may try out these criteria of behavioural capacity and available neural mechanisms in relation to the question of whether animals can be said to perform abstractions. After language, this is the most popular dividing line between animals and men, Locke and Romanes for instance giving it pride of place as a peculiarly human faculty. Kenneth Craik (1943, p. 72) pointed out that, unless one adopts the practice of putting the question in the form 'do animals abstract like men?' the distinction loses much of its force. Abstraction means neglecting particulars, and this is easy, not difficult. Craik's example is a photoelectric cell counting objects passing by on a conveyor belt. Every particular characteristic of the objects is neglected in favour of the non-specific factor of whether the photo-cell beam is broken. Similarly, very rudimentary mechanical devices can respond to weight irrespective of shape, height irrespective of width, or speed irrespective of what it is that is moving. Is this what is meant by abstraction? It seems to be partly what Locke meant (cf. pp. 23), since his example is the abstract perception of 'whiteness' irrespective of whether it occurs in snow or milk. This degree of abstraction could be achieved by a sophisticated version of Craik's photoelectric cell, and a Pavlovian experiment could easily show monkeys salivating to anything white. It is reasonable to conclude that when Locke said 'brutes abstract not' he was simply wrong.

However, although Locke was quite specific about the abstraction of general ideas such as whiteness as an underlying ability, the reason why this ability has been erroneously raised to such a high position in the panoply of intellectual capacities is probably because of the existence of abstract *words* for such things as whiteness. The special thing about human abstraction probably boils down to the use of verbal labels.

I have already mentioned, in discussing Pavlov's experiments, that Locke's assertions about 'compounding' not being present in animals can be shown to be false, by behavioural testing. It is still common to discuss animal perception in terms of isolated particulars—a robin being said to recognise another robin only in terms of redness, for instance. It may be the case that isolated stimulus qualities can exert a powerful influence on animal behaviour, especially for young animals or creatures such as the frog, which has highly specialised responses to anything that moves like an insect. Similarly, it is sometimes claimed that 'cross-modal' perception—recognising an object by touch, sight or sound as the same thing—is a specifically human capacity (e.g. Geschwind, 1965). Sophisticated behavioural tests have confirmed that monkeys and chimpanzees are perfectly capable of recognising objects in alternative modalities such as touch or sight (Weiskrantz, 1977) and these add to the evidence that this form of human abstraction is shared at least by other primates. This is a case where further behavioural tests can be expected to provide stronger evidence. But it ought to be stressed that object recognition is a general function of the animal sensory systems rather than something confined to primates—a cat is superbly equipped to recognise a mouse by sight, sound, smell and touch, and it is more likely that the cat's perception of 'mouse' relates to all four sources of information than that it responds quite independently to each modality. A visual sense which was not correlated with touch and sound would be much less useful than one that is, and the vertebrate brain is often described as a set of correlation centres which exist precisely to accomplish the integration of information from the various modalities.

Thus, while it is perfectly legitimate to emphasise that animals do not think abstract thoughts in the sense of using abstract words rather than concrete words, and in the sense that human abstract thought requires the grammar of language or a symbolic system such as mathematics, it is quite wrong to push limitations on abstraction back to elementary forms of object perception. In direct opposition to Locke, I would maintain that the dog's perception of his master occurs as a compound of voice, shape and smell, rather than 'so many distinct marks'. What the dog cannot do is say to himself that he is one of the interacting elements in a master-dog situation. But this is a limitation in language, not in perception.

Memory and learning

Lloyd Morgan maintained that any animal capable of learning from experience could only do so by calling up conscious memories of previous occasions in order to guide present acts. He did not say that much-practised skills and drills could not become routine and automatic, but rather that the early stages of practice that are necessary to establish unconscious habits must require conscious effort, and the active recall of mental images. The thrust of behaviourist scepticism, beginning with Thorndike, and exemplified by Hull and Skinner, has been to suggest that learning can take place without any inner memories or mental processes of any kind. It has to be acknowledged that there are many forms of learning for which this is undoubtedly true.

First, adaptive changes in behaviour resulting from experience can be observed in animals or parts of animals with access only to neural mechanisms so rudimentary that the existence of mental processes which normally require an intact human brain seems extremely unlikely. Learning of a sort can be demonstrated in isolated ganglia of cockroaches and slugs, decorticated rats, the human foetus, humans in a vegetative coma, and isolated parts of the spinal cord in humans and other mammals.

Second, there are many forms of human learning which can take place without any indications of subjective awareness. We are not necessarily aware of the movements of individual muscles which must be co-ordinated by experience in learning to play tennis (an example Thorndike was fond of) or of the movements our eyes must make when scanning a printed page—still less of the learned neural processes which enable us to recognise letters and words. It has been repeatedly pointed out that children learn a good deal more grammar while in blissful ignorance of its existence than when they are required to develop conscious memories about its describable forms.

But because *some* kinds of learning are apparently unconscious and automatic, and do not involve the subjective inspection of recalled memories of past events, we should not make the behaviourist mistake of concluding that *all* forms of learning have a similar character. Only the doctrinaire ever gave credence to the proposition that we could account for human psychology without including unexpressed mental events; but demonstrating similar processes in animals is a much more difficult matter. The traditional touch-stone, still in use, is the goal-directedness of animal behaviour (e.g. Tolman, 1932; Bennett, 1976; Dickinson, 1985). The animal runs through a maze, or climbs a tree, because it remembers there is something it wants that can be obtained by these activities. This in itself is not good enough: Thorndike was able to claim that we may occasionally make a tennis stroke which has a purpose, without thinking about its purpose until afterwards, if at all, and that animals might do this sort of thing all the time. Similarly, it can be claimed that a cruise missile behaves in a goal-directed and purposeful way, but we would not believe that the cruise missile therefore has intentions and memories like our own, even if, like other manufactured robots, its actions were determined by prior experience.

The only way out is to make detailed examination of the extent to which the behaviours and neural mechanisms observed in animals are like those of our own which we identify with memory. I will return to this topic in a later chapter, but it seems to be becoming clear that detailed evidence suggests that laboratory animals have memories, or expectancies about the future based on experience. Lloyd Morgan may have been right to say that conscious memories guide learned actions in so far as the typical laboratory tests of animal learning have to be interpreted as expectations concerning future events, as well as mechanical elicitations of a response (Mackintosh, 1983). Put in another way, this means that it makes sense to say at least some of the time that Pavlov's dogs salivated because they believed that a buzzer should be followed by food, Thorndike's cats released latches because they remembered that this would allow them to get out of confinement, and Skinner's rats pressed levers because they expected, on the basis of previous experience, that this would enable them to eat food pellets.

Language and thought

As I pointed out at the beginning of Chapter 1, for some purposes it is perfectly reasonable to define 'thought' as something that only man is capable of, and to then say that everything that might occur in the brains of animals should be called something else. The disadvantage of this strategy is that it encourages the belief that every mental process which in ourselves becomes tied up with verbal expression is necessarily absent in all other species. Because we have a word for whiteness, and our own perceptual activities tend to become locked on to our words, many have followed Locke in asserting that species which lack a word for whiteness are therefore not able to isolate this quality perceptually. Because we practically always can put words to our memories and anticipations, we assume that without the words, memories and anticipations cannot exist. When we use a name for individual objects, such as 'the FA cup' or 'the White House' it is clear that using the name embodies a great deal more than sensory information about the objects. Indeed we can use the names perfectly well without ever having seen or touched the FA cup, or the White House. However vague our notion of the meaning of names may be, it is clear that there is much that is independent of the sorts of immediate physical knowledge that can be assumed to be available through animal senses. When we talk of 'the author of the anonymous letter', or 'inaudible sound frequencies', we make use of linguistic abilities that seem to be peculiar to our own species.

It is clear, therefore, that there must be mental processes made possible by language, which cannot take place without linguistic competence and experience, and which must be denied to animals. The argument is whether language-dependent mental processes are grafted on to, or perhaps develop from, more elementary inner representations and ideas which arise in the brains of animals, or whether, if linguistic devices are excluded, nothing is left which bears any resemblance to human perception, memory, and subjective awareness. I hope to support a strong form of the first alternative: that language-dependent mental processes can be accomplished in the human brain only because animal brains in general work in terms of perceptions, memories, concepts and ideas. Without such internal referents, there would be little point in evolving whatever it is that enables human brains to exchange information via speech. Rigid and restricted methods of communication might be useful if, for instance, instinctive cries of alarm elicited flight in other members of a species, without any intervening inner mental pictures of predators. It is conceivable that fairly elaborate exchange of information between ants or between bees takes place like this, by way of elicitation of preprogrammed response plans. But it is patently obvious that the way human speech works is that someone having the idea of bananas can produce a corresponding idea in someone else simply by saying 'bananas'.

Now, one might suppose that the ability to have the idea 'bananas' depends on the possession of language, and thus that the ability to have ideas evolved after, or in step with, the evolution of language. This is the familiar theory put forward by Locke, that the ability to have abstract ideas is a uniquely human achievement, and a prerequisite for speech, since words are only useful if they are connected to ideas. My proposal is that rather good 'abstract ideas' for such things as bananas were available *before* the evolution of human language. Thus chimpanzees may have the idea of a banana (and related concepts such as 'lots of bananas'), bears may have a pretty clear idea of 'honey', and cats of 'mouse', even if they do not have words for them. The general theory behind this is that a function of brains is to provide an internal model of reality, or something like it (e.g. Craik, 1943; Bindra, 1976) and that ideas are necessary because they correspond to external realities. Thus the original purpose of brains is to internalise the objective external world, and the external world is usefully described in terms of complex relationships and associations, amounting to relatively abstract ideas. Once this inner network of ideas is re-externalised by mapping them on to verbal utterances, new possibilities for the mental manipulation of ideas emerge. Spoken words are themselves both external objects and voluntary actions. Internalisation of words, and relationships between words, clearly allows for a new realm of inner ideas, not necessarily identical with the internal representation of more tangible physical realities. In the human species, at present, and certainly in its more academically inclined members, mental processes driven by words tend to dominate.

To test the hypothesis that there is such a thing as pre-linguistic thought, one might first wish to examine the psychological processes of young children, in whom ideas might occasionally run ahead of speech, or in adults deprived of language by deafness, or damage to the brain. However, my interest is clearly in the demonstration of non-linguistic mental abilities in other species. This may be done through the investigation of perception and action, if this provides evidence of classification, categorisation and compounding of ideas, and the activation of inner memories and expectancies. A more immediately appealing tactic is to make non-linguistic mental events manifest by forcing animals to reveal their inner cognitive organisation in a way analogous to human speech. The last ten years have seen an enormous amount of effort devoted to the inculcation of human-like modes of communication of ideas in chimpanzees, the species where this tactic should have the greatest chance of success. If a chimpanzee could be persuaded to speak English, or properly utilise the gestures of a sign language like those used by the human deaf, this would certainly provide a short cut to the discovering of what normally goes on in chimpanzee minds. Unfortunately, no chimpanzee has yet been found that can reproduce the remotest approximation to human speech, and it is still unclear whether the numerous apes that have been trained to mimic sign-language-like gestures are doing very much more than what a parrot can do with speech-like vocalisations. However, the evidence produced in these exercises must be important, whichever side it supports, and I shall review it in Chapter 9.

For the present I simply assume that mental states of all kinds are properties of brains, and that it is therefore possible to consider mental evolution as an aspect of brain evolution.

4 The phylogenetic scale, brain size and brain cells

Even if one is convinced that all mental processes, whether in man or in animals, depend on the activities of the brain, it does not follow that all psychological investigations can be replaced by the examination of brain tissue. However, if the assumption that mental states reflect brain-states is taken at all seriously, then it is clear that the physical structure of animal brains must be taken into account in any theory about the existence of mental activity in animal species. In this chapter I will therefore examine the evidence concerning the anatomical and physical characteristics of vertebrate brains. Inevitably, some of this evidence is rather technical and detailed. But first we should consider the broad and general question of the physical evolution of the brain. A concept which has the immediate appeal of simplicity is that vertebrate brains can be placed on an evolutionary scale of excellence, with the human brain coming at the top of the scale as the end result of a long series of brain improvements. There are many dangers and difficulties in this idea of a phylogenetic scale, but clearly we should expect to place physical brain characteristics within an evolutionary context, and I shall start with a brief account of vertebrate evolution. This will, I hope, clear the way for an examination of two specific issues: the nature of the variations in the quantity and the quality of brain tissue across vertebrate species. The underlying question is of course the extent to which animal brains are similar to the human brain. If the human brain is quite radically different from the brains of all other animals in its physical characteristics, then one might conclude that human mental processes could not possibly have counterparts in other species. But if, as I think the evidence will suggest, the physical superiorities of the human brain are a matter of degree, then one may argue backwards, and say shared brain processes imply shared mental processes. This argument does not depend on any particular course of vertebrate phylogenesis, or even on evolutionary theory, but of course we would expect species differences in brain anatomy and physiology to reflect evolutionary relationships.

The phylogenetic scale

Evolutionary theory is often vague and indefinite, but it can hardly be ignored if we are to make systematic comparisons of any kind between species. The most controversial and dubious aspects of the Darwinian theory of natural selection have to do with gradual progression and its causes, and many of the assumptions about these aspects made in discussions of psychological differences between species can be severely criticised (Hodos and Campbell, 1969). Part of the explanatory value of Darwinian theory is the concept of a gradual step-by-step sequence of design improvements, with superior designs supplanting the inferior (Yarczower and Hazlett, 1977). But we cannot use this idea to rank species on a single ladder of ascending complexity. Hodos and Campbell argue that there can never be any valid classification of species based on a linear grading, and say that the use of terms such as 'the phylogenetic scale', 'the Great Chain of Being' or 'Scala Naturae' has been grossly misleading. They would prefer to abandon even such familiar dichotomies as that between higher and lower vertebrates. This would be an uncomfortable abstinence in comparative psychology since the framework of progressive increases in intelligence, brain size, or learning ability is a very common assumption. It is very hard to avoid dealing with the proposition that animals in general have cognitive abilities that are inferior to those of the human species, and that some animals have less cognition than others. In itself this implies a scale of psychological complexity, but it is difficult, if not impossible, to give such a scale any biological meaning. The most obvious attempt to give evolutionary backing to intuitive ideas of progress in psychological complexity is in terms of an historical account of vertebrate ancestry. The three main objections to this are: (1) accounts of phylogenetic sequence in vertebrate evolution are highly speculative; (2) convergent and parallel evolution resulting from similar ecological specialisations in unrelated groups mean that ancestry is not always important; and (3) what is known about the evolutionary tree of vertebrate development cannot possibly be mapped on to a single linear scale.

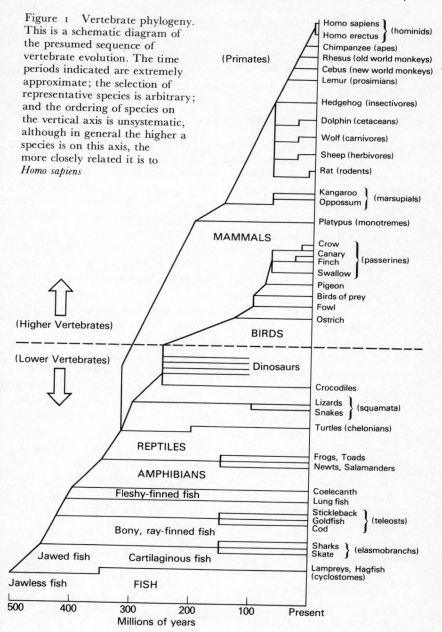

Figure 1 Vertebrate phylogeny. This is a schematic diagram of the presumed sequence of vertebrate evolution. The time periods indicated are extremely approximate; the selection of representative species is arbitrary; and the ordering of species on the vertical axis is unsystematic, although in general the higher a species is on this axis, the more closely related it is to *Homo sapiens*

Given these and other criticisms of the phylogenetic scale we should be wary of all general theories of vertebrate brain evolution. But the extent of the disparity between species genealogy and the assumption of an ordered scale, as well as the give and take between ancestry and ecological specialisation, deserves closer analysis.

Sequence and relations in vertebrate ancestry

It would be wonderfully convenient for the purpose of comparative experiments if vertebrate phylogeny *had* proceeded in a strict linear succession. The story has sometimes been presented almost as if it did—as if a swimming chordate with no jaw developed a minimal brain and became a lamprey, which survives as the oldest vertebrate but which was superseded by animals with jaws and a bony skeleton in a series of improvements by which fish changed into frogs, frogs turned into lizards, lizards turned into birds, birds turned into rats, rats turned into monkeys, and monkeys turned into man. If things had happened like this, then we would have some reason to expect that we should be able to plot increasing levels of psychological complexity by making comparisons between living representatives of each of the stages. But in fact, the family relationships between living species are rather involved and complicated. What can be done, with a considerable amount of speculation, is to chart roughly the evolutionary tree of the vertebrates, to show relationships between taxonomic divisions above the species level such as classes (for instance birds and mammals) and orders (for instance rodents and primates). A diagram of this kind is shown in Figure 1. Rather than providing a linear scale of vertebrate species it can be seen that comparisons between living animals have to be judged against a variegated pattern of phylogenetic relatedness, recency of origin, and species specialisation. In other words the vertical axis of Figure 1 does not represent a single biological dimension, although it is certainly true that species towards the top are more closely related to man than species near the bottom.

To go back to the beginning of the story, the earliest vertebrate fossils are indeed of jawless fishes, and there are surviving jawless fishes in the lampreys and hagfishes (cyclostomes). Lampreys and hagfishes are therefore conveniently called primitive. But their lifestyle is highly specialised: they are parasites and scavengers depending on much more recently evolved fishes. The habits and instincts of the living parasitic cyclostomes cannot therefore be representative of the original, and now extinct, 'primitive vertebrates'. (There might have been a short and drastic period of mutual cannibalism, but things could hardly have started that way.) We must do the best we can with whatever evolutionary left-overs are available, and therefore we assume that the brains of lampreys and hagfishes are more like primitive vertebrate brains than are those of other species of fish. To support this assumption, we may appeal to the necessarily vague 'principle of conservation', which says that essential features of organisation and structure, once evolved in a group of animals, will be retained in all the direct descendants of the group (Stebbins, 1969; Jerison, 1976). But there is always the danger that modern lampreys and hagfishes have developed their own specialisations, and that this makes them differ significantly from the original jawless fish that they are presumed to represent.

The earliest jawed fish provide the next most ancient branch of the vertebrate tree, and this branch divided, about 500 million years ago, into fish whose descendants now have skeletons composed of cartilage, and those which gave rise to the numerous living tribes of bony fish. Although many changes may have taken place in 500 million years, modern cartilaginous fish (sharks and rays) are usually considered to represent very old vertebrate stock. The vast majority of modern species of fish evolved in several stages from primitive bony fish through a line in which isolated examples, such as the garpike and sturgeon, remain from otherwise extinct radiations. The modern bony majority, the *teleosts* (e.g. goldfish, cod, perch) come from a line of ray-finned fish (*actinopterygians*) which diverged more than 400 million years ago from the fleshy-finned orders (*sarcopterygians*) whose more substantial appendages provided the basis for the limbs of amphibians, and thus for the limbs of all other land-going vertebrates. It is fair, then, to regard the teleosts as phylogenetically very remote from birds and mammals, even though the teleosts did not become common until the Cretaceous period (about 100 million years ago), and in this sense are almost as *recent* as birds and mammals.

Amphibians as a class, arriving about 350 million years ago, are clearly ancestral to later land-based vertebrates; but the common modern amphibians, the frogs and toads, are highly specialised as jumpers and insect catchers and cannot be taken as early kinds of reptile. The early reptiles themselves, having come into the possession of a mode of reproduction which allowed them to exploit purely land-dwelling lifestyles (as their eggs could be laid on land), diverged into both mammals and birds, and surviving forms such as lizards and snakes. In a typical evolutionary quirk, reptile groups which remained loyal to sub-aquatic environments, the turtles and crocodiles, are among the survivors.

The fossil record for birds is poor, and as a class they are sometimes treated as 'glorified reptiles', rather unjustly in view of what I shall say later about their psychological capacities. Bipedal, highly visual reptiles developed feathers some 50 million years after quadrupedal, nocturnal, smell and hearing specialists grew hair, and thus birds could be regarded as more recent than mammals. Intermediary species which can be classified as 'mammal-like reptiles', then 'reptile-like mammals', provide fossil evidence for the connection between reptiles and mammals, and living species which are different again from these seem to have part-mammal and part-reptile characteristics. The monotremes—the duck-billed platypus and two species of spiny anteater—lay eggs but suckle their young, and one of the spiny anteaters carries its eggs about in an external pouch (*Tachyglossus*: Griffiths, 1978). The more numerous marsupials (e.g. the oppossum or the koala bear) suckle their young, and do not lay eggs, but, lacking a placenta for the internal nourishment of their offspring, give birth very early in foetal development. One reason for regarding this as an intermediate level of reproductive strategy is that marsupials were once very much more widespread, but were superseded by placental mammals.

The ancestral placental mammals were rather unimpressive, small, shy, nocturnal insectivores, according to the usual interpretation of fossil evidence. If we are to believe this, the hedgehog is closer to the typical primitive placental mammal than any living species is to a primitive amphibian, reptile or bird. Unflatteringly, it is the primitive insectivores, represented by the hedgehog, which are the ancestors of the modern primates (which include monkeys, apes and man). The early branching off within mammals was fan-like, rather than step-by-step, and there is therefore no question of a rat or a cat representing an intermediate stage along a line stretching from hedgehogs to monkeys. The rapid fan-like branching out of mammalian orders, 50-60 million years ago, meant that rodents, carnivores, insectivores, primates and so on followed separate lines of development (see Figure 1, p. 117). Although mammalian species fall within families, and the families fall within orders, descent alone cannot be used to put them into a natural hierarchy. We may put primates at the top of the mammalian scale because we are primates, but no one has discovered any other reason for singling out this particular branch of the phylogenetic tree. In particular, recency of origin of a species or group, in so far as this can be guessed at, has very little relevance. For instance, rodents first appear in the fossil record rather later than primates, and may be derived from primates, and Old World rats and mice (murids) are a particularly recent family, first appearing only 10 million years ago. Recency in the fossil record does not allow one to put Old World monkeys above Old World rats (Radinsky, 1976). Because of this lack of phylogenetic distinction between the various orders of mammals, and because of the uncertainty and irregularity of vertebrate evolution which led to mammals, we must accept the caution that a continuum of living species with man at the top is an arbitrary and unfounded invention (Hodos and Campbell, 1969). But, although vertebrate evolution cannot provide a neat and linear scale of superiority, we are not left with only confusion and anarchy in phylogenesis. It is illegitimate to regard animal species as small steps made towards the human species, but there is no reason why we should not work backwards, and construct an explicitly anthropomorphic scale in terms of *phylogenetic relatedness to man* (or even in terms of superficial similarity to man). If we simply wish to classify other species according to how close they are to our own species in the phylogenetic tree, there is no great problem in identifying other primates as more like *Homo sapiens* than other mammals, or in saying that mammals in general should share more human characteristics than other classes of vertebrate. By being explicitly anthropomorphic we can provide some justification for the use of a natural scale.

A second and quite different reason for not completely discarding the notion of a natural scale is that the theory of progression in evolution, or *anagenesis*, still carries a certain amount of weight (Rensch, 1959; Jerison, 1973; Gould, 1976; Yarczower and Hazlett, 1977). It is not unreasonable to suppose that, other things being equal, evolution via natural selection should lead to increases in the complexity, variety and efficiency of life-forms. The question is whether such general theoretical changes can be related to specific issues such as the increase in the size of the brain during vertebrate evolution without the commission of the vitalist and teleological errors discussed by Monod (1972) and Hodos and Campbell (1969). I shall come back to the issue of progressive increases in brain size shortly, and theories of evolutionary changes in the complexity of brain organisation come up in the next chapter: in both cases there are obvious connections with arguments about animal cognition.

For the moment, if we simply assume that thought and cognition are special characteristics of the human species, Figure 1 provides a rough guide for estimating genealogical relationships with other vertebrates. These may or may not give a useful indication of which species are most likely to exhibit approximations to human psychological qualities. But in asking questions about thought, one is inevitably being anthropomorphic, and the first hypotheses would be that chimpanzee cognition is more similar to human cognition than is that of other mammals, mammalian brain function is more like human brain function than is reptilian brain function, and so on. Purely on the basis of ancestry, human characteristics should be traceable through primates and insectivores, to primitive mammals, and then back to reptiles, thus bypassing all other mammalian orders and all birds. One problem with this is the enforced absence of the most interesting members of the sequence: primitive hominids, early anthropoids, primitive mammals, and early, non-specialised reptiles. The strategy usually recommended for minimising this problem is to study species which come as close as possible to the supposed lines of descent, that is to compare man with chimpanzees, then monkeys, then hedgehogs, then opposums and then turtles (turtles being optimistically considered to represent primitive reptiles—Riss, 1968a; see also Diamond and Hall, 1969; Hall and Ebner, 1970; Ebbesson and Northcutt, 1976). However, this strategy has rarely been followed by psychologists and, instead, vast amounts of the available evidence from behavioural experiments come from domesticated species of teleost (goldfish), bird (pigeon), rodent (rat) and mammalian carnivore (cats and dogs).

There are compensations in adopting a resolutely non-phylogenetic strategy of comparisons, since even the most sensible assumptions about ancestry are still subject to the difficulties arising from convergence, and ecological specialisation. The general pattern of vertebrate phylogeny necessarily points to relations between broad groups or classes of species, there being important common attributes within each group. Thus one emphasises the breathing of amphibians, the terrestrial egg of the reptiles, the feathers of birds, and so on. But an important aspect of evolutionary theory not represented in diagrams of phylogeny such as Figure 1 (p. 117) is the adaptive radiation of particular groups into different habitats. A factor which arises from this is *convergence*, which means that species with very different ancestries may independently evolve similar characteristics: the usual example is the streamlined shape which appears in fast-swimming sharks and teleosts, and in marine reptiles and marine mammals. On the other hand, species with a good deal of common ancestry may adopt radical specialisations, so that within the same group there may be many different forms. Within mammals, for instance, there are aquatic forms, amphibious forms, ground feeders, arboreal feeders, insectivores and carnivores, among others, all with specialised anatomical features. Even within orders, similar species may share some features because of inheritance from 'common ancestral stock', and other features because of convergence, while being separated by idiosyncratic species specialisations (Martin, 1973). Shared features due to common ancestry are said to be *homologous*, but shared characteristics resulting from convergence are distinguished from these as *analogous* (Simpson, 1953). The decision as to whether a particular feature is shared by two species because of analogy or because of homology is not always clear cut, but if species behaviour as well as anatomical structure may be determined by specialisations which override phylogentic factors, then great care must be taken with the psychological implications of any purely genealogical comparisons. Hodos and Campbell (1969) make the case that psychology may reflect the current lifestyle of a species, rather than its pedigree.

In the extreme, this implies that general questions based on phylogeny, such as whether the learning abilities of fish differ from those of birds, may be completely misleading. A goldfish may be representative only of goldfish and not of teleost fish as a group, and the pigeon may have evolved behavioural characteristics which serve as a poor guide to the traits of other birds. However, there is a theoretical alternative to the uninviting prospect of treating each species as a law unto itself. This is to follow for ecological classifications as well as, rather than instead of, phylogenetic taxonomy. (In Julian Huxley's terms, we can classify species into *clades* of ecological specialisation as well as into phylogenetic *grades*: Gould, 1976.) There may certainly be striking analogies between the psychological capacities of species, based not on common ancestry but on common behavioural functions. An example is the vision of owls and cats. Phylogenetically these families are from different classes, but both are composed of carnivorous predators, and include species that can be said to have specialised as nocturnal mouse catchers. Such owls and such cats have binocular vision which is remarkably effective at low levels of illumination, and which seems to involve similar brain mechanisms (Pettigrew and Konishi, 1976). One may speculate that the anatomical analogies in perceptual apparatus should be accompanied by psychological analogies in the ways in which the apparatus is used, and that stealth, patience and rapid attack should be required of mouse catchers, whether they are owls, or cats. In general, just as species in different classes may arrive at similar anatomical solutions to problems associated with particular ecological niches, so there may be some degree of equivalence in the psychological capacities of such species. But an owl is still a bird, and a cat is still a mammal: ecological specialisations do not necessarily abolish all phylogenetic differences.

Thus, although we might circumvent all the difficulties of genealogy by adopting the principle 'ecology overrides phylogeny', this would be going too far. Phylogenetic position clearly limits the available ecological options (only warm-blooded vertebrates could hunt mice on cold winter nights) and the fact that there may be analogies of behavioural function does not mean that ancestry is always irrelevant. In fact, the analysis of the diversification of species into ecological specialisations can be used to support the idea that a particular ancestry brings with it a flexible potential, rather than only a fixed and static species-specific inheritance. The classic example of a natural experiment which illustrates the potential for adaptive radiation into varied ecological niches is the case of the Galapagos finches. The Galapagos are volcanic islands, only about 20 or 30 million years old, which have been colonised by chance arrivals from South America, which is several hundred miles to the east. Several species of the birds observed on the Galapagos are clearly recognisable as South American, and some may be very recent immigrants, but there are fourteen unique species of finches. Although the presumed ancestor of all these fourteen species was a seed-eating ground finch, there is now a wide divergence in their eating habits (Lack, 1947; Young, 1962). Five species remain ground feeders, although two in this category feed predominantly on cactus. But several species have become insectivorous, and this dramatically violates normal finch behaviour patterns. The convenient anatomical measure of divergence in the Galapagos finches is the shape of the bill, but presumably behavioural adaptations to suit warbler-like and tit-like habits have become necessary in the species with warbler-like and tit-like bills. And although one would have thought that variation in bill growth should be the simplest and quickest mechanism of adaptive radiation, the insectivorous Galapagos finch that mimics woodpeckers (*Camarhynchus pallidus*) is a major star of behavioural evolution, since instead of having a long woodpecker-like bill, it uses its short finch's bill to hold cactus spines, with which it picks out insects from crevices in trees.

From the point of view of Darwinian theory, the Galapagos finches are important because the existence of fourteen new species in geographic isolation suggests that their origin should be attributed to the natural selection exerted when a seed-eating ground finch found itself in novel conditions of life. The example could also be taken as an illustration of ecology overriding phylogeny, since the ancestral seed-eating has been displaced by cactus-eating or insect-eating in some of the descendants. But the Galapagos finches can be used equally well to emphasise that phylogeny is more than a reflection of ecology, in the sense that the original seed-eating species was not eternally bound to its seed-eating habits, but possessed the potential for adaptive radiation into the fourteen new ecological niches. Critics of phylogenetic comparisons, such as Hodos and Campbell (1969), imply that each species is bound to a particular ecology and that a single species should thus never be taken as a representative of its family or class. But the possibility of adaptive radiation means that each species must represent something more than its own ecological specialisation. It was because the ancestral Galapagos finch was a bird that it could be the progenitor of other species of bird, and it was because it had the brain of a bird that its descendants could develop new ranges of bird behaviours.

There is thus a case for saying that every species must to some extent be representative of its class and grade, and that to this extent comparisons between individual species in different vertebrate groupings should not always be dismissed. More generally, phylogenetic classifications of some kind or other are essential in any discussion of brain evolution.

The physical characteristics of vertebrate brains

Although animal behaviour and its relation to evolution may be studied without reference to brain mechanisms, as it typically is by ethologists (Eibl-Eibesfeldt, 1970; this methodology is explicitly advocated by Dawkins, 1976a), there is a long tradition in comparative brain anatomy and physiology which deserves to be recognised and which currently seems to be undergoing a minor revolution (Cajal, 1911; Kappers, Huber and Crosby, 1936; Elliot Smith, 1910; Hodos and Karten, 1970; Macphail, 1982). Part of the reason for the changing of views lies in technical advances, and it is instructive to consider the sorts of evidence accumulated by these brain sciences.

Techniques of brain study

Evidence about the brain itself includes how much it, and its constituent parts, weigh; what the individual cells in various brain regions look like; where the axons of these cells go to; and the extent to which brain cells respond electrically when the sense organs are experimentally activated or when the animal is doing things of its own accord. Conversely brain cells themselves can be electrically stimulated, to see what behaviour this produces, or groups of cells can be damaged and subsequent changes in psychological capacities assessed. Slightly more detail concerning these techniques is given below.

Gross anatomy
The more directly observable physical features of the brain, such as overall size and shape, have been responsible for some of the most far-reaching speculations about brain function and importance. Total weight or volume of the brain provides an objective and unambiguous scale and indeed cranial volume in cubic centimetres continues to be used as the major index in the study of human evolution based on fossil skulls (Pilbeam, 1972). Considerable emphasis has also been given to the relative mass of different parts of the brain, especially in comparisons between 'higher' and 'primitive' structures, such as the ratio of cerebral hemisphere size to brainstem size (Portmann and Stingelin, 1961, in birds; Passingham, 1975, in primates: see below and Figure 4, p. 175, for descriptions of brain parts). The general shape and arrangement of vertebrate brains has been assessed in terms 'fissurisation' (foldings of the surface), and 'flexure'—the bending and realignment of parts—which appears to change the longitudinal layout of the fish brain into the more compressed and spherical shape of the brain of birds and mammals (see Figure 3, p. 150). The form and

size of fossil brains is sometimes inferred from 'endocasts': a fossil skull may be filled with a suitable material such as latex rubber in order to produce a rough copy of the original brain surface, and sometimes naturally occurring endocasts are found (Jerison, 1973).

Microscopic anatomy and histology
Brains are solidified by *in situ* perfusion or by later immersion in a solution such as formalin and may also be frozen or embedded in wax before a set of slices a few microns thick are removed by a microtome and mounted on slides for microscopic analysis. There is a vast array of photographic and staining procedures for bringing out different features of 'cellular architectonics'. The silver impregnation methods developed in the late nineteenth century by Gogli and Cajal provided the tool for much of standard comparative anatomy, but there have been relatively recent improvements in this technique. The silver methods of Nauta and Gygax (1954) and Fink and Heimer (1967) are of particular importance for the tracing of degenerating nerve pathways, while the study of cell-body architecture has benefited from electron-microscopy. Many of the new ideas about brain circuitry in animals have resulted from the more powerful silver methods. If cell bodies are destroyed, their axons and axon terminals (which make up nerve tracts or pathways in the brain) atrophy within a matter of days, and if the animal is then sacrificed and the degenerating pathways are located by these histological techniques, functional relationships between parts of the brain may be discovered.

Of course even the modern methods are not infallible, and it is always possible that the pattern of connections manifested by degeneration is subtly different from that of an undamaged brain. But confirmatory results may be obtained from another technique, which involves the transport of radioactively labelled protein tracers down functioning axons ('autoradiography': see, for instance, Cowan *et al.*, 1972). For example, radioactively labelled proline or leucine may be injected into the eye, and then some days later the animal may be sacrificed and its brain prepared for sectioning in order to map out the paths followed in the brain by the optic nerve. The cross sections taken from the brain are simply coated with photographic emulsion, and left until residual radioactivity has drawn visible silver grains into the places reached by the proteins which travelled down the optic nerve. A refinement of autoradiography allows cells in the brain to be marked according to their degree of activity: if a monkey is given an intravenous injection of labelled 2-deoxyglucose and then exposed for about an hour to vertical stripes, immediate autoradiography picks out cells in visual projection area on the surface of the monkey's brain. It is deduced that these cells were activated by the vertical stripes, and therefore absorbed glucose, to fuel their activity, to a greater extent than other cells; and the organised layout of the cells conforms to the results obtained with other physiological methods (Sokoloff, 1975; Hubel, Wiesel and Stryker, 1978).

The degeneration method and the use of radioactively labelled proteins give an idea of the neural pathways out from a particular point to other parts of the brain. It is also helpful to examine which tracts feed into a particular brain structure. Fortunately some substances—as it happens, horseradish peroxidase and egg albumen are convenient ones—are moved backwards along nerve axons ('retrograde transport') and are microscopically visible (Lavail and Lavail, 1972; Kristensson and Olsson, 1974). This has allowed the filling in of some of the gaps in the pathways discernible with the anterograde techniques (Benowitz and Karten, 1976) as well as the plotting out of the whole range of inputs into particular structures (Brown *et al.*, 1977). By combining retrograde and anterograde procedures, reciprocal connections between interacting brain areas can be observed (Jacobson and Trotanowski, 1975).

Brain chemistry
The study of brain chemistry is now an extremely active research area, the main questions revolving around the nature of synaptic transmission, and the distribution and function of the various different neurotransmitter substances (Warburton, 1975). In some instances the distribution of brain chemicals may provide evidence of homologies between brains in separate vertebrate classes (Juorio and Vogt, 1967), but on the whole biochemical data have played a relatively small part in comparative investigations (Pearson and Pearson, 1976) since in the main the emphasis is on the biochemistry shared by phylogenetically disparate animals, as in the use of rats to study the brain chemistry of human schizophrenia (Carlsson, 1978) or in the use of goldfish to provide a model for the biochemistry of memory (Agranoff, 1972).

Electrophysiological measurement of brain activity
General electrical activity can be detected with electrodes placed on the surface of the skull, and gives the familiar electroencephalogram

(or EEG) of brain rhythms. More detailed knowledge can be obtained by recording from individual brain cells or groups of cells—advances in electronics and in the production of fine electrodes make this tactic readily available. The most successful application of this methodology is probably in the study of the visual system: spots or bars of light, of various sizes and with different directions and speeds of movement, are projected on to given points on the retina of the eye and the resulting electrical activity is detected in the retina itself, in intermediary stages of the optic pathways, and in the visual areas of the cortex of mammals. Individual cells may then be classified according to their 'receptive fields'. (A receptive field is the area of the retina which, when appropriately stimulated, causes a particular cell to respond electrically: Kuffler, 1953; Hubel and Wiesel, 1962.) Other sensory modalities are open to the same kind of analysis: the cortical neurons which respond to the touching of points on the body surface can be mapped (e.g. Woolsey, 1965) and the destiny of the information received by an individual whisker on the nose of a mouse can be discovered (Welker, 1976).

Electrical stimulation of the brain
The position of brain structures in terms of three-dimensional spatial co-ordinates has been ascertained in many species by histological methods and compiled into stereotaxic atlases. Thus stereotaxic instruments can be used to insert electrodes or surgical tools into predetermined places. Apart from recording, this means that small electrical currents can be instigated via implanted electrodes wherever the experimenter chooses. Reportable sensations in man and an array of natural acts in animals (eating, attack, vocalisation, etc.) can be reliably elicited in this way (Penfield and Roberts, 1959; Valenstein *et al.*, 1970). Not surprisingly, such stimulation also produces emotional and motivational effects, even in the absence of stereotyped behaviours, but often related to them. The examination of 'pleasure and pain areas' in various species has been a source of immensely important data over the past three decades (Olds and Milner 1954; Olds and Olds, 1963; Valenstein *et al.*, 1970; Benninger *et al.*, 1977).

Experimental interference with brain function
One of the oldest forms of evidence about brain function comes from human clinical neurology—information concerning the behavioural effects of brain damage caused by disease, tumours and accidents or by

remedial surgery connected with these factors. In animals, experimental damage to the brain has been used for more than 150 years in the search for explanations of brain function. Other kinds of experimental interference include the administration of drugs and the application of electrical currents to suppress local brain action. There are logical difficulties in interpreting the effects of localised brain damage, which cannot always be overcome, but the combination of data from this sort of study with knowledge assembled from other kinds of investigation often provides the only way of making inferences about brain function. The difficulties arise mainly from the complexity and flexibility of brain circuitry which make it hazardous to assign particular functions to physically identifiable structures. It has often been pointed out that even with standard man-made electronic circuits such as those involved in a television set it is unwarranted to infer component function simply from component damage or removal. If poking a screwdriver into a section of a television circuit produces picture fuzziness, it does not follow that the section damaged is normally a fuzziness inhibitor—which would be the natural conclusion of a physiological psychologist. However, it is hard to see how else we are to proceed except by building up a collection of pieces of evidence about correlations between structure and function, and experimental alterations of structure are frequently useful as tests of hypotheses which may be derived in the first instance from anatomical and physiological descriptions of brain circuits.

The overall size of vertebrate brains

One of the most straightforward kinds of comparison between animal brains is simply the measure of their overall size. We should expect gross size to bear some relation to total number of neuronal elements available in a given brain, and hence overall size ought to provide a rough estimate of its computational power (Von Neumann, 1951). Certainly one of the most frequently heard explanations for the superior cognitive capacities of modern man is the relatively large volume of his brain. Despite the apparent directness of this argument, however, there are numerous subtleties and pitfalls which require extremely careful logical navigation.

The first consideration is that overall changes in size may involve complex changes in physical proportions. Some of these follow from the elementary mathematical differences between the effects of size changes on surface areas and on volumes. Surface areas are critical: in loss of heat from the body; in the space available for chewing and for absorption in the intestine; in the cross-section and therefore the strength of the bones; and, in more intellectual functions, surface areas determine the space available for the retina and for the mammalian cerebral cortex. Volume (or weight) is most crucially correlated with total number of cells. The mathematical law is that area increases as the square, and volume as the cube, of linear dimensions. Therefore small animals have a relatively high ratio of body surface to internal volume, and this ratio must systematically decrease as linear dimensions increase. Another deduction, which goes back to Galileo (1564–1642) is that large animals must need bones which are relatively much thicker than those of smaller animals. The deduction which concerns us here is that, other things being equal, the ratio of surface area to internal volume of a large brain must be very much less than the ratio of surface area to internal volume of a small brain.

There is another point, however, that we must deal with first, and this is that although as animals become larger we might expect them to need large bones to support themselves and large digestive systems for their nutritional requirements, there is less reason to suppose that they should need particularly large eyes and brains, since what has to be

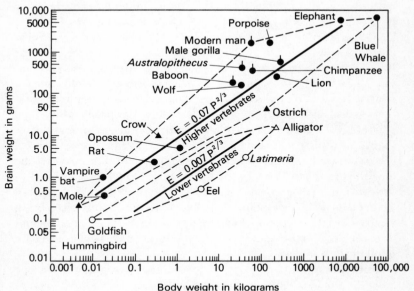

Figure 2   Brain weight as a function of body weight (from Jerison, 1973; see p. 132)

seen and understood by a large animal does not necessarily differ very much from what has to be seen and understood by much smaller creatures. This point was put forward long ago by von Haller (1762)—more recent reviews of various biological corollaries of size increases have been provided by Rensch (1959) and Jerison (1973). Notwithstanding the antiquity of the groundwork provided by von Haller, there is still a good deal of confusion about the relationship of brain size to body size. This arises because there are two essential propositions which seem to point in opposite directions. The first proposition is that larger animals have brains which are absolutely larger than the brains of more diminutive creatures. Second, the brain of a large animal is smaller, relative to its overall body weight, than would be expected by strict repetition of the proportions seen in a little animal. It is important to bear in mind both these opposing ideas—the brain tends to become absolutely larger, but relatively smaller, as body size increases.

Most systematic studies of brain and body weights across different species suffer from arbitrary selection of species and even more arbitrary selection of individual animals to represent a particular species (Sholl, 1948). However, allowing for a generous margin of error, the data used by Jerison (1973) provide a basis for discussion, and one of Jerison's plots of brain weight against body weight is reproduced in Figure 2. The data are shown as points within two statistically separable polygons. It is vital to stress that the logarithmic co-ordinates used for the plot mean that a straight line sloping upwards does *not* indicate that brain weight is a constant proportion of body weight. Such a relationship would produce a line with unit slope, with the intercept on the vertical axis indicating the constant of proportionality. The gradient of less than 45 degrees represented by the continuous line in Figure 2 means that brain weight tends to increase from species to species with a fractional power of the body weight. For instance, the line fitted for higher vertebrates makes brain weight proportional to the two-thirds power of body weight. ($E = .07P^{0.6667}$, where E is brain weight and P body weight). The extent to which this gives brain weights for large animals which are dramatically smaller than would be expected by extrapolation of strict proportions can be illustrated by numerical examples.

Using the formula $E = .07P^{0.6667}$, an animal weighing in at one kilogram would be expected to have a brain weight of 7 grams—seven-thousandths of its mass. A species ten times larger would not have a ten times bigger brain according to the equation: a 10 kg body weight gives an expected brain weight of only 32.5 gm, not the 70 gm which would come from strict proportion. The heavier the animal, the greater the disparity: the formula gives a 100 kg animal a brain of 150 gm rather than 700 gm, and a beast of 10,000 kg (a large elephant, say) gets a brain of only 3 kg, not 70 kg. On the other hand animals weighing less than the 1 kg example we started with get relatively large brains by the application of the formula. A rat or a pigeon with a body weight of 250 gm gets a 3 gm brain—not much it seems to us in our 1,500 gm wisdom, but quite a bit more than seven-thousandths of its body weight. Such is the make-up for brains in even smaller animals that a sparrow's brain (1 gm), as a proportion of its body weight (20 gm), is larger than a man's.

Clearly body weight must be taken into account in deciding whether a particular species's brain is 'large' or 'small', but since a sparrow devotes a twentieth of its mass to its brain, while the human brain is only a fiftieth of the human body weight, an adjustment must be made for absolute size, and assuming that the brain is proportional to the two-thirds power of body weight is the best adjustment available. Given this, what can be inferred from the data presented in Figure 2? First, it is gratifying to see that modern man does have a large brain for his size, since he is further above the line than any other species. Certain other animals, in particular the crow family and the dolphins and porpoises, also show up with larger brains than would be called for by the two-thirds power of their body weight, but to a lesser extent than ourselves. Statistically speaking, the most obvious separation between groups of animals occurs between higher vertebrates and the rest. The difference between mammals and birds within higher vertebrates does not reach statistical significance, and neither does the difference between reptiles and fish (within lower vertebrates a reptile of a given size tends to have a smaller brain than a fish of the same weight: Jerison, 1973). However, it is apparent from Figure 2 that, although higher vertebrates have larger brains than lower vertebrates of equivalent sizes, the way in which brain weight increases with body weight is just the same in lower and higher vertebrates.

We now have two theoretical questions about the empirical facts distilled from the data: why do higher vertebrates devote more of their weight to the brain than lower vertebrates—and why is vertebrate brain weight proportional to the two-thirds power of body weight? It might be hoped that the large brains of higher vertebrates could be clearly ascribed to a high value placed on brain functions in these species. This may turn out to be the case, but it is difficult to decide whether lower vertebrates, because of their meagre intelligence, make do with less brain tissue, or alternatively whether, because of their cold-blooded metabolism, they can afford to carry a greater mass of flesh and bone. It is usually taken for granted that the smaller brain indices of lower vertebrates indicate their lesser intelligence, perhaps quite rightly, but in the absence of independent assessment of psychological capacities the argument tends towards circularity. (Smaller brains occur in less intelligent animals, which we know are less intelligent because they have small brains.) An example of the problems lurking among the generalities is the case of sharks, regarded as a primitive order of fish, who seem in any case to have rather large brains, but whose intelligence quotient, if it is calculated on the basis of body weight, must be upped a bit by their use of a cartilaginous skeleton, which is lighter than one of bone. Jerison (1973) concludes in desperation that sharks are not to be considered as fish, and are therefore not lower vertebrates after all, but intermediates, thus saving his distinction between the brain size of higher and lower vertebrates, but throwing away part of the traditional phylogenetic scale.

The theory which Jerison defends is that lower vertebrates have small brains because of the primitive nature of their psychology, and that early mammals also had small brains for the same reason. The crucial increases in mammalian brain size which supposedly took place during the last 50 million years or so can only be quantified by heavy reliance on estimates of brain size from endocasts of fossil skulls and guesses at body weight based on what remains of fossil skeletons. It seems plausible that there was selection pressure on brain effectiveness caused, for instance, by competition between and within mammalian herbivores and mammalian carnivores, but the evidence in support of this hypothesis remains very sparse (cf. Simpson, 1953). Even in the case of modern species which are unquestionably large-brained by comparison with other modern species, such as man or the dolphin, fossil evidence to show when the increase in brain size took place is hard to come by, although there is little doubt that hominid species prior to *Homo sapiens* already had large brains (Pilbeam, 1972; Jerison, 1973).

Jerison's conclusion, however, is clear, and worth repeating:

> The evolution of intelligence occurred mainly within mammals and only in a casual way in birds, if one defines intelligence as the capacity to learn new response patterns in which sensory

information from various sensory modalities is integrated as
information about objects in space. (Jerison, 1973, p. 433)

The main difficulty with this is that the brain size data do not support
such a clear distinction between mammals and birds. The data as they
stand say only that cold-blooded animals, with the notable exception
of sharks, tend to have smaller brain weight/body weight ratios than
the warm-blooded vertebrates, which include both birds and mammals. But since mammals are in general bigger than birds they also in
general have bigger brains, and it is perfectly legitimate to argue, as
does Rensch (1959), that absolute size of the brain may be a more
valuable pointer to absolute intellectual capacity than any brain/body
ratio. Accepting this would oblige us to consider whether an ostrich is
more capable than a small monkey and whether an elk has greater
psychological capacity than a chimpanzee.

This brings up the question of the interaction between body size and
brain function which we started off with. The problem of why a
particular species has the body size that it does is difficult enough in
itself. There are some disadvantages in being small (for instance,
excessive heat exchange via the body surface) and there are also
disadvantages in being very large (mechanical awkwardness in
locomotion and simple weight support—these factors, and the techni-
calities of food supply, are perhaps sufficient to explain why the largest
mammals tend to be herbivores). It is obvious that flying imposes a much
lower limit on size than swimming—it is hardly surprising that there
are no whale-sized birds. But the various limits on size leave a very
large range of possible sizes, and many groups of animals seem to have
adopted varying proportions at different stages of evolution. 'Cope's
Law' says that there is a progressive tendency for species to get bigger
and bigger as they evolve, but there are numerous counter-examples
(Simpson, 1953).

The point of psychological interest is whether animals which
happen to have different gross weights *need* brains with different
capacities. On the face of it, the behaviours to be controlled by the
brain of a gorilla are not radically more demanding than the
behaviours of a very small monkey. The same thing could be said of an
elk and a miniature deer, or a tuna and stickleback. Other things being
equal it is arguable that, due to reduced urgency for nutrition, and
greater immunity from predators, large animals have a somewhat
easier life than small animals, and therefore less need of intelligence.

But suppose we simply assume that roughly equivalent demands are placed on the brain, whatever the scale of the body whose actions need to be supervised. One hypothesis which would follow from this is that an increase in overall size should be a short-cut to greater sophistication of behavioural control, since a large animal should have available more brain capacity to devote to behavioural problems which are essentially the same as those faced by its less well-endowed brethren. The main argument against this is the trend noted above for increases in body size across species to be accompanied by what seems to be an effort to cut down on the proportion of body weight taken up by the brain. This trend suggests the alternative hypothesis—that variations in body size will take place with minimal modification of brain capacity, and hence the range of brain sizes will be very much less than would be expected on the basis of the range of overall dimensions of body size. The connection of brain weight to a fractional power of body weight, as shown in Figure 2 and discussed above, provides a measure of support for this hypothesis of conservation of brain capacity. More detailed confirmation can be obtained in the case of very closely related groups of species. Here, it is found that brain weight is proportional only to the cube root of body weight, rather than to the two-thirds root—in other words there is even less variation in brain size between closely related species of different sizes than there is between unrelated species. Illustrative examples can be drawn from families which include miniature or pigmy subspecies. The pigmy chimpanzee (*Pan paniscus*) has a brain which is virtually identical in size to that of the very much larger main species *Pan troglodytes*, and similarly within *Homo sapiens* a pigmy body type is accompanied by a normal size of brain. Breeds of domestic dogs and chickens show very large variation in overall dimensions with very little change in absolute brain size (Rensch, 1959; Jerison, 1973). If dolphins and porpoises are regarded as pigmy species of odontocete whales, their very high brain-weight to body-weight ratios could come under the heading of the defence of brain size against overall size variation.

It is clear that primates as an order have large brains, over a wide range of body sizes from squirrel monkeys to gorillas, but it is equally clear that an exceptional expansion of brain size took place in the hominid lines ancestral to modern man. The available fossil evidence suggests strongly that related hominid species with approximately similar body sizes possessed brains with weights varying from 500 gm (*Australopithicus boisei*) and 600 gm (*Homo habilis*) to 1000 gm (*Homo erectus*) and 1500 gm (*Homo sapiens Neanderthalensis*: see Jerison, 1973, p. 398). In hominid species, therefore, it looks as though there was a very special kind of selection pressure towards larger brains, but it should be emphasised that this selection pressure began to operate at the early stages of hominid evolution, long before the emergence of *Homo sapiens*. The brain of an orang-utang of roughly human body size weighs about 350 gm. This had been doubled by the stage of *Homo habilis* investigated at Olduvai Gorge, who probably walked erect and made primitive tools, although without the benefits of a thumb as opposable and as useful for precision grips as that of modern man (Leakey *et al.*, 1964). A similar degree of brain enlargement may also have been achieved as much as 2.6 million years ago by yet another hominid with bipedal habits (Leakey, R., 1973).

A brain three times as big as the orang-utang's appears in *Homo erectus*, who used fire and undoubtedly hunted and made tools, and left evidence of cannibalism, but who probably did not have such more advanced characteristics as care of the sick, burial of the dead and drawing on walls. The typical brain size of modern *Homo sapiens*, roughly 1100 to 1500 gm, or about four times bigger than the size of the orang brain, was reached, and possibly exceeded (there are examples of cranial capacities of 1700 gm) by later Neanderthals, who qualify as *Homo sapiens*, but are denied full *Sapiens sapiens* status, despite evidence of ritual burial of the dead and their 'Mousterian' stone technology which produced a great variety of scraping and cutting tools by the detailed working of stone flakes. The relation of brain size to tool-making is not at all clear. The earliest known stone implements are from the Olduvai Gorge; they consist mainly of pebble-tool choppers made by knocking off flakes from two sides of a lump of rock and using the remaining sharp core without further dressings of the edge (Oakley, K. P., 1972). However, even at this early stage, before the major expansion of the human brain, there may have been some trimming and sharpening both of the cores and of the initial bits chipped off (the primary flakes). Also, and even more remarkable at this primitive stage, there was 'machine tool' production, that is the use of special hammer stones and anvil stones as 'tools for making tools'. It is thus no simple matter to tie intelligence via brain size to the level of stone technology accomplished, although the variety, sophistication and delicacy of construction of stone tools are said to increase during the course of human evolution. In any event Neanderthal man, although technically accomplished, did not leave behind enough by way of artifact or ornament to indicate that he possessed the aesthetic sense usually attributed to *Homo sapiens sapiens*. One view, albeit very flimsily based on inferences about Neanderthal vocal tracts, is that Neanderthals were not capable of the full range of human speech (Lieberman, 1975). In spite of (and possibly because of) this, Neanderthal brains are indistinguishable from those of modern man on the grounds of size except in so far as they are actually larger.

The expansion of the human brain thus began and ended before the appearance of the species we recognise as ourselves. It thus did not occur because of modern civilised habits, although these may only be feasible with a brain that is already enlarged. Since hominid brain expansion predated modern civilisation, it may perhaps be included within the scope of discussion of vertebrate brain evolution. Purely in terms of size, the extent of human brain expansion can be kept within natural proportions by comparisons with larger mammals (see Figure 2 and Quiring, 1950). Gram for gram, man has the body of an orang-utang and the brain of a large walrus. Conveniently, a stubby-limbed North American rhinoceros (*Teleocerus*), now extinct, once had a brain listed at the same weight as man's—1500 gm. Modern rhinoceruses and hippos are slightly bigger animals but, curiously, they have brains of only 600 or 700 gm. The African elephant is an immense animal with rather more brain than Jerison's equation would predict—5000 gm, four times larger than yours or mine. The biggest brains of all are of course those of the large whales, but they are not very much bigger than the elephant's. The brains which come closest to man's in terms of relation to body size as well as in terms of absolute size are those of the small whales, the dolphins and porpoises. These brains are rounder and more encephalised than man's and have 'hyperfissurisation' of the cortex, that is the surface foldings of the cerebral cortex are more extensive than the surface foldings of the human brain. Brains like this, of human size or larger, occur in animals that would only be expected to have brains of about 250 gm, according to Jerison's equation based on body size.

Brain size and neuron density

Leaving aside man and the dolphin, the general rule seems to hold fairly true that the absolute weight of the brain increases as the two-thirds power of body weight, and therefore as the square of the length or height of a species. Although this means that large animals will tend to have smaller brains in direct proportion to body weight than little animals, one would not expect this to be much comfort to the latter, faced with the problems of processing information with a smaller absolute amount of neural tissue. Irrespective of scale, the only reasonable assumption is that computing power or efficacy of behaviour-controlling function is proportional to the available number of neuronal elements in the central nervous system (Von Neumann, 1951). On the whole bigger animals are bigger because they are composed of more cells than smaller animals, and this holds roughly true of the brain, but there are several features of microscopic brain organisation which point to the neural luxuries enjoyed by large animals and the neurological thrift required of small animals.

Over and above species-to-species difference, smaller vertebrate brains are composed of smaller neurons, more densely packed together, so that a gram of brain tissue in a small brain may contain many more neural elements than a gram of tissue from a large brain. The brain as a whole obviously consists not only of neurons but includes the associated blood supply, ventricular system and covering membranes. Mixed in with the neurons themselves are large numbers of supporting or interstitial cells of various types especially glia, or neuroglia. The density of neurons can be increased either by reducing their size, or by cutting down on the amount of non-nervous brain tissue. Both these features occur in smaller brains, at least within mammals, from whom most of the quantitative data have been collected. Many types of brain neuron increase in size with the overall size of the species (see Rensch, 1959; and Tower, 1954). This is particularly visible in the length of the dendritic tree of cortical neurons (Bok, 1959). Since glial cells fill in the gaps between dendrites it is to be expected that larger brains should have a relatively high proportion of glial to nerve cells, and Tower and Young (1973) found a very orderly relationship, with glia/nerve ratio increasing with the one-third power of mammalian brain weight. The end result is that, in the cortex of mammals, neuron density varies inversely with brain weight to the one-third power. (The range is from thousands to hundreds of thousands of neurons per cubic millimetre.) Thus although large brains contain more neurons, they do not do so in strict proportion to their size. In fact the relation between total number of neurons and brain size, estimated in this way, is rather similar to the relation between brain size and body size: bigger animals have bigger brains, but not in strict proportion; and bigger brains have more neurons, but not in strict proportion.

The combination of these factors means that bigger animals have more brain neurons, but extra brain neurons come only in proportion to, very roughly, the square root of extra body weight. This still leaves small animals with less powerful brains, but suggests that there is a tendency to conserve brain power in smaller mammals by allotting a generous fraction of the total of the animal's cells to brain neurons. One might put it the other way around, and say that large animals are a lot less profligate with neurons than they could be. Despite the cut-back on brain neurons in large animals, one can still argue, following Rensch (1959), that because bigger animals have more brain cells greater intelligence may come as an accidental fringe benefit of any increase in scale.

Practically all of the data on variations in neuron density with brain size come from mammals. It is worthy of note that the human brain appears to have just about the cortical neuron density that would be predicted by extrapolation from other mammalian brains of different sizes: the human brain is exceptional in terms of its mass in relation to body weight, but not in terms of its internal cell density. It seems a reasonable hypothesis that smaller brains should have higher neuron densities in other vertebrate classes apart from mammals and this suggestion has been made in the case of birds by Kappers (1947). Data for birds are rather variable, and Pearson (1972) is doubtful about the correlation between brain size and cell density. It is surely no accident, however, that the highest cell densities quoted by Pearson (from Stingelin, 1958) occur in the Goldcrest (*Regulus*), the tiniest of all European birds, and the next highest neuron density occurs in the Goldfinch (*Carduelis*), which is not very much bigger. Larger birds such as the cuckoo or pigeon have lower brain-cell densities. Pearson (1972) is worried that a couple of fairly big species seem to have higher brain-cell densities than they should, but since these species turn out to be a crow and a macaw, we might be forgiven for assuming that their unexpectedly large number of brain cells is explicable in terms of the reputed high intelligence of birds in the crow and parrot families.

Miniaturised brains in teleost fish

The problem of cramming an adequate amount of behaviour-controlling mechinery into an extremely small body is most acute in the teleost fish (which include goldfish, minnows, sticklebacks and guppies). Many species of teleost fish are very small, by mammalian standards, even when adult, but it must also be considered that the teleost brain has to control free-swimming behaviour in the even more minute fry of these species. Possibly because of this need for compactness (see Aronson and Kaplan, 1968) but calling for special attention in any case, teleost fish have an unusual method for the embryological development of the forebrain. In all other vertebrate classes the forebrain grows from a U-shaped neural tube when the outside walls rise and turn inwards, to form the cerebral hemispheres. This is known as *evagination*, and except in the primitive cyclostomes (in which the walls never turn downwards, leaving a single internal space or ventricle) the walls curl in, down and around to make a cross-section of two separate hemispheres each with a hole in the middle (the holes being the lateral ventricles). A cross-section through the frog forebrain, for instance, looks like two misshapen doughnuts, side by side, with a lot of wasted space.

In teleost fish, although there is considerable variation from species to species, forebrain development occurs when the two side walls of the neural tube expand *outwards* at the top, pushing the inside faces close together and swelling out and around, leaving no space for internal ventricles. This 'eversion' during the development of the teleost forebrain makes it rather difficult to find which bits go where, by comparison with other vertebrates, but gives a pleasing sense of economy of design to the forebrain section of a stickleback or goldfish, and suggests that the psychological capacities of the teleost forebrain may be slightly greater than we might expect simply on the grounds of its external dimensions.

A further special aspect of the teleost forebrain, which is extremely pertinent to lesion studies of its function, is that the embryological instructions for growth are retained in the adults of many species. This means that the forebrain can regenerate after local damage, so that the reappearance of efficient behavioural organisation after lesions to a particular part of the forebrain does not imply that that part of the forebrain is not important; an alternative possibility is that it is of such importance that arrangements have been made for effective regrowth after damage. Regeneration of central and peripheral nervous system can also occur in amphibians (especially in the larval stage), and the capacity for some adult brain growth is apparent in elasmobranch fish (Leonard *et al.*, 1978), but effective regrowth of the damaged adult brain is most remarkable in small teleosts (see Segaar, 1965, for a review). An example of highly organised regrowth in the adult teleost brain, which is scarcely credible by comparison with the very limited peripheral neural regeneration seen in higher vertebrates, occurs after the surgical removal of parts of the sending or receiving ends of the optic tract. The major connection in the teleost visual system is between the retina of the eye and the contra-lateral optic tectum of the midbrain (see Figure 4, p. 175). This connection is topographically arranged so that each point on the retina goes to a corresponding point in a systematic two-dimensional array on the tectum. Suppose that one half of the tectal array on one side is cut out. In theory, the fish becomes blind in the part of the visual field which normally projects to the portion of the tectum which has been removed. But, over a period of months, what happens is that the remaining terminals of the optic nerve move over, and the severed half of the optic nerve sticks itself on to the intact area of the tectum so that a complete, although compressed, visual picture is recovered (Sharma, 1972; Yolen and Hodos, 1976). On the other hand, if half the retina is removed, the connections from the remaining half spread out to make use of the entire optic tectum (Schmidt *et al.*, 1978). The way in which such intelligent-seeming regrowth of adult neural circuits occurs is probably the same as that used in the initial embryological growth of all vertebrates (Miller and Lund, 1975). But in the small brains of lower vertebrates it is perhaps more important to retain the capacity for organised growth in the adult than it is in the larger brains of higher vertebrates, where recovery of function after brain damage can be more readily accomplished by reliance on the tissue that is left.

The neural components of vertebrate brains

Although the weight or volume of animal brains is easily inspected, it might be more to the point to go to a microscopic extreme, and ask whether vertebrate brains may differ in the neural components of which they are made. Is the tissue in the brain of a shark or a frog the same stuff as that which gives the human brain its remarkable intellectual powers? Surprisingly perhaps, the answer, as far as we can tell, is yes (Kuhlenbeck, 1967, 1970; Kappers *et al.*, 1936; Sarnat and Netsky, 1974). Some brain cells, such as the giant Mauthner and Muller neurons in the medulla of lower vertebrates (Zottoli, 1978) are specific to certain classes, but on the whole the transition from one vertebrate class to another is not marked by radical changes in the nature of brain neurons. Many comparisons of neurons in brains are based on what the cells look like after staining with metallic ions, which is rather remote from an assessment of what they can do, but more detailed structural descriptions via electron microscopy and electrophysiological and biochemical studies of neuron activity at present suggest similarities in the modes of operation of neurons in the various vertebrate classes, rather than differences.

It should be recognised that there are specialisations of shape of cell, and of nerve-fibre structure, for different parts of the brain (see below) and knowledge of the crucial interactions between neurons, at synapses, is expanding very rapidly. Therefore it is possible that phylogenetic changes in the sophistication of neural operation remain to be discovered—a persistent hypothesis is that there exists some as yet unknown microscopic detail in the fine structure of the human brain which results in a qualitative change in function (e.g. Popper and Eccles, 1967). But the most common assumption is that changes in brain function have evolved by changes in the amount of brain tissue and its arrangement, rather than by radical alterations in the nature of its constituent elements. As an example, one may quote the distinctive and easily recognisable cells of the cerebellum, the small 'granule' cells and the Purkinje cells, which occur in all vertebrates. Not only is the physical appearance of these cells similar in the shark, frog and cat, but analysis of their electrical responses, in the shark, shows that with these vertebrates 'already in evolutionary development the cerebellum had achieved most of the characteristic features of the neuronal machinery in the mammalian cerebellum' (Eccles *et al.*, 1970).

If there is a typical component for the vertebrate brain, it is a 'multipolar' neuron, in which the cell body gives off several twig-like dendrites (fibrous extensions of the cell body which receive input) as well as an axon (the output line of the cell). The axon may also branch out to provide multiple terminations, providing several synapses with the dendrites of other neurons. Human axons vary in length from less than a millimetre to almost a metre (as part of a nerve or fibre tract). The basic idea is still that neurons act as logical switching elements, amplifying, inhibiting, gating and recording neuro-electrical impulses rather like the components of a computer or pocket calculator (Sommeroff, 1974). The most general categorisation of vertebrate neurons is in terms of the multipolar characteristic as opposed to the more primitive unpolarised type (no distinction between the axon and the dendrites), the bipolar type (a single dendrite and an axon) and the unipolar type (dendrite and axon arising from a single stem). All types except the multipolar occur also in the nervous systems of invertebrates (Kuhlenbeck, 1967). These categories are supplemented by classifications based on the physical shape of the cell body (pyramidal, fusiform, stellate, granule and so on) or of the dendrites (Purkinje cells, for instance, can be recognised by their very extensive and distinctive dendrites). Axons may be graded according to their length and thickness and to their degree of surrounding insulation (myelination) as well as by their shape or pattern (e.g. 'mossy' fibres and 'climbing' fibres). The interaction between axonal terminations and the dendrites of other neurons takes place by the release of chemicals, and neurons can therefore be classified according to which of the numerous known 'neurotransmitter substances' is employed (e.g. noradrenaline, acetylcholine, dopamine).

Although some cell types are restricted to certain vertebrate classes, the main impression is of the repeated use of the same cell types in widely varying species. Long *et al.* (1968), for example, in an investigation of the fine structure of elasmobranch brains, found the same basic neuron categories in sharks as the ones which occur in mammals. This goes for the non-neural brain cells too: although more use may be made of neuroglia in the larger mammalian brains, most of the many kinds of supporting brain cells found in mammals occur not only in sharks but also in the even more venerable lampreys (Pearson and Pearson, 1976, pp. 48–9). We may conclude, I think, that the major process in brain evolution has been in the deployment of brain cells rather than in the design of the cells themselves, although this does certainly not preclude cellular changes as well. Ideas as to how redeployments of brain cells may have come about, in terms of changing functions of different divisions of the vertebrate brain, are dealt with in the next chapter.

5 The functional organisation of the vertebrate brain

Concepts of phylogenetic improvement in the organisation of the vertebrate nervous system have been (Bastian, 1880; Romer, 1949) and are (Razran, 1971; Romer and Parsons, 1977) rampant in accounts of comparative neuro-anatomy. This could be because such concepts are accurate reflections of fact, but the reason may have more to do with the visibility of a topographical progression of structures in the plan of the vertebrate brain, which has in the past drawn evolutionary hypotheses irresistibly towards it. The human brain can be said to consist of the hindbrain, the midbrain and the forebrain, and almost every account of brain evolution incorporates to some extent the notion that each part was physically or functionally added at successive stages of phylogenetic development. A pleasing orderliness would prevail if the ancestors of vertebrates made do with only a spinal cord, to which a hindbrain was added for the benefit of the primitive cyclostomes, needing the assistance of a midbrain for the control of higher fish behaviour; the forebrain arriving in a diminutive and rudimentary aspect for the purpose of life on land, and showing only a partial elaboration in the warm-blooded but instinct-dominated birds, before fulfilling its destiny with the flowering of the cortex in mammals, which has been permitted to enshroud and overwhelm the now-redundant former stages by the rationality of man.

One still has a sense of regret that this charming and convincing tale must be discarded. The weight of evidence is now if anything more in favour of the unhelpful suggestion, bravely canvassed on some occasions (e.g. Heier, 1948), that all of the fundamental parts of the vertebrate brain were present very early on, and can be observed in lampreys. In fact the strictly additive story has always had the disadvantage that all the physical divisions of higher vertebrate brains appear in the lower classes, and the most popular hypotheses incorporate their presence in the notion of *encephalisation of function* (Weiskrantz, 1961; Jerison, 1973). The essential doctrine of encephalisation of function is that the superficial layout of all vertebrate brains was present in the original versions, but that there has been an evolutionary trend which moves psychological functions further and further forward in the central nervous system, from the spinal cord through the midbrain to the cerebral hemispheres. Although this has often been accepted without question, it is best to be suspicious of all purported evolutionary trends of this type (Simpson, 1953). The evidence which can be put forward in favour of encephalisation is of two kinds: first, the relative size of different brain structures; and second, more detailed experimental information bearing on their psychological importance. As far as size goes, there is no doubt that the relative size of different parts of the brain varies from species to species, and it is also beyond dispute that the relative size of the cerebral hemispheres is greater in the 'higher' vertebrates, and that the cerebral hemispheres of the human brain are exceptionally large. Jerison (1973) suggests that we should regard these facts as evidence for encephalisation of *structure*, rather than for encephalisation of *function*. These are two separate theories, since encephalisation of structure simply means that the forebrain tends to expand its size, while encephalisation of function implies that the reason for the expansion of the forebrain is that it takes over jobs previously done by lower brain divisions. One of the earliest and most explicit accounts of encephalisation of function refers to the 'migration of the dominant controlling centre' (Bastian, 1880). Before going into these ideas any further it would be as well to establish the layout and terminology for these areas of the brain which are to be distinguished (see Figures 3 and 4). Brief inspection of the outer surfaces of the brain frequently permits the identification of the cerebral hemispheres, the optic lobes, and the brainstem, and these boundaries may be confirmed by large-scale dissection. But, as reference to standard works will show, more detailed dissection and microscopic examination reveals a bewildering number of separately identified nuclei and fibre tracts (Gray, H. 1967; Pearson and Pearson, 1976; Kappers *et al.*, 1936). In giving convenient labels to brain structures such as the cerebellum, the hippocampus, or the pituitary gland, it should not be forgotten that the names mask several orders of complexity—the named organ does not necessarily have only one sort of function but may incorporate dozens of separate nuclei, cell types and neural pathways. The nomenclature I shall use here is fairly conventional.

The spinal cord

There is no difficulty in identifying the spinal cord as a distinct structure in the vertebrate nervous system, which serves to transmit information between the head and the body, but which also plays some part in the organisation of bodily activities. Even in higher vertebrates, we know that the running movements of a chicken may be co-ordinated by the spinal cord in the absence of a head, and that many reflexes can be elicited from the spinal cord of mammals when the connection with the brain has been lost (Sherrington, 1906). Leg withdrawal, away from irritating stimulation, can be observed in cats whose spinal cord has been severed above the relevant limb ('spinal' cats: Groves and Thompson, 1970) and a full range of sexual reflexes including erection, pelvic thrusting and ejaculation can be produced by tactile stimulation of spinal dogs (Hart, 1967). Similar spinal reflexes exist in all mammals, including man. Usually, higher brain centres are considered to modulate spinal activity by inhibitory influences as well as by taking active control. One can, if pressed, voluntarily inhibit the built-in spinal reflexes which would otherwise produce the withdrawal of one's hand from a flame. Motor activities such as movements of limbs are referred to as the skeletal functions of the spinal cord; vegetative activities such as digestion are referred to as autonomic processes. Our concern with thought might at first sight imply little interest in the autonomic control of digestion, perspiration and the like, but autonomic responses are often important indicators of inner mental states. Emotional feeling is intimately related to the racing heart and moist palms quantified by psychophysiologists, and the effect of external stimuli on glandular secretions of the stomach led Pavlov to the study of conditioning (see Chapter 3).

The brainstem and cerebellum (hindbrain)

The initial swelling out of the spinal cord when it reaches the brain, variously called the brainstem or the medulla, contains many nuclei known to have particular sensory and motor functions. Information about sounds, motion detected in the inner ear, tastes and visceral states enters the brain here, and relevant motor reactions may arise directly from brainstem nuclei. A very obvious addition to the brainstem is the cerebellum, which is usually visible as a large external bulge. There is almost universal agreement that the cerebellum is specialised for the automatic fine co-ordination of fast movements. There is also a consensus that the hindbrain in general and the cerebellum in particular has undergone relatively little change 'in the course of evolution'. We should regard this assumption of lack of phylogenetic change in the hindbrain with some suspicion—it is not so much that there is no evidence of elaboration and specialisation in hindbrain structures but rather that a contrast is drawn with more radical developments which are presumed to have taken place in the forebrain. In particular the cerebellum is large and well differentiated in higher vertebrates, with strong connections (via the pons in the brainstem) with the cerebral hemispheres.

Apart from specialised sensory and motor nuclei, the brainstem contains a non-specific network of neurons of a relatively simple shape (Ramon-Moliner and Nauta, 1966) which act in concert without depending on any particular sensory modality. This network is known as the *brainstem reticular formation*, although it extends down into the spinal cord and forward through the midbrain into the thalamus. The function of the reticular formation appears to be to determine a general level of sensory alertness (something interesting in one modality thus engages the others) and also, by the descending rather than the ascending part of the system, to influence the overall intensity of muscular activity. It has a pervasive role in the degree of activation or 'arousal' of the brain, but also uses particular channels for the sensitisation of perceptual mechanisms and for the control of such things as muscle tone and respiration. Although both the form and the function of the reticular system are phylogenetically primitive, this brainstem mechanism has to be taken into account in sophisticated discussion of human attention and awareness. In combination with other brainstem circuits, the reticular formation controls states of consciousness and the sleep-wakefulness cycle.

The spinal cord and the brainstem together provide the site for the *lower motor system*—a pool of interneurons which, though not themselves directly connected to muscles, serve as the 'final common path' for several sources of brain output to muscles.

The midbrain

It is at the level of the midbrain that the battlelines of phylogenetic theories are usually drawn, since the hindbrain is taken as common to all vertebrate classes, with regions above competing for the privilege of dominating it. In the lamprey, shark, cod, frog, alligator or pigeon there is a distinctive midbrain feature in a pair of clearly visible optic lobes (collectively referred to as the tectum, or optic tectum). In the lamprey and in many teleost fish the optic lobes are larger than the cerebral hemispheres. In these and in all other non-mammalian species the midbrain tectum is the main (but not the only) recipient of optic nerve fibres. A common conclusion drawn from these two anatomical facts is that the midbrain is a visually driven 'highest correlation centre' in fish (e.g. Romer, 1962). The optic lobes receive auditory and somatosensory inputs from the brainstem, and send back massive outputs to hindbrain motor nuclei in non-mammals—it is thus assumed that the midbrain supervises hindbrain functions in these cases. In mammals the tectum is hidden from external view: it is re-named (the superior and inferior colliculi for the visual and auditory centres) and sometimes forgotten. One of the clearest examples of the encephalisation of function theory is the supposition that in mammals the relative reduction in size and the change in appearance of the midbrain has been accompanied by a sweeping degeneration of its function, connected with the substitution of the forebrain as the chief destination for visual information. If the forebrain, and in particular the cerebral cortex, performs in mammals the analyses, associations and directions left to the midbrain in lower species, then the mammalian midbrain should indeed be redundant. However Weiskrantz (1961), among others, voiced doubts about the evolutionary logic of developing a new organ to do the same job as an old one, and subsequent anatomical and behavioural evidence suggests that the difference between mammalian and non-mammalian midbrain function is not as clear cut as the encephalisation of function doctrine proposes.

The thalamus and hypothalamus (diencephalon)

The next step on the linear progression from the spinal cord to the nose end of the central nervous system is the region of the forebrain known

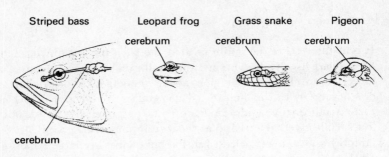

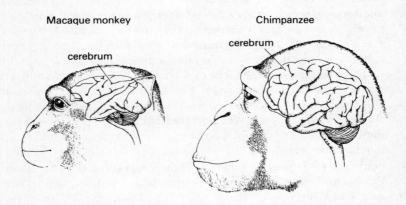

Figure 3   The external appearance of vertebrate brains. A
selection of vertebrate brains drawn to the same scale. The
cerebrum, or forebrain, is labelled, and can be seen to increase in
size through the series, although due allowance should be made
for the overall body size of the animals involved. The opossum,
for instance, would weigh at least four times as much as the
pigeon, while its brain is only a little larger than the pigeon's.
On the other hand a cat and a macaque monkey may weigh

Opossum

cerebrum

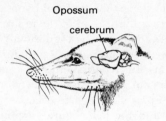

Cat

cerebrum

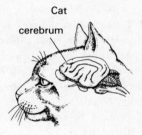

Man   cerebrum

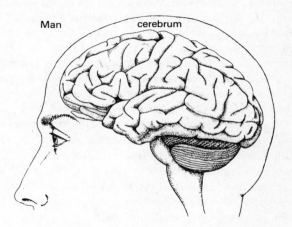

about the same amount (say 4 kg) overall, but the cat's brain would be under 30 gm, and the monkey's brain over 60 gm. The spinal cord is visible in all cases and the cerebellum, just above the spinal cord and finely convoluted, can be seen clearly in the pigeon brain, and in the larger examples. The optic lobe, or tectum, of the pigeon midbrain can be seen as an oval below the cerebrum. (From 'The Brain' by D. H. Hubel. Copyright 1979 by *Scientific American*, Inc. All rights reserved) as the diencephalon, which includes the thalamus and hypothalamus. These two structures give a further illustration of the multiplicity of purposes served at each stage of the anatomical progression. While the thalamus (in the upper part of the diencephalon) contains sensory projections and association circuits, the hypothalamus underneath it is related to visceral and metabolic functions (among other things, the hypothalamus controls the pituitary gland). The effects of surgical damage to the hypothalamus, and the behavioural responses produced by its electrical or chemical stimulation, support the general designation of the hypothalamus as a centre of drive and motivation.

There are a number of opinions as to how the diencephalon fits into the pattern of encephalisation. A rather unusual assertion is made by Rose (1976), who says 'It is the THALAMUS which is dominant in amphibia. ... In evolutionary terms, the thalamus was not to remain dominant for long—just enough for the regions of the thalamencephalon to sprout the pineal gland, the hypothalamus and the pituitary' (Rose, 1976, p. 167: original capitals). Others hold quite different views: 'In fishes and amphibians the tectum appears to be the true "heart" of the nervous system. ... The thalamus proper is in lower vertebrates an area of modest importance' (Romer, 1962, p. 44). Rose's assertion carries the implication that the hypothalamus, the pituitary and the endocrine (hormonal) system governed by it had to await the arrival of land-going vertebrates. It is a safer bet that the traditional characterisation of the hypothalamus as the 'head ganglion of the autonomic nervous system' applies to all vertebrates. We may note that an important aspect of the relationship between the hypothalamus and the pituitary gland in mammals—the secretion of hormones by the hypothalamus itself—was first described in a teleost fish (Scharrer, 1928). Comparative study of the pituitary and the endocrine system has tended to follow, rather than lead, comparative neuro-anatomy, and has not given rise to such strong theories of phylogenetic progression (Bentley, 1976). It is not the case that hormonal control is a primitive characteristic from which higher vertebrates become emancipated, although this has sometimes been suggested (Beach, 1947): the pituitary may be said to increase in complexity and organisation in higher animals with as much justification as most other brain structures, and possibly the most singular achievement of mammals—lactation—has required its own endocrine specialisations. Oddly, the gonadal (sex) hormones appear to be identical, from fish to man, despite the astounding range of sexual practices which they sustain. Even the development of lactation in mammals did not require a unique mammalian hormone—the same chemical which induces milk production in mammals (prolactin) is found in other vertebrates. A few non-mammalian species, notably pigeons, manufacture milk-like substances with which the young are fed, in response to prolactin (Chadwick, 1977). It seems clear that the functions of the hypothalamus and the pituitary do not fit neatly into the doctrine of progressive encephalisation.

Sensory representation in the thalamus

In man, the thalamus is often referred to as a 'sensory clearing house', 'sensory relay station', or 'antechamber to the cerebral cortex' (e.g. Elliot, 1963). This is because all sensory information, with the single exception of olfactory input, gets to the forebrain only after passing though the thalamus. It may be convenient at this point to look at Figure 4 (p. 175) which illustrates, for instance, that cutaneous sensation (from the skin) must pass successively from the spinal cord through the brainstem, midbrain and thalamus before reaching the mammalian cortex. As the reader might by now have come to expect, this linear sequence of sensory stages has been rudely transformed into a theory of phylogenetic progression and thus the thalamus is likely to be regarded as phylogenetically advanced. One theory (supported by Rose, 1976) is that the thalamus originally succeeded the midbrain as the dominant correlation centre in amphibians or reptiles, but then became reduced to merely passing on sensory information to the superior cortex of mammals. A contrasting suggestion is that the thalamus in lower vertebrates is merely an extension of the dominant midbrain serving in a rudimentary way to connect audio-visual matters in the tectum with smells in the cerebral hemispheres. On this view the thalamus only really developed to relay detailed sensory projections to the cerebral cortex of mammals (Diamond and Hall, 1969; Romer, 1962).

The latter used to be the main theory: lacking cortex to relay to, the non-mammalian thalamus is diffuse and underdeveloped and works together with non-cortical parts of the hemispheres as a controller of reflexes. But in the last ten years or so anatomical evidence has mounted against it. It is now apparent that the thalamus in reptiles and birds contains sensory projection nuclei comparable in organisation and complexity to those in the thalamus of mammals (Nauta and Karten, 1970; Webster, 1973; Hall and Ebner, 1970; Karten,

1979). This is not to say, of course, that the thalamus is identical, or entirely equivalent, in fish, amphibian, reptile, bird and mammal. Differences between the classes there certainly are (Riss *et al.*, 1972) but they need to be interpreted cautiously, and the characterisation of the dorsal thalamus as a uniquely mammalian acquisition, which was added to primitive ancestral thalamic nuclei which suffice for lower vertebrates, is becoming increasingly outmoded.

The cerebral hemispheres (cortex, corpus striatum and limbic system—the telencephalon)

The forebrain is traditionally divided into the diencephalon, which I have just discussed, and the telencephalon, which is more conveniently referred to as the cerebral hemispheres. It is the evolution of the cerebral hemispheres which is given most weight in theories of how higher forms of intelligence emerged from the shadows of lower vertebrate life. The hemispheres are clearly visible as paired bulges at the front of all vertebrate brains, but show an undeniable trend of increasing size in some degree of correspondence with the notorious phylogenetic scale (see Figure 3, p. 150).

It is equally undeniable that the cerebral hemispheres form a substantial part of the brains of even the lowest fishes and that they are especially large in sharks. The direction of theory about divisions of function within the hemispheres has thus tended towards the general principle of finding important parts in the hemispheres of mammals, and less important parts in the hemispheres of lower vertebrates. In man, almost the entire surface of the hemispheres is covered by a thin cladding of grey matter, the neocortex or cortex, which is composed of six layers of neurons. Rather similar types of nerve-cell are seen on the surface of the cerebral hemispheres of reptiles and birds (Webster, K. P. 1973), and to a lesser extent in fish and amphibian brains (Pearson and Pearson, 1976). But the mammalian cortex provides a special kind of neural organisation, and the outside, or pallium of the hemispheres does not have much significance in non-mammalian classes. Within the hemispheres there are of course bundles of nerve axons (fibre tracts) connecting various regions of cortex one with another and with other forebrain structures. These connecting pathways form the white matter, which takes up a considerable proportion of the internal volume of large mammalian brains. But the interior of the hemispheres also contains solid nuclei of neurons which can be grouped into either the corpus striatum (the basal ganglia) or the telencephalic components of the limbic system—a heterogeneous collection of structures which includes the hypothalamus and other parts of the diencephalon.

Mammalian cortex

Although the mammalian cortex is considered as a single entity for the purpose of comparison with other vertebrate classes, it is composed of nerve-cells which differ in shape, size, and dendritic structure, and this provides a basis for distinguishing its several laminations and for mapping slightly different kinds of neocortex that are distributed over the brain surface. The identification of six separate layers of neocortex is reasonably clear, although the boundaries between the layers are not always particularly sharp. Mammalian cortex can be divided into categories of complexity, with the six-layered neocortex said to be phylogenetically newest, 3-layer archi-cortex or 'allo-cortex' the oldest, and 4- or 5-layer paleo-cortex or 'juxta-allo-cortex' intermediate. The differentness of mammalian cortex from the reptilian version has been a matter of some dispute, but the detailed comparisons made by Poliakov (1964) led him to emphasise the similarity between reptilian cortex and the simpler kinds of mammalian cortex as they occur in, for instance, hedgehogs.

The distribution of various types of cell-predominance in the cortex of many mammalian species was mapped by A. W. Campbell (1905) and Brodmann (1909) and found to follow family relationships between species so that the map of the human brain is very similar to that of the chimpanzee (Kappers *et al.*, 1936).

The advantages of spreading out neurons in a two-dimensional array on the brain surface would appear to lie in the ease of access thus given to underlying connecting fibres; the same plan of neuronal elements on the surface, with connections radiating out from inside, appears in the hindbrain cerebellum and optic lobes of birds and lower vertebrates (and mammals). The disadvantage of such a system is that when overall brain size expands, the surface area increases with only the square of linear dimensions while internal volume increases with the cube, and thus the relative amount of space available on the surface will become unduly limited. A numerically convenient example is to imagine constructing a hypothetical brain or micro-computer by placing 1 mm-square memory element plates on the exposed five surfaces of a 1 cm cube, this 1 cm cube being filled up with little 1 mm cubes for internal connections. This would give 500 surface memory elements and exactly twice as many (1,000) internal programming elements. Now suppose you decide to double the size of this imaginary device, keeping to the same plan, and using the same components. Choosing a 2 cm outer cube would allow you 8,000 units for internal programming and, according to the original proportions, there should be one memory plate on the surface for every two of these. Thus 4,000 'cortical' elements are called for. But on the surface of your 2 cm cube there is only room for half that number (2,000) on the five sides (400 to each 2 cm square side). To keep to the original proportions more surface space is needed, and one obvious solution is to corrugate the sides of the cube.

Something very like this solution seems to have been adopted in all orders of mammals, including monotremes and marsupials. In every order, small animals have smooth-surfaced cerebral hemispheres, but larger animals of the same type, who have larger brains, have an increasingly convoluted surface of the hemispheres, allowing them not to get too far away from the proportion of cortical area to brain volume used by the smaller members of the order. In fact, one of the older findings of comparative anatomy, the 'Law of Baillarger and Dareste' (see Kappers *et al.*, 1936, pp. 1518ff.), is that the folding of the surface of the hemispheres does not quite maintain the ratio of surface area to volume, so that larger brains usually have more internal volume, and more white matter, per square inch of surface cortical grey matter (Baillarger, 1845; Dareste, 1862). A quantitative confirmation of this finding has more recently been published by Elias and Schwartz (1969).

The whole question of progressive increases in brain size, and their possible implications for intelligence, is exceedingly complicated, as we have already seen. It is at first sight very odd, however, that the layout of the mammalian forebrain, with seminal interchanges between an outer crust and inner nuclei, would be more directly applicable to a small-sized system, while the arrangement which appears in the other higher vertebrates, the very much smaller birds, relies on connections between solid, non-surface neuronal structures, a plan which creates fewer problems of scale when used in larger brains. It is tempting to suggest an historical account for this discrepancy, since the fossil evidence has always been interpreted as showing that mammalian features first appeared in very small animals, and that the birds on the other hand arose from a line of very much larger reptiles, the same line that bred gargantuan dinosaurs. (There has been speculation that dinosaurs were warm-blooded, and were the immediate ancestors of birds, and Jerison concludes that dinosaurs had a normal relationship between brain weight and body weight: they were not exceptionally small-brained, and the absolute volume of a large dinosaur brain would have been several hundred times larger than that of a small mammalian brain.) It would be a pleasing illustration of the role of accident and conservatism in brain evolution if this is indeed the case and large mammals, such as ourselves, have had literally to go into convolutions to adapt what started as a small-brain design, whereas the plan originally used by large reptiles is now seen to best advantage in a sparrow.

The corpus striatum (the basal ganglia)
In mammals the floor of the hemispheres is occupied by several nuclei surrounding the thalamus and collectively called the corpus striatum or the basal ganglia. The 'striatum' in the name derives from the striped appearance of the cross-section of these structures, but this striping is on a somewhat different scale from the fine layering of the cortex. However, in both cases it is alternations of layers of cell bodies with layers of fibres that produces the striping. The main role assigned to the corpus striatum in mammals is as a stage of the 'extra-pyramidal' motor pathway, which sends efferents down through the midbrain and brainstem reticular system to the spinal cord and the cranial nerves. This is as distinct from the 'pyramidal' pathway which connects pyramidal cells in the motor cortex directly to the lower motor neurons, without any relays at intermediate levels. When in higher mammals the cortex is supposed to control voluntary, intelligent and skilled activities via the pyramidal pathway, the corpus striatum has been left stranded with instinctive, stereotyped and mechanical functions. Put crudely, the cortex has been assigned the thoughtful and the corpus striatum the unthinking aspects of motor control.

It suits the principle of encephalisation to allow for stability of function in this instance: since the hemispheres of reptiles and birds contain a large identifiable corpus striatum and very small amounts of rudimentary cortex, it would follow that the activities of both birds and reptiles should be largely instinctive, stereotyped and mechanical, even though the hemispheres of a bird may be as big as those possessed by a mammal with the same body weight. However, while the psychological capacities of reptiles remain obscure (Burghardt, 1977), the performance of birds on the standard tests of learning ability does not always suffer by comparison with mammals. And neuro-anatomists have now discovered that connections to parts of the striatal mass of the hemispheres of reptiles and birds are at least analogous and possibly homologous to the connections between the thalamus and the neocortex of mammals (Nauta and Karten, 1970; Webster, 1973; Ebbesson, 1980). Cells in these sensory pro-jection areas of the avian striatum react in the same way as the corresponding cells in mammalian cortex in electrophysiological experiments (Revzin, 1969; Pettigrew and Konishi, 1976; Karten, 1979) and lesions to the visual projections in the bird striatum can be shown to affect performance on behavioural tests of visual perception (Stettner, 1974; Macphail, 1975; Hodos, 1976).

Apparently mammals have adopted a particular form of con-struction of the cerebral hemispheres, relying heavily on the spreading out of neurons in the cortical sheet over the surface, while in birds functionally similar neurons are compressed into a more restricted region, previously identified as the *hyperstriatum* or 'Wulst' which can often be seen as a bulge somewhere on the top of their cerebral hemispheres. The Wulst is confined to birds, and there are many variations of terminology applied to the thalamic projections of non-mammalian hemispheres, but there is a measure of agreement that the telencephalon of reptiles and birds (and possibly of fish and am-phibians also) can be divided into an 'internal striatum', which corresponds roughly with the corpus striatum of mammals, and an 'external striatum' plus remaining bits of primitive cortex (which tend to be fused with the external striatum in birds but occupy a more separate location in most reptiles). On the anatomical evidence to hand it is not unreasonable to suppose that the external striatum in non-mammals has some functions in common with mammalian cortex. Some such degree of similarity between the cerebral hemi-spheres of mammals and other vertebrates is assumed in Figure 4 (p. 175).

The limbic system (hippocampus, septal area, amydala, etc.)
One of the constancies of vertebrate brain geography is that the olfactory sense projects directly into the cerebral hemispheres without the intervening relays in the brainstem, midbrain and/or thalamus

which apply to all other sensory modalities. Either the entire cerebrum, or some part of it, can therefore be identified with olfaction. For lower vertebrates (fish, amphibians and reptiles) the telencephalon has frequently been called the 'smell brain', with the explicit assumption that it has only a marginal role in any other function. The endearing simplicity of this assumption has recently been shattered by a single blow: when olfactory pathways are picked out by modern histological methods, it turns out that these projections are confined to only a small part of the cerebral hemispheres, even in sharks (Ebbesson and Northcutt, 1976). The structures which have a relatively close connection with olfactory pathways are part of what is known as the limbic system. In birds (which have rather little sense of smell), higher mammals, and probably in vertebrates generally, the limbic system is the locus of brain circuits which are fundamental to bodily needs and drives, and to motivation and emotion.

It is usually held that the limbic system has had a long and fairly stable evolutionary history, and the limbic system is sometimes characterised as the 'reptilian core brain' or the 'proto-reptilian brain' (Isaacson, 1974). This may be misleading: it is certainly wrong to say that the mammalian brain contains within it a limbic system similar to that of a reptile, on which the mammalian cortex has been superimposed. A palliative is supplied by extensive evidence of evolutionary changes within the limbic system, which is involved in human emotion and feeling and also in the emotional aspects of human communication and language (Lamendella, 1977). However, it should be remembered that there is no simple phylogenetic sequence of modality dominance, with smell a primitive vertebrate specialisation and hearing and sight later refinements, which would support the theory that the limbic system began as a set of structures exclusively concerned with olfaction but gradually and continuously changed in its functions as the importance of olfaction declined.

Sight was one of the earliest vertebrate inventions and specialisations, and this fact is used in connection which the argument for midbrain dominance in fishes and amphibians. Mammals, as a class being originally nocturnal, first discounted vision, and emphasised smell and touch very much more than reptiles or birds. It is arguable that both mammals and birds made a quantum leap in techniques for hearing, by re-assigning bones which are part of the jaw in reptiles to a sound-transmitting job in the middle ear. The need in mammals for brain apparatus to codify the additional auditory information thus obtained is given great play by Jerison (1973), but touch and smell are better candidates for modalities which led to mammalian distinctiveness, as they are not well developed in birds. The continuation, or possible re-emergence of vision as a dominant modality in tree-living insectivores, and primates, is a special factor: lower vertebrates and birds generally have good colour vision whereas mammals other than primates generally do not have colour vision—having lost it, we assume, during the early phases of nocturnality. The main point is that in so far as the limbic system is concerned with olfaction, there is no reason to suppose that it is of great importance to highly visual species, and these include the majority of non-mammalian vertebrates, and in particular the majority of reptiles. (One well-known reptile, the arboreal chameleon, has such well-developed eyes that it is referred to as a 'living microscope': Walls, 1942.)

Perhaps it is a mistake to group the various limbic structures together too firmly in the first place. The *hippocampus* is cortex, actually on the surface of the hemispheres (dorso-medially) in most non-mammals, but submerged down at the bottom of hemispheres in most mammals. There are only three cellular layers to the hippocampus, which perhaps makes it second-rate cortex in mammals, but this is as good as cortex comes in other classes. From the hippocampus, the *fornix* provides extensive two-way connections with the hypothalamus (terminating in the mammillary bodies). Non-cortical limbic components in the telencephalon include (1) the *amydala*, which is continuous with the basal ganglia or internal striatum and, like the hippocampus, is well connected with the hypothalamus (via the *stria terminalis*); (2) the *septal area*, which has anatomical pathways both to the hippocampus (via the fornix) and to the hypothalamus (via the *median forebrain bundle*). As well as the hypothalamus, other parts of the diencephalon such as the anterior thalamus and the habenular nuclei are also considered to be part of the limbic system. The above description is for mammals, but homologous components and connections of the limbic system are ascribed to most other vertebrates (Kappers *et al.*, 1936).

It is obvious that there are extremely rich interconnections within the limbic system, and the effects of electrical stimulation and lesion damage also provides justification for the belief that the limbic structures act in concert in a manner which suggests emotional regulation of one sort or another. The pattern of interconnections, along with analyses of cell types, is what has led to the identification of limbic structures across vertebrate classes. But of course it is extremely unlikely that what is identified as the hippocampus in lampreys, the septal area in a frog, or the amydala (archistriatum) in birds, has the same functions as the corresponding brain regions in a mammal. There is certainly no reason to regard the limbic system as especially reptilian.

The two halves of the brain—bilateral organisation and decussation

One almost universal feature of vertebrate brain organisation, which I have so far conveniently ignored, is the existence of separate circuits for inputs and outputs to and from the left and right sides. Bilateral symmetry of the body is a fact of life for all vertebrates but the importance of separate consideration of the two halves of the bilaterally symmetrical vertebrate brain arises partly because of the special role apparently played by an asymmetrical assignment of duties in the human brain. The human left hemisphere seems to dominate the right in the control of speech and language, skilled manipulation, reasoning, and conscious experience, while the right hemisphere holds sway over emotion, intuition, and unconscious thought (Gazzaniga, 1975; Corballis and Beale, 1976; Dimond, 1972). This kind of division of labour with a line of lateral demarcation between the hemispheres is thought by some to be one of the dimensions on which the human brain differs from that of other vertebrates (Levy, 1969, 1977), but the general problems associated with categorising information into left and right are by no means confined to the human species.

In all vertebrate classes, there is separate neural input from the left and right sides of the body, from the left and right eyes and ears (or lateral pressure sensors), and from the left and right olfactory bulbs. Similarly there is separate neural output to muscles on the left and right sides of the body. We may ask, what would be the simplest and most primitive way of fitting together these four lines of information—left and right input, and left and right output? Anatomically it would be most straightforward to keep all left-side lines of information on the left of the brain, and all right-side lines on the right of the brain, but this by itself would have the rather serious disadvantage of isolating one half of the body from the other. In order to co-ordinate the whole animal we should want both sides of sensory input to eventually get to both sides of motor output, and this would clearly require some kind of interaction between the two sides of the brain. The simplest solution would seem to be to put left-side information in the left half of the brain, and right-side information in the right half of the brain, but to cross-connect the two brain halves. In the typical vertebrates solution the two halves of the brain are indeed cross-connected, but in addition left-side information is put on the right side of the brain and vice versa.

The basic switch, which means for instance that the left hemisphere tends to control the right limbs, is referred to as 'crossed-lateral control' and no one seems to know why it takes place. If the two halves of the brain are going to be cross-connected anyway, it seems to be an unnecessary complication. Sarnat and Netsky (1974) suggest that crossed-lateral control arose in the first place because of a primitive need for left-side input to be converted to right-side output, and vice versa. In *Amphioxus*, the swimming chordate supposed to represent a vertebrate ancestor, there is a powerful coiling reflex produced by the contraction of muscles on the side opposite to the one prodded. But this does not take us very far in explaining why, in vertebrates, *both* left-side tactile input *and* left-side motor output tend to be localised in the right side of the brain.

By comparison, the reason for direct connections between the two sides of the brain is obvious. If an animal is to act as an integrated whole, and not as two independent halves, shunting circuits across the brain are clearly required. Pathways strung across from similar points on either side of the central nervous system could do this job. Usually such tracts are called commissures, and Kappers *et al.* (1936) make a sharp distinction between these and 'decussations' which occur when fibres from a certain point on one side of the brain cross over to a quite different location on the other side. However, it seems possible that 'partial decussation' could serve as a sort of diagonal commissure. In partial decussation connections up and down in the nervous system are to both the same and the opposite side, and thus information could be diagonally distributed across the midline as an alternative to the up-and-across method.

For whatever purposes, all vertebrate brains make very extensive use of both commissures and decussations. Ventral and dorsal commissures occur within all vertebrate spinal cords. Similarly, commissures directly traversing the brain are found in the brainstem, the cerebellum, the midbrain and the forebrain, with some degree of regularity in the various vertebrate classes. Emphasis is usually given to forebrain commissures, partly because a major new tract, the corpus callosum, evolved to interconnect the neocortex in the two hemispheres of placental mammals. It should not be forgotten, though, that other forebrain commissure can provide for hemispheric cross-talk in the absence of the corpus callosum. Monotremes and marsupials possess mammalian hemispheres but lack the corpus callosum, and rely on having large anterior and hippocampal commissures. The forebrain anterior commissure is phylogenetically very stable, being present in lampreys and sharks, and retained in higher mammals and man adjacent to the front end of the corpus callosum itself (Putnam *et al.*, 1968). Other forebrain cross-connections vary more from class to class and also vary within classes. Lampreys and teleost fish are assigned a dorsal forebrain commissure, and sharks have a number of commissure-like paths including the superior telencephalic commissure associated with 'hippocampal' areas. In amphibians the superior forebrain commissure has rather different terminations, and there is a separate hippocampal commissure, giving three main links between the cerebral hemispheres altogether. All extant reptiles have a hippocampal commissure in addition to the anterior commissure, and lizards and snakes have a third one, again considered to be associated with the hippocampus (Pearson and Pearson, 1976).

Interhemispheric connections are still somewhat mysterious in birds, since functional interaction is more obvious than the anatomical routes, but the anterior commissure in birds, like that in mammals, contains a section that terminates in the amygdaloid ('archistriatal') regions (Kappers *et al.*, 1936; Pearson, 1972; Cuenod, 1974). Mammals retain a separate hippocampal commissure in the psalterium (composed of crossing fibres from the fornix) as well as the anterior commissure, along with the new corpus callosum.

Apart from direct transverse commissures, there are many decussations or diagonal crossings, especially in the course of sensory input and motor output, in all vertebrates. In general decussations are partial, involving same-sided as well as opposite-sided transmission. Given the profusion of commissures and decussations in all vertebrate brains, it is reasonable to assume that much information is in principle transferable from side to side. When I deal with other aspects of brain design, looking primarily at relations between hierarchically organised 'up–down' stages of processing, interaction between the two halves of what is through and through a paired system will be taken for granted. However the functional effectiveness of lateral co-operation (or in the case of cerebral dominance, lack of co-operation) is subject to experimental test. In general animals appear to experience little difficulty in giving universal application to information received from one side of the body. For instance, visual stimuli received initially by one eye, are normally recognised by the other eye, even in animals (such as the goldfish) where there is a complete decussation of the optic nerves (Ingle and Campbell, 1977). Phylogenetic theory would suggest that the channel of transmission in this case should be the midbrain commissures of the optic tectum, but it would appear that, even in the goldfish, forebrain decussations are involved in the transfer of visual information.

The replication of visual information is a clear example of the necessity of bilaterally available representations: an object seen with one eye, or in one half of the visual field, needs to be registered in both sides of the brain if an animal is not to be constantly surprised by each turn of its head. But as well as the requirement for duplex representation, there is also a need for some separation, so that the animal codes whether a seen object is on the left or the right. Perfect duplication of information would lead to trouble in distinguishing left and right. To a degree, such difficulties occur, especially in animals and children (Corballis and Beale, 1976). The importance of separating left and right is more obvious in the case of motor instructions than it is in perception—we must be able to lift one leg or the other, and not attempt to lift both at once. The presence of some degree of equivalence between motor commands to our own right and left limbs is apparent in the traditional problem of making circular movements on the stomach with one hand while doing non-circular pats on the head with the other. But in general limbs must work in conjunction, doing different things at the same time, even in the case of the movements of fins in fish. The brain must be able to label left and right in terms of motor commands at the same time as being able to recognise equivalences between left and right perceptual input. Conceivably, the need for left/right differentiation is the reason behind the peculiar crossed-lateral layout of sensory and motor pathways. Since any neuron which crosses the midline of the brain must violate strict mirror-plane bilateral symmetry, brains organised on the crossed-lateral plan with left-sided input and output going to the right half of the brain (and vice versa) have an additional source of structural asymmetry by comparison with the more obvious design of keeping all left-side information in the left half of the brain (Walker, 1981). This might explain a curious exception to the crossed-lateral plan. The vertebrate rule is that sensory and motor pathways tend to cross from one side of the body to the other side of the brain but a major exception to this rule is that smells received by one nostril go into the cerebral hemisphere on the same side. If it is generally important to code sensory and motor information according to whether it pertains to left or right peripheral organs, but not important to code smells according to whether they are received by the left or right nostril, and the crossed-lateral layout serves the purpose of left/right differentiation, then the absence of crossed input from the nostrils makes sense.

The optic chiasma

The best-known example of the general rule of sensory decussation is that in the majority of vertebrate species the retinal output from one eye goes to the midbrain or thalamus in the opposite half of the brain. Most non-mammalian species have their eyes pointing sideways, and this means that a large part of the left visual field goes to the right side of the brain and vice versa. Some mammals, especially carnivores and primates, have less panoramic visual fields because both eyes point forward to survey more or less the same scene. An advantage of this is that for an object in the near distance the slight differences between the images projected onto the left and right retinas can be used to give the impression of depth. Perhaps in order to capitalise on this possibility, most mammals have partial decussation of the optic nerves, so that the left visual field, as seen by *both* eyes, goes to the right side of the brain and the right visual field, as seen by *both* eyes, goes to the left half of the brain.

The crossing of the optic nerves before they enter the brain is called the 'optic chiasma' in both mammals and non-mammals. Usually the optic chiasma is a total decussation in non-mammals, and a partial decussation in mammals, but there are some exceptions to this. At least two kinds of mammal, with little else in common, have total crossing of the optic nerves. These are the dolphins and whales, and the guinea pigs, which both have their eyes so much on the side that there is almost no overlap in the independent fields. By and large, mammals with side-directed eyes have almost completely crossed optic nerves, and those with both eyes pointing forward, pre-eminently primates, have a relatively even partial decussation at the optic chiasma. The mammalian type of partial decussation at the optic chiasma is occasionally seen in lower vertebrates: in some amphibians; snakes and lizards; the sole living representative of the immediate precursors to teleost fish (Northcutt and Butler, 1976); and adult lampreys (Kennedy and Rubinson, 1977). Birds, turtles, teleosts and sharks all seem to conform to the non-mammalian pattern of total optic nerve crossing (Ebbesson, 1970). Whether or not the partial decussation of the optic chiasma that sometimes occurs in lower vertebrates is utilised for stereoscopic vision has not been behaviourally tested, but in the case of the teleost precursor, the long-nose gar, its ecological niche as a fast predator, chasing and catching fish that swim in front of it, implies that binocular distance perception would be a help.

Whether or not stereoscopic depth perception is possible in birds (which have totally crossed optic nerves) *has* been tested. As long as the individual fields of view of the two eyes overlap, and these fields can be compared at some stage, for instance by the use of midbrain or diencephalic commissures, there is no reason why stereopsis could not be accomplished without the mammalian convenience of partial decussation at the optic chiasma. That stereopsis occurs in many birds has often been suspected, but an ingenious and conclusive test has been performed on the falcon, by fitting a bird with goggles which allowed the placement of red and green filters over the separate eyes, and presenting it with the well-known Julesz type of array, by which three-dimensional subjective effects are produced in human observers due to disparities between red and green elements. The bird was successfully trained to fly only to the 'three-dimensional' displays, thus demonstrating that it possessed a mechanism for the perception of depth and distance by binocular disparity. Such a mechanism would undoubtedly be of real use in chasing and stooping on other flying birds. Cuenod (1974) and Pettigrew and Konishi (1976) have demonstrated that what happens in the owl and the pigeon, and probably in many other avian species, is that although the optic nerves themselves are totally crossed, bilateral projection from each eye to both cerebral hemispheres is brought about at the 'supra-optic decussation', which goes through the midbrain just above the optic chiasma itself, but is a visual projection pathway from the thalamus to the telencephalon. This means that the Wulst (hyperstriatum) of the owl hemispheres is able to react to binocular stimulation in roughly the same way as the cat's visual cortex, even though the binocular information has come via a different route. Like the cat, the owl's eyes are pointed straight ahead, and no doubt depth perception is as useful to the owl, when pouncing on a mouse, as it is to the cat.

Apart from the use of binocular vision for depth perception at short distances by birds, it is likely that many of them assess long distances by bobbing their head up and down to take successive looks at objects with the same eye from different positions. The cocking of the head to look at the same object with either eye alternately is another strategy which may expand the possibilities of binocular perception with side-facing eyes. Thus, although mammals possess a peripheral splitting of visual input, and a cortex for the analysis of binocular comparisons, it certainly does not follow that mammals are the only vertebrate class capable of seeing in three dimensions.

Brain asymmetries and human speech and handedness

The vertebrate brain, like the vertebrate body, is superficially remarkable for its anatomical symmetry. One half of the central nervous system is generally taken to mirror the other although marginal violations of mirror-plane symmetry must occur at the midline in cross-connections. A notable exception to the bilateral symmetry of visible gross anatomy is common in lower vertebrates in the habenular nuclei, which are an otherwise insignificant part of the diencephalon, usually classed as olfactory centres and components of the limbic system. The habenular nuclei on the left and right are markedly asymmetrical in lampreys and hagfish, sharks, and some teleosts and amphibians (Braitenberg and Kemali, 1970). The largest side is the right in the lowly cyclostomes, the left in the sharks and some frogs, and variable from species to species in the teleosts.

Not surprisingly, rather more attention has been given to the fact that anatomical asymmetries are measurable for certain areas of the cortex of the human cerebral hemispheres. Cunningham (1892) observed that the upward turn of the Sylvian fissure is more acute in the right hemisphere of the human brain than it is in the left. The Sylvian fissure divides the temporal lobe below from the frontal and parietal lobes above, and Geschwind and Levitsky (1968) examined a roughly triangular portion of the upper surface of the temporal lobe, inside the Sylvian fissure, termed the 'planum temporale'.

Measurements of the longitudinal extent of this area gave average figures of 3.6. $\pm$ 1.0 cm in the left hemisphere and 2.7 $\pm$ 1.2 cm in the right hemisphere, the left figure exceeding the right in 65 of the 100 brains studied. On its own this is a less than compelling variation in physical structure, but of course the favouring of the right hand over the left for writing and other manual skills has been a fact of human life throughout recorded history (Hardyck and Petrinovich, 1977) and the restriction of the more sophisticated mechanisms governing speech to only one hemisphere, which is usually the left, has now become equally well established (Gazzaniga, 1975; Warrington and Pratt, 1973). That there are implications for theories of cognition is clear, although exactly what the implications are is somewhat less than clear.

In the context of animal thought it is obligatory to consider the extreme possibility that all forms of cognition are completely dependent on an exclusively human degree of anatomical asymmetry and lateralisation of function in the cerebral hemispheres. We must therefore examine briefly how asymmetrical functioning in the human brain might be related to the more general questions of symmetry and duplication of function in the vertebrate nervous system. I will deal with handedness and speech separately, and ignore for the present the many other interesting but subtle specialisations of the two halves of the brain that have been detected (Walker, 1980; Denenberg, 1981).

Handedness
The fact that each human limb tends to be served by the opposite side of the brain is not, of course, remarkable. What is distinctive about human handedness is that one side of the brain, and therefore one hand, appears to be better than the other. Vertebrate species apart from ourselves seem to be wonderfully ambidextrous, both in the sense that individuals are capable of performing most skills necessary to them with either side of the body and in the sense that when individual side preferences can be found, they are distributed very evenly within the species. It should be noted that in a given population of rats, or monkeys, most individuals will prefer a particular forelimb for a simple task such as reaching out for food, but there will be the same number of 'left-handers' as 'right-handers' (Peterson, 1934; Lehman, 1978; Collins, 1977).

What can have induced the human species to become predominantly right-handed? There is no shortage of theories, but a specialisation of some sort would seem to be the most obvious advantage of manual asymmetry. Reserving the left hand to place over one's heart is one of the oldest and least plausible theories, but incorporates an interesting feature—the task of the 'non-preferred' hand. For purely one-handed activities the usefulness of not being ambidextrous is obscure, given the assumption that the massive human corpus callosum should enable skills to be transferred from one limb to the other. If, however, there are important activities in which the two hands do different things then a degree of isolation of the separate skills might be helpful. The manufacture of stone tools is a distinctively human, two-handed and asymmetrical skill which was sufficiently important during the period of human evolution to have supplied a unique selection pressure. As the nature of the paleontological evidence suggests that it began at least two or three million years ago and continued while the brain grew from about 500 to about 1300 gm, the manufacture of tools seems on obvious candidate for a selection pressure for a 'holding and hammering' specialisation.

Reconstructions of tool-making techniques, and the habits of modern Australian aborigines, imply that the way to make stone tools is to hold a flint or bauxite core against the body or against an anvil stone, with the left hand, and swing at it with a hammer stone held in the right hand. Although we have difficulty in making different ballistic movements concurrently with separate arms, as in the rubbing and patting trick, we are well adapted for gripping and holding firmly with one hand while making finely controlled movements with the other. The utility of being able to do this could be a reason for the development of an asymmetry in arm use, but it does not of course explain why it is the right hand, rather than the left, which gets the more interesting work. Perhaps this was arbitrary, or due to a slight left-brain physiological superiority. But it must be pointed out that the left hand, and the right hemisphere, are not devoid of the biological capacity for carefully and finely controlled movements. The left hand of a virtuoso violinist may be said to accomplish the highest form of human manual dexterity. Usually when one hand is selected for delicate movement, we plump for the right, but if the left is forced into service it is not necessarily found wanting. The use of the left hand for the fingering of the violin and similar stringed instruments (and more recently for the fingering of the valves of the French horn) is almost certainly an historical accident, due to the preference for holding things with the left hand while making ballistic movements on or around them with the right. But such accidents serve as a useful indication that some human asymmetries result from culture and convention as much as biological predestination. It should be remembered that handwriting, which is used as the modern index of human lateralisation, is confined to the last few thousand years at most, and to the last few hundred for all but a tiny fraction of each human generation. It is thus supremely irrelevant as a selection pressure, though perhaps not quite so irrelevant as a connection between human lateralisation and language.

Human language
The universal use of spoken propositional communication by the human (or a pre-human) species was undoubtedly a Rubicon whose crossing led to new pastures of group activity, social organisation and, eventually, civilisation, which are denied to all animals that remain on its other side. The fixation of the mechanisms which enable the use of so decisive a facility on only one side of the brain is something of a puzzle—if ever there was a case for doubling up on brain circuits as a fail-safe device, language would surely be it. A number of speculations on this theme may be presented. First, it is conceivable that language was not of such overwhelming importance at earlier stages of human evolution as it is in modern literate societies. Second, assuming that language is crucial, being able to accomplish speech with only half a brain has its points as a form of insurance. Language is not genetically restricted to the left side of the brain since damage to this hemisphere (or its removal), in childhood, means that the remaining right hemisphere does the job. There is very little firm evidence to support the contention that those left-handers who use the right side of the brain for all, or part, of speech control suffer from significant impairment of speech or other faculties (Hardyck, 1977). Needing only one side of the brain for speech might thus be supposed to be somewhat safer than needing both, but duplicating speech mechanisms on both sides would be safer still.

An argument for the non-duplication of language mechanisms in the two cerebral hemispheres is that space which would be taken up by duplication can be put to better use (Levy, 1969). Given that unilateral brain injury is not a major feature of the human condition (at least in the absence of car accidents and strokes) it would perhaps be unduly cautious to waste brain space by the duplication of any function that is not inherently bilateral. The theory that when the left hemisphere takes command of speech the right hemisphere is freed for other duties such as spatial awareness, and non-verbal imagination and intuition thus provides an explanation for cerebral lateralisation in terms of evolutionary economy, and has been broadly supported by various kinds of psychological testing since it was first put forward by Semmes (1968) and Levy (1969).

A difficulty with this strict division of labour theory is that it is perhaps more convincing than the data requires. For performances other than linguistic ones, differences between the hemispheres are more a matter of degree (and a matter of serving the two sides of the body) than a revelation of qualitatively quite different modes of functioning. Further, theoretical advantages of strong lateralisation imply severe deficits if it is much reduced, and the absence of catastrophic impairments in the capacities of moderately left-handed individuals whose brains tend to be anatomically and functionally symmetrical (Hardyck, 1977; Lemay, 1976) indicates that brain lateralisation is not a necessary condition for the attainment of uniquely human cognition.

What then are the implications of asymmetries in human brain function for the psychological gap between humans and other animals? Man seems to share with other animals the general duplication of the nervous system, both in terms of the normal programming of two-sided behaviours and in terms of the ability of one hemisphere to take over whole-brain capacities after damage to the other in childhood. But for speech and handedness the typical adult human brain appears to follow a very distinctive strategy which involves specialisation of the left half of the brain for these functions. If the demands of human thought and intellect are so much greater than the demands placed on the brains of other species that a unique division of labour, even in an enlarged brain, has been necessary to meet them, this certainly widens the gap between human and animal cognition. On the other hand, if lateralisation of brain functions confers so much benefit on man, should we not expect that similar strategies should have been resorted to at least occasionally in other species, which may have more limited need for cognition but have equally limited amounts of available brain tissue? Unfortunately evidence which bears on this last question is not easy to come by. However, a single finding of some significance concerns vocalisation in birds.

Vocalisation in birds as in man is controlled by apparatus which does not require independent movements in its left and right halves. It may be that the lack of necessity for equal but independent representation of the two halves of the speech apparatus was an important factor in the evolution of human brain asymmetries, as similar asymmetries appear to occur in song birds. A series of experiments by Nottebohm seems to have established beyond doubt that in several species of seed-eating passerines the left side of the brain and the left side of the peripheral nervous system is predominantly responsible for controlling song in the normal adult males (Nottebohm, 1971, 1976, 1977, 1979; Nottebohm *et al.*, 1976). In the birds studied (the canary, the chaffinch and two species of sparrow) the organ of sound production, the syrinx, has muscles on the left and right sides, and each set responds to a separate branch of the hypoglossal cranial nerve. The left-hand set of syrinx muscles in considerably larger than the right, which is in itself suggestive, but clear results are obtained by severing the nerve to the left-hand muscles and comparing the effects of this operation with the effects of cutting the nerve to the muscles on the right side of the syrinx. If the cut is on the left, all, or almost all, of the syllables previously used by the canary (in a range of 20–40 syllables, identified by an auditory spectrogram) are lost, whereas if the right-side muscles are inactivated vocalisation even immediately afterwards is virtually unchanged, with only one or two syllables missing at the most. Since, in the canary, the left hypoglossal nerve comes from the left side of the brain, one might expect left-brain dominance of vocalisation in the canary, and other experiments confirm that this is so.

In man, there is a region of the frontal lobe of the left hemisphere which is called Broca's area because a French neurologist of that name discovered that patients in which it was damaged suffered from a form of aphasia. In the canary, there is a region in the left hemisphere which perhaps ought to be called 'Nottebohm's area', since Nottebohm claims that lesions at this place cause a major disruption of song. It is located in the external striatum (at the caudal or rear end of the hyperstriatum ventrale) which has been assumed on other grounds to be analogous to the cerebral cortex of mammals. Although lesions to this area in the left hemisphere resulted in the immediate loss of almost all song, lesions placed at the corresponding point in the right hemisphere allowed more than half of the usual syllables to be reproduced immediately after the operation in a pattern that to the human ear was indistinguishable from the pre-operation performance.

The prognosis for language disturbance (aphasia) which results from brain damage in human patients is not good, but significant recovery is not at all uncommon either spontaneously or with the assistance of speech therapy, especially after relatively clean lesions due to accidents or war wounds rather than strokes or tumours (Goldstein, 1948; Paradis, 1977). Nottebohm's canaries, even those which suffered a profound impairment of song, made a good recovery after the brain lesions in the course of the next year. Another parallel with human language mechanisms is that if the left branch of the hypoglossal nerve going to the syrinx is cut in young birds, the right-side structures very quickly take over the control of song. Whether or not auditory perception or comprehension of sounds is as much lateralised in the song-bird brain as vocal production seems to be remains to be seen. Acoustic lateralisation of a completely different kind is known in several species of owls, some of which have very pronounced physical asymmetries of the external ear, consistently in all individuals. It is presumed that the left/right differentiation in these cases is for the purpose of localising sounds in the vertical as well as the horizontal plane (Norberg, 1977).

It would be curious indeed if of all vertebrates only song birds, owls and humans benefited from relaxations of bilateral brain symmetry. But there is increasing evidence that left/right distinctions in brain function of one sort or another are not particularly uncommon (Walker, 1980; Denenberg, 1981). Unfortunately it is still by no means clear whether lateralisation of human brain function is foreshadowed in other primates, and this is obviously a crucial point. In terms of anatomical inequalities, Cunningham (1892) found that human Sylvian fissure asymmetries had counterparts in the great apes, and large monkeys, and this has been confirmed by Yeni-Komshian and Benson (1976), Lemay and Geschwind, (1975) and Cain and Wada (1979). In terms of recognition of species-specific cries Petersen *et al.* (1978) claim that left-hemisphere processing in Japanese macaque monkeys is analogous to that of humans listening to speech, and Dewson (1977) has also produced data that appear to demonstrate preferential use of the left hemisphere for complex auditory functions in monkeys. The best assessment at present is, in my view, that asymmetries of brain function as such are not a human prerogative even though one of the things that is lateralised—language—is. Cerebral lateralisation is neither a necessary nor a sufficient condition for human mental activity and therefore we need not suppose that degree of brain lateralisation determines the extent to which an animal species may be said to possess cognitions.

Hierarchical design in vertebrate brains

I shall now ignore the question of side-to-side interactions in the brain, and return to the idea that progression along the tail-end to nose-end axis of the brain is the fundamental dimension of vertebrate brain evolution. A rough plan of the anatomical relationships between the longitudinal divisions of the brain which I reviewed earlier in this chapter—hindbrain, midbrain and forebrain—is shown in Figure 4. A speculative simplification which is shared by phylogenetic theory, human neurology and other attempts to give an overall description of brain function (Riss, 1968a; Pearson, 1972) is the identification of a hierarchy of levels of brain activity. At the lowest level, the spinal cord clearly supplies the most direct route there is between sensory input and motor output. At the highest level, some regions of the mammalian cortex receive sensory information which has been successively transformed, filtered and classified at previous stages, and other regions of the cortex initiate actions which may be given more detailed organisation by lower brain divisions. Between the spinal cord and the cortex, the brainstem, midbrain, cerebellum, thalamus and corpus striatum can be assigned particular intermediary roles. Clearly an underlying assumption is that the higher levels of brain organisation are linked with complex forms of cognition and thought while lower levels are concerned only with more mechanical and reflexive matters.

It is hard to imagine how any sense could be made of the workings of the brain without some such assumption of a hierarchy of levels or progression of forms of integration, but a number of reservations ought to be expressed before I make further use of this kind of concept. First, many important details are necessarily ignored: identifying levels of function makes things more intelligible, but the levels may in some senses be convenient fictions. Second, if divisions of function are made, it is almost inevitable that one succumbs to the temptation of imposing spurious meanings on the divisions. As a cautionary example, even the split between sensory and motor functions is sometimes regarded with suspicion.

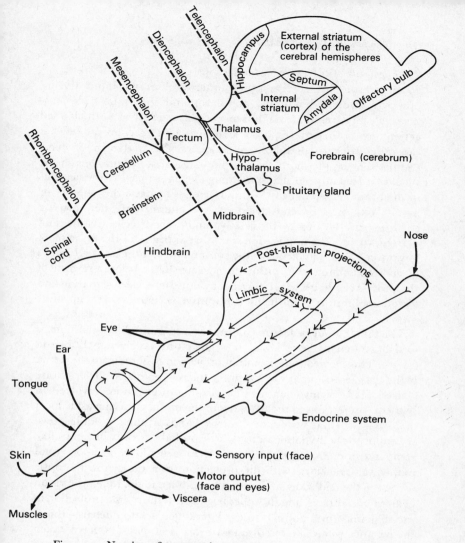

Figure 4 Naming of parts and general layout of the vertebrate brain. The top diagram is a rough sketch of the anatomical relationships between the structures usually identifiable in any vertebrate brain. The bottom diagram shows schematically the points of entry of the major sensory nerves, and grossly simplified pathways of neural connections within the brain (see text). In mammals and birds, the forebrain is larger than indicated here, and the brain as a whole is compressed over the long axis (see Figure 3). In mammals, post-thalamic projections are composed of the neocortex of the cerebral hemispheres. (After Nauta and Karten, 1970)

The complexity of the sensory and motor systems

By interpreting brain organisation in terms of sensory input moving upwards through hindbrain, midbrain and forebrain tiers, progressively more remote from the sense organs themselves, with planned actions, co-ordinated response sequences and mechanical reflexes cascading back to peripheral muscles, one is in danger of over-emphasising simple input and output categories. To counter this, it should be remembered that something like 99 per cent of the neurons in the brain and spinal cord cannot be classified as either sensory or motor, but may be considered as an 'intermediate net' coming between strictly sensory or strictly motor nerve cells (Nauta and Karten, 1970). The implication is that what begins as the firing off of sensory cell axons, and ends as the contraction of muscles, is subject to an enormous fanning out within the nervous system before a reversal of this process converges to produce behaviour. In between sensation and action the brain of even the most primitive vertebrate has a life of its own.

The fanning out of sensory information to multiple destinations is well illustrated by the review of the visual pathways given by Ebbesson (1970). This showed that the initial projection of fibres from the retina of the eye goes to as many as five or six different points, in all vertebrate classes. (This is not counting the possible duplications involved in bilateral projections to the two sides of the brain.) Leaving aside most of these, which may have rather narrow bands of function (for instance the input to the hypothalamus, which probably assists in things like responses to changing day-length), there are still two major visual pathways. One starts with the projection from the eye to the optic tectum in the midbrain, and is usually assumed to dominate the vision of lower vertebrates, and the other begins with the retinal projection to the thalamus (in mammals to the lateral geniculate nucleus—this is the instance where the forebrain pathway is supposed to have 'taken over' vision from the midbrain pathway). All vertebrates make use of this kind of double vision, possibly because one pathway detects moving objects while the other analyses stationary patterns. But several nuclei in the thalamus are involved in each case, and exceedingly complex transformations and abstractions may take place in the cerebral hemispheres, even in lower vertebrates such as sharks (Graebner, 1980).

Using at least two parallel but complementary interpretations of sensory input for a single modality may be the rule rather than the exception. Acoustic information from each mammalian ear goes to two nuclei in the brainstem, and from them goes either direct to the thalamus (the medial geniculate nucleus) or, by a separate route, relays in the midbrain (the inferior colliculus) before going up through the thalamus to auditory cortex. Similarly it is well established that in mammals there are at least two projections of the body surface on the cortex (Adrian, 1941; Woolsey, 1965). Motor traffic also passes down double or triple lanes before converging on to muscles, the main distinction being between the pyramidal path direct from motor cortex to the spinal cord, and the extra-pyramidal circuit through non-cortical forebrain structures and the midbrain and brainstem, with detours taken by both to pick up elaborations of assignment in the cerebellum.

Clearly, much of the richness and variety of the central nervous system is lost if we condense function down to sensation, action, and correlations between the two: one should use terms like 'sensory' and 'motor' not as labels for elementary categories but as synonyms for problems whose practical solution required the evolution of an organ as complex as the brain, and whose interpretation in neuropsychological theory is still tentative.

Hypotheses of phylogenetic change in brain organisation

Bearing in mind the limitations of the basic concepts, we can now examine more closely ideas about how the organisation of vertebrate brains may change from class to class. Most of these ideas can be subsumed under the general heading of encephalisation, but I believe that speculation under this heading covers a multitude of theoretical sins, which I intend to categorise as hypotheses concerning take-over, addition, and conservation of function.

Take-over of functions

The most common form of the doctrine of encephalisation presupposes that behaviour-controlling functions become progressively concentrated at higher brain levels (that is, towards the front of the longitudinal layout: Figure 4, p. 175). This notion has been applied to the evolution of vertebrates from invertebrates, the evolution of successive classes of vertebrate, and to differences between and within mammalian orders. With mammals, encephalisation is taken to mean corticalisation. It is often assumed, for instance, that primates, being more advanced, make greater use of their cortex than rodents or carnivores, and similarly that man is more dependent on cortical functions than prosimians, monkeys or apes, in that sequence of other primates.

The origin of the take-over of function hypothesis is that the business of any given part of the central nervous system can be seen in broad terms as the interpretation of sensory information and the control and organisation of behaviour. Once this is done there is a tendency to want to appoint some brain division as 'in charge' of all the others, and this sets the stage for phylogenetic take-overs of the executive position. The dominance of a particular brain level is often linked with the duties of correlation, integration or association, so we may find references to the midbrain as the dominant correlation centre, or to the thalamus as the most highly developed mechanism of association, in a certain group of vertebrates. The 'migration of the dominant controlling centre' (Bastian, 1880) appears to involve the stripping of the correlative and associative assets of the fish and amphibian midbrain by the reptilian and higher vertebrate forebrain. The phylogenetic take-over is not thought of as complete until the rise of cerebral cortex, and therefore the midbrain is considered to be a going concern in reptiles and birds, finally going into liquidation only in mammals. As a consequence of the take-over by cortex the formerly dominant centre may be expected to become almost vestigial and in mammals the midbrain is often given credit for little more than a few minor reflexes. On the other hand when the midbrain remains the seat of sensory integration and action the forebrain as a whole ought to be no more than up and coming. It can hardly be said to be vestigial in fish and amphibians, but in these classes the forebrain is sometimes viewed as merely a holding company for olfaction.

The take-over idea is supported by obvious differences in the physical proportions of the brains of the various classes, but it is open to various objections. Weiskrantz (1961) doubts the evolutionary logic of competition for business within reproducing units. If non-mammalian vertebrates were already equipped with efficient midbrain functions, what was the point of shifting these functions to a new location? One obvious answer to this sort of question is that the evolution of brain organisation took the form of adding extra or different capacities, rather than the migration of executive centres from one location to another. This gives another version of the encephalisation principle—the hypothesis of addition of functions.

Addition of functions

It is reasonable to assume that the elaboration of higher brain levels adds something new in terms of behavioural capacities. This is the root idea of most psychological discussion of phylogenetic comparisons, and is given detailed support by Riss (1968a), Riss *et al.* (1972), and Diamond and Hall (1969) among others. The cortex in particular ought to allow for *better* or *more* associations, correlations, integrations and so on. If there are significant differences in brain organisation between the vertebrate classes then, provided that we test numerous animals to encompass idiosyncratic species specialisations, systematic differences in the psychological abilities of the classes should emerge. This was originally one of the goals of comparative psychology: the problem is that after about a century of experimentation, there is little agreement even on whether such psychological dimensions exist (Hodos and Campbell, 1969; Warren, 1974; Bitterman and Woodward, 1976). Part of the difficulty undoubtedly lies in the naivety of the phylogenetic expectations as exposed by Hodos and Campbell (1969). However, I refuse to abandon the expectation that chimpanzees may be demonstrated to possess psychological capacities which are superior to those of the goldfish. The current failure to distinguish between the abilities of the vertebrate classes rests largely on the adoption of standardised conditioning techniques which may indeed produce much the same outcome when applied to a wide variety of species, and alternative strategies of assessment may be more successful in revealing cross-species differences in brain power. But it is necessary to acknowledge that behavioural evidence suggests that widely disparate species have a good deal of associative, correlative and integrative abilities in common, and this would imply that the doctrine of encephalisation must come to terms with constancies as well as changes in brain function.

Conservation of functions

If one reliable universal principle can be distilled from the study of evolutionary changes in brain and behaviour, it is that there are no universal principles. However, allowing for numerous exceptions, the sweeping generalisation I shall attempt to defend for the rest of this chapter is that vertebrate phylogenesis reflects conservation of functions, rather than take-overs or additions. The essence of this hypothesis is that *all* vertebrate brains are built on more or less the same plan, give or take a few special adaptations for particular species and orders. The hypothesis was formulated as the *Conservation Principle* by Stebbins (1969) and endorsed by Jerison (1973, 1976). It states that the functions of brain divisions and brain pathways are preserved through phylogenesis, rather than altered.

It should be emphasised that the Conservation Principle does not entail the assumption that the brain remained utterly unchanged throughout vertebrate evolution: even if the general role played by a certain brain division is always the same, the importance of that role may change, and it may be performed with a greater or lesser degree of expertise. The importance and effectiveness of particular brain structures should, according to Jerison, vary to conform with two other principles: the *Principle of Adaptation*—species ought to have evolved brains appropriate to their particular needs (an animal which depends for its survival on the sense of smell should have efficient olfactory apparatus); and the *Principle of Proper Mass*—the amount of use given to a brain structure should bear some relation to its size (large olfactory bulbs should be better than small ones).

One could choose to believe in the Conservation Principle without knowing what any of the supposedly constant functions of particular brain structures were, but clearly the principle would be more plausible if it was possible to say what it is that is conserved. Claims of this kind are either tentative or trivial, but it is worth listing some presumed constancies. It is not being unduly speculative to say the spinal cord *always* subserves some local reflexes and transmits information to and from the brain. The brainstem is *always* the main site of the reticular activating system, and contains nuclei associated with the sensory and motor cranial nerves which go to the head and the face and the viscera. In species which are not blind and deaf, there will be some visual and auditory processing in the midbrain. The midbrain certainly plays a larger part in the processing of visual information in fish and amphibians than in other classes, but the type of visual processing may perhaps be constant across classes—the midbrain appears to be specialised for reacting to movements in the visual field and detecting location in the field, and is said to ask 'where is it?' visual questions in mammals. In *all* vertebrates the thalamus receives inputs direct from the eye and contains nuclei which can be characterised as sensory projections in vision and other modalities, from the brainstem and midbrain. It is likely that post-thalamic projections of sensory information are universal: they are certainly not confined to mammals, having been very reliably demonstrated in birds, reptiles and sharks (Nauta and Karten, 1970; Ebbesson, 1980). Certainly, the elaboration and extent of post-thalamic projections varies from class to class, but their functions may show some constancies: visual post-thalamic projections, for instance, may contribute to object recognition (answering 'what is it?' visual questions) in all classes. The internal striatum of the telencephalon is generally regarded as furnishing some basic control over movement and action, perhaps being concerned with relatively slow and sustained directions. The cerebellum is *always* firmly identified with motor co-ordination, and may be especially adapted for the sequencing and timing of movements which need to be put together quickly (Kornhuber, 1974). The limbic system as a whole, or some of its constituent parts, is specifically involved with olfaction, but also appears to exert a regulating effect on instinctive and motivated behaviours, which leads to its identification as the source of instinctual drives and emotions in *all* vertebrates (Isaacson, 1974).

Given that this list establishes a certain minimal plausibility for the slogan of phylogenetic conservation of function, let us now test the virtues of the conservation idea against the take-over and additive versions of the encephalisation principle by considering more fully two particular issues. First, is there sound evidence of the atrophy of lower levels of brain function as a consequence of the elaboration of higher circuits, as the take-over version implies? And second, does the enlargement of the forebrain, which undoubtedly takes place in higher vertebrates, bring about completely new psychological capabilities, as would be predicted by the additive theory, or does it expand and develop functions which can already be seen to be present in the lower vertebrate forebrain?

Evolutionary development in non-forebrain structures

Encephalisation in its purest form would have it that, with the rise of the forebrain and the formation of its cortical crust, hindbrain and midbrain foundations should become vestigial evolutionary relics, or vanish altogether. It is apparent that this did not happen—the question is only whether the hindbrain and midbrain suffer any predations at all from the imperialism of the forebrain, or whether their functions remain fixed, or whether they undergo parallel improvements. We may briefly say that the spinal cord shows considerable change from class to class with the cord of the cyclostomes being particularly rudimentary (Kappers *et al.*, 1936). Elasmobranch fish can be said to possess the prototype spinal cord for other vertebrates with the separation of dorsal afferent and ventral efferent roots, but many fairly obvious new adaptations, such as local enlargements for the control of limbs and tails, occur in amphibians and reptiles. Some of the most peripheral elements of the nervous system, such as the somato-sensory nerve endings which feed into the spinal cord, show a pronounced elaboration in mammals (although birds have relatively little tactile sense, presumably because of the sensory limitations of feathers as opposed to hairs, and have noticeably small dorsal roots in the spinal cord). However, there is some tendency for the spinal cord of higher vertebrates to become simplified, in the sense of having specialisations for single-synapse reflexes, which do not occur in the spinal cords of lower vertebrates.

The brainstem, while retaining its primitive and reflexive characteristics, undergoes progressive evolutionary changes, as may be illustrated by the importance of the facial nerves and their corresponding cranial nuclei in mammals. Chewing, tasting, facial expression and hearing all require the operation of cranial nuclei, and one would presume that the refinements of muscular control in the cranial regions necessary for song in birds and speech in man should be represented in some way in relays in the brainstem. The modality of taste is strong in many teleost fish (which may have taste buds outside the mouth, or covering the whole body) and in mammals, while reptiles and birds apparently have very few taste buds (sometimes only 40–60 in birds, although the gustatory sense is nevertheless a powerful influence on their behaviour—Garcia *et al.*, 1977). The change from a 'lateral line' external pressure sense, and other methods of detecting vibration in fish, to hearing techniques more appropriate for airborne sounds, must have been paralleled by changes in the brainstem, where auditory input enters the brain. Reptiles have no external auditory canal, and lack the complex sound transducing mechanism of levers in the inner ear, but the more sensitive hearing of birds and mammals had more effect on the growth and specialisation of lower brainstem nuclei than it did on the pattern of auditory connections to higher centres, since the latter show a 'remarkable resemblance' in reptiles to those observed in birds and mammals (Foster and Hall, 1978).

The cerebellum attains healthy, highly fissurised proportions in the larger sharks, and the same cerebellar components, such as Purkinje cells with climbing-fibre and mossy-fibre input to their elaborate dendrites, are thought to be involved in cerebellar activity in all vertebrates (Llinás, 1970). Although the direct connection from the motor cortex of the cerebral hemispheres to the spinal cord is a mammalian speciality and is therefore given much significance, there has never been any suggestion that the cortex has taken over cerebellar functions: if anything, the size and differentiation of the cerebellum increases with the size and differentiation of the cerebral hemispheres, and the cerebellum is thought to show improvements in internal organisation for the purpose of skilled rapid locomotion in the higher vertebrates.

One would be very hard-put, therefore, to support a claim that the hindbrain—the brainstem and cerebellum—degenerates in structural or functional importance as the midbrain and forebrain which surmount it expand. As far as the midbrain goes, no one denies that it retains well-developed functions in birds, and, as will be emphasised when I discuss perception (Chapter 7), midbrain pathways are present in mammals, and even in primates have much more than the marginal role in visual perception that was accorded to them twenty years ago (Humphrey, 1974; Weiskrantz, 1977). The Conservation Principle seems to apply reasonably well to non-forebrain structures—they do not wither away or substantially change their function as a consequence of phylogenetic progression. One could incorporate the stability of hindbrain and midbrain functions into the additive version of encephalisation if the major point of addition was narrowed down to forebrain expansion. It is all very well to have the Conservation Principle apply to the supposedly more ancient brain divisions: but how can it be relevant to later modifications?

Evolutionary conservation and development in the forebrain

In the forebrain the evolution of the thalamus has usually been supposed to have proceeded hand-in-hand with corticalisation, so that the mammalian 'neo-thalamus' appears only in primates (e.g. Diamond and Hall, 1969). In contrast, the status of the corpus striatum is thought to be very stable. Differences in the complexity and size of the forebrain limbic structures (for instance the hippocampus) are extremely obvious, and are certainly in the direction of progressive development of the limbic system along with the rest of the cerebral hemispheres, but there is still a tendency to regard the limbic system as the 'regulator of the reptilian core brain' (Isaacson, 1974) and therefore primitive.

I put the case in the previous section that, whatever new capacities might have accrued as a result of the development of the cerebral hemispheres, these capacities are not accompanied by under-employment of other brain regions. The higher cerebral attainments occur in conjunction with, and not instead of, other functions of the brain. Given this pointer, how can we characterise cerebral, or cortical activity? The obvious, usual, and possibly correct rule of thumb is that the cerebrum is the seat of mentation—of contemplation, inference, reason, volition, anticipation, foresight and cognition generally. There are many variations on this theme. The crux of any treatment of cognition in animals is of course the apparently qualitative difference between human faculties and those of all other beasts. This is frequently dealt with by adopting some form or other of the *human cortex hypothesis*: the assumption that the human cerebral cortex, or some portion of it, is so superior in its quality or quantity to all other mammalian cortices, that virtually no mentation or thought is conceivable in any brain except our own. A sophisticated Cartesian version of this hypothesis is the one put forward by Eccles, who proposes that a small and as-yet-unidentified population of neurons in the cortex of the human left cerebral hemisphere is in communication with a disembodied and reasoning soul. Many less explicitly Cartesian theories attribute unique properties to one or both of the human hemispheres. Less radical proposals identify either the cortex of primates, or the association cortex of all mammals, with cognitive functions. Anatomically the strongest case is that the mammalian neo-cortex in general differs so much from any other kind of vertebrate brain tissue that mammals should be set apart from all other classes. The difficulty in this case is that psychological tests of cognitive capacity do not clearly separate mammals from vertebrates lacking a neocortex, if the latter happen to be birds. Evidence from behavioural experiments, reviewed in later chapters, supports a rather more general anatomical suggestion, the *post-thalamic hypothesis*: post-thalamic forebrain circuits, whether cortex or not, mediate the more cognitive of psychological capacities. Since post-thalamic circuits are more pronounced in higher vertebrates, both birds and mammals, and take up an increasing proportion of tissue in large mammalian brains, the usual expectation of greater cognition in primates and other large-brained mammals is thus retained. But anatomical and physiological evidence now suggests that post-thalamic sensory projections are a small but significant reality in the forebrains of lower vertebrates. The post-thalamic hypothesis therefore implies, as an aspect of the Conservation Principle, that some degree of cognition is a vertebrate universal. At the moment this has an extremist and unlikely ring to it, but an examination of some of the relevant data may make it seem somewhat less outlandish.

Forebrain and cognition in non-mammals

It is appropriate to begin with Flourens (1794–1861), who may be regarded as one of the earliest supporters of the post-thalamic hypothesis. In a series of clear and simple experiments, Flourens surgically removed the cerebral hemispheres of frogs, pigeons and chickens, and made careful observations of their behaviour after they had recovered from the operation. In some cases he cut successive slices from the hemispheres, in separate operations. His conclusion was that in these animals the cerebral hemispheres are the organ of 'feeling, willing and perceiving'. A frog with no forebrain he described as having 'lost all volition', and a chicken with a similar deficit could be kept alive, and could stand up and move about, but had to be hand fed (Flourens, 1960). By experiments of this kind, Flourens established the traditional functional divisions in the vertebrate brain, identifying the brainstem as the centre for vital and visceral reflexes, the cerebellum as the organ of balance and movement, and the cerebrum as the seat of intelligence and will.

However, Flourens's contention that the cerebral hemispheres in amphibians and birds control volition and cognition has often been rejected. There is more than a suspicion that the rejection derived from phylogenetic dogmas, rather than contradictory evidence, but two empirical generalisations have seemed to go against Flourens. First, many have claimed that the removal of all or part of the forebrain has a negligible effect on the behaviour of non-mammals; and second, it is argued that such behavioural effects as do occur can be interpreted in terms of the role of the forebrain in olfaction (Aronson, 1970; Ebner, 1976). Underlying these points is the assumption that non-mammals do not possess anything approximating to volition or intelligence, and therefore have no need of an organ which subserves these faculties.

It is not too much of a caricature to present the following as the source of considerable confusion in theories of forebrain function:

The forebrain is of little importance in this species. Animals with extensive forebrain damage can be kept alive indefinitely and show locomotion in response to tactile stimulation. Several workers have shown that classically conditioned reflexes can be established in forebrain-ablated subjects, and therefore the forebrain is not necessary for associative learning in this species. The domination of social behaviour by olfaction in this species is illustrated by the fact that forebrain-ablated subjects show no signs of aggression, reproduction, or other instinctive social behaviours.

The disparity in this invented paragraph is between the retention of limited locomotor and sensory abilities and the capacity to perform at a satisfactory level on standard laboratory tests of conditioning, and the complete disruption of behaviour as observed from the standpoint of clinical or naturalistic assessments. The varying inferences which may be drawn from performance in laboratory tests of conditioning were discussed in Chapter 3: the main point is that evidence of 'associative learning' is obtainable at very low levels of nervous system organisation, if a simple enough experimental procedure is used. With more demanding tasks, deficits in the learning of both teleost fish (Farr and Savage, 1978) and sharks (Graebner *et al.*, 1978) follow forebrain damage. There is sufficient, though limited evidence to suggest that some forms of learning are impaired by lesions of the cerebral hemispheres in amphibians and reptiles (Aronson, 1970), and quite small localised lesions of the hemispheres of birds produce reliable deficits in certain kinds of acquired discriminations (Macphail, 1975; Stettner, 1974).

If volition is measured as the occurrence of spontaneous actions, then there has been widespread confirmation of Flourens's finding that damage to the forebrain reduces volition, since spontaneous action is lost after removal of the cerebral hemispheres in amphibians, reptiles and birds (Aronson, 1970; Ebner, 1976). A forebrain-ablated bird may 'fly' if thrown into the air, but unless some similarly drastic goad is imposed on it from without, it will just sit still with ruffled feathers. Forebrainless frogs may snap at passing insects, but without eating the target if it is caught, even though the swallowing reflexes are still intact. Coupled with the almost complete absence of social and reproductive behaviour, these findings ought to be sufficient to illustrate the biological necessity of a functioning forebrain for these species.

The alternative suggestion that the forebrain in lower vertebrates is used exclusively for olfaction is now no longer very plausible. Anatomical and physiological data show that in teleost fish (Scalia and Ebbesson, 1971), sharks (Ebbesson and Heimer, 1970), amphibians (Vesselkin *et al.*, 1971) and reptiles (Ebner, 1976) olfactory projections are more limited than had previously been assumed, and on the other hand visual and auditory projections to the telencephalon appear to be available. Even if the cerebral hemispheres were used only for olfaction, there would not be much point in it if there were not outputs to other brain divisions. But since there are specific groups of motor cells in the hemispheres that put out efferent fibres which reach midbrain and hindbrain motor systems, and which may go as far as the spinal cord in the case of sharks (Ebbesson and Northcutt, 1976) and also in birds (Adamo, 1967), there is support for the interpretation that the hemispheres of lower vertebrates are involved directly in the initiation of action.

We can say fairly firmly then that the forebrain in lower vertebrates ought not to be dismissed as merely an extension of the olfactory bulbs but may supply, albeit on a very limited scale, the same sort of facilities for behavioural control as are provided by the cerebral hemispheres of mammals. But what are these facilities? In a very general way, it may do no harm to retain the old characterisations of perception, volition and intelligence, not because these are entirely satisfactory, but because attempts to go beyond these intuitive categories have not yet added very much to the conclusion reached by Flourens:

Animals without cerebral lobes have therefore no perception, no judgement, no memory, no volition, because there is no volition when there is no judgement, no judgement when there is no memory, and no memory when there is no perception. (Flourens, 1824; see Boring, 1950, p. 77 ff.)

This is in accord with Flourens's belief in the unitary action of the hemispheres, but various distinctions between the functions of fore-brain components are possible. For some purposes, it is useful to draw lines between perceiving and knowing, localised in the sensory thalamus and the post-thalamic projections, feeling and wanting, supposedly the main business of the limbic system, and acting, mediated by both the internal striatum and the higher motor centres of the external striatum or cortex. Each of these could be analysed in greater detail into several substages, even on the basis of current knowledge, but if forebrain function can be given any overall defining features it is probably in terms implying values, perception, memory and action. One way of incorporating these things into a single package is to speak of goals. Nauta and Karten (1970), for instance, see vertebrate forebrain function as 'the perception of goals and goal priorities, as well as the patterning of behavioural strategies serving the pursuit of these goals'. To narrow down some of the ways in which the vertebrate forebrain may be a very sophisticated kind of goal-seeking device, we may consider intermodal abstraction, selective information pick-up memory, anticipation and choice of action. I will discuss perception and memory in some detail in later chapters but give now these briefer comments.

Crossmodal abstraction
Especially in higher vertebrates, the independence of an animal's actions from specific individual cues is often apparent—a goal can be identified by *either* taste, or smell, or visual pattern, or spatial position, or sound, or touch. Experiments with rats performed with the intention of finding the single crucial cue that controls behaviours have shown that, for instance, the identification of a female by a male can occur in any sense modality—males deprived successively of each sense continue to attempt to mate a female as long as any sense modality at all remains (Beach, 1942, 1947). Similarly, rats deprived of vision, smell, or muscular feeling will negotiate a maze successfully with whatever information is left to them (Honzik, 1936; Hunter, 1940). When a rat encounters a novel object it will be seen, sniffed, whiskered and listened to—subsequent identification may be based on any or some of these modalities.

Many aspects of sensory-motor co-ordination, such as the main-tainance of visual fixations during movements of the head and body, are definitely wired in to the midbrain and hindbrain; but the identi-fication of an object independently via information from alternative modalities may require forebrain intervention. Indeed, until recently it tended to be assumed that the transfer of sensory qualities between modalities, as when something that feels round to the touch is also expected to look round when it can be seen, was unique to man (Geschwind, 1965). Monkeys and apes have, however, also been persuaded to exhibit competence at such tasks (Weiskrantz, 1977) and specific cross-modal associations, as between the sight and sound of predators or between the smell and sight of prey, would be of great use to other animals. In mammals, the mechanism for making cross-modal abstractions or associations has been identified as cortex which is not closely tied to a particular sense—'association cortex'—and larger brains have a greater proportion of this available (Penfield, 1966), but behavioural data to show whether and how cross-modal abilities vary with brain size are almost wholly lacking.

Selective attention

Being relatively remote from the peripheral sensory pathways, forebrain structures are in a prime position to filter out relevant details from the 'blooming, buzzing confusion' of sensory bombardment from the environment. Overall amount of reaction to stimulation is probably governed by the reticular activating system (pp. 148) which specifically does not belong exclusively to the forebrain. But valuing, searching for and picking out certain details within a given sensory modality is widely supposed to be one of the higher aspects of perception and cognition (Neisser, 1967, 1976). There is no shortage of explicit theories as to how selective attention might work in animal behaviour (Sutherland and Mackintosh, 1971; Andrew, 1976), and there is a considerable body of experimental data available for review (see Chapter 7). Although selective attention is not necessarily only a forebrain function, it seems likely that switches of attention are very much a part of the interactions between the limbic system and the thalamic and post-thalamic stages of sensory pathways.

Memory and anticipation

It should not be difficult to find agreement that memory for perceptions and actions, and anticipations of future events, are more likely to be dealt with in the cerebral hemispheres than in the spinal cord. The difficulty is in measuring memory and anticipation in animals with any confidence. Given the possibility of verbal formulations, we have very little doubt about our own memories and future plans, and very elaborate (although perhaps very irrelevant—Neisser, 1976) experimental techniques can be employed for the analysis of human memory (Brown, 1976; Baddeley, 1976). But, although the more anthropomorphic among us may incorporate memories and expectancies into our theories of animal behaviour (Tolman, 1932, 1949), it is surprisingly difficult to produce convincing experimental proof that any animal has any memory or foresight at all. A major advance, of course, is the development of gesture language training for apes, which allows these animals to give fairly firm indications of what they want next, though they do not appear to have much interest in recounting what they did last. And some quite simple modifications to traditional laboratory tests seem to allow the measurement of a sort of short-term memory for stimuli in birds and mammals (Medin *et al.*, 1976; see Chapter 8 below).

Choice of action

Instead of manifesting robot-like certainty, many animals give a reasonable imitation of being individuals in whom 'nothing is so habitual as indecision'. Reluctance to plump for one action over another is apparent both in natural behaviour (where it deservedly receives much attention from ethologists under the heading of 'conflict': Hinde, 1970), and in laboratory tests, where the latency of response may sometimes provide a useful behavioural index, but at other times be a considerable annoyance to the experimenter. McFarland (1976) has emphasised that the ordering and timing of numerous incompatible but necessary activities is an everpresent problem of behavioural organisation and has suggested that some positive momentum for any action already under way is essential to prevent continuous dithering between possible responses. Categories of natural and artificial decisions range from the sequencing of foraging, resting, grooming and courting to the choice between a left and right turn in a laboratory maze. A fundamental conflict is that between caution and risk, with 'fight or flight' as an example. Fear of danger or of the unfamiliar is often finely balanced against curiosity and physical needs.

Forebrain involvement in these decisions is indicated by the results of lesion experiments, especially when limbic structures are damaged. A very broad description of 'lack of inhibition' can often be applied to mammals with limbic lesions, and there is some basis for more particular speculations. For example, the amydala appears weighted to promote both caution and aggression. Damage to this area in primates results in tameness, passivity and a marked lack of discretion in feeding and sexual activities (Kluver and Bucy, 1937). A not dissimilar syndrome is observed after equivalent forebrain lesions in Mallard ducks (Phillips, 1964). On the other hand septal area lesions produce a touchy, sensitive and occasionally vicious animal in the normally amenable laboratory rat (Grossman, 1967). It would be foolish to draw detailed conclusions from this, but given the anatomical relationships within the limbic system one is bound to entertain the idea that the amydala and the septal area act in tandem, and have opposing effects on mood.

Clearly, mood and emotion in animals should be closely related to social behaviour. Even the most rudimentary social behaviours, such as flocking and schooling, require subtle co-ordination of the individual with the group, and in teleost fish and reptiles, as well as birds and mammals, social interactions in general can be said to be notable casualties of damage to the telencephalon (Aronson, 1970; Phillips, 1964; Tarr, 1977; Rosvold *et al.*, 1954). The dimensions of social choice engendered by communal living have been put forward by some as the driving force behind the evolution of the intellectual powers of the cerebral hemispheres of primates (Humphrey, 1976), and while there are problems in this argument, it is useful to bear in mind that the regulation of social interactions may be one of the more demanding tasks performed by the vertebrate central nervous system.

In any context, a fundamental question about the initiation of action is the extent to which the selection of an act is governed by the anticipation of its consequences. This is another case where plausible theories are difficult to pin down in terms of behavioural predictions—how are we to distinguish between an animal governed by useful reflexes and one responding to intelligent expectations? Not very easily, but there is a certain face validity to the argument that being able to anticipate the consequences of actions should have considerable survival value. While it is evident that the anticipation of consequences has proved to be an elusive form of animal cognition, it is certainly something we should look for in the cerebral hemispheres rather than elsewhere.

Evolution of the vertebrate brain—conclusions

Evolution means nothing if not changes in the complexity of biological systems over time, which account for the development of the enormous variety of plant and animal species in terms of their genesis in earlier and simpler forms. The translation of the notion of increasing complexity into animal psychology has, however, produced many errors and misconceptions. Animal species that we may now observe, and whose brain function we wish to explain, do not fall directly into a scale of brain excellence. First, the family relationships between orders and classes of species is rather involved, with numerous branchings: deciding which species are more primitive, or more advanced, than others, is very difficult. Some kind of classification of animals cannot be avoided, of course, and the obvious starting point for theories of brain evolution is that the earliest vertebrates were fish, and were more like lampreys than they were like any other surviving species of fish. Amphibians derived from an intermediate stage of fish evolution, and reptiles derived from early amphibians. All these are 'lower vertebrates': birds and mammals, which arose from different branches of reptiles, are 'higher'. By and large, the brains of higher vertebrates are much bigger than the brains of lower vertebrates, and are therefore, perhaps, better.

Irrespective of size, all vertebrate brains can be described by reference to the same component parts, most simply in terms of the hindbrain, midbrain and forebrain divisions. There has been a tendency to say that the hindbrain is very old and primitive, the midbrain is intermediate, and the forebrain is modern and advanced. It is true that the forebrain of lower vertebrates is relatively small, and that in the larger brains of higher vertebrates, it is the forebrain which has expanded most in size. This is most obvious in man, whose brain is extremely large, and physically dominated by the cerebral hemispheres of the forebrain. It thus seems to follow that the forebrain is the most important part of the brain for intelligence, thought and cognition. However, I have supported the idea that the functions of the different divisions of the brain are more or less the same in all vertebrates, and that therefore we should expect these higher psychological functions to be present roughly in proportion to how well the forebrain seems to be developed. A fish, frog, or lizard does not have very much by way of cerebral hemispheres, and should therefore have very little cognition. But this little is a much more generous allowance than that given by other theories, which say that such forebrain as is present in non-mammals is not used for cognition, or attention, or learning, at all, but is only there to respond to smells, or to program primitive instincts. These other theories are probably wrong, because the cerebral hemispheres of lower vertebrates share several anatomical and physiological characteristics with the cerebral hemispheres of mammals, and the hemispheres of lower vertebrates should therefore have some psychological functions in common with the forebrain of mammals as well. What these functions are exactly is difficult to say, but emotions, plans for action, goals and values, and the selective direction of perception, seem to require the operation of the higher levels of the brain. Direct evidence about these functions, in terms of how animals normally behave, and what their capabilities are in psychological tests, is not easy to produce, but I shall go on to discuss these sorts of evidence in later chapters.

6 The life of vertebrates and the survival value of intelligence

It may be a comforting and valid truism that the brain integrates and controls behaviour, but clearly we ought to be able to say something rather less vague in the context of the theories of brain evolution which I discussed in the last chapter. The basic biological requirements are to survive and multiply. Animals, both vertebrate and invertebrate, are distinguished first of all by movement, and this entails in itself a special imperative for the organisation of behaviour. Functions such as nutrition, excretion, respiration and reproduction are universal, and criteria based on the psychological processes by which these are accomplished are as important as any others for distinguishing animals from plants, vertebrates from invertebrates, and classes of vertebrate from each other. Our concern is whether there are systematic differences between vertebrate species in the way in which the brain operates, and more specifically whether there are differences between vertebrates which can be related to the high degree of intelligence we would like to attribute to animals most like ourselves. Some account must be taken then of the natural behavioural categories of moving, feeding and breeding—is there anything in these which implies an evolutionary necessity for the development of more and more elaborate psychological processes? First we might examine what ought to be a simpler question—is there any logical progression to improvements in the purely physical apparatus of the body which underlies a progression of methods by which it is governed?

Bodily evolution and brain evolution

Analysis of gradual improvements in bodily efficiency—via the evolution of better limbs, better digestive systems and so forth—is as fraught with theoretical difficulties as the argument for successive improvements in mental abilities (Simpson, 1953; Rensch, 1959). However, it is often stated that there is a phylogenetic trend towards physical independence from the environment. There are certainly particular instances, at least, where an emancipation from the demands of exterior geography seems to have occurred: amphibians and reptiles 'conquered the land'; the higher vertebrates, being warm-blooded, are less dependent on external temperature and climate. The distinction between the higher, warm-blooded (homiothermous) classes and the lower, cold-blooded (poikilothermous) classes is especially interesting, as it provides a correlation between a major metabolic change and a possible psychological step. If there is a qualitative jump in psychological capacity from the cold-blooded reptiles to the warm-blooded birds and mammals, then an obvious hypothesis is that brain efficiency was in some way substantially improved by the faster energy metabolism of the latter. Since documenting the qualitative difference in brain efficiency in psychological terms is so difficult, such hypotheses are not easily tested.

However, a curious principle is illustrated by the shift to better internal temperature control, the principle being that the higher vertebrates can as readily be seen to have superior vegetative or mechanical properties as psychological or mental ones. The higher animals may have better 'reflex programming' as well as, or even instead of, improved cognitive abilities. Recent investigations of reptiles have shown that many species go to elaborate *behavioural* lengths to ensure a similar degree of control of internal temperature as that achieved much more easily by birds and mammals. Reptiles such as lizards and snakes may spend a considerable proportion of the day in basking in the sun, altering body posture, or else burrowing to cooler levels of sand, in order to maintain body temperature. I would argue that the brain functions required to govern these behaviours involve more, rather than less, cognition, compared to the methods of temperature control evolved later by mammals. These include shivering, raising and lowering of fur, sweating, and 'non-shivering thermogenesis' (internal metabolic production of heat): these are brainstem reflexes while the reptilian methods seem purposeful by comparison. The instrumentality of reptilian temperature-changing behaviours is attested to by large numbers of experiments in which external temperature is used as a goal to support learned artificial responses (Burghardt, 1977). Lizards will learn to press levers to turn on a gently warming sun-lamp, and in other experiments have learned to respond appropriately to a buzzer used as a conditioned warning signal for an imminent unpleasant degree of heat (by moving out of the way in time—Yori, 1978). Mammals, of course, are just as capable of performing simple learned acts to ensure a comfortable external temperature: the point is that they have superior peripheral and autonomic methods of temperature control as well. It should be noted that perspiration is as much an indication of human uniqueness as the more valued faculty of inspiration in intellectual and artistic endeavours: anthropoid apes do not have sweat glands like ours and thus their skin is more obviously non-human than their brains (Weiner, 1971).

Specialised bodily devices to serve the needs of particular species are of course innumerable, from worm-like appendages which lure prey to the mouths of fishes and reptiles to the retractable claws of the cat family. It is not obvious that such specialisations follow progressive phylogenetic rules, or that they can be related to changes in brain organisation, although in many cases psychological adaptations must exist to allow a species to take advantage of its external equipment. Two physical types of advance may be mentioned, however, which apply to vertebrate classes, and therefore might be considered to have phylogenetic implications, although in both cases the bodily mechanisms appear to simplify the demands placed on the brain.

First, the mechanical advantage of neutral buoyancy in water that is enjoyed by teleost fish has received many plaudits. Because of their possession of a 'swim bladder', relatively little body movement is needed to maintain orientation in modern teleosts. On the other hand, sharks and other elasmobranchs sink to the bottom if sufficient lift is not given by swimming movements. The hydrodynamics are pretty straight-forward, but the central nervous system of sharks has to be capable of continuous operation in the case of swimming movements. The movement co-ordinating structure—the cerebellum—is extremely prominent in sharks, but this may have more to do with skill than with continuous operation.

Second, consider the task of programming reproductive behaviours in the higher vertebrates. The supreme evolutionary achievement of mammals could be said to be the development of psychologically foolproof reproductive devices, while birds need very elaborate behavioural organisation and control to achieve the same ends. The mammalian placenta and breast require minimal motor skills or cognitive sophistication for their effective deployment, and in the majority of species relieve the male from any parental responsibilities whatsoever. But the birds, lacking these organs, need behavioural programs for nest-building, and highly sophisticated strategies for incubation, then feeding, of the young. These activities typically require the active co-operation of both parents. Without labouring this point, it should be clear that the mammalian pattern of reproduction involves physical, as much as mental, adaptations, and that, rather than necessitating superior mental abilities, it could be argued that the physical evolution of mammals is such that fewer demands are placed on the brain. One has to say, therefore, that if mammals are cognitively superior to other classes, it is as much because the brain is freed from the more immediate biological duties as because features such as warm-bloodedness and breast-feeding would be logically impossible in the absence of superior intelligence.

Clearly, speculation about biological needs for intelligence is extremely hazardous. On the one hand, natural selection via the survival of the fittest seems to imply that everything that has evolved has been absolutely necessary for survival, and that anything inessential will eventually be lost. On the other hand, the most potent condition for adaptive radiation, and thus evolutionary invention, is lack of competition, when interesting divergences may be rewarded rather than punished (Rensch, 1959). It is perhaps a better universal rule that whatever is sufficient, survives: and the criterion for sufficiency is always a complex combination of habitat, relations with other species, and specialisation. Various sufficient solutions to common problems of behavioural control may be achieved in different vertebrate (and invertebrate) classes; and therefore a statement of the problem does not imply a universal solution. Nevertheless, something may be gained from reviewing general categories of task which vertebrate life may present to the brain, and the most elementary categories are movement, food-finding, and reproduction.

Movement and knowledge of space

Seasonal migration, defence of home territory, and systematic search for food by foraging or predation are common vertebrate characteristics and may require navigational skills and spatial memory to varying degrees. One of the jobs of the vertebrate brain can therefore be said to be the detection and storage of geographical information and its use in directing locomotion. This is sometimes merely taken for granted, but a specific proposal is that mammalian brains at least are constructed so as to contain 'cognitive maps' of the outside world, which may be consulted as the need arises. The comparative question is whether fish, amphibians, reptiles and birds have less reliable or accurate maps, or some more primitive method of accomplishing adequate orientation in space. Migration and the defence of territory are not, of course, confined to mammals. Reproductive migrations occur in lampreys as well as, more dramatically, in eels and salmon and other teleost fish, and in some frogs, and reptiles such as the green turtle. This animal swims 3,000 miles to a small Pacific island to lay its eggs, the young then having to swim 3,000 miles back to the South American coast. It has been suggested that in this case the migration results from the geological movement of the breeding islands over many generations (Carr and Coleman, 1974).

If any class is especially prone to migrations, it is of course the birds, who possess the physical capacities for extensive travel, and have in some cases insectivorous feeding specialisations that make migration, if not hibernation (Aristotle's explanation for the absence of swallows in winter), mandatory. The study of bird migration has tended to be a specialised subject area, not always fully examined for its psychological implications (Dorst, 1962; Mathews, 1955; Schmidt-Koenig, 1975; Schmidt-Koenig and Keeton, 1978). The main point is that behavioural programming by the central nervous system must be very considerable for any systematic migrations, but that some processes, such as the following of chemical traces suspected to be used by salmon, may be regarded as less complex than the celestial navigation and the use of memorised visual landmarks which are among the methods used by bird species. It is also important to note that birds are sometimes very flexible when it comes to migration—probably much more flexible than lower vertebrates. Many European species not dependent on summer flying insects appear to make individual or group decisions about whether to make winter migrations, or stay put. The individual decisions may be determined primarily by climate, since a major source of variation is that the same species may have quite different patterns of migration, depending on its breeding locations: the robin, which sits through the winter months in England, abjures the more severe Northern European winters, and migrates from Scandinavia to North Africa, and to the Near East from Russia. This is not only a matter of inherited regional differences, since in Germany some robins migrate while others do not. In populations exhibiting this sort of 'partial migration', there is usually a tendency for females to travel more than males, and young birds sometimes migrate in populations where the older birds are more sedentary.

In any event it is clear that avian brain design must incorporate a substantial capacity for storing geographical information, and this may be done in a more sophisticated way than that employed by lower vertebrates. Little is known of what brain structures might be involved in the direction of bird migrations, although in mammals the hippocampus is supposed to be the major repository for spatial information (O'Keefe and Nadel, 1978). The spatial functions of the hippocampus have not been investigated in other vertebrates, and it does not appear to be anatomically prominent in birds (Pearson, 1972), but it is a reasonable guess to suppose that forebrain structures play some part in navigation and landmark recognition in birds, if not in all vertebrates.

As always, the problem is that species with what we would assume are vastly different cognitive capacities display superficially similar behavioural patterns—I strongly suspect that the psychological mechanisms used to direct long-distance travel in the robin are more complex than those utilised by the eel, but I cannot prove it. Long-distance migration is perhaps the most spectacular example of a behavioural ability which is difficult to tie down in terms of cognitive aspects of brain function, but spatial ability in general tends to share this feature. Movement in space is an everpresent part of animal life, and so one can hardly claim that advanced cognitive mechanisms are necessary to achieve it.

Another conventional subdivision of spatially-directed behaviour, apart from migration, is 'territoriality'. This has been widely canvassed as an underlying motivational factor in animal behaviour, but rather less attention has been given to the intellectual requirements of categorising geographical stimuli sufficiently well for them to acquire their emotional significance. Even for invertebrates, some sort of home base can be seen to direct movements, as in the systematic, if slow, perigrinations of limpets to and from the same spot (the consensus is that limpets and other molluscs follow their own mucus trails on their homeward journeys: Cook and Cook, 1975; Mackay and Underwood, 1977). The occurrence of such apparent spatial competence in organisms with little apparent means of neurological support should be a caution against reading too much into the spatial characteristics of movement in lower vertebrates, but territory defence in the stickleback, whose behaviour is relatively well known (Tinbergen, 1951; Van Iersel, 1953), goes beyond limpet-like routines, since it involves constructed, visually detected landmarks. The male stickleback digs out small holes around the circumference of its territory as a by-product of social interactions with its neighbours—border disputes include mutual digging activities. In a sense the most ubiquitous territorial landmark is other species-members—if a certain distance is always kept between individuals, this in itself establishes 'personal space'. Particular instinctive cues may simplify the task of species recognition: colour (redness for the robin and stickleback); vocalisation, pre-eminently in bird-song but also in frogs; and scent—many mammalian species have scent glands which are rubbed on the ground or on trees to provide cues of location and possession, or an economy is achieved by pressing other bodily functions into geographical service, as in the pungent urination of dogs and cats. One might ask, to what extent does the olfactory discrimination of the social significance of urine by dogs demand higher cognitive capacities than the use of colour by fish? Phylogenetic theory would imply that social interactions in fish are reflexive and mechanical, whereas mammalian behaviour must be more flexible and cognitive. This might be supportable by sufficiently detailed experimental comparisons, and we should expect to be able to show higher divisions of the brain are involved in the territorial behaviour of mammals. However, such sketchy data as exist suggest that it would be premature to assume that territorial behaviour in fish is under the control of the brainstem, whereas leg-cocking in dogs is cortical: it has been found both that subcortical mechanisms are involved in the socio-sexual behaviour of dogs and that forebrain centres regulate instinctive behaviour in fish (Hart, 1974; Aronson, 1970).

It is worth putting in another word at this point about the bird/mammal distinction. Birds display a very noticeable collection of complex species-specific behaviours, and thus have often been regarded as being dominated by fixed and stereotyped instincts, 'with little of the learning capacity which in mammals is associated with the development of the expanded cerebral cortex' (Romer, 1949, p. 585). I shall discuss later (Chapters 7 and 8) the performance of birds on laboratory tests of learning, but we can note here the considerable flexibility of many avian species in selection of breeding habitat—in particular their use of the human urban environment. The resemblance of buildings to cliffs is probably responsible for the large urban populations of pigeons and house-martins, but even so, the shift from cliffs to cities implies a certain range within any stereotopy adapted originally to a particular type of territory. The rapidity of the transition of a species to a man-made adaptive zone is illustrated by the herring gull, whose 'fixed action patterns' of social behaviour were documented by Tinbergen (1953) on sand dunes in Holland, but which has been seen in growing numbers as a roof-top nester in coastal towns in Britain (and in Central London) during the last few years. Gulls nest on cliffs, as well as on dunes, and so could be said to be capitalising on natural instincts; but the capability to nest and establish family and flock social organisation on either dunes, cliffs, or town buildings, suggests some rather more subtle adjustments to ecological opportunities than would be provided by a very rigid set of fixed behavioural patterns.

A distinction needs to be made, of course, between adjustments to new environments by genetic change through selection, which may occur in the simplest of organisms (as in the emergence of drug-resistant strains of bacteria) and the behavioural variations possible within a genetically homogeneous population. One interpretation of the advantages of a larger or better central nervous system is that the same brain can cope with a wider range of environments—*either* by containing a larger set of instinctive behaviours, *or* by providing the means for learning from experience.

Locomotor and manipulative skills

Given that movement in space occurs at all, a further variable is simply mode of locomotion. The biologically most primitive way of getting about for vertebrates is the lamprey-like undulation of a long body, used by many invertebrates, and returned to successfully by eels and snakes. The emergence of paired fins, and then paired limbs, has been thought to require more sophisticated muscular control, but the spinal cord and hindbrain alone can accomplish a satisfactory degree of limb co-ordination: birds whose forebrains have been removed can manage flight, as well as bi-pedal walking (though not the trickier manoeuvres of take-off and landing). It might be suspected that the primate facility for tree-climbing and two-legged running should be associated with outstanding brain power, but both activities are performed with considerable success by lizards.

The prominence of the cerebellum in the delicate programming of postural balance and rapid movements has already been alluded to, and is usually confirmed by at least temporary motor incapacities following cerebellar lesions. Considerable recovery of ability often follows initial losses due to cerebellar lesions, however, even in the case of climbing by racoons or primates (Wirth and O'Leary, 1974). A strong anatomical case can still be made for the encephalisation of motor control in mammals, because of the presence of the pyramidal tract direct from the motor cortex to the spinal cord. This is not an absolutely clear mammalian prerogative since analogous, if less substantial, connections have turned up in birds and reptiles, and even sharks (Ebner, 1976; Ebbesson and Northcutt, 1976). It has always been obvious that shark, teleost, reptile, bird and mammalian brains can all be used for fast swimming, just as analogous streamlining of the body has evolved in the relevant species, but the acrobatics of dolphins and seals may manifest an additional dimension of muscular control superimposed on the basic necessities by large mammalian brains.

It is possible that higher vertebrates in general are capable of more complex motor control than lower, and have more varied methods of locomotion available within a single species. One could cite in support of this the multiple gaits of horses, or the walking, running, climbing and swimming of man, and the rat. But to be fair, one would also have to consider the multimodal locomotion of the duck, which can swim, dive, walk and fly, and the frog, which can both jump and swim. Reptiles, though often appearing ungainly, can show a good turn of speed when necessary. Crocodilians and turtles are elegant and skilled underwater, if clumsy on land, and the change of gear from slow four-legged walking to fast two-legged running in frilled lizards may be an example of reasonably complex reptilian locomotion. Fish might be thought limited by their watery environment, but some species (e.g. lung-fish and mud-skippers) have useful if rudimentary land-going abilities. Lampreys as well as salmon leap into the air in the course of their up-river migrations, and the flying fish can traverse up to 400 metres in a single airborne glide. Even casual observation of a domestic goldfish is sufficient to reveal an extraordinary number of combinations of fin and tail movements. It is thus difficult to be convinced that complexity of locomotion as such was the driving force behind brain evolution.

Manipulation may be a special category of muscular co-ordination. Primate handgrips of varying degrees of precision have been the subject of detailed study (Napier, 1960) and the use of the forelimbs for manipulation rather than locomotion has been given considerable emphasis in theories of the origin of human intelligence. In general higher vertebrates use all four limbs for locomotion but both primates and rodents (and dinosaurs and kangaroos) use the forelimbs also for pushing, holding or digging. As rodents are usually thought of as a rather lowly order of mammals, the fact that they possess manipulatory skills provides another perturbation on the phylogenetic scale. Beavers rival birds in instinctive architectural abilities and young mice and rats can be surprisingly adept at ape-like brachiation, when they swing from the roof bars of cages, or are trained to climb wires. Some aspects of manipulation in mammals are undoubtedly controlled by the pyramidal tract from the cerebral motor cortex. Heffner and Masterton (1975) rated 69 species of mammal for 'digital dexterity' and found a correspondence between this rating and the anatomical intimacy of pyramidal fibre terminations with spinal motor neurons, although there was no correlation with the thickness of the tract. Either the lack of forelimbs or the absence of the pyramidal tract may preclude manual dexterity, but the emphasis on hands may be slightly misleading, since it disguises the fact that the behavioural purposes served by the forelimbs are in some vertebrates equally well administered by the nose, mouth, trunk or bill. Among mammals, the trunk of the elephant and the nose of the dolphin may be exceptional, but many herbivores use snout, horns or lips in a manipulatory fashion (the llama has independently mobile separate halves of the upper lip and, in each cerebral hemisphere large independent somato-sensory projections for the ipsi- and contra-lateral halves: Welker *et al.*, 1976).

In birds the bill is a manipulatory device, and an extremely effective one for use in nest-building, food carrying, preening, digging and tool-handling (in the Galapagos finch/woodpecker). Two examples may be given to illustrate interesting analogies between bill-use and hand-use. The European oystercatcher uses its bill to open up shell fish—a task requiring some skill in humans equipped with a hand and a knife. The unexpected aspect of this is that it is a learned rather than inborn skill in the oystercatcher, with the magnitude of the educational problem indicated by the need for several months of supervision and supplementary feeding of the young by the parents, by the variation in the opening techniques finally mastered, and, most emphatically, by the high mortality rate among slow learners (Norton-Griffiths, 1969). Given the high mortality rate in the young who never learn the shell-opening skill, one would have thought that oystercatchers should be in the throes of developing a stereotyped and species-specific fixed-action-pattern for this purpose, but the advantages of trial-and-error learning over fixed instincts may be manifested in the fact that the oystercatchers studied by Norton-Griffiths were feeding on mussels, not oysters: trial-and-error allows more ecological flexibility. An apparently unique *lack* of flexibility in bill-use occurs in the New Zealand wryneck, whose beak curves strongly to the right. This kind of built-in 'handedness' is extremely rare in vertebrates, and appears to be associated with the manipulation of pebbles: the wryneck inserts its bill under the left side of pebbles and turns them over to the right.

Many species of fish manipulate stones or vegetation, either in the course of foraging, or more elaborately in the construction of nests. The mouth in these species is the manipulatory organ—fish mouths are obviously not the equivalent of bird bills in this respect but some fish, including the much-studied stickleback, build quite respectable nests. Modern reptiles do not appear to utilise manipulative skills in any sense of the term, and heaps of vegetation (cobras) and holes in sand (turtles) represent the extremes of reptile nest-building. But numerous extinct reptiles including many dinosaurs and many species implicated in mammalian evolution (therapsids) are assumed to have walked on their hind legs, and to have had forelimbs specialised for manipulative clawing. Control of forelimb movements is no doubt more skilled and expert in mammals such as rodents and primates (and in carnivores like bears and racoons) than it was in extinct reptiles. But detailed control of head movements, involving the cranial nerves, is also an example of sophisticated motor programming, especially in birds.

Feeding strategies

Type of feeding is one of the major candidates for the determination of behaviours by aspects of ecology, as opposed to phylogenetic inheritance. The broadest distinction can be made between carnivorous and herbivorous habits, but there are several useful sub-categories within each of these, and a further line to be drawn between specialised and omnivorous species. The first point is that most types of feeding occur within each extant vertebrate class, with the possible exception of modern amphibians (the initial amphibian radiation having become largely extinct). Quite clearly different problems of behavioural control are presented by reliance on an unconcentrated but stationary diet of grass or leaves on the one hand, and a specialisation in catching highly nutritious but alert and mobile prey, on the other. But both types of problem have been effectively solved in fish, reptiles, birds and mammals. All these classes include foragers and browsers, and predators of various kinds. A meaty diet will not involve the excitements of the chase if it is acquired by scavenging on already dead prey or on shellfish. But capture by stalking, chasing or ambush is sometimes supposed to require the development of cunning or intelligence. A standard explanation for the explosion of human intelligence beyond the already high standards of the primate order is that our ancestors underwent an ecological transition from a fruit-eating arboreal primate, via a foraging terrestrial ape, to a co-operative hunting hominid (Jolly, 1972; Pilbeam, 1972).

Intelligent and co-operative pack hunting is found in wolves and other canids, but pack hunting as such works successfully in dogfish and the teleost barracuda (although claims of intelligent herding or 'nursing' of prey by sharks and barracuda should perhaps be treated sceptically). It is curious that although birds are often intensely social and communicative, there do not appear to be any co-operative hunting species, although there is often group activity for defence against predators (mobbing) and some hawks and falcons, as well as vultures, have very gregarious habits. Solitary ambush and stalking may be associated with cunning or foresight when these techniques are utilised by mammals, but individual hunters such as the pike or eagle (or any number of lower vertebrate or invertebrate predators) may occupy a similar ecological niche without the benefits of mammalian cognition. The main assumption is that mammalian predators depend more on learning, and the practising of their skills, especially through play, while those in other classes rely on fixed instincts of attack. However, many attack patterns are definitely inborn in mammalian carnivores, since appropriate behaviours can be elicited by the electrical stimulation of the brains of naive animals (Roberts and Berquist, 1968) and species-specific actions such as neck-biting can appear fully-formed without practice, as has been observed in the pole-cat (Ewer, 1973). No doubt parental tutelage, and practice, refines these skills.

Clearly intelligence is not a necessary condition for ecological status as a predator, and thus if intelligence of some kind is associated with mammalian hunting practices, it is the phylogenetic mammalian characteristic, rather than the ecological role, which is important. Even if it were possible to show that it was the requirements of hunting which led to the development of cunning and foresight in mammalian carnivores, this would still leave the problem of how to account for the brains of mammalian herbivores. Consumption of vegetation often sustains large bodies, and as a consequence some mammalian herbivores, such as the elephant and elk, have enormous and elaborately convoluted brains. In my view it is unnecessary to try and identify ecological needs served by these large brains, since I believe that their size and organisation are determined mainly by phylogenetic factors—any large mammal will have one. However, it has been suggested that brain power in mammalian herbivores can be put to the uses of (a) defence against predators (Jerison, 1973); (b) locating and remembering sources of food; and (c) maintaining social organisations which facilitate (a) and (b).

There are special difficulties in accounting for why primates should require more brain power than other orders of mammals, and in assigning the human-like brains of the great apes ecological causes. Because of its large size the gorilla suffers from little predation and the adult orang-utang prefers solitude to elaborate social interactions. Although the gorilla forms 'extended family' social groups, interactions within these groups are not noticeably more complex than those found in lizards, chickens or rodents. Gorillas also appear to be less playful and curious than their smaller relatives, the chimpanzees, their daily life being a repetitive round of eating, digesting and heedlessly defecating enormous quantities of vegetable matter (Schaller, 1963). Several observers have concluded that the gorilla is a stupid animal, but training with gestural sign-language suggests that it has abilities equivalent to those of the more obviously alert chimpanzee (Patterson, 1978) and the development of cognitive capacities during the first 18 months of life is much the same in gorilla and human infants (Redshaw, 1978). Although we might expect that such measured intelligence should exist because of its survival value to the species, the lifestyle of the gorilla suggests a contrary hypothesis—that intelligence as assessed by these methods is purely incidental to the ecological niche occupied by the species.

The problem of apparently useless organs is not unfamiliar in evolutionary theory—blind species may retain eyes, and appendages such as the antlers of deer may reach a size out of all proportion to their superficial usefulness. It often has to be assumed that vestigial organs or other anatomical features are retained only because they are genetically linked to other more useful structures (Simpson, 1953), and Darwin supposed that some anomalies, such as the webbed feet of non-aquatic geese, were evolutionary accidents, supporting the haphazard element in natural selection. Darwin's alternative explanation for anatomy or behaviour that lacked conspicuous survival value was that it arises from sexual selection, which may be at odds with more mundane utility. The antlers of deer are selected for during male competition for females (predators being kicked rather than butted). Sexual benefit may outweigh other biological costs, or species may be sufficiently well adapted to carry otherwise unnecessary secondary sexual apparatus. Conceivably, therefore, some form of sexual selection acts on primate intelligence. In the case of the gorilla, at least, the social structure revolves around a dominant male, who has first call on both food and sexual partners (Schaller, 1963). However sexual activity itself is extremely perfunctory and infrequent in gorillas, and so sexual competition between males is not a very obvious factor.

To return to feeding strategies, the gorilla is an example of a species with quite a varied diet, even though it only eats plants. In general it is assumed that omnivorous species need to be more flexible in their food selection, and more amenable to trial-and-error learning, than specialised feeders. As many as 100 different plant species may be eaten by the gorilla (Schaller, 1963) and perceptual identification of these, together with knowledge of their location and the season when they are available, and the skills involved in their collection (such as tree-climbing, bark stripping and digging), could be put forward as the tasks to which gorilla intelligence is directed. Classification of plant species has sometimes been said by anthropologists to be an early and important form of human cognition (Lévi-Strauss, 1962) and it might not be too far-fetched to consider gorilla communities as utilising a similar kind of knowledge, in a non-verbal form. Among birds, the crow family have large brains for their size, and typically consume a wide range of edible materials. Jackdaws for instance may take eggs or young from other birds' nests, pick insects from the backs of sheep, and forage for fruit, worms, shoots and grain, and anything else that is going. Such habits are sometimes said to be indicative of advanced phylogenetic status. But many birds have similarly catholic tastes, especially those commensal with man such as sparrows, pigeons and seagulls. There are plenty of omnivorous or scavenging fish, and modern amphibians have been characterised as 'not particular in choice of diet' (Young, 1962).

At one end of any dimension based on diet selection one would have to put filter-feeding Baleen whales, possessors of the largest known brains, whose feeding strategy of swimming with an open mouth through seas rich in small invertebrates seems almost equivalent to breathing food, and would hardly be put at the top of a list of activities requiring high brain power. Similarly, living in trees and eating whatever leaves and fruit come to hand seems an undemanding, even idyllic, existence. But this is a rough description of the ecological niche of South American monkeys, and a fairly accurate account of the feeding habits of one such species, the Howler monkey, which is the fortunate beneficiary of a digestive system which can cope with mature leaves and unripe fruit, as well as more palatable ripe and juicy fruit and tender shoots and buds. Typically tree-living primates *drop* half their food to the ground, and eat only a small fraction of what is readily available—they are not 'food-limited' (Jolly, 1972). This relationship to the food supply does not suggest a selection pressure to evolve intelligence in order to gather food more efficiently. If anything it prompts the speculation that the *lack* of selection pressure allowed the emergence of primate intelligence as a luxury not available to species more hard-pressed (Kummer and Goodall, 1985). Cogitation may, like other civilised pursuits, be a product of surplus, leisure and excess, and not a consequence of struggle, deprivation and need.

In any event, the idea that diet determines destiny, in terms of brain evolution, is difficult to sustain except by hand-picked examples. The most common example has it that man shares intelligence with primates because of arboreal fruit-eating, and with wolves because of co-operative game hunting. But there is little systematic evidence that fruit-eating, or hunting, is associated with intelligence in other instances. Even the more general idea that flexibility in diet selection is somehow correlated with brain development runs into difficulties in accounting for apparently intelligent specialists (aquatic mammalian fish-eaters) and comparatively dull all-rounders (such as the rat).

Reproduction and other social interactions

Reproduction, and genetic reduplication, must be the most funda-mental of all biological imperatives. The reproductive success of a species, more than anything else, is of immediate importance for its survival and adaptive evolution. It is therefore worth asking whether reproductive strategies have any bearing on brain evolution. The aspect of reproduction which at first sight has phylogenetic implications is parental care, since this is prominent in mammals and birds but relatively rare in lower vertebrates. Except in very unusual cases, fertilisation, usually via copulation, is indispensable for all vertebrates, but courtship and mating take various forms, ranging from completely indiscriminate mating with external fertilisation in many teleost fish, to elaborate courtship with permanent pairing of the couple, which is common in birds and occurs occasionally in mammals. It should come as no surprise that there is no clear correlation between reproductive strategy and phylogenetic status.

Cyclostomes

The sexual behaviour of lampreys is relatively well known, and certainly involves minimal post-natal parental duties, since the two adults invariably die after mating (Breder and Rosen, 1966). Marine lampreys migrate up rivers, in some species several hundred miles, to mate. Although these fish represent the most primitive vertebrates, there is an interesting complication in their mating, since they construct, sometimes communally, circular egg-laying sites. The lampreys make use of their jawless sucking mouths to remove quite large stones from the circular area, and place them round the circumference to form a low parapet. If enough stones are available, some are also used to form a barrier upstream from the circle. A single pair or, more often, several pairs, share in the construction of this spawning site: recognition of species and sexual identity is an obvious perceptual requirement, and is probably aided in many species of lamprey by colour cues, since variegated colouring appears during the reproductive season. The motor co-ordination needed for copulatory spawning is simplified by the male being able to attach its mouth to the female's head. Excited, violent and repeated copulation, which produces synchronised ejaculations of eggs and sperm, begins on completion of the nest construction, and extends to permutations of couplings when several pairs have made the same site. These ritual acts of the most primitive vertebrates, taking place within a laboriously constructed circle of standing stones, are strangely reminiscent of some ideas about human Mesolithic relics such as Stonehenge. Without succumbing to biological mysticism, it is possible to point out that migration, colour vision and social co-operation to produce constructed environments appear at the lowest phylogenetic vertebrate stage that we can now observe. This should emphasise that we must look for subtle changes in the cognitive control available to other species, and that a behaviourist principle of examining only the most superficial characteristics of actions is likely to be of little use in the comparative study of brain evolution.

Sharks

The reproductive biology of sharks poses another problem for theories of progression in phylogenesis, since it is evident from the existence of male intromittive organs that fossil sharks relied on internal fertilisation, and modern sharks either lay skinned, reptile-like eggs or, in other species, give birth to live young. In some of these the foetal young are nourished by a mammal-like placental organ. The psychological implications of this 'advanced' biology are not clear, since there is no reason why reproductive sophistication should not be accompanied by primitive behavioural reflexes. It is maintained that no parental behaviour occurs in sharks, but this is based on lack of observations of the newborn, rather than positive identification of parental apathy (Breder and Rosen, 1966). If we were to use the argument popularised by Dawkins (1976b; Hamilton, 1964) we would expect that the investment of the genes in internal fertilisation and maternal nourishment during gestation should be followed by protective parental behaviour to guarantee reproductive dividends. For instance, the basking shark, a large filter-feeder, endures a pregnancy of two years to produce a single offspring. It would seem foolishly parsimonious not to program some maternal interest in the post-natal welfare of the infant. In fact it is suggested that female sharks generally do indeed seek out favourably shallow waters in which to give birth, but it would not be surprising if some social interaction between mother and infant were eventually to be discovered.

Reptiles

This last guess is nourished by the fallibility of the traditional belief in the incapacity of reptiles for parental responsibilities. It is true that in the case of the vast majority of modern reptile species biologists pay far more attention to the reptilian amniote eggs (as the precursor of the reproductive methods of higher vertebrates) than do the reptile parents. Nevertheless, forms of incubation of the eggs are found in some species of the squamata (lizards and snakes) and elaborate parental care occurs, it is now believed, in most crocodilians. The Nile crocodile mother guards with a high degree of maternal intensity the mud nest in which the eggs have been laid, responds to vocalisations from the young to assist emergence from the eggs, and then ensures their safe transition to water by carrying them to it in her mouth (Pooley, 1977). One cannot claim, then, that the reptile brain as such is incapable of sustaining maternal instincts.

Teleost fish and amphibians

Reproductive habits in these lower vertebrates are marked by incredible diversity, and it is certainly not possible that they suffer from behavioural simplicity. Extensive accounts are available (Breder and Rosen, 1966; Noble, 1931) but we may note the well-documented responsibilities of the male stickleback for nest-building, egg-fanning, and nest-protection, and the organised vocal competitiveness of many anurans (frogs and toads) during courtship. In non-mammals the female is not anatomically predestined to provide post-natal care for the young, and most conceivable possibilities of single-parent and two-parent involvement with eggs and young can be found in some or other teleost or amphibian species. Mouthbreeding, and production of milk-like secretions by both parents are examples from teleosts, and in amphibians, though typically neo-natal survival is guaranteed by large numbers of free-swimming larvae, there are salamanders which are viviparous, a tree-frog in which eggs develop in a womb-like sac under the skin of the mother's back, and a tongueless aquatic South American toad (*Pipa*) in which the young grow in individual pits in the mother's back, emerging only when metamorphosis is complete. In other such 'marsupial' species of toad the bearing of the young, either on the back or, less conveniently, in the mouth, may be the prerogative of the father; similarly in the European 'midwife' toad (under suspicion of non-Darwinian tendencies for other reasons) it is the male which carries the eggs wrapped around its legs for safe-keeping.

Birds

The extremely taxing parental duties of most birds are attributable perhaps to the liabilities of warm-bloodedness in the absence of mammalian organs for the internal and external nutrition of the young. Behaviourally a binary division has been made between altricial (or nidiculous) avian species, in which the relatively helpless young are fed in the nest for protracted periods, and those which are precocial (or nidifugous), where more mobile young can leave the nest immediately after hatching to search for their own food. In these latter, the connection between parent and young is not broken after hatching: considerable interest has been attracted to the apparently haphazard process by which the young form social attachments to (usually) the female parent during the first day or so of their post-hatching life. The interest is in the importance of individual experiences: the young will 'imprint' on almost any suitably sized, but preferably moving object which is presented to them during the 'critical period' (Sluckin, 1964; Hinde, 1970). In other words, there is little in the young by way of an instinctual perceptual image of the species parent, and it is left largely to chance that the thing they imprint upon will have appropriate social consequences—but of course in the absence of human intervention this is usually a fairly safe bet.

Partial features of the natural parent may assist the imprinting process, especially in ducks, where the 'following response', which is the initial behaviour required, is elicited more readily if a waddling movement and a regular quack-like sound accompany the artificial stimulus-object used in imprinting experiments (Ramsay and Hess, 1954; Hess, 1959). However, the crucial psychological mechanism appears to be the formation of a memory of whatever is responded to first during the first few hours when movement is possible after hatching, and this allows for unnatural stimuli to be substituted for the species parent (notably the figure of the ethologist Konrad Lorenz, who first drew attention to the phenomenon).

In the case of nest-rearing species, it is the natural instinctual cues which elicit the responses given by the infants to the parents which are given pride of place. The classic ethological studies of nestling herring gulls and thrushes by Tinbergen showed that certain visual cues in the profile of the adult's head are crucial 'trigger features' which elicit the begging responses of the young. These in turn stimulate the adults to place food into the mouths of the most insistent nestlings, if necessary after first regurgitating it. In the herring gull, the trigger features which attract the young's response of pecking at the parent's bill include the redness and contrast of a small patch on the bill, to which pecking is directed. There are certain variations in such stimulus factors among even closely related species of gull (Weidmann, 1961) but begging and parental feeding show some constancies in form over many groups of altricial birds, which is sufficient to ensure cuckoos a choice of foster-parents. Transfer of affectionate and caring emotions across species is of course not unknown in mammals and in primates: Tinbergen has gone as far as to suggest that there are aspects of the appearance of the young which have very general effects in calling forth appropriate emotions in adults—in mammals he supposes that smallness of the body and roundness of the head serve as 'releasing stimuli' of this kind.

The finding that there appear to exist instinctively coded stimulus-response connections in young birds was used by Tinbergen (1951) to support his concept of the 'Innate Releasing Mechanism': this idea is simply that particular vertebrate species will respond in fixed ways to only certain innately determined stimuli. The impression that only rigid inbuilt reflexes are available to the species studied is, however, false. A careful reading of Tinbergen's methods reveals evidence of the normal plasticity and change in 'species-specific' behaviours due to individual experience which is not always made use of in ethological theorising. For instance, Tinbergen and Kuenen (1957) reported that they used great caution in feeding young thrushes during tests of their reactions to artificial stimuli, since if a very natural stimulus was presented without subsequent feeding the infants very quickly refused to respond to it as they should, whereas if by chance a 'wrong' stimulus was given just before feeding, the fledglings tended to treat the wrong stimulus thereafter as a natural releaser. There is no reason to doubt that nestlings come equipped with appropriate instinctive preferences, but the readiness of nestlings to learn at least as flexibly as precocial young in reaction to novel experiences is often ignored (Eibl-Eibesfeldt, 1970). Conversely, precocial young have need of instinctual preferences and fixed action patterns if they are to be successful in their first foragings for food. Mallard ducklings have been shown to have a preference for pecking at green, rather than at other hues, which is rather unexpected, since they initially eat dark invertebrates and not green vegetation; but it is conceivable that reactions towards greenness assist in directing their behaviour to where these may be found (Oppenheim, 1968).

In general, the social interactions of parents and young suggest that the brains of birds must encode a considerable amount of innate information in terms of both releasing stimuli and the organisation of instinctive fixed-action patterns. However, these brains must also be well adapted to the behaviour-controlling method of learning from experience. Apart from the refinement of motor skills, the main category of experiential learning involves perceptual recognition of known objects. The imprinting process in precocials such as young geese or chickens is a clear example of this, but it is likely that young nestlings often learn to recognise their own parents. In herring gulls the young learn to recognise the individual vocalisations of their own parents (Tinbergen, 1953; this also occurs in terns—Stevenson *et al.*, 1970).

The use of vocalisation in birds for species and individual recognition and for social communication is of course a rich and highly specialised area of study (Thorpe, 1961), and is not exclusively related to reproduction, but I would like to draw on it here for implications concerning the capacities of bird brains. First, bird vocalisation clearly requires elaborate control of the vocal organs, and there must be similarly complex auditory analyses for the recognition of distant songs and chirps, and for the monitoring of self-produced output. As we have seen, there is evidence that in some species at least the two halves of the brain are unequally involved in the control of vocalisation (Nottebohm, 1977), a design characteristic which is also typical of the human brain. A further question is whether the efficiency of bird vocalisation is determined by in-built genetic specification, or whether it is educable by individual experience alone—this also has some interest in the context of debate about the neurological underpinnings of the complexities of human language (Lenneberg, 1967). A subtle balance of advantages between reliable and rigid pre-wiring of behavioural outcomes on the one hand, and the variable but plastic results of determination by experiential factors on the other, is illustrated by the varying weights attached to these two influences on vocalisation in different bird species. At one extreme young birds completely isolated from all external sounds, from birth, are able to produce extremely complex songs specific to their species, given time for maturation and individual practice (for example, the song sparrow; Mulligan, 1966). More commonly, a rudimentary version of natural songs (or a complete vocal repertoire in species with only a crude range of sounds) may be possible in individual birds deprived of the opportunity for vocal learning. Sound production of this kind may occur even when individuals are isolated from the sound of their own voice, by neo-natal deafening (deafened juncos and white-crowned sparrows produce rudimentary songs—Konishi, 1963, 1965; domestic chickens and ring-doves show a relatively complete range of species-specific vocalisations after neo-natal deafening—Konishi and Nottebohm, 1969). In some species, young reared in groups but isolated from adults can develop normal species-specific songs by singing at each other, even though individuals reared alone produce abnormal and idiosyncratic sounds (white-crowned sparrows—Marler, 1970). In all these cases the species involved are obviously relying to a large degree on genetic inheritance of detailed motor patterns, or of 'auditory templates' as the goals for vocal practice (Marler, 1970). This is probably more a matter of executive brain routines than peripheral constraints in the sound-producing apparatus, since the structure of the distinctive avian sound-producing device, the syrinx, changes very little from species to species.

At the other extreme, imitating species such as parrots and mynah birds quite clearly are capable of producing sounds that are not genetically programmed. It now seems likely that these species are not so unusual in their capacity for auditory imitation as they are in their readiness to use human sounds as their model. Many other species pick up sounds as they go along, but imitate conspecifics, which makes the imitation very much less obvious to the human observer (Marler, 1970; Waser and Marler, 1977). The functions of vocalisation include isolation of local groups within a particular species as well as species recognition and the identification of individuals: the function of imitation is presumably partly to promote the learning of local or familial dialects. Various aspects of the auditory pattern may be used for different purposes: the decision 'that is not my species' must be a lot easier than 'this is an unfamiliar member of my tribe of my species'. For species recognition, genetically built-in determinants of vocal production and auditory perception is a possibility and very rapid learning of slight individual variations may be imposed on this. The speed with which recognition of individual parents can be acquired is illustrated by the 'His Master's Voice' experiments performed by Stevenson *et al.* (1970) on young terns: these responded immediately to tape-recordings of their own parents (by cheeping a greeting, and walking towards the loudspeaker) but ignored other tern calls, even those recorded from other adult members of their own colony.

Vocal recognition among the adults of some species may be more arduously acquired. There is an East African shrike in which

> two members of a pair learn to duet with one another and, while adopting certain phrases and rhythms which are

characteristic of the locality, work out between themselves duets which are sufficiently individual to enable the bird to distinguish and keep contact with its mate by singing duets with it (or, to be more exact, singing antiphonally with it) in the dense vegetation in which they usually live. (Thorpe, 1974, p. 116: see Thorpe, 1966, 1972)

This involves a clear element of song composition in addition to imitation. However, both the composition and the imitation are constrained within a range peculiar to the species. In general, if imitation in any species is to be useful, it is important for the young to imitate the right thing. Marler (1970) refers to the inherited 'auditory template', which may not be sufficient to generate complete song in isolated birds, but enables young in the natural environment to single out the noises produced by their own species instead of trying to imitate the entire dawn chorus. The experimental basis for this concept is that isolated white-crowned sparrows learned by imitation if they were played tape-recordings of adult song of their own species, but paid little attention to the songs of other species. The force of the concept is therefore attentuated by the fact that the experiments were performed on nestlings which had had several days of natural existence—and feeding by their natural parents—before they were removed from the nest and artificially reared (Marler, 1970). Bearing in mind the extreme rapidity of visual imprinting in ducks and geese, and of visual learning in nestling thrushes (Tinbergen and Kuenen, 1957) and that terns appear to recognise the individual voice of their parents when only four days old (Stevenson *et al.*, 1970), early experience in the nest could be at least partly responsible for the later recognition of species-specific song in white-crowned sparrows.

However, it is a safe generalisation that innate factors at least partly determine the form of song in most species; but that it is also very common for young birds to imitate the vocalisations of individuals with whom they have social interactions. This may in some degree be due to mere propinquity, as is imprinting in parent-following species, but selective imitation is the norm. Nicolai (1959) found that a male bullfinch fostered by canaries was prepared to imitate canary phrases, but this did not prevent him from successfully courting a female of his own species, which allowed the observation that the canary phrases were transmitted secondhand to the next generation. Human whistled tunes, remote from any natural template, were also transmitted through bullfinch generations in this way. Other finches selectively imitate whatever paternal model is provided (Immelman, 1969).

The same sort of imitation is the basis of the extraordinary performances of domesticated parrots and mynah birds (and budgerigars) since in the wild these species learn the vocal signals of their own families or communities (Bertram, 1970). There are also well-known species which, although giving less spectacular impressions of human speech in captivity, mimic other species of bird in the wild (the mockingbird and the starling). Mimicry tied within genetic relationship is more obviously functional, and whether starlings or mockingbirds gain any biological advantage from their vocal promiscuity is difficult to establish. Imitating other species might be the result of general imitative tendencies gone awry, and raises the issue of vocalisation in excess of natural utility. Given an adaptive value for the production of vocal signals, either instinctive or learned, there may arise an independent motivational system for vocalisation, which under some conditions could produce vocal performance far in excess of the marginally usefully biological requirement. Thorpe, a distinguished authority, has suggested that such a dissociation between drive and utility can be seen in the singing of the blackbird, which emits hurried, imperfect and less pleasing songs during the crucial phases of courtship, nest-building and parental care, but indulges in more elaborate, inventive, and well-practised sound sequences when freed from these reproductive responsibilities by the end of the breeding season (Thorpe, 1972).

Mammals

The biological techniques employed for mammalian reproduction could equally well be assumed to minimise the cognitive load placed on the brain, as to require a newer and higher psychological level. This is especially true in the case of co-operative parental care, which is typical of birds, but rare among mammals even in primates. However, the dependency of mammalian infants on their mothers provides greater opportunities for social learning than usually occur in lower vertebrates. Yet the constancies of mammalian anatomy support a certain diversity in patterns of parental care and social structure. The tree shrew, which is sometimes used to represent a primitive primate for the purposes of comparative brain anatomy (although this is a very dubious practice—Campbell, 1966) has an absolute minimum of parental care. The infants are born in a nest separate from that used by the parents for sleeping, and left entirely unattended except for a ten-minute period once every two days, when the mother returns to perfunctorily squirt milk (a highly concentrated type) into their mouths (Jolly, 1972). Unusually limited maternal activity also occurs in some small New World monkeys, in which the father carries and cares for the infant continuously except for the short intervals when it is handed over to the mother for breast feeding. On the whole, though, the involvement of the male parent with the care and rearing of the young is extremely limited in primates (Mitchell, 1969). This is also the case with herbivorous mammals, where males of some species form separate groups, and only interact with females during the formation of harems or of mating pairs.

It is possible that a line should be drawn between carnivorous mammals and all others, for patterns of parental care. Certainly neo-natal carnivores are less able to fend for themselves than the young in hard herbivores, which are up and about soon after birth. Similarly the transition to grazing after weaning can be accomplished without very much parental attention, but providing food and training for infant meat-eaters which are as yet incompetent to hunt for their own food is a major task for the carnivore parent which, like many birds, must bring solid food to the young at some stage of their development. The most elaborate parental and community organi-sation is found in the canids (dogs, foxes, jackals and wolves), where males will hunt to bring back food for both young and the maternal females (Fox, 1975). This has been taken to suggest that human sex roles evolved while hunting was the main source of food, although the appeal of the analogy with wolves is somewhat reduced by their habit of food-sharing by regurgitation. The forming of social attachments between pairs ('pair bonding') may be needed to ensure parental co-operation in canids and may be facilitated by the nature of copulation in these species. Typically in a watchful mammalian ungulate, although there will be great competition between males to establish sexual access to females, copulation itself is brief and perfunctory—in some species faster than the human eye can follow (Grant's gazelle: Walther, 1972)—and clearly requiring little by way of interpersonal relationships. In carnivores generally copulation is a more protracted and involved activity, and in the canids prolonged personal contact is guaranteed by an anatomical copulatory lock, produced by a bulbous expansion at the end of the penis. Although in domesticated dogs wolf-like male responsibilities have been lost, it may be assumed that in wild canids physical attachments reinforce even more lasting social bonds. It should be noted that while 'two-parent' families appear to be universal in canids, but do not occur in our close relatives the chimpanzee and the gorilla, the gibbons (the 'lesser' apes) are found in nuclear family groups (one adult male, one adult female, and their young). The diet of gibbons—fruit and leaves which they find in trees plus some insects and bird's eggs—does not differ dramatically from that of chimpanzees, and it is therefore a mistake to assume that it was necessary for an ape to become a co-operative hunter before the two-parent family group could make an appearance in the larger primates.

Where there is any social organisation at all in mammalian species, it may be said that a network of social relationships in the family, pack or herd needs to be mastered by each individual and that this is the primary task for which mammalian intelligence evolved (Humphrey, 1976). However, it is difficult to support this by comparisons between relatively solitary mammalian species and their more gregarious counterparts (such as comparisons between orang-utangs and chimpanzees): indeed it is not immediately obvious that mammalian social structures are such that they would require more elaborate forms of cognition than those of birds or lower vertebrates. Complex social hierarchies can of course been seen in the 'pecking orders' of birds (and are very highly developed in corvids such as the jackdaws studied by Lorenz, 1966), and social hierarchies can be observed in reptiles (particularly in the social lizards: E. O. Wilson, 1975). Therefore it is not very plausible to suggest that social organisation as such is the prime mover behind the evolution of intelligence, even though it may well be the case that the range of learned social relationships which occurs in higher vertebrates can exceed that which is possible in lower vertebrates. It could be that it is the gradual learning of individual social relationships, rather than simply the existence of social interactions, which distinguishes mammals from other vertebrate classes. The imprinting of parent-following birds on artificial objects seen soon after hatching is certainly more abrupt than the imprinting of hand-reared sheep and goats on their human foster-parents or the identification with humans which develops in the domestic carnivores (cats and dogs). Any line drawn between birds and mammals on this count must, however, be blurred, since Klinghammer (1967) has shown that gradual and cumulative social learning takes place in many altricial birds, and very early experiences are important in the taming of mammals (Scott, 1962). The general view is that gradual learning from experience is supremely important in mammals, but on the other hand it is assumed that most of the social signals in mammals are innately programmed (e. g. 'appeasement gestures' and the social significance of tail position in wolves, and facial expressions in primates: Lorenz, 1966; Eibl-Eibesfeldt, 1970). The soundest hypothesis would seem to be that both birds and mammals make use of a large amount of social learning, by comparison with lower vertebrates.

Aggression and altruism

No account of social relationships in vertebrates would be complete without due consideration of aggression and competition between members of the same species, and the relation of such hostile interactions to an opposite category of co-operation, affection and self-sacrifice. It should first be emphasised that either hostile or co-operative interactions between members of the same species should be kept distinct from between-species factors. Predation, and defence against predation, provides an obvious example of what would appear to be competition between species, and there are many subtle cases of parasitic or symbiotic relations between species. But it is relationships between individuals of the same species which have most immediate theoretical interest. It is clear that many vertebrates have very systematic and time-consuming forms of ritual competition and fighting between individuals of the same species. The rituals frequently include 'appeasement' mechanisms involving submissive gestures, which may prevent fights between species members extending to the death of the losers (Lorenz, 1966). It is certainly common practice to conduct hostile interactions with the weapons of proud display, strutting and threatening postures, and mutual vocal abuse. But biting, kicking and goring are also resorted to, and fairly serious wounding, sometimes obvious from the scars of successful veterans, takes place in species as far removed as fighting fish, domestic chickens, and elephant seals.

As usual, we may ask if there is any evidence for a phylogenetic progression in the utilisation of aggression, and to what extent aggression requires higher forms of intelligence. And, given the prevalence of within-species aggressive interactions in all vertebrate classes and orders, we can again dismiss the idea that a particular category of behaviour will distinguish one class from another, even though the human species may exhibit interspecies hostility to a very pronounced degree. It is likely, of course, that in lower vertebrates interpersonal unpleasantness is based on innate and reflexive reactions while higher vertebrates and mammals especially may make use of greater foresight and cunning to implement malevolent intentions. But equal weight could be given to the proposition that even in higher vertebrates aggression is predominantly reflexive, emotional and innate, and that even in man violent impulses provide evidence for the retention of primitive methods of behavioural control (though insight and imagination may in some instances be employed in the service of reflexive revenge and resentment).

A stronger argument can be made for a phylogenetic progression in the use of altruism, particularly if one assumes, optimistically, that human individuals show exceptional care and concern for fellow species members (when they are not being callous or cruel). Care of the sick and injured as well as the young and helpless is certainly a characteristic of human, as opposed to animal, societies. However, one cannot adopt this as a source of more general phylogenetic hypotheses. In the first place, the analysis of the genetic basis of altruistic behaviour has to be made independently of the ancestry of a particular species, following the argument that altruism should only be programmed towards individuals closely related to the benefactor, irrespective of the behavioural or psychological mechanisms involved (Hamilton, 1964; Dawkins, 1976b). Also there is a confusion between altruistic motives and the means or tools available for putting them into practice.

The distinction between means and ends was very clearly expressed by Lorenz (1966) in his discussion of aggression, and the same point applies equally well to altruism. According to Lorenz, man is not necessarily more dominated by aggressive motives than other species, but has access to weapon-making skills and social institutions which vastly amplify the damaging results of individual aggressive feelings. The same could be said of more laudable behavioural categories: it is difficult to decide whether the human species has exceptionally powerful helpful impulses, or merely unique medical and social technologies for improving the welfare of others. It would be reassuring to believe that the increased mammalian capacity for cognition improves the expression of friendly impulses by allowing more imaginative identifications with the predicaments of others, but it is always difficult to disentangle emotion and cognition. It is usually convenient to assume that such altruism as may occur in lower vertebrates (as in the parental behaviour of sticklebacks and toads) is merely a product of mechanical reflexes, whereas in higher animals emotion and cognition develop hand in hand. But there is a well-grounded alternative opinion that emotions and instinctual drives are biologically stronger and phylogenetically more primitive than the rarified realms of cognition. According to this, animals are both more emotional, and less intelligent, than people. It seems reasonable that cognitive abilities should always be to some extent the servants of emotion. While in lower vertebrates very highly charged behaviours may be directed by relatively simple perceptions, emotional drives in brains better equipped for cognition should be modified by imagination and inference.

One can only say that behaviour in all vertebrate classes appears to be very well organised within the category of aggression and competition, whereas the category of affectionate and co-operative social interactions is more problematical, but is sufficiently well represented to account for social affinities and group behaviour in a wide variety of vertebrate species.

Reward and punishment

In theories of animal behaviour deriving from laboratory experiments there is a fundamental division between the motivational systems for reward and punishment, which cuts across natural categories of behaviour such as food-seeking or social interaction (Hilgard and Bower, 1975; Mackintosh, 1983; J. A. Gray, 1975). A similar division has been proposed from the standpoint of neuroanatomy (Riss, 1968b). Rewards imply a motivational system for the maintenance and repetition of activities which satisfy some criterion of value while punishment should serve to reduce and discourage disadvantageous or dangerous behaviours. A major feature of theoretical accounts of animal behaviour is the proposition that one or both of these motivational systems promote the learning of relatively arbitrary responses (Hull, 1943; Mackintosh, 1983; see Chapter 3, this volume). But it has been much emphasised recently that natural, species-specific behaviours are closely entwined with supposedly arbitrary reward and punishment (e.g. Seligman, 1970; Hinde and Stevenson-Hinde, 1973; Bolles, 1972). Indeed it is possible to start at a purely reflexive level, and yet categorise inbuilt and automatic behaviours as either positive and 'appetitive' (causing increased contact with eliciting stimuli) or negative and aversive (reducing contact with environmental signals): this is the initial step suggested by Riss (1968b). The question is how far natural vertebrate behaviours arise from automatic elicitation of responses which are appropriate for the feeding strategies, reproductive patterns and all other necessary activities. In the case of higher vertebrates at least, the apparent direction of behaviour with respect to external goals, and the relationship between organised actions and ostensible needs, are usually taken to imply that inner motivations modulate elicited reactions to external stimuli.

It is here that behavioural flexibility and arbitrary learning become important as criteria for the necessity of inner motivation. If a mammal maintained its body temperature only by changes in metabolism, shivering, and raising or lowering its fur, that might not be sufficient to convince us that there was any need for body temperature to have psychologically motivating properties. If on the other hand it is shown that the animal will learn to turn a wheel to alter the intensity of a heat lamp used in a laboratory experiment, it is hard to resist the conclusion that the arbitrary response of wheel turning is motivated by the goal of physical comfort. It is true that the sucking reflexes of a newborn mammal, or the efforts of a newly hatched cuckoo to turn out all other eggs from the nest in which it finds itself, may appear to be motivated, but any stereotyped and rigid sequence of responses could surely be satisfactorily preprogrammed as a set of inbuilt reflexes.

There is little likelihood of establishing clear and agreed definitions of whether a given behaviour should be regarded as motivated or not, and all speculation about inner drives which may provide causal explanations for observed behaviours is open to criticism (Hinde, 1959). However, apart from the criterion of arbitrary learning and behavioural flexibility, it is possible in some cases to anchor psychological processes of motivation to particular kinds of brain process. It is generally supposed that shifts in emotional mood, and the selection of behavioural priorities, are a function of the forebrain limbic system. Electrical activation of various parts of the limbic system can provoke natural behaviours such as attack and copulation in birds and mammals in a way which suggests that normal moods and drives are being mimicked (Glickman and Schiff, 1967; Valenstein *et al.*, 1970). The most revealing phenomenon is, however, that experimental animals will perform relatively arbitrary behaviours if electrical stimulation of points in the limbic system is used for reward or punishment. In higher vertebrates it is possible to suggest that limbic pathways correspond to subjective pleasure and pain, since electrodes surgically implanted in their brains appear to provide internal sources of reward and punishment which are detached to some degree from inbuilt motor patterns. Animals desist from any action which results in stimulation of the 'pain centres' and energetically repeat simple behaviours which are made to bring about activation of the 'pleasure centres' (Olds and Milner, 1954; Olds and Olds, 1963; Benninger *et al.*, 1977). It is regrettable that the vast majority of experimental studies of this 'self-stimulation' phenomenon have been confined to mammals and in particular to the rat and the monkey. Several attempts to reproduce self-stimulation in birds have been successful (e.g. Macphail, 1966; Andrew, 1967; Delius *et al.*, 1976; Zeigler *et al.*, 1978), but systematic comparisons of a greater number of species, from all vertebrate classes, in terms of their susceptibility to this artificial source of motivation, would be extremely valuable. At present there is very little evidence to suggest whether self-stimulation, of the kind found in mammals and birds, can be successfully reproduced in any lower vertebrate species. The existence of 'pain' and 'pleasure' centres in the brains of goldfish has been reported (Boyd and Gardner, 1962) but without any convincing behavioural data, and there does not appear to have been any investigation of self-stimulation using reptiles or amphibians.

Sleep and dreams

If the most obvious and universal feature of vertebrate behaviour is apparently purposeful activity, the next most general aspect of vertebrate behaviour is a regular alternation between periods of rest and periods of action. Vertebrates are hardly exceptional in this respect, but we are reminded daily that many mammals spend a considerable proportion of their lifetime in a peculiar sort of suspended animation, marked by unresponsiveness to external events, in direct contrast to the characteristics of alertness and intelligence. I am referring of course to the daily cycle of sleep and waking, rather than seasonal hibernation. The problem of the function of sleep still remains to be solved. One extreme theory is that sleep has no function, other than to ensure conservation of energy during periods of enforced idleness in species which can only engage in their normal activities during part of the day/night cycle (Mednis, 1975). Alternative theories suggest that the special activities of the brain during sleep are intimately related to its successful function during wakefulness (Oswald, 1962; Jouvet, 1975). Apart from theories concerned with purely physiological needs (for instance, for some sort of recharging of stores of neuronal transmitter substances) the most interesting theories for present purposes concern the role of thought during sleep, in the form of dreams. Vivid and memorable human dreams have always provided compelling evidence of thought processes detached from action, and from immediate reality, although as often as not dream content is assumed to have a deeper meaning, or a greater psychological significance, than more mundane waking experience. However, why dreams should occur at all presents a biological puzzle. Are dreams a spurious and unnecessary artifact of sleep, or are they crucial biological events, sufficiently important to require long periods of 'down-time' for the normal brain? It is still rather uncertain how far the human brain suffers a serious loss of efficiency if it is deprived of sleep, whether by the demands of an experiment, idiosyncratic personal routines, or clinical abnormalities (Meddis, 1975; Dement, 1960; Oswald, 1962). There is certainly a disparity between the strongly felt need for sleep which most of us experience, and the difficulties experienced by psychologists trying to demonstrate fundamental deficits resulting from temporary sleep-deprivation. By and large, keeping people continuously in bed with absolutely no form of distraction ('sensory deprivation'), that is imposing ideal conditions for sleep, even for a few days, is more likely to produce psychological disturbances than keeping them awake, and bombarded with sensation, for a similar period of time. It is possible that the biological need for sleep is somewhat less fundamental than our individual drives might lead us to believe. If so, this would support the speculation that the 'sleep instinct' exists to serve a diurnal cycle for the regulation of physical activity rather than to set the stage for dreaming, or to support a necessary form of mental or physical restoration.

However, a strong hypothesis has been put forward by Jouvet (1967, 1975), who has been responsible for localising some of the brainstem mechanisms which control sleep and dreaming. This hypothesis is that dreams function as mental rehearsals for instinctive performances. The main reason for supposing that dreams are a running through of built-in perceptual, motor and emotional programs, rather than a consolidation or organisation of life memories, is that sleep and dreaming are most prevalent in the newborn and young (in man and other mammals). However, this is not a strictly necessary deduction. One could equally well put forward the theory that neonatal (and even prenatal) experiences and sensations are sufficiently radical and new as to require more consolidation and organisation, via re-running and compiling during sleep, than the predictable happenings of adulthood. An intermediate position would be that mental rehearsal could accomplish both a running-in phase for instinctual programs and a means for repetition and elaboration of individual life experiences. An obvious source of evidence for deciding the relative importance of instinctual and experiential factors in dreaming is of course phylogenetic comparisons, and received opinion here is definitely that it is the species which are presumed to rely most heavily on learning from experience, that is mammals and preeminently man, in which dreaming sleep is most apparent.

Before looking more closely at the comparative psychology of sleep, we need to define some relevant terms a little more clearly. Electroencephalography—the measurement of rhythmic fluctuations of electrical potentials picked up from surface or implanted electrodes on or inside the head—is the technique used to make relatively unambiguous and quantitative assessments of sleep. It can be combined with direct observation of rapid flickering movements of the eyeballs which is a convenient outward sign that inner events reportable as dreams are taking place. In a normal sleep sequence, before any dreams are to occur we must close our eyes and wait for a special sort of muscular relaxation, most evident in the neck. EEG recordings (electroencephalograms) show that if we are awake with the eyes open, there are fast (about 40 cycles per second), desynchronised (irregular) and shallow (low voltage) brain rhythms. Once the eyes are closed, but depending on our state of relaxation, a more regular medium frequency and medium voltage rhythm appears—this is the famous alpha rhythm aspired to as a measure of the success of meditative techniques of self-control. During the first hour or so after dropping off to sleep there is a gradual transition to 'slow-wave sleep' in which there are long (5 per second) waves on the EEG record of a distinctly higher voltage than alpha rhythms or the desynchronised waking pattern (200–300 microvolts as opposed to 30–50). It is customary to distinguish four stages of depth of sleep during the transition from drowsiness to slow-wave sleep, but these are rather arbitrary distinctions imposed on a continuous shift. The most interesting change in sleep state, which is quite unmistakeable, occurs normally when one and a half hours of the drift down to slow-wave sleep have been followed by a further half an hour of this state. The change is to a new state variously known as REM (rapid eye movement) sleep or 'paradoxical sleep'. The distinguishing features indicated by these terms include a rapid flickering of the eyeballs (easily observed even when the eyes are closed in most mammals) and the appearance of fast, low-voltage EEG patterns which would otherwise be characteristic of an awake and alert animal. Originally, the similarity of the EEG records in this phase to those of attentiveness led to the idea that REM sleep was 'light' (Kleitman, 1939; Oswald, 1962). But behavioural indications, such as how easy it is to wake someone up from REM sleep, and how long they take to show physical reactions to external stimuli, do not support this conclusion, and extensive experimentation with cats seems to have established that by most criteria, dreaming sleep is 'deep' (Jouvet, 1967). The term 'paradoxical sleep' is used precisely because electroencephalographic brain waves are characteristic of attentiveness, but there is little reaction to the outside world. This is a vital point for theories of the biological function of paradoxical sleep, since Oswald (1962) and Ullman (1959) supposed that the attentiveness indicated by EEG records meant that this was a phase of greater external vigilance, and that REM sleep served a 'sentinel' function. If Jouvet is correct in the finding that REM sleep is not accompanied by any increase in sensitivity to external dangers, then the 'sentinel' theory must be dropped. This leaves the way clear for theories of the internal utility of REM sleep, most obviously for theories of the biological function of dreaming. People woken from REM sleep can almost always report vivid dreams, while those woken from other phases of sleep usually cannot, and therefore it is assumed that dreaming and REM sleep are closely related.

Animals, of course, do not give verbal accounts of dreams. But it is clear that in general the sleep of mammals can be divided into slow-wave and paradoxical phases, on the basis of brain activity, in exactly the same way as this is done for human sleep. The anatomical and neurochemical aspects of the brain mechanisms which govern sleep and dreaming are almost certainly held in common by man and other mammals, and most of the experimental work on the brain mechanisms which control the sequence of sleep phases has been performed on cats (Jouvet, 1967, 1975). Certain brainstem centres, but not the cortex, must be intact if the normal cycle of sleep phases is to occur. Raphe nuclei in the pontine region of the brainstem, and especially their constituent neurons which contain the neurotransmitter serotonin (5-hydroxytryptamine or 5-HT) are important for the induction of slow-wave sleep. Destroying these neurons produces insomnia, and boosting them by drug treatments leads to a dramatic increase in both slow-wave sleep and succeeding phases of paradoxical sleep. Clearly, other brain circuits are involved as well—we know that stimulants such as caffeine or amphetamine (Benzedrine) may prevent sleep, and these are drugs which facilitate pathways which use the transmitter substance noradrenalin. The appearance of the paradoxical or REM phases of sleep seems to require yet another process which involves the neurotransmitter acetylcholine, since 'anti-cholinergic' drugs selectively prevent this phase while leaving slow-wave sleep undisturbed. 'It is evident that the appearance of PS (paradoxical sleep) is protected by a delicate succession of biochemical mechanisms' (Jouvet, 1975). The interactions between these mechanisms is not completely understood, but there is a further very important experimental fact. This is that the paradoxical lack of behavioural arousal during REM sleep may not be seen if another brainstem nucleus (the locus coeruleus) is lesioned. When this is done in cats, sleepwalking, or 'pseudo-hallucinatory behaviour' occurs during the REM sleep phases. They jump about, adopt aggressive postures and expressions and hiss and growl, or move their front paws as if playing with a mouse: all this with their eyes almost closed, and with frequent bumping into walls. This is powerful evidence for dream-like programming of instinctive behaviour patterns during paradoxical sleep, and supports the impression which one gets from watching twitching and growling in 'dreaming' dogs and cats. Less obviously, it suggests that brain instructions for action are usually present during REM sleep, but are normally suppressed—behaviour itself is de-coupled from brain representations of behaviour. This clutch mechanism between activity in brain circuits and motor implementation does not seem to apply to the eyes, since it is their extensive movements when other behaviour is lacking which typifies paradoxical sleep. It could be that eye movements are excluded from the de-coupling system simply because they do not matter—it makes very little difference to the sleeping animal whether eye movements occur or not, whereas sleepwalking can obviously lead to trouble.

The alternative view is that eye movements are present in paradoxical sleep for more positive reasons. It has been suggested that they are in some way necessary for 'looking at the pictures' in dreams (Oswald, 1962, pp. 128–34). There is also a theory that the single function of paradoxical sleep is to provide extra practice for conjugate eye movements, which are necessary for following objects or scanning the visual field with both eyes in parallel (conjugate eye movements are used by primates and to some extent by mammalian carnivores with front-facing eyes). This theory (Berger, 1969) may seem plausible if one assumes that paradoxical sleep occurs only in primates and mammalian carnivores, but it founders on the fact that the dreaming phase is prominent in many species which could have very little use for conjugate eye movements. There is extensive paradoxical sleep in the mole, which is quite blind (Allison and Van Twyer, 1970), and mammals with eyes that face to the side may exhibit the brain rhythms characteristic of human dreaming, notably the opposum (Van Twyer and Allison, 1970) and the rat (Jouvet, 1975).

Sleep and dreaming and mammalian habits

In order to assess general theories of the biological or psychological functions of sleep, it is clearly necessary to take into account species differences, and to compare sleep in the various vertebrate classes. It is probable that sleep is associated with many complex physiological cycles, but in the context of the cognitive aspects of brain function the most interesting theory is Jouvet's idea that the distinctive dreaming phases of sleep (that is in the paradoxical, REM state) function as periods for the mental rehearsal of instinctive behaviours. I have noted above that when phylogenetic comparisons are considered, dreaming sleep appears to be paradoxical in more ways than one. It is curious that mammals, supposedly less governed by instinct than other vertebrate classes, should need special attention to instinctive behaviours. Also, if dreaming is specifically mammalian, it would be unusual as a mammalian speciality in appearing to survive the removal of the cerebral cortex. Conceivably, as the mammalian brain adopted a heavy reliance on learning by experience, mediated by cortical memories, remaining instinctual programs require extensive rehearsal to fit in with the general plan. However, any universal principle applying to mammals as a whole needs to be modified in the light of the diversity of the habits of individual species.

It is sometimes claimed that ruminant herbivores, such as sheep, cows and goats, do not sleep at all, since sheep may not lie down during the night, and cows and goats, even when lying down, usually keep their head up and their eyes open, and continue to chew the cud. Careful observation and EEG recording suggests that these species may accomplish some sort of sleep, which includes brief periods of dreaming, even while chewing the cud with their eyes open (Oswald, 1962), but obviously they obtain fewer of the benefits that sleep may provide than rats, cats or monkeys. Similarly, marine mammals, including both whales and seals (the latter having the front-facing eyes of carnivores) usually sleep for brief periods under water, interrupted by the necessity of coming up for air. Breathing in these cases imposes special limits on sleeping patterns, and for ruminants the utility of nocturnal chewing and vigilance against predators may impose equally strong ecological pressures against prolonged somnolence (Allison, 1976). But within the limits set by ecological specialisations it is still conceivable that paradoxical sleep plays a distinctive part in mammalian brain function. Since human dreams provide such clear examples of mental experiences freed at least temporarily from external behavioural realities, the fact that similar brain processes to those involved in human dreaming can be observed in other mammals is certainly worth remembering.

Sleep and dreaming in non-mammals

From the point of view of progressive phylogeny, it would be convenient if dreaming were confined to mammals, since this would support a firm line of demarcation between thinking and dreaming vertebrates and reflexive lower forms. It is hardly surprising then, that in the absence of data to the contrary, the assumption has often been made that 'the physiological state associated with dreaming is a very old and basic characteristic of mammalian life' with the corollary that in all non-mammals this state is absent (Snyder, 1966). But we can now, with some confidence, eliminate this clear typology, and allow birds, at least, a dream life not very different from that of mammals. It may be that a firm distinction will eventually emerge between the higher, warm-blooded vertebrates, which dream, and the lower, cold-blooded animals, which do not, but the data on sleep in fish, amphibians and reptiles are at the moment very sketchy.

The vast majority of birds, although early risers, are strongly diurnal, needing the clear light of day to make use of their excellent visual sense. On the hypothesis that a sleep instinct exists to ensure nocturnal quietude (Meddis, 1975), birds would have as much need of it as mammals. There are nocturnal birds of course, such as owls and nightjars, and one cave-dwelling species has apparently evolved a sonic system similar to that of bats for dark flying, but these species usually doze off during the day. Many perching birds sleep standing up, on one or both legs, and might be thought therefore to sleep lightly, especially as a sick or anaesthetised bird will quickly fall off its perch. However, successful perching during sleep is brought about partly by an anatomical arrangement of muscles in which the grip is tightest when the main muscles are relaxed. Lack of muscle tension in the neck is quite apparent from the habit of dropping the head and tucking it under a wing. Non-perching birds such as ducks, and birds which sleep in burrows or nests, can adopt even more restful postures for sleep. None of this, of course, implies the existence of dreaming or paradoxical sleep, and initially EEG recordings were taken to suggest that although birds showed evidence of the REM sleep state, they were in it for a negligible amount of time—less than 1 per cent of the total sleep periods (Klein, *et al.*, 1964; Tradardi, 1966). More extensive observations have now established that, in the limited number of bird species studied, the total duration of sleeping, and the proportion of sleeping time spent in the paradoxical phase, are both comparable to the figures for mammals. Up to 50 per cent of the day is taken up by sleep, and about 10 per cent of sleep is occupied by the paradoxical state: this is for the pigeon (Goodman, 1974), and for two birds of prey (Rojas-Ramirez and Tauber, 1970). An interesting test case for the hypothesis that paradoxical sleep exists for the purpose of producing eye movements arises in owls, whose tubular eyes are so firmly fixed in their sockets that no movements can occur in any circumstances.

Berger and Walker (1972) duly reported that there are no rapid eye movements during sleep in the burrowing owl, but EEG recordings made it plain that desynchronised brain rhythms are present in this species nevertheless.

Since the birds so far studied show mammalian amounts of paradoxical, 'REM' sleep, by the criterion of electroencephalographic measurements, even if eye movements are limited, or absent altogether, we may safely conclude that the electrical brain rhythms characteristic of dreaming are not a mammalian preserve. Any generalisations about sleep in lower vertebrates would be very much less safe. The simplest assertion is that lower vertebrates do not sleep at all, and that if they have periods of 'behavioural rest' there is no brain-state which corresponds to the paradoxical phase in birds and mammals (Allison, 1972; J. M. Walker and Berger, 1973). Let us look first at the question of sleep/wakefulness cycles, leaving aside the division of sleep into paradoxical and other phases. The main difficulty with amphibians and reptiles is that so much time is spent in behavioural torpidity that whether this should be regarded as sleep or 'just resting' is largely a matter of opinion. (Consider the problem of an awake, but resting, tortoise.) Even those who have devised electroencephalographic methods which give some indication of brain-states for reptilian sleep and wakefulness are forced to admit that there are long periods of time which have to remain unclassified by these methods (Flanigan, *et al.*, 1974). However, many reptile species have very definite diurnal cycles of behaviour. Crocodilians typically spend most of the night in water, emerging for an early-morning bask in the sun (Lang, 1976), and many lizards seek out favourable locations in trees or stonework for their nocturnal state, whatever this may be. In these species, behavioural signs of sleep, such as marked attenuation of reactions to external stimuli, closing of the eyes, and muscular relaxation, are relatively unambiguous.

In fish, on the other hand, and especially in sharks, which need to keep moving to maintain buoyancy, the difficulty is in finding a sufficient lack of activity to qualify even as resting. But it has been claimed that, in teleost fish at least, periods of active swimming may alternate with periods of floating which are passive enough to suggest sleep (e.g. Shapiro and Hepburn, 1976; Tauber and Weitzman, 1969, say eye movements may be observed during the periods of behavioural inactivity in some species). Even with sharks, it is possible that phases of lowered sensory alertness could occur during mechanical and automatic continuation of swimming. It is not possible to say, therefore, that sleep, as behavioural quiescence, is absent in lower vertebrates, although it is not unreasonable to speculate that the brain-states which control sleep in higher vertebrates are different from those which govern cycles of behavioural activity in other classes.

Some have sought to support the distinction between brain mechanisms controlling sleep on anatomical grounds. The brainstem nuclei associated with the reticular system, which have been firmly implicated in the control of sleep cycles in mammals, in particular the raphe nuclei and the locus coeruleus, are very similar in birds and mammals, and appear to be identifiable in reptiles, but have been presumed to be absent in fish and amphibians (Kappers *et al.*, 1936; Allison, 1972). It would be unwise, however, to place too much emphasis on this aspect of brainstem anatomy, since cell areas in the reticular system of sharks and frogs have been labelled as raphe nuclei in more recent reports (Smeets and Nieuwenhuys, 1976; Opdam *et al.*, 1976). But we can note in passing that this is a case where the evolution of the hindbrain, as opposed to the forebrain, assumes considerable theoretical importance, even for a cognitive process (dreaming).

Although the brainstem structures which are required for paradoxical sleep in mammals are present in reptiles, the electroencephalographic evidence concerning this type of sleep in reptiles is extremely sparse. There is a report of behaviourally observed rapid eye movements during the sleep of chameleons, which is theoretically important, if it is reliable (Tauber *et al.*, 1966). These arboreal lizards adopt a resting posture along a branch as dusk approaches, and close their eyes (and retract their eyeballs) when it gets dark. After this the grip of the feet relaxes and, especially during the first half of the night, there are periods, about 5 minutes in length, when the eyes can be observed in rapid movement. Tauber *et al.* (1966) could not differentiate between the eye-movement periods and other periods of sleep on the basis of EEG recordings, but these were clearly different in sleep and waking, showing distinctive irregularly spaced spikes during sleep, and rapid low-voltage saw-tooth patterns during waking. Spikes, or 'sharp-waves' have also been recorded during behavioural sleep in tortoises (J. M. Walker and Berger, 1973), iguanid lizards (Flanigan, 1973) and crocodilians. In the iguanids, 'behavioural sleep' is identifiable by a flat-out posture, and greatly reduced reactivity (Flanigan, 1973; Tauber *et al.*, 1968). Such behavioural indications of sleep must be less obvious in tortoises, but in these animals there is pharmacological evidence that EEG spiking is analogous to EEG slow-waves: the same drug, atropine sulphate, increases both slow-wave sleep in mammals and spiking sleep in tortoises (Hartse and Rechtschaffen, 1974). In iguanids, sleep deprivation amplifies the spikes recorded in subsequent sleep (Flanigan, 1973).

It thus appears that while reptiles may have periods of inactivity and reduced alertness which are accompanied by characteristic EEG patterns and which therefore appear to correspond in some degree to the slow-wave sleep periods seen in mammals and birds, there is little to suggest that reptiles typically exhibit anything which corresponds to paradoxical sleep. It is therefore tempting to assume that this dreaming state has evolved only in the higher vertebrates. The simplest interpretation of this would be that paradoxical sleep began as a device for ensuring a modicum of metabolic activity in warm-blooded animals undergoing energy-conserving quiescence (Zepelin and Rechtschaffen, 1974). A word is thus in order about forms of behavioural arrest other than sleep. Physiologically, anaesthesia shows some similarity to slow-wave sleep, and as a rule, a drug which anaesthetises one vertebrate will also put out all others. At any rate, some sort of temporary brain shut-down, leading to a collapse of the sensory and motor systems, can be induced in all vertebrates by chemical interference with brain activity (or by a sufficiently vigorous knock on the head). A more specialised self-induced slowing down of body and brain activities occurs in hibernation, which is used in several orders of mammals (most commonly in rodents), one order of birds (caprimulgiformes), one order of reptiles (chelonians) and in isolated amphibian species (Mrosovsky, 1971). It is assumed that brainstem mechanisms are involved in the programming of hibernation, and the clearly apparent metabolic functions here suggested comparisons with sleep. A less obviously functional phenomenon is the so-called 'animal hypnosis' (preferably, 'tonic immobility: Maser and Gallup, 1977) which may be induced in species in all vertebrate classes by certain forms of physical restraint.

Obviously, the suspension of normal behavioural reactivity can occur in varying circumstances and for various purposes, and the basic diurnal cycle of sleep and rest is at once too complicated and too simple to be given explanations in terms of psychological utility. Yet the dreaming phase of sleep stands out as a special case. The subjective intensity of human dreaming has always provided a pointer to the separation of mental experience from external reality. The opportunity to rehearse and elaborate internal schemata in the absence of external necessities may or may not be a crucial requirement for higher vertebrate adaptability, but the bare fact of the existence, during paradoxical sleep, of electrical indices characteristic of waking brain-states without neural input and output in the sensory and motor systems, suggests that brain representations of external events have attained independence from the external events themselves. Since this fact applies to higher vertebrates, but not to lower vertebrates, it deserves a great deal of attention in theories of mental evolution.

Vertebrate life and vertebrate brain powers—conclusions

The review in this chapter of various natural categories of behaviour which stand in need of control by the brain does not reveal a single condition of life or psychological requirement as a pressure towards successive improvements in brain capacity. Any account of the anatomical evolution of the vertebrate brain must allude to greater physical size of the brains of higher vertebrates, in which the forebrain appears to have been most subject to evolutionary changes. But it is not clear that in terms of biological functions the brain of one vertebrate class serves a set of purposes which are radically different from those achieved by brains in any other class. The problem is that most behavioural programming needs, such as the reception of visual information, the selection of feeding strategies, and the control of social interactions necessary for reproduction, span the entire panorama of vertebrate species. Presumably the answer is that the same be-havioural tasks can be accomplished in different ways, but this means that we cannot simply say that a brain of one type is necessary for predatory habits while a brain of another type must evolve for any fruit-eating species; or that migration absolutely requires any parti-cular form of brain organisation; or that a social species has to be more intelligent than a solitary species. In this sense phylogenetic status, with all its theoretical faults as a concept, may be a more reliable guide to the psychological capacities of a species than its ecological niche. Pri-mates are intelligent because they are primates, not just because they live in trees, eat fruit, and form social groups. Clearly this brings back anagenesis, or 'evolution above the species level' with a vengeance, since we are left with the vague notion that a phylogenetic progression in brain capacity exists regardless of the specialisations of individual species. And in terms of the behavioural categories selected here, there is not so much a progression as a simple dichotomy between higher vertebrates and lower vertebrates: in most cases where it is possible to suggest a form of mammalian superiority, the mammalian characteristic is seen in birds as well. This applies to such varied features as the importance of parental care, elaborate vocalisation, complex social organisation, flexibility in innate behaviour patterns, learning by individual experience and learning by imitation. It applies also in two cases where aspects of brain functioning can be examined directly: sensitivity to the emotionally rewarding or punishing consequences of motor responses is studied by allowing animals to turn on or off small electrical currents delivered to certain forebrain structures—this works for both mammals and birds but has not as yet been demonstrated in other classes; the changes in electrical brain rhythms which occur during human sleep can be found in mammals and birds but not in lower vertebrates. Results such as these confirm the traditional opinion that the brains of mammals support forms of learning and cognition which are superior to those found in reptiles but do little to strengthen the assumption that there is a clear psychological separation between mammals and birds. However, it is on the whole remarkably difficult to infer psychological capacities from the natural behaviours required of particular species or groups of species. An alternative source of evidence is laboratory testing of psychological capacities, and it is the results of such experimentation that I shall turn to in the remaining chapters.

7 Modes of perception

Perception, very broadly, refers to the utilisation of the organs of sense. Human perception, though, is often defined in terms of the use of the senses to acquire conscious knowledge of the outside world, with the existence of a human mind being assumed as the destination which sense data may reach. Less tendentiously, we could discuss perception, in a more modern phrase, as the processing of information received via the sense organs. Even in this case, there are many problems in trying to compare the perception of men and animals. For human perception, the inner organisation of knowledge needs always to be considered as one of the determinants of what is sensed. Context, expectancies, the synthesis of pieces of sensory information into coherent perceptual wholes: these are variables of crucial importance in theories of human information processing—but to what extent do these things affect the perceptions of animals? At the extreme, human perception may be characterised as a sequence of intentional perceptual acts, requiring selection, choice and effort. Does this mean that human perception is fundamentally different from the activation of the sense organs of animals? Philosophical views on fundamental differences between human and animal perception, particularly those of Locke, have been discussed in Chapters 1 and 2. Here I shall attempt to start again from the beginning: using first, information from laboratory tests of the perceptual capacities of animals, by which some of the questions about the limits of these capacities can be answered by reference to behavioural data; and second, modern knowledge, such as it is, of how brain processes are involved in perception.

Modalities and qualities in perception

The easiest distinctions to make about perception concern the method of operation of the external sense-organs. The eyes are clearly different

237

from the ears and we can say that acquiring information through the eyes is vision, and acquiring information through the ears is hearing, without fear of contradiction. This is a distinction between sensory *modalities*, and it is obvious that we can separate out five modalities of external perception—vision, hearing, touch, taste and smell—according to whether the eyes, the ears, the skin, the tongue or the nose can be identified as the source of particular sensations.

This is simple enough, but once we begin to enquire as to what kinds of information can be transmitted by each modality, things become rather more complicated and subjective. These types of information can be discussed as stimulus *qualities*, and it should be emphasised that stimulus qualities which are subjectively obvious to ourselves can only be attributed to the operations of perception in other species on the basis of physiological and behavioural evidence. One stimulus quality is common to all modalities and that is intensity. We should expect sense organs to be capable of reacting differentially to a bright light or a dim light, a loud or soft sound, intense or mild pressure on the skin, and so on. As far as the transformation of external events by sense organs goes, we may safely assume that differentiation between bright and dim lights is not a uniquely human accomplishment, although whether a bright light is perceived as having something in common with a loud noise in any other species is something which would require experimental confirmation.

There are many stimulus qualities which are specific to particular modalities, and there are some, like intensity, which may or may not apply to more than one modality, depending on the capabilities of the animal involved, and perhaps on prior experience. Colour, and certain aspects of brightness and shape, apply to vision; pitch and timbre to hearing; sweetness and bitterness to taste. Interactions between these are an interesting aspect of human subjective experience—we speak of warm colours and sweet sounds—and have been investigated under the heading of 'synesthesia', but there are little or no data on whether similar subtleties might be apparent to animals. However, the independence of the mental analysis of stimulus qualities from the immediate activities of particular sense organs is clearly one of the ways in which 'higher' forms of perception may differ from 'lower'. This sort of distinction is one I wish to emphasise by referring to different 'modes' of perception.

Reflexive and cognitive modes of perception

The use of the term 'modes' as well as 'modalities' may appear unnecessarily confusing, but the distinction I want to make is really a very straightforward one. It is possible to purchase equipment which will arrange that one's garage door opens whenever a car appears before it—similar devices make walking though the compartments of trains very much easier than it used to be. On simple behavioural grounds it might seem that the doors, or the sensing devices connected to them, are 'perceiving' the cars or persons which present themselves in appropriate places. No one would suppose, however, that such perception has a great deal in common with the processes which take place in our own brains. It might be claimed, in the Cartesian tradition, that such mechanical or electronic arrangements should be taken as analogies for animal, as distinct from human, perception. It is necessary, therefore, to attempt some sort of categorisation of modes of perception that do or do not mirror various aspects of our own perceptual abilities.

Reflexive perception

To start with, we can pick out the simplest possible kinds of reactions to stimuli, reactions analogous to the opening of a door in response to the breaking of a photocell beam. It is unlikely that any response of organic tissue is quite as simple as this, but, clearly, some reactions of very simple animals to external stimulation, and some of the reflexive responses of more complicated animals, ought to be separated out. A single cell, either as a single-celled animal, or as a specialised part of a mammal, may respond to touch, temperature, or chemical stimulation, in particular ways. The spinal cord of vertebrates, even in isolation from the brain, allows for a variety of limb movements in response to touch, and for reactions of the digestive system to internal forms of stimulation. There is a sensitivity to events here, which is a characteristic of perception; but the nature of the stimulating events, and the individual response to them, is relatively fixed and rigid. The fixity and rigidity is relative to the greater complexity and malleability of higher forms of perception—it would be a mistake to oversimplify the characteristics of even these simpler forms of organic response to stimulation. We can assess the reflexiveness of these stimulus-response relationships both in terms of the complexity of the stimulating event, and of the flexibility of the forms of response to it. In some cases the information which is 'recognised' even by a single cell may come in quite an elaborate form, as in the 'recognition' by mammalian immune mechanisms of cells which belong to the individual animal rather than to another animal of the same species. In other cases, as in the scratching reflexes of decerebrate frogs, the perceptual input may appear rather rudimentary, but the nature of the response to the input may be complex. The way in which tactile end-organs pick up chemical or mechanical stimulation at some point on the skin of a leg of the decerebrate frog is easily explained: the way in which the spinal cord reacts by bringing up the other foot to just this point to make wiping movements has to be interpreted in terms of quite elaborate motor organisation.

But in all these cases there is a restricted category of stimulating event and the only way in which this stimulus can be said to be perceived is that there is an immediate and preprogrammed response to it. It is improper to think of even spinal reflexes as completely fixed and isolated from one another, but there is an important distinction to be made between, on the one hand, the sensing of stimulation which takes place in the organised movements of swallowing, the unconscious co-ordination of particular muscles in walking or standing, or the accommodation of the lens of the eye to objects at different distances, and, on the other hand, such things as the perceptual experience of recognising another person in a photograph or noticing that traffic lights have turned from red to green.

Cognitive perception
The characteristics of human perception of events include some kind of detached knowledge which is not tied exclusively to a single form of response, and which is typically (though not universally) available to some system of verbal description. Perception in this sense is closely linked to memory—we not only perceive that the traffic lights have changed, but remember that we have just perceived this; we not only recognise someone, but we know *that* we have recognised him. This is not to deny the reality of unconscious or 'subliminal' forms of human perception, but to acknowledge that human perception usually needs to be accounted for in terms of complex inner mental organisation. The more serious theories of human perception have to say that when a person sees something, he acquires a belief, or has an idea, about what it is that he is seeing. Such a concept is made more technical, if it is said

that visual information is assimilated into a 'schema' (the term used by Piaget and Neisser), but the main thing is that there is a cognitive aspect of perception and this is quite different from reflexive reactions to stimulation such as the contraction of the pupil in response to bright lights or a jerk of the arm when the finger touches a burning-hot plate.

Modes, qualities and modalities in human and animal perception

There will surely be little disagreement that distinctions can be drawn between reactions to events of a 'knee-jerk' reflex type, and more knowledgeable ways of extracting information from the environment by the use of the senses. There is considerable difficulty, however, in coming to decisions about whether the utilisation of the senses by animals falls into one category or the other. Part of the difficulty arises, I believe, from the tradition, examined in earlier chapters, of assuming that all animal perception is of the reflex type unless it can be shown otherwise. That this assumption is unrealistic and misleading can be shown by examining the functional relationship between the modality of sensory input and the perception of stimulus qualities.

The essence of reflexive perception is that information is confined within the modality in which it is received. A touch on the skin is a touch on the skin, rather than the presence of another animal. But is this the way that the senses are normally utilised by, for instance, the cat? If my cat is sitting down, and I lightly snap my fingers behind her head, I may observe one ear, and then both ears, turning towards the sound. This can be put down to a sophisticated auditory reflex. If I snap my fingers a little louder, however, I would expect to see not just the ears, but the whole head turn with the eyes firmly fixed on my hand. And it would not be surprising if the whole animal then turned and moved, and came and sniffed the hand and rubbed her head against it, making contact with the whiskers just before the final rub with the cheek. Would it be reasonable to construe this sequence as a succession of reflexes, each isolated in particular modalities of hearing, vision, smell and touch? I suggest not, and that on the contrary, the brain of the cat is organised so as to connect and correlate the various modalities, one with another.

The information within one modality may take part in various specialised reflexes, but can also be put towards an interpretation, schema, or belief about the current state of affairs in the world which is cognitive *because* it can be applied across modalities and across a certain range of changes of time and place. After rubbing one cheek against my hand, the cat may turn around, losing sight of the hand, and come back to rub its other cheek. In ordinary language, the cat knows that the hand is there. I am not suggesting that the cat knows as much about me as I know about the cat, but I would argue that, in terms of immediate perception, the cat knows that the hand is there in much the same way that I know that the cat is there.

The most abstract and overriding, and the most useful, perceptual quality which is independent of modality is something that may be termed *object identity*. By this I mean that the cat perceives a 'thing' rather than a sensation, and that its perception of the thing must consist of a collection of bits of knowledge. The hand is something that looks solid, can be rubbed against, will smell and feel like a hand, and will do the things hands normally do. This is not to claim that the cat mentally runs through a list of this type every time it sees a hand, but that when it sees a hand, a complex mental process of recognition takes place. This sort of hypothesis may be theoretically debatable, and difficult to subject to experimental testing. But I believe that we know enough about the behaviour of mammals, and the brain mechanisms available to them, to make it extremely plausible, and that experimental data of the kind to be discussed below will support it.

If the extent to which animals analyse (and synthesise) their environment into 'things' is difficult to determine, it may be easier to isolate rather less abstract stimulus qualities which, while they may serve as attributes of things, can be derived more obviously from correlations between sensory modalities, or from specific features within sensory modalities. Isolating sensory qualities is certainly a more speculative matter than differentiating between modalities, and no doubt there are considerable differences between species or between classes of animal, but let us look at the possibility that animals may perceive such qualities as location, movement and object identity with a certain degree of independence from particular modalities.

Location and movement

Location presupposes some minimum case of object identity, since one has to ask 'location of what?' But given some rudimentary classification of stimulus events such as the identification of a touch on the skin, or the identification of an insect via the visual 'bug detectors' of a frog, then these events may be given a location in terms of 'where exactly is the body surface touched?' or 'where is the visual field and at what distance is the detected bug?' Now in the case of the scratching reflexes of a frog, or the tongue-throwing response of the same animal, it is possible that location is not a cross-modal quality, since receptors on the skin surface may have rather direct connections with the muscles used in the scratching reflex, and the transformation of data from the eye which indicate the angle and distance for effective tongue-throwing may take place in a reflexive and automatic way. But in the case of mammalian predators locating prey, then scenting, sighting, hearing, and touching might be expected to work in a co-operative fashion. This is especially obvious if the activation of one modality leads to orientation, or investigation with the others. The co-operation of the eyes and ears of the cat has already been emphasised, but a correlation between visually detected closeness and touch with the whiskers and skin seems equally likely. In mammals with weak vision, which are often classed as 'primitive', such as the hedgehog, or the mole, the joint use of smell and touch to establish 'cognitive maps' may be more important than the combination of vision and hearing.

Either for touch, or for vision, perception of the position and posture of the animal's own body has to be taken into account for the accurate perception of the external world. If we look at a door while turning our head to one side, we do not sense the door turning, although the image on our retina moves: the inner sensing of the movement of our head is used to compensate for the movement of the retinal image. If I close my eyes and touch several mugs on the table, I know which mug is closest because it is the mug I touched when my arm was flexed, even though the tactile sensation in my fingers might be the same in this case as in touching a mug with my arms stretched out. It is highly unlikely that other mammals manage without a very similar kind of co-operation and compensation between different forms of perception, and the assessment of external information in terms of the position and movement of the body of the receiving animal is a necessity throughout most of the animal kingdom.

The interaction between internal and external senses is especially necessary in the perception of external movement. Specialised receptors respond when a visual array moves across the retina, or a tactile stimulus moves past the whiskers or skin. But animals need to know, surely, whether it is they or external objects, that are moving.

Incoming information from external-movement detectors must be constantly monitored in terms of the motor activities currently being performed. This need not count as a particularly cognitive form of perception—it is something taken for granted as a continuous and unconscious adjustment necessary to maintain human perceptual reality (otherwise the room would seem to spin every time we turned our heads). However, it can be used to illustrate the fact that very basic ways of perceiving and interacting with the environment are not as simple as they seem, and that the perceptual apparatus utilised by vertebrates simply for movement from place to place may require a considerable degree of internal organisation and interpretation.

Object identity and value

Neisser (1976) has stressed the analogy between human perception and the activity of picking apples from a tree. Apples do not attempt to force themselves down our throats, he says, and neither do perceptual experiences force themselves upon us. Rather, we ourselves select and choose among sense impressions. On what basis do we make the choice, and to what extent can animal perception be said to be similarly a matter of selection? One of Neisser's examples was the selective ability of human subjects watching sporting events on a television screen to attend to a coherent sequence of visual images, even in the face of confusion introduced by the superimposition of recordings of more than one game on the same screen. Overtly passive watching of a television screen can be taken as a supremely 'cognitive' mode of perception, in so far as information may be absorbed in the absence of any direct effect on behaviour, reflexive or otherwise. But the input of information is clearly not emotionally neutral—one could say that even the minimal effort required to maintain eye-contact with the screen is maintained only so long as there is at least a momentary interest in the scene depicted and that passionate involvement with unfolding human dramas thus represented is not unusual.

Assigning values to purely visual images may be a peculiarly human characteristic—the question is not whether animals could show an equivalent interest in moving pictures, but whether there is an element of choice and direction in the way they gather information from the real environment. Do animals categorise certain perceptions as good or bad, desirable or undesirable, to be sought out or to be avoided? It would seem hard to deny that there are motivational or emotional connotations to perceptions that are related to basic drives of hunger, thirst and reproduction but there are clear differences of opinion as to whether the emotional aspects of such perceptions work in a reflexive or cognitive way. A hungry animal must be said to perceive food, if it eats the food, but it is often difficult to decide whether, for instance, an innate reaction to the smell of food leads to reflexes of biting, salivating and swallowing, coupled with a degree of temporary excitement and emotional arousal, or whether, as well as this, there is a more dispassionate perception of food as a 'thing which may be eaten'.

This was one of the questions addressed in Chapter 3, in the comparison between stimulus-response and cognitive theories of animal behaviour, where I argued that laboratory rats and pigeons, to say nothing of monkeys and chimpanzees, are capable of remembering and anticipating both perceptions of food, and such things as where the food should be, and what actions might be necessary to obtain it. If this argument is accepted, the *value* of objects is clearly one of the determinants of object perception by animals. At its simplest, this is an assertion that animals categorise objects into 'good to eat' or 'not good to eat': by reviewing laboratory experiments on animal perception one might be led to believe that this is the *only* perceptual categorisation of objects ever made by sub-human species. It may be the case that a large part of animal perception is constrained by the Darwinian imperatives of searches for food, safety and social experience, but these constraints are undoubtedly overemphasised by the more abstruse restrictions of the search by animal psychologists for effective experimental techniques. In particular, there is very much more laboratory data on what hungry animals can perceive about stimuli associated with experimental food rewards than there is on what animals normally perceive in the course of their natural movements and social interactions. Another limitation of the available experimental data is that it is heavily weighted towards vision. This is partly because it is technically much easier to present animals with particular visual arrays than it is to arrange controlled delivery of specific smells, tastes or tactile sensations, but also because the modality of vision involves especially interesting theoretical problems. In a subsequent section I will review a number of experimental findings which bear on the degree of cognitive organisation involved in visual perception by animals.

Cognitive organisation in animal perception

The application of rigorous experimental techniques to the study of animal perception has had rather mixed effects. On the one hand, unequivocal evidence is available to document the sensitivity and functional effectiveness of animal sensory systems. In some cases, such as Kalmus's careful study of the ability of dogs to identify human individuals by scent (Kalmus, 1955) the results reaffirm conclusions arrived at by more naturalistic observations. In others, such as the experiments in Pavlov's laboratory (discussed on pp. 65ff) which established the sensitivity of dogs to the rhythm, timbre and sequence of musical notes, systematic investigation has allowed the detection of sensory capacities which might have gone unnoticed by the more casual eye. There is no doubt about the advantage of conventional and reliable experimental techniques in instances such as these. But if there has been a drawback to the use of standard experimental procedures, it has been in the way in which the restricted performances demanded of experimental animals have given apparent support to the absurd theoretical proposition that the only variation possible in an animal's reception of external events was in the instigation, or non-instigation, of an immediate overt behavioural reaction.

In Pavlov's experiments on the conditioning of salivation to various sounds, for instance, one dog might salivate to the note of middle C whether played on a clarinet, organ pipe, or tuning fork, but not to any note more than a semi-tone different in pitch, however played, because only middle C signalled food. But another dog might salivate to any note whatever played on a clarinet, and not to any sound made by an organ pipe or tuning fork, because for this dog, notes from a clarinet but not from any other instrument had been used as the indication for food. Pavlov himself spoke of such results in terms of lower and higher kinds of auditory analysis. Subsequently, however, there has been a tendency for other theorists to ignore such questions, and to make the assumption that the perception of the sound stimuli must occur in an identical way for both dogs (and that in so far as it is mentioned, the dogs listen and hear in the same way), the difference between the dogs salivating to different sounds being that the response of salivation attaches itself to a different subset of possible auditory patterns (e.g. Spence, 1936). It may not seem as though the form of this description is very important, but it means for one thing that the theoretical emphasis very much concerns the response which happens to be used in a particular experiment; the problem with this is that the overt response (in this case salivation) may be the least interesting aspect of the perceptual ability being studied (in this case hearing). More specifically, the response-based description misses out the possibilities of perceptual learning, and selection and choice within perception. Another form of description would emphasise that the first dog had learned to pay attention to pitch, while the second had learned to recognise the sound of a clarinet, but chose, for good reason, to ignore pitch.

In fact, there is overwhelming evidence suggesting that the second form of description, that which emphasises selection and learning during the process of perception, is more accurate than the first, which is limited to responses which happen to be made as a consequence of stimulus input. Species commonly used in the laboratory, such as dogs and cats, rats and pigeons, can be shown to organise and direct their perceptual activities independently of the movements and bodily reactions measured to assess these. The evidence is extensively reviewed by Sutherland and Mackintosh (1971) and Mackintosh (1974), and can be put under two general headings. In the first place, the effects of perceptual training are *not* inextricably tied to particular overt responses. Suppose the two hypothetical dogs described above, one trained to salivate to middle C whatever instrument it is played on, and the other trained to salivate to the sound of a clarinet irrespective of pitch, were given a new test, which did not involve salivation, but which required the same perceptual discriminations. This is easier said than done, but we may imagine the two dogs lifting their paws in response to a middle C, or to a clarinet note, respectively. We should definitely expect some *transfer* of the effects of perceptual training, so that the animal which was already in the habit of noticing middle C should find it easy to apply this perceptual habit to a new task, and the dog which had already learned to recognise the clarinet should continue to recognise it even when salivation was not called for. Comparisons with animals lacking the previous training would of course be needed, but I think few theorists would really want to stake very much on the claim that recognition of a clarinet takes place in the salivary gland, when it came to the point.

Actual experiments along these lines are rare, but Lawrence (1949, 1950) successfully demonstrated transfer of perceptual learning between different response tasks using visual discriminations in rats. The fact that vision in rats is very poor, and is not particularly amenable to the effects of experimental training gives these results additional weight. A much more frequently performed type of experiment is one in which there is a change in response output with similar perceptual requirements, simply reversing the response rule. The dog trained to salivate to the sound of a clarinet, but not to an organ pipe, could be retrained so that the organ pipe was the positive stimulus, leading to food, and the clarinet was the negative one, no longer signalling the food. The usual initial effect of such a reversal is total confusion, although oddly enough there are certain conditions under which rats with long experience of a difficult visual discrimination can accomplish a relatively rapid reversal of response (the 'overtraining reversal effect', see Mackintosh, 1974, pp. 602–7). However, a standard kind of experiment, which gives exceedingly reliable results, is to wait until responding has settled down after the first turn about, then to reinstate the original conditions, then to reverse the stimuli again, and so on. The results of this 'serial reversal learning' procedure are that the long-suffering animals eventually become adept at switching into the required pattern of responding at a moment's notice, making few mistakes at any stage. Chickens and pigeons, for instance, will learn to peck a red disc but not a green one as long as red is 'correct', and indicates that food is available; and then to switch to pecking at green, but not red, as soon as the experimenter reverses the conditions (Levine, 1974). There are various other implications of this, to do with the ability to remember which signal is correct at any particular moment (see Mackintosh, 1974, pp. 608–10); but clearly the animals must pay close attention to the colour of the stimuli in the absence of a consistent code by which a single colour is connected to a single response.

Apart form directly chopping and changing between the responses animals are supposed to make as a consequence of their perceptions, the independence of perceiving and responding can be illustrated by the transfer of perceptual effects from one set of stimuli to another. It can be argued, for instance, that training a dog to salivate only to middle C must have had the general effect of inducing attention to pitch, if subsequent training to salivate to other individual notes is facilitated. Also, we can certainly say in general that it is possible to draw an animal's attention to a particular sensory *modality* by the use of rewards or punishments—pigeons which show no sign of noticing tones played into a Skinner box where they are performing a learned response rapidly acquire a sensitivity to the auditory quality of the tones if the presence of a tone is made significant as a predictor of their food rewards (Jenkins and Harrison, 1960). Much more detailed focusing of attention is possible *within* particular modalities, however, as in the case of selective attention to the pitch, or intensity, of sounds; or the shape, instead of the colour, of visual displays. Given some variety of visual stimuli in initial training, such as presentations of squares and circles which may be red or yellow, then animals trained to pick out red, but not yellow displays, irrespective of shape, are, not surprisingly, more ready to make distinctions between other colours (blue and green, say) than animals set up to ignore the original colours, and pick out individual shapes (see Mackintosh, 1974, pp. 597–8, on 'Intradimensional and extradimensional shifts'). Thus animals may be trained not only to pay attention to one modality rather than another, but also to notice (or ignore) certain qualities within a particular modality.

Various experimental permutations and combinations of the kinds of stimuli presented to animals, and the nature of the overt responses the animals are persuaded to make when the stimuli occur, all support the hypothesis that the perception of the stimuli is in some sense independent of particular overt responses made to the stimuli. In other words the mode of perception demonstrated in these experiments is cognitive rather than reflexive, using the terms as discussed above. The degree to which it is cognitive may be rather limited, but it is well worth stressing that animals do not just make certain responses to immediately present events, but selectively and actively perceive things *about* stimuli, which allow them to behave appropriately under experimental conditions. In Piaget's terms, stimuli can be 'accommodated', leading to the formation of new perceptual schemata, rather than merely 'assimilated' into currently available reactions.

Perhaps the clearest demonstration of the detached and selective character of animal perception, in contrast to the notion that environmental events force themselves willy nilly through the sensory receiving apparatus and out to automatic responses, is the finding that experimental subjects can change, as it were at will, from noticing one thing to noticing another about the same set of sensory information before them. One kind of procedure which allows this sort of demonstration is referred to as 'conditional discrimination' and an experiment reported by Reynolds (1961) serves as an example. Pigeons were shown four visual stimuli, in a repeated succession. These stimuli consisted of white shapes in a coloured background: a blue circle, a blue triangle, a red circle and a red triangle. One way to demonstrate the perceptual combining of visual features would simply be to train the birds to respond to only one of these stimuli—the blue triangle say—which could be done with no difficulty. What Reynolds did instead was to show the perceptual isolation of the features of colour and shape in the visual displays in front of the birds, by training them, at a signal, *either* to select both triangles, irrespective of colour (by pecking at them), *or* to select both red stimuli, irrespective of shape. The instruction as to which selection to make was given by the illumination of different light bulbs to the side of pigeons. Logically, performing this task might seem to be an unnecessarily complex achievement for pigeons as a species to have evolved, or for individual animals to trouble to demonstrate. Functionally, however, it makes sense for visual analysis to proceed on an if-then basis, to the extent of for instance putting the detection of hawk-like features along with things moving in the sky, but grain-like features together with little things lying on the ground; and, more generally, the use of visual perception for such activities as foraging for food may be advanced by selective capabilities. It has often been suggested that foraging birds and mammals may activate 'search images', so that they may be looking for moths at one point, and beetles at another (Croze, 1970; Murton, 1971; Krebs and Davies, 1978). This means moths will be more readily detected while they are being searched for, even though other prey are then more likely to be missed. If this is so, then in terms of perceptual organisation it means that there must be a moth-schema, or a moth-recognition procedure, that can be selectively brought into play to modify from within receipt of messages from without.

Dimensions, analysers, descriptions and representations

Even the bare facts of the visual recognition of objects at different distances and in different places in the visual field require a theory of perceptual analysis of some sophistication (Sutherland, 1959). This is not quite so clear in the case of other modalities; but if we rub our palms over the corner of a table, and then feel the same corner with our fingers or forearm, there is a 'corner' quality to the sensation which is generalised over the body surface, and over different intensities of pressure, which corresponds to 'pattern recognition' at different locations and distances in the visual field; and we expect a dog to recognise 'his master's voice', or the sound of a clarinet, as a category of auditory pattern, despite considerable variations in the dimensions of absolute pitch, and intensity.

The general type of theory put forward to account for the facts of perceptual recognition, especially in the case of vision, is known as 'feature analysis' (Selfridge, 1959; Sutherland, 1959, 1968; Frisby, 1979). Such a theory presupposes the existence of a hierarchy of analysers, each level capable of detecting perceptual features progressively further removed from the detailed reality of neural activity transmitted from the sense organs. The now traditional example is the invariant recognition of the many different patterns of light impinging on the retina of the human eye which may be classified as a letter 'A' (e.g. Neisser, 1967). At the first level of analysis, we might imagine detectors of light and shade at every point in the visual field. Then we would need a level at which lines were distinguished from background, and the length and angle of dark or light lines on the retina coded. After this, we must have detectors for various arrangements of lines, which can code such aspects of the arrangements as 'two legs at the bottom', 'horizontal cross bar in the middle', 'corner point at the top'. Finally we end up with an 'A' analyser, which recognises 'A's of various sizes, and in different typefaces and handwritings. This last stage is by far the most perplexing, since it must put in the same category capital 'A's with round or pointed tops, printed lower case 'a's, and the enormous range of handwritten capital and lower case 'A's. In practice, and especially for difficult-to-read handwriting, we should expect our 'A' analyser also to guess the presence of 'A's on the basis of context, and surrounding information, as in the sequence T-H-squiggle-T. This means that a single analyser has been given rather a big job, and it is arguable that in saying that there exists a final 'A' analyser, we are simply translating the fact that we can recognise 'A's into a different terminology.

Sutherland (1968) broadened the concept of the final analyser by referring to 'structural descriptions' which enable a comparison to be made between current patterns of stimulation and previously established criteria of form. As with final analysers, the crucial point about structural descriptions is that they include several quite different alternatives and incorporate wide ranges of variation. The internal structural description of an 'A' would have to contain a similar amount of information as is given in the form 'Anything *either* with two angled lines meeting in a point at the top with a cross bar half way down *or* something similar with a rounded top *or* a circle with a vertical line of the same height touching at the right *or* etc'. Clearly one does not expect such a description to be written out in code somewhere in the brain, but the structural aspect of the description is that neurons or sets of neurons in the brain correspond in function to analysers or feature detectors, at various levels of the hierarchy of analysis, and are connected together in parallel in such a way that the possibilities of a serial, written out, description are mimicked. The emphasis on structure as a fixed set of relationships is in some ways unfortunate, however, since one of the peculiarities of perception which I have just emphasised in the case of pigeons is that descriptions are flexible, and can be rapidly changed. The emphasis in Sutherland and Mackintosh's account of analysers as they are theoretically derived from experimental studies of animal perception (Sutherland and Mackintosh, 1971) is that analysers are 'switched in' or 'switched out' according to their current usefulness to the animal. In human perception, direct instructions such as 'look for all the vowels, and ignore capital letters' radically alter the way in which visual information is processed.

I shall prefer, therefore, to use the term 'inner description' to refer to the criteria which, as an aspect of perceptual processing in the brains of animals, are used as the basis for recognition and classification of experienced events. Another rather similar theoretical term is 'representation' often used to imply that an animal is assumed to conjure up some sort of remembered perception of an event (e.g. Rescorla, 1979, 1980). It will be convenient to use these two terms, 'inner description' and 'representation', to make the kind of distinction emphasised by Bindra (1976, see pp. 99–102, this volume) between relatively permanent cognitive organisation and an activated memory, or image. 'Inner description' is my preferred version of Bindra's term 'gnostic assembly' or any other form of cognitive organisation necessary for object recognition, while 'representation' I will try to reserve for cases of particular mental images or memories of events which are assumed to direct sensory activities, searches for objects, or goal-seeking actions. The distinction is not always easy to uphold, and 'inner description or representation' abbreviated 'IDR' is a useful reminder that the shorter word 'idea' covers much the same ground.

The naming of hypothetical mental states or properties is of course a dangerous step, because, for people if not for animals, the use of a name gives rise to a sense of reality, and the 'thinghood' of what the name refers to, that may turn out to be spurious. Thus, little importance should be attached to the names themselves; what matters is that, in order to account for cognitive modes of perception, which are measurable in terms of reactions given to certain sets of external stimuli, it is necessary to posit the existence of forms of analysis of picked-up or received sensory information which might just as well be called 'central cognitive structures' or 'schemata' (as they are by Neisser and Piaget) or 'small-scale models of external reality' (as they are by Craik, 1943), as inner descriptions and representations. In other contexts, it is apt to refer to similar facets of mental organisation as 'memories' or 'expectancies', emphasising that mental representations of events can be tagged as past and future, to the extent that we might be able to deduce the existence of an apprehension that 'something important is going to happen soon' or a sense that 'it's been a long time since anything happened' with only the vaguest knowledge of particulars.

However, the main point is that it is the capacity for complex perception, exemplified by visual pattern recognition of variable and disparate forms of the letter 'A', which requires us to consider these perceptual descriptions or schemata. Could it be the case that these complex forms of perception are a property of only the human mind, so that there is no need to assume that the necessary kinds of mental organisation exist in other animals? In previous sections I have argued that animal perception is cognitive, in so far as attention to such stimulus dimensions as pitch and colour, and to cross-modal qualities such as distance and spatial position, is free from particular behavioural reactions, and selective attention of this kind can be seen to vary. But perhaps this is true only for relatively simple forms of perceptual analysis, so that the perception of certain colours, tastes, smells, sounds and rudimentary features like touched corners or seen dots, curves and straight lines, may be subject to context and selective attention, without being capable of being formed into the more elaborate descriptions needed for human perception. Animal perception is often discussed as if this were the case: and certainly, just as there is much in animal (and human) reactions to sensation that is reflexive, there are many ways in which very simple cues of brightness, temperature and so on, influence animal behaviour. But consider how it comes about that a pigeon recognises another individual (as occurs for instance, in parent-young and parent-parent social activity). Or how a dog recognises particular human individuals. Although more direct methods, such as the detection of scents by dogs, may have their uses, it would considerably expand the adaptiveness of animals' perception if objects could be recognised by assessment of the same range of sensory evidence that is surveyed in human pattern recognition. Also, the anatomy and physiology of the sensory organs and associated brain systems in mammals suggests they possess the same sort of physical machinery that accomplishes the schemata and inner representations of human perception. Perhaps we ought not to rely on these hints and suggestions, but fortunately it is possible to obtain additional evidence from behavioural tests.

Experiments in two-way classification and visual concepts

In fact we can look first at evidence that the pigeon visual system accomplishes the recognition of the letter 'A' by feature analysis of the same sort as was put forward as a theory for the human ability. The experimental technique which provided this evidence is not necessarily ideal, but is used very generally: it is one in which animals are trained to sort stimuli according to a two-way classification. For the animals, the classification is based on a 'food' versus 'no-food' dichotomy. Probably this makes the type of perception involved something of a special case, in that the sort of looking done in the context of food-seeking may differ from that done in, for instance, the homing or social interaction of birds. Manipulating the availability of food is, however, an invaluable method for the experimental study of animal capacities, and if unusual perceptual acts not apparently connected with the animal's normal food-seeking behaviours can be thus observed, this is all to the good in demonstrating the flexibility of the perceptual mechanisms.

In the experiment reported by Morgan *et al.* (1976) pigeons were initially trained to look at 40 slides showing the letter 'A', and 40 slides showing the numeral '2'. These were back-projected one at a time, for an average of half-a-minute each, onto a small screen. Unusually, the experiment was conducted on free, rather than captive, birds, so the screen was in an apparatus presented at an outside window, rather than inside a small Skinner box. Several fantail pigeons living wild in Cambridge voluntarily took part in the experiment because, by pecking the illuminated screen, they could produce food from an automatic dispenser. However, in accordance with standard laboratory procedures, food was only forthcoming if they pecked the screen while a letter 'A' was shown, and was not available when the numeral '2' was shown. (In this instance, the birds were allowed to peck at grain for three seconds at the end of every presentation of an 'A', provided they pecked first at the screen.) The results, for the three pigeons studied, were fairly straightforward : these birds pecked 2 or 3 times per second at the 'A's, and infrequently or not at all at the '2's. In a sense this is unremarkable, since a two-way classification of 'A's and '2's is not the same as the identification of 'A's from all other letters and similar shapes. There are a number of distinct clues, any one of which will differentiate between 'A's and '2's, for instance a curve as opposed to a point at the top, or legs as opposed to a horizontal line at the bottom. However, I have not yet mentioned a crucial point: in the 40 slides of each category ('A' or '2'), eighteen different typefaces (from commercial designs) were used. Thus, although all the 'A's were capitals, some had rounded tops instead of pointed tops and there were variations in the size, thickness, and style of the lettering. Furthermore the introduction of 22 new typefaces, after the initial learning, did not cause any disturbance of the discrimination between 'A's and '2's. Therefore any individual features which might have been used by the birds, such as the tops or bottoms of the figures, needed to work over a considerable range of precise forms of retinal stimulation.

To get a better idea of exactly what aspects of the lettering were being picked up, two further tests were made. Bits of 'A's and '2's, and upside down and partially rotated whole 'A's and '2's were shown to the first three birds in the same way as the normal stimuli, and two other pigeons who learned the original discrimination were then shown one at a time, a complete set of the letters of the alphabet (in the upright capitals of a single script). The results of these additional tests are revealing, although not absolutely clear. The birds were keen on an upside down 'A', and the top or bottom of an 'A' separately, but not on an 'A' on its side, or on the separate angled sides of an 'A'. Of the other letters of the alphabet, R, H, X and K were responded to almost as if they were 'A's, and E, S, C, G, I, J, L and Z were treated as if they were '2's, and not responded to at all. W, N, M, B, and U got some attention, in decreasing amounts, with progressively fewer responses being given to Y, T, F, D, V, O, P and Q.

What may we conclude from all this? It looks very much as though 'feature detectors' for 'apex', 'legs' and 'horizontal line in middle but not bottom', were utilised, with the presence of any one of these features eliciting some responding. Enclosed regions and T-junctions, which are also present in 'A's, did not seem to be picked up in isolation, since P and E were a long way down the list. 'Curved top' and 'flat bottom' which are present in '2's, may have been counter-indications to responding. Although this evidence by itself is rather limited, it points firmly in the direction of a form of perceptual analysis in the bird visual system more like a general purpose pattern-recognition device, and less like a restricted set of reactions to peripherally built-in cues such as brightness, colour and movement (Blough, 1984).

The reader may experience some reluctance to take seriously the notion that the pigeon eye and brain should recognise letters in anything like the same way as the human eye and brain, since, after all, what would be the point of a bird evolving an ability to deal with letters, and surely the human eye must have special ways of reacting to the printed word, since we all do so much reading. There is something wrong with this objection. The human visual system was not designed so that it could recognise letters; rather, letters were invented because they could be processed by the human visual system. Speech and language go far enough back to be specially built-in to the human brain, and that may be why we take the trouble to read and write, but reading and writing themselves are comparatively recent developments, and their visual components have to be accomplished with an eye and brain evolved for a life of illiteracy.

If, on the other hand, one is tempted to argue that discrimination between 'A's and '2's is too simple an achievement on which to rest the attribution of perceptual schemata to pigeons, consider some of the other two-way classifications which these birds can apparently make when shown pictures by means of a slide projector. In the original experiment of this type (Herrnstein and Loveland, 1964), it is extremely difficult to suggest individual visual features such as 'apex' or 'curved top' which could have served to simplify the pigeon's perceptual task, because the two categories of visual scene were colour slides showing people, versus colour slides not showing people. Over 1,000 slides of town and country landscapes were used, half of them containing one or more persons, in foreground or background, standing or sitting, clothed or unclothed, and often partly obscured, with the other half similar scenes containing no people. Each day birds were shown 80 slides, one at a time, for roughly a minute per slide. In this experiment, the conventional tactic was used of putting the birds inside a box, with slides rear-projected on a screen a couple of inches square on one of its walls. Of the 80 slides, half would contain people, and the other half not, these two categories always being mixed in a random order. The bird's concern was to activate a food hopper, which it could do by pecking a hinged switch to one side of the projection screen. The bird did not, in this case, have to peck the screen itself: such factors often make a big difference to the observed sensitivity of animals to external stimuli, since their attention is sometimes narrowly focused in the direction of their actions, but experiments such as this one show that pigeons need have no great difficulty in looking at one place before pecking at another.

The critical aspect of the experimental arrangements, readily detected by the birds, was that as long as one or more persons were present in the view projected on the screen, there was a small chance that pecking the adjacent switch would trigger the food hopper, allowing them access to grain for a few seconds. The odds were such that on average the hopper could be operated just once for each slide with a person in it, but the exact time when this would happen was unpredictable (a 'variable interval' schedule of reinforcement: see pp. 92ff.). When no person was shown on the screen, food was *never* available.

As would be expected if information was more direct (by such categories as triangles for food and circles not), the birds, after a week or so of training, responded more vigorously when the slides which did contain people were displayed, and after a few more weeks made a very clear discrimination between the two categories. For almost all the slides with people, their reaction was measurable by the fact that they pressed the switch about 50 times during the minute each was presented. By contrast, for the scenes without people, the pigeons did nothing, or made fewer than 10 pecks.

Each day a random selection of slides was made from the collection of 1,000, so the birds had no opportunity to learn very specific stimulus features. There was thus no doubt that the 1,000 or so visual displays were being put into two categories, and the most obvious interpretation is that a sufficiently complex inner description, or visual concept, of 'people' was being utilised. Experiments using almost identical techniques have established that similar two-way classifications of slides can be made, by pigeons, according to whether the slides are of pigeons or other birds (Poole and Lander, 1971); of oakleaves or leaves from other species of tree (Cerella, 1979); of scenes with trees or similar scenes without trees (Herrnstein *et al.*, 1976;

Herrnstein, 1979); of scenes with versus scenes without bodies of water (Herrnstein *et al.*, 1976); and of scenes with versus scenes without a particular human being present (Herrnstein *et al.*, 1976).

In my view, the theoretical implication of these results is that the normal mode of visual perception in birds is the formation and comparison of inner descriptions or perceptual schemata. What I mean by this is that the birds use their eyes to perceive things, rather than using them as collections of isolated detectors for qualities such as brightness and colour. This is not saying a great deal, though it is useful to have experimental support for the ability of birds to do more than react to simple inbuilt visual signals. Many more detailed theoretical questions remain to be answered. Herrnstein *et al.* (1976) suggest that the visual capacities, hence inner descriptions, exhibited by the birds have 'something to do with evolution' and that the object categories for trees and bodies of water are 'somehow represented in the genes'. But there was very little evidence to justify this, since the birds classified slides according to the presence of 'trees' or 'water' no more readily than they classified slides according to the presence of 'people', or according to the presence or absence of a particular young woman. It is not very sensible to suggest that domestic pigeons come equipped with a complete set of perceptual schemata for all the things they are likely to encounter in the modern world. Whatever natural predilections or preferences may be characteristic of the species, it seems to be the case that the pigeon brain is capable of rapidly forming descriptions of a very wide range of visual patterns (Herrnstein, 1985).

In the phrase used by Cerella (1979), 'concept formation is spontaneous rather than deductive'. This refers to his result that a generally applicable description of some types of pattern can be formed on the basis of one example, and does not have to be distilled from a wide variety of experiences. At any rate, this happened with the outline of an oak leaf in Cerella's experiments, in that the training given, of classifying one oak leaf against leaves of numerous other trees, or even, in one experiment, experience of pecking at one example of an oak leaf outline, without the benefit of other comparisons, enabled pigeons correctly to classify new oak leaf examples. Not too much should be made of this, perhaps, since one oak leaf outline looks very like another, by the standards of variability which apply to pictures of different individual human beings in different postures and from different angles, but it serves to emphasise that the original point of talking about 'descriptions' was that the descriptions should be sufficiently general to cover a variety of different instances, and, in the case of 'A's, several quite different forms.

The amount of experience needed to establish perceptual schemata of different visual categories ought therefore to vary to some degree according to the complexity of the category. There has as yet been little systematic investigation of this possibility. It is a matter of laboratory experience that simple discriminations, such as black versus white, for any seeing animal, and red versus green for animals such as the pigeon with strong colour vision, are formed more readily than discriminations which we should expect to be more difficult, such as a differentiation between two similar shapes of grey, or between two lines at slightly different orientations. It is common practice to distinguish between 'easy' and 'hard' discriminations, and to suppose that laboratory animals required to perform a hard discrimination will learn to do this more quickly if they have previously mastered a related, but easier form of it (see Mackintosh, 1974, p. 595 and Terrace, 1963). One would think, therefore, that it would be possible to demonstrate, because of prior experience or inherent complexity, that, for instance, pigeons can distinguish between individual pigeons more easily than between individual humans, or that they can distinguish between the two species more reliably than they can distinguish between individuals of either species.

Little evidence pertinent to this topic is available. Herrnstein (1979) suggests that, rather surprisingly, pigeons learn to notice the presence or absence of trees in visual displays just as quickly as they learn to notice the presence or absence of a loud tone, and just as quickly as they distinguish between closely similar colours. By comparison, although aerial photographs showing man-made objects are successfully sorted from those not doing so (Lubow, 1974), pigeons are reported to be relatively poor at classifications of line drawings (Cerella, 1975) or at detecting the presence of object categories such as bottles or vehicles in photographs (Herrnstein, 1979). The precise nature of visual information which can and cannot be satisfactorily classified by pigeons therefore remains to be determined. Very little is known of how other species (even monkeys) might perform on similar classification tasks. A theoretical possibility is that the inner descriptions of visual information may not be confined to visual analysis. If, for instance, there is an evolutionary basis to the visual categories of trees and water, as Herrnstein *et al.* (1976) suggest, one would suppose that the description of 'trees' should include some estimate of value, and association with the possibilities for perching, and that 'water' should be even more definitely valued, and should have associations with taste and the actions of drinking.

Abstract qualities in vision—regularity and irregularity of configuration

The advantage of the two-way classification experiments discussed above are that the results are easily summarised and give clear support to the view that animal perception allows the detection of categories of reality which correspond to what we ourselves comprehend as natural or unnatural objects, rather than being limited to the transmission of isolated elements of sensation. The experiments may be less than conclusive, but the results fit well with theories such as that of Craik (1943) to the effect that perception in general must ultimately be understood in terms of its function in providing inner representations which parallel external events. It is unfortunate that data from species other than the pigeon are not available, but the study of primate cognition, which will be discussed in a later chapter, provides a wealth of evidence that inner descriptions of object categories are not confined to humans and pigeons.

There are, of course, many other forms of experiment by which the nature of animal perception can be assessed, but these are subject to great difficulties of interpretation. In between experiments on the detection of simple stimulus qualities such as colour and brightness, and the attempts to demonstrate the utilisation of visual concepts at the level of object recognition, there are some experiments which imply the operation of intermediate levels of perceptual analysis. At first sight, the traditional 'oddity problem' can be put under this heading. If a chimpanzee is several times shown two cups and a spoon, placed in a line, and rewarded for picking up the spoon, whatever position it appears in the line, it would be very foolish if, on first being shown two spoons and a cup, it did not pick up one of the spoons. However, if, over a longer period of experience, it is always rewarded for picking the cup from a line of two spoons and a cup, but the spoon from two cups and a spoon, it may very well adjust its selections according to this rule. If it did so, some would undoubtedly say that it had 'solved the oddity problem', since in each case it would be picking what in fact was the 'odd one out' of the three objects. But the evidence as it stood then would allow us to infer very little about any inner conception of 'oddity' by the animal. It might have learned only to pick up an unduplicated spoon and an unduplicated cup, without being able to extrapolate from this experience when confronted with two saucers and a knife. This would involve, certainly, the perception of duplication in the case of cups and spoons, but without the extraction of a general principle that isolated objects should be picked up and duplicated ones left alone. Very careful experimental designs are required to decide how specific particular perceptual strategies are. However, with visual stimuli, and one odd out of three stimuli presented at once, it is probably the case that a much more general rule of 'oddity' is perceived by chimpanzees than by pigeons. That is, chimpanzees who have been trained to select a red disc from two blues and a red, but the blue one from two reds and a blue, continue to apply the rule of oddity if the objects presented are changed to triangles and squares. (Strong and Hedges, 1966; Bernstein, 1961). Pigeons require prolonged training even to perform correctly in picking out the odd colour, when two colours are unevenly distributed in three patches, and show few signs of having grasped a principle when tested with a new pair of colours, let alone after a shift from colour cues to shape cues (Zentall *et al.*, 1974; Urcuioli, 1977).

Rather surprisingly, it is very difficult to interpret such apparently obvious differences in perceptual capabilities between species. Perhaps the first hypothesis would be that mammals, with brains much more like our own than birds, should perceive visual stimuli in terms of more abstract rules than birds. But mammals other than chimpanzees and monkeys, even cats and racoons, have shown little sign of a clear superiority over pigeons on oddity problems (Strong and Hedges, 1966), and some species of birds other than pigeons may demonstrate monkey-like levels of abstraction on visual tasks—canaries (Pastore, 1954) and rooks (Wilson, 1978) seem to generalise oddity from one set of visual cues to another (Mackintosh *et al.*, 1985).

Although a difference between chimpanzees and pigeons is not necessarily an instance of a universal gulf between birds and mammals, it may represent the superiority of primates over all other animals, and this possibility will be considered in a later chapter. For the present I want to examine not the way in which modes of visual perception may vary from species to species, but aspects of the analysis of the visual field which may to a large degree be shared by a great variety of vertebrate species.

Some characteristics of the oddity problem point to a rather general property of vision, and that is the detection of irregularities and discontinuities in patterns of retinal stimulation. Even within the retina, and at the lowest levels of any hierarchy of visual analysis, it is contrasts and differences between adjacent parts of the visual field which serve as the units of stimulation. At some subsequent level, it seems likely that discontinuities in the visual field as a whole attract special attention. A single dark spot set against an otherwise blank background has much more subjective significance, to the human observer, than a dark spot in the same position which is only one among a multitude of similar spots scattered over the visual field. Is this a product of human awareness; or is human subjective experience in this case a product of forms of visual analysis which are shared by other possessors of the vertebrate eye? And what if our attention is drawn, not to a single spot against a featureless background, but to a single large spot in a scattered array of small spots, or a single cross in a regular array of noughts of the same size? Should we assume that a pigeon, or a cat, is subject to the same kind of perceptual effect?

Any attempt to explain how the visual system works in species other than ourselves would have to consider this possibility, and there is a certain amount of evidence from behavioural experiments to suggest that the mechanisms which underlie many subjective effects in human visual experience, such as the 'figure-ground' effect by which one item stands out from a background, have counterparts in other species.

For instance, the oddity problem itself can be conceived of as a test of the 'figure-ground' effect—how easy is it for animals to pick out the odd item out of a collection of repeated elements? This question applies to any particular set of elements—clearly only species with good colour vision will pick out a figure of one colour from a ground which is of a different colour, but equally bright. And a species which is very sensitive to discontinuities in colour may not be able to respond to triangles hidden in an array of squares. If we were sure that both these perceptual effects occurred in the same species, it would still be an open question whether an animal of this species trained to direct a response at a discontinuity of one type would feel obliged to make the same response when first presented with a discontinuity of the second type.

A confirmation of the figure-ground sort of perceptual effect within a conventional oddity detection task performed by pigeons has recently been obtained by Zentall *et al.* (1980). Pigeons were shown a row of three adjacent discs, each about half an inch in diameter. When two discs were red and one green, pecking at the green one was rewarded; when two were green and one red, pecking at the red one was rewarded. The birds failed to learn this task when the two conditions were randomly alternated. There would of course be no problem for the birds in always picking out the same colour, irrespective of its position in the row—it is having to ignore any preference or learned rule of pecking at a particular colour which makes the problem difficult, and allows in this case the assessment of the extent of the contrast between duplicated and non-duplicated colours.

The most revealing test in the experiments of Zentall *et al.* (1980) involved presenting pigeons not with a row of three discs, but with an array of 25 of them (in a five by five matrix) with the same alteration as before: either one disc was red with the other 24 green, or vice versa. In this case the animals quickly learned to peck only at the 'odd' stimulus wherever it appeared, with almost 100 per cent accuracy. The obvious implication is that the perceptual contrast between one odd element and an alternative which is very extensively duplicated is much more detectable than the contrast between a single element and an alternative only duplicated once.

Especially with colours, it is easy to imagine this as an immediate and automatic effect, similar to the perception of a black dot against a continuous white background, or a white spot against a black background, and an aspect of automatic methods of processing of visual information. That colour is not the only type of visual information processed in this way is indicated by some results used by Sutherland to support his theory of structural descriptions in animal vision.

First we may consider an experiment on the perception of regularity in black and white checkerboard patterns by rats. Although some rodents, such as squirrels, have good vision, the rat as a species is not noted for the acuity of its eyesight. (Furthermore albino varieties of laboratory rats, like other albino mammals, have, as well as difficulties due to lack of pigmentation in the eyes, oddities in the visual pathways in the brain.) Visual discriminations can be obtained in rats, however, especially if a rule of 'look before you leap' is engaged by forcing the animals to jump towards placards on which various shapes and patterns are drawn. By offering the animals a choice of two placards to jump to, a kind of two-way classification of visual displays can be obtained. In the experiment reported by Sutherland and Williams

(1969) rats (not albinos) were given the choice of either jumping towards a completely regular 'checkerboard' pattern (of 16 black and white squares), or jumping to a similar display which contained a 'mistake' in the form of a displaced pair of component squares, so that there was a row of 3 black squares over 3 white ones at one place in the array.

If the rats were rewarded only for jumping to the regular pattern, then, characteristically, they took a long time to manifest accurate visual discrimination, taking about 2 weeks, at 10 choices per day, to reach a criterion of not more than one wrong choice per day. Now one's initial hunch about the visual processes taking place during this period would be that the animals were learning to look for the 'row' of black or white squares in a particular place. Something of this kind probably did occur, since irregularities in the lower half of the display screens, where rats tend to concentrate their attention, were picked up soonest. However, this was not the only thing going on, because, after they had other experience of three sessions of an irregular pattern, the rats managed to sustain their correct choices when new instances of an irregularity were introduced.

Sutherland's conclusion from this was that rats form and store highly abstract rules describing the pattern of visual input which they are exposed to. One could argue about exactly what 'abstract' means in this context, but it is clear that something *about* the patterns, in terms of regularity and irregularity, is abstracted from the visual arrays, something which is independent of the *exact* sequence of light and dark squares. Quite possibly, the analysis of light and dark squares is related to the analysis of the array of red and green circles by the pigeons in the oddity experiment of Zentall *et al.* (1980), discussed above. Subjectively, certainly, there is to a human observer something immediate and automatic about the way in which an irregularity in a checkerboard pattern stands out from the rest, just as one picture hanging askew on a wall demands attention. Conceivably, part of the aesthetic appeal of repeated motives in wallpaper patterns, friezes and similar forms of decoration, is that the regularity and symmetry is perceived as a quality of visual input. It is unlikely that laboratory animals care very much about regularity and the symmetry of repetition in this sense, but the Sutherland and Williams experiment suggests that rats are capable of noticing regularity, at least as a property of checkerboards, and Delius and Habers (1978) have shown that pigeons can classify shapes into categories of symmetrical and non-symmetrical about the vertical.

A second experiment demonstrates a similar distinction between regular and irregular figures, but is notable because the subjects were goldfish, which, although they have quite mobile and sensitive eyes with better quality retinas than the rats', might not be expected to have enough brain circuitry beyond their eyes to do more than detect exact repetitions of particular patterns of retinal stimulation. But, according to the data collected by Bowman and Sutherland (1970), this is far from being the case. Visual perception in the goldfish may be studied successfully by a number of methods, but one of the most direct is to obtain two-way classifications by eliciting the choice of one of a pair of figures shown to the fish at the same time. In this experiment the fish were shown a perfectly square piece of black plastic sheet, and a square identical except for a bump on the top, at the end of their tank, one shape being baited with food, and the other not. Under these conditions, goldfish very rapidly demonstrated their visual acuity by learning to swim to the shape at which they had previously found food. (Some were trained with the ordinary square baited, others with the bumpy square baited.)

The question is, what mechanisms of analysis of visual information allow for such a discrimination? The bumpy square presented a rather greater area—is it discriminated on the basis of greater total area, or possibly by the presence of an additional area of blackness in a position at the top of an ordinary square? Such hypotheses can be tested by giving trained fish new pairs of stimuli which they have not seen before. If only total area were detected, then a smaller bumpy square or a square with a chunk carved out, might be confused with the ordinary square. In fact no such confusions were observed. The rule apparently being followed by the fish was that any square with a sudden break on the side where the bump was on the original bumpy square, should be treated as a bumpy square. In a rather subtle extra test, the fish were shown the ordinary square, but with an extra vertical strip of plastic just in front of it, giving a two-dimensional outline like the bumpy square. If only the outline of the pattern of illumination impinging on the retina was important, the goldfish might have been forgiven for responding to the compound stimulus as if it was bumpy. But this did not happen: a square with the site of the original discontinuity occluded by the overlaid strip was responded to randomly, as if (quite rightly) it might or might not have had an irregularity at the hidden place.

The whole experiment (Bowman and Sutherland, 1970) was more elaborate than this, with a number of forms of the original irregularity, and of subsequent test figures, presented to different fish. All the results, however, were consistent with the conclusion that the information picked up from the original displays was 'highly abstract', at least by comparison with the supposition that the only capacity contained within the eye and brain of the goldfish is the connection of exact patterns of retinal stimulation with particular swimming movements.

That goldfish trained to swim to a square with a small triangular extension on the top side will also swim to a circle with a small semi-circular bite out of the top, might be thought to indicate only a certain vagueness about their vision. It should be emphasised that their acuity is not in doubt, and that they are perfectly capable of picking out circles from squares, and bumps from gaps, if the occasion requires it. Presumably there are limits on the complexity of visual descriptions that can be utilised by fish, and we should expect these limits to be set very much lower than those for the pigeon, and for the nature of their perceptual schemata to be quite different from those of the chimpanzee. Behavioural evidence for such species differences is difficult to obtain, but it is a step of some importance to discover that even a vertebrate as small and as psychologically insignificant as a goldfish appears to subject visual information to such varied levels of analysis.

Comparative anatomy and physiology of the visual system

The behavioural evidence suggests that goldfish can detect a visual category or quality of 'irregularity' over a wide range of immediate physical stimuli, and that pigeons can combine features which may have a similar degree of remoteness from particular patterns of light into classifications which approach the complexity of a description which will allow the visual identification of a letter of the alphabet, or of human presence. Unless such evidence is seriously flawed, it implies the availability of biological machinery appropriate for these tasks.

In fact, only if one held simple-minded views about evolutionary scales of excellence would one doubt whether lower animals like the goldfish and pigeon had *eyes* which were sufficiently developed to serve in the recognition of complex visual patterns: we may still be surprised that their brains are capable of dealing with the richness of the information supplied by their eyes, but this may be a case where experimental studies of the psychology of animal perception forces a re-evaluation of the theories of brain function.

Although there are enormous gaps, there is sufficient knowledge of the basic anatomy of vertebrate vision to allow for some comparisons to be made between the machinery itself, and the way it works (see, Walls, 1942; Rodieck, 1973; Kruger and Stein, 1973; Masterton and Glendenning, 1979). The first point is that the eye itself displays more uniformity in structure, from species to species and from class to class, than any other organ of the body. In terms of the peripheral origin of sensation, therefore, human vision is less distinguishable from that of other vertebrates than is the case with other sensory modalities. For touch, for instance, the difference between skin and scales gives no common starting point to the perceptions of fish and mammals. And while the hair cells which convert vibrations into nerve impulses are essentially similar in all vertebrates, the development of sound-transducing organs is quite different in fish and air-living classes, and there are radical changes in the structure of the ear between amphibians, reptiles, birds, and mammals.

The eye of all vertebrates works like a camera, in that light reflected from objects is passed through a transparent lens to be focused on a sensitive film of tissue a short distance behind. In fish and amphibians the lens is moved backwards and forwards for focusing, as in a camera, but in reptiles, birds and mammals, the lens is thickened or made thinner by the tightening or relaxing of muscles. The very first visual distinctions are thus those between crisp and fuzzy images, fed back into focusing mechanisms. The light-sensitive tissue at the back of the eye, the retina, works in a more or less similar way in all vertebrates, although there are certainly plenty of differences from species to species. Receptor cells which are most sensitive to dim light ('rods') are distinguished from those somewhat less sensitive, but useful for high acuity, and for differential response according to wavelength, as the first step in colour vision ('cones'). Several other types of cell, within the retina, intervene between the detection of light by the receptor cells, and the 'ganglion' cells which provide the output from the retina to the optic nerve, and which are thus the point at which information from the eye is passed on to the brain.

There are two points of some controversy here: first, how complicated is the information that retinal ganglion cells send back to the brain in different species, and second, how much does the brain act back on the ganglion cells or other parts of the retina, to tune them selectively? But an agreed general concept is the 'receptive field' of cells (Kuffler, 1953), meaning the patch of the retina which, when stimulated by an appropriate pattern, will make a cell fire off nerve impulses. The typical type of pattern which activates retinal ganglion cells is a small spot of light surrounded by darkness, or black dot surrounded by light ('centre-surround fields'). These have been measured most clearly in the cat and monkey, but are also apparent in goldfish. In frogs, pigeons and rabbits, somewhat more complex visual events seem to be detected within the retina, such as lines or dots moving in a particular direction. This has given rise to the idea that mammals such as the cat, the monkey and man have rather simple retinas, waiting to analyse shape and movement until the 'on/off' sort of information has reached the brain, whereas less complicated animals get a greater amount of feature analysis over with before transmitting messages down the optic nerve. De Monasterio and Gouras (1975), however, who found some movement sensitive cells in rhesus monkey retinas, suggest that this distinction may have been overplayed. In the human retina, about 125 million primary receptors (rods and cones) converge, through the intervening network within the retina, on less than 1 million ganglion cells, so a good deal of summarising must go on in this case. Subjective detection of moving lights occurs for such rapid movements that Wertheimer and McKee (1977) think movement detectors in the human retina are a possibility, and the separation of different types of information according to different sorts of fibres in the optic nerve, in monkeys and cats, has become more and more apparent (Lennie, 1980).

For most intents and purposes, the retina can be considered to act independently of the brain. There is some evidence, however (e.g. F. A. Miles, 1970), that in pigeons and chickens the brain may act forward to the retina to maintain the sensitivity of certain ganglion cells. It is sometimes suggested that similar modulating of signals from the retina, by outgoing impulses from the brain, occurs in other species such as the cat and monkey, but whether this is a very important influence on the way the retina transforms the optic image is doubtful (Rodiek, 1973).

The relative importance of vision in vertebrate evolution

It is fairly safe to say that the eye, and in particular the retina of the eye, is a very sophisticated device for transforming optical images into activity in the optic nerve, in all classes of vertebrate, and in the goldfish, pigeon, rat and monkey in particular. Many (though not all) of the psychologically interesting questions have to do with what happens to neural activity at the other end of the optic nerve. A peculiarity of visual perception is that the usual phylogenetic hierarchy of brain function, in which we should expect that the brain of the monkey has more in common with that of the rat than with that of the pigeon and goldfish, conflicts with the similarities of the visual input to the brain in fish, bird and primate. The similarities are (a) colour vision, and (b) foveal vision: they may be deceptive, and are probably best explained in terms of their absence in mammals other than primates.

The 'bottleneck' theory of the evolution of vision in mammals (Masterton and Glendenning, 1979) has it that early mammals were nocturnal, and thus less sensitive to colours. Living in complete darkness may mean that species lose vision altogether (as in the case of moles and blind cave-living fish) relying on touch and/or smell. Occasionally species evolve spectacular alternatives to vision, as in the echo-location systems of bats and dolphins and the electric field method of some species of fish living in very muddy rivers. It is therefore not implausible that early mammals sniffing around in the dark for roots and grubs might have de-emphasised vision in general. To the extent that vision was retained, in these nocturnal species, sensitivity to dim light, rather than acuity, would be at a premium and therefore a retina composed largely of rods would have been necessary, and hence colour vision would be lost. Finding safety in trees during the day, instead of prowling about at night, and specialising in a diet of fruit, may be supposed to have led to the invention of acute colour vision, with cones as well as rods in the retina, in only the primates among mammals.

Apart from sensitivity to colour, one of the crucial aspects of the human eye is the use of a fovea, and an 'area' of the retina. The 'area' is a circular patch in the middle of the retina which has a high concentration of cones, giving high acuity, and the fovea is a depression in the middle of this, which leaves only a thin covering above a small spot with no rods and a high density of closely packed cone receptors. The fovea is what we look at things with, and the use of this place on the retina is crucial for detailed human vision. Characteristically, human vision is to a large extent foveal vision. (It has been claimed, for instance, that reading is only possible when the images of words fall on the fovea: Rayner and Bertera, 1979.) No mammals apart from primates have foveas (though some, such as the cat, have central areas where rods or cones are concentrated). But many species of marine teleost fish, and of reptiles and birds, do have foveas in their retinas. It is not uncommon for birds to have two fovea in each eye, and on structural grounds, birds can be said to have 'better' fovea—deeper and steeper pits—than man or the monkey. The duplication of foveas in the eyes of bird arises because of the relative immobility, and lateral placements, of the eyes. Foveas in the centre of the retina face to the side of the bird, and are therefore used for accurate fixation at each side, but foveas at the outer sides of the retina allow for binocular inspection of objects in front of the bird. Hawks, eagles, swallows and terns are among the birds with two well-developed foveas in each eye; more common is one central fovea, as in the pigeon or sparrow. As well as the central fovea, the pigeon has a special 'pecking field' in the upper side quadrant of each retina, which is distinguished by red oil droplets as filters for the cones. Some birds (such as gulls) and some mammals (such as rabbits), have a horizontal stripe of densely packed receptors, thought to be used for fixation of the horizon.

To the extent that the phenomena of human vision depend on the fovea itself, therefore, some human specialisations might be shared with birds: more generally, vision in particular species must depend on the characteristics of the retina and comparisons between species must take this into account. It can usually be taken for granted that a predominance of cones over rods in the retina is backed up by brain mechanisms which compare the output of different types of cones to produce sensitivity to colour. The legendary acuity of birds of prey can be understood in terms of the excellence of their retinas—the fovea of a large hawk (*Buteo buteo*) is packed with cones at a density eight times greater than that found in the human fovea, and, as in the human case, almost every receptor is represented in the optic nerve. Even the non-foveal parts of the retina of these birds would be expected to have twice the resolving power of human acute vision.

Thus the information which the eye sends to the brain in non-human primates is very similar to that sent from the human eye, and the amount of information derived from the eye in other species, especially birds, may match or exceed that which the human brain receives. For ourselves, we know that visual information is eventually transformed into the images and illusions of our subjective perception. How are the reports dispatched from the retina interpreted in the brains of other animals?

The receipt of visual information in the vertebrate brain

The complexity of this topic cannot be underestimated. The points I wish to make here are comparatively few. The main one is that our knowledge of the brain mechanism involved in human vision is based on evidence from animals, and in particular from cats and monkeys. In terms of physiological mechanisms, it is not at present possible to claim that human visual perception is in any way significantly different from that of the rhesus monkey or chimpanzee. However, there are apparently very radical differences between the brain mechanisms used for visual perception by mammals and those used by other vertebrates, differences already referred to in Chapter 5, and we need to return to the question of whether mammalian vision is therefore more cognitive than that of the other vertebrate classes, in the light of the behavioural data which suggests that goldfish and pigeons can form abstract and complicated perceptual schemata from visual experiences.

Visual cortex; area 17; striate cortex—the mammalian super-retina

The three terms 'visual cortex', 'striate cortex', 'area 17', are used interchangeably to refer to the critical arrival point of retinal messages in the mammalian brain ('V1' is yet another synonym). Perhaps as many as three-quarters of the fibres in the optic nerve relay in the thalamus (in the lateral geniculate nucleus; see Chapter 5 for thalamic functions) which sends the message of each of these fibres directly to the striate cortex, on the surface of the brain, right at the back of the head in man, and in a similar position in other mammals.

Great advances have been made in the last twenty years in the study of the structure and function of this area of primary visual cortex, and much has been made of what has been discovered (Hubel and Wiesel,

1962, 1974, 1977; Berkley, 1979; Blakemore, 1975; Frisby, 1979). The basic technique of these investigations is to take electrical recordings of the activity of individual cells in the striate cortex of lightly anaesthetised animals, while spots of light of different shapes and sizes are moved over various parts of the retina (see Chapter 5).

Perhaps the most striking and fundamental fact about the organisation of visual cortex is that it provides a point-to-point map of the visual field. If we were to look at a large letter 'A' in front of us, the pattern of activity in visual cortex would also form a letter 'A', though of a peculiar sort, since it would be upside-down, and laterally reversed after being split middle to sides. In other words, if we looked at a large poster saying 'VISION', someone looking at the back of our head, if he could detect cortical activity, would see a rough outline of the letters, all upside-down, in the order I, O, N; V, I, S. The semi-colon indicates that the letters I, O, N, in the right half of the visual field would be written across the left hemisphere while V, I, S would be on the cortex of the right hemisphere. The connections between the hemispheres for the striate cortex are concentrated in the parts of the cortex that represent a straight line right down the middle of the visual field (Zeki, 1978a). It is legitimate, then, to think of the visual cortex as providing a 'picture in the head', since topological relationships in outside two-dimensional space are repeated on this surface of the brain. Apart from being inverted and split, the cortical picture is stretched out in the middle and compressed at the fringes, since space on the cortex is allocated roughly according to receptors in the retina, which are themselves more concentrated in the middle.

The current theory of what is actually going on in striate cortex is rather involved (Hubel and Wiesel, 1977; Frisby, 1979) but can be given a rough paraphrase. The striate cortex, on which the transformed retinal image is displayed, is made up of a mosaic of small blocks, each one or two millimetres square. Within each block are columns of cells which respond to edges, slits (light against dark) or lines (dark against light), of one particular angle or orientation. These columns are arranged into the blocks (often called 'hypercolumns') so that a complete set of possible orientations is covered. Within one hyper-column, there are different slabs for each eye (in cats and monkeys, with front-facing eyes, everything is seen with both eyes). Individual cells in any block can be found which detect stationary edges, slits or lines in very precisely defined positions in the visual field ('simple' cells); other cells respond to the movement, within small areas, in a given direction, of an edge or line at a certain angle ('complex' cells) and yet others select lines moving over their area of the retina which are of a certain preferred length (hypercomplex' cells).

Thus it is as if the visual field is plotted out in squares, and a separate block of cortex assigned to each square of the visual field, so that for each square, the same set of questions can be asked—is there a light/dark edge in this square?—what angle is it at?—is it moving? and so on.

This is all good to know, and it provides confirmation of the physical existence of the lower levels of feature analysis discussed earlier in the chapter. But, as was emphasised then, these levels are only the most rudimentary beginnings of visual perception. The 'hypercolumn' theory tells us that if a particular form of the letter 'A' is flashed on a particular part of the retina, we can expect a particular set of firings of cells in the visual cortex. But it tells us almost nothing about how 'A's in different typefaces, at different positions in the visual field, are all recognised as 'A's. If the goldfish or pigeon retina were able selectively to respond to edges and movements in certain places in the same way (Maturana and Frenck, 1963) we would still be left with the puzzle of why the goldfish may swim to *either* a square bump, *or* a circular notch, as instances or irregularity, since different cells should be firing in these cases, to say nothing of the differences in firing patterns from the pigeon retina to slides of a clothed standing, or unclothed reclining person, both of which may elicit the same behavioural response (see above).

Since the striate cortex is a stage in the visual perception of mammals, and we would presume that mammalian vision is even further removed from reactions to individual edge movements than that of goldfish and pigeons, the fact that small regions of this cortex contain cells capable of detecting a wide range of visual features in corresponding small areas of the visual field does not take us very far towards understanding how inner descriptions, which could enable us to perceive objects, rather than edges, might be constructed. The features detected in the one thousand or so little blocks of striate cortex described by Hubel and Wiesel (1977) must obviously be fed into further stages of comparison, abstraction and interpretation. One question is simply how far these further stages are incorporated into the striate cortex itself, and how far they depend on other parts of the brain—in particular, areas of cortex surrounding the striate visual projection, conveniently termed the 'extra-striate' areas.

Striate cortex is known according to its stripes: all cerebral cortex has a 3- to 6-ply lamination of layers identified by the size and shapes of the cell-bodies they contain, and within this layering there is an alternation of cell-bodies and horizontal connecting fibres. In striate cortex a middle sheet of horizontal connecting fibres is thick enough to be visible to the naked eye as a white stripe between two grey ones in a fresh cross-section. Thus although recent discoveries have led to stress on the vertical columns passing through the layers of cortex, since the functional homogeneity of columns (all cells in the same column responding to lines at the same angle for instance) can be fairly easily demonstrated, *horizontal* connections, between adjacent columns or between adjoining patches, are just as fundamental to the anatomy of cortex in general and striate cortex in particular.

Facilities thus exist for an enormous amount of lateral interaction between closely adjoining areas of striate cortex (Fiskin *et al.*, 1973). There is considerable sense therefore in the theory that several stages of abstraction and perceptual construction take place immediately, within the striate cortex itself. Even principles derived from psychological examination of subjective visual experience can be applied here. I have mentioned the subjective immediacy of the 'figure-ground' distinction. Similar configurational qualities described by introspective 'Gestalt' theories of the first half of the century were 'proximity', 'similarity' and 'grouping'. At one level, seeing continuous lines and figures and continuous movements may result from lateral filling in and synchronisation between adjacent sections of striate cortex. Seeing dots in groups of the same size, and noticing irregularities of colour and shape, could also be manifestations of lateral comparisons across the visual field as it is represented by cellular activity in this part of the brain (see Frisby, 1979, pp. 110–12, and Marr, 1976; 1982).

But even if the output from this primary visual projection in the mammalian brain takes a great deal of account of configurational aspects of patterns of light impinging on the eyes, it is unlikely that this output alone provides a useful description or schema for object recognition. Interactions within the striate cortex are almost certainly responsible for the difference between what we see with one eye alone, and what we see with both eyes open at once, but subjectively, under normal conditions, this does not amount to very much. Conceivably, a cup of tea two feet away, and the same cup ten feet away, although activating a much larger area of striate cortex in the first case than in the second, might produce patterns of striate activity with something in common, but subsequent stages in the visual pathway would be better placed to detect the commonality. For one thing, if the further-away cup was in the right half of the visual field, but the closer cup was to the left, the initial descriptions would be in different hemispheres.

In any event, there is sufficient anatomical evidence to make it clear that many important aspects of visual perception occur outside the primary projection from the retina to the striate cortex. This is admirably summarised by M. Wilson (1979). In part the evidence can be understood in terms of what happens to visual information after the striate cortex has done its job of constructing a 'primal sketch' (Marr, 1976) from the optical image in the eyes. But directions as to what is to be looked for in the optical image may be given *before* the construction of any sketch. What is known about anatomical pathways suggests that there are cycles of perceptual analysis in which questions and answers are continuously passed round between numerous stages in the visual pathways, the striate cortex standing out because it contains the most faithful reflection of reports from the retina.

Objects and abstractions in extra-striate cortex

Apart from the horizontal passing of information across short distances within the layers of cerebral cortex, the fact that the cortex itself is in a thin sheet means that there is plenty of space for outputs into the great tracts of white matter underneath the cortical grey, these tracts being made up of nerve fibres carrying impulses across to different surface regions, and down to the thalamus and other internal brain nuclei. The general plan of output from the striate cortex is that information is passed forward, from its location at the very back of the brain, first to the surrounding cortex of the occipital lobes, then further forward to the cortex in the parietal lobes, getting closer to tactile sensory projections, and further forward to the temporal lobes, getting closer to auditory projection areas. An advantage of having the middle of the external visual field located around the outside of the striate mapping is that the detailed and concentrated information from the fovea is right at the point where the transition to further stages of analysis takes place (Cowey, 1979).

Topographical maps of the visual field appear to be repeated several times after the initial striate projection, and it may be that each of these additional maps is specialised in certain features, such as colour comparisons, movement comparisons, left-eye/right-eye comparisons for depth perception, and so on (M. Wilson 1979; Zeki, 1978a, 1978b; Cowey, 1979). Because of the techniques of physiological investigation, cells which respond to certain classes of stimuli, in certain positions in the visual field, are the easiest to identify. But of even more interest would be regions in which position in the visual field is irrelevant, and cells do not respond consistently to particular simple visual features, because their job is to pick up more complex features, such as a discontinuity in an otherwise continuous line, or the occlusion of one object by another, over large sections of the optical image. The crucial thing about such higher-order analysers is that they must be optional—irregularities might be important in one context but not in another, and the main theme of the first part of this chapter was that analysers should be capable of being 'switched-in' or 'switched-out', according to circumstances. The technique of recording from individual cells in restrained and anaesthetised animals may not be as helpful for identifying these more flexible stages of visual analysis, which are important precisely because they are *not* inevitable responses to certain exact patterns of retinal stimulation. It is therefore hardly surprising that the use of these techniques has not allowed such detailed and systematic mapping of the functional arrangements of extra-striate visual cortex as has been possible for the more reflexive reactions of cells in the striate, 'first-stage' visual projection. Areas outside primary sensory projections have indeed often been defined as 'silent', since they usually do not manifest electrical activity in response to local stimulation at peripheral sense organs. However, when cells *can* be found outside the primary and secondary sensory cortex which respond to any sort of sensory input, the results are of exceptional interest, even if, and perhaps especially if, the spatial arrangements of the cells do not fall into any obvious architectural plan.

The results obtained by Gross and his colleagues from the cortex in the bottom part of the temporal lobe in the brains of monkeys come under this heading (Gross *et al.*, 1972; Gross, 1973; Gross *et al.*, 1974). Cells in this area often respond to complex visual patterns, which may appear in wide areas of the visual field, and some cells respond if the patterns are presented to either the left or to the right visual field. Stimuli which are moved towards or away from the animal, so that the exact size of the image on the retina changes, are often very effective. Particular stimulus shapes such as a circle, a circle with a toothed circumference, or a semi-circle, may be 'recognised' by particular cells, from retinal images of different sizes and at different positions. One cell was found which gave little or no response to any of these shapes, but fired vigorously whenever an outline approximating the shape of a monkey's paw was presented. This region of the brain ('infero-temporal cortex'), which is in fact closer to the main auditory receiving areas than it is to the striate cortex, may thus be the location of the more abstract parts of perceptual description, in the sense that it receives combinations of inputs which characterise objects, rather than specific and localised visual experiences (Gross and Mishkin, 1977). If the striate cortex exemplifies a 'world of features', it is left to other regions to perceive the 'world of things' (Wilson, 1979). It is the primate temporal lobe, which receives visual information rather indirectly, that is the 'organ of categorization par excellence' for seen events (Weiskrantz, 1974, p. 202).

Old wine in new bottles—the primitive tectum and the primate pulvinar

One reason for interest in the extra-striate cortex, which is beyond the main pathway from the mammalian eye to the mammalian brain, is that there is a relatively large amount of it in human and primate brains. The part of the thalamus which relays to and from the extra-striate cortex is also enlarged in primates, and given a special name, the 'pulvinar'. But, as with the other primate specialities of colour vision and the central fovea, this brings us back again to the submammalian classes including the fish and the birds. For the pulvinar receives some of its input, even in the highest primates, from the quarter or more of the optic nerve which splits off from the main mammalian projection, and goes first to the tectal areas of the midbrain (in mammals the main part is called the 'superior colliculus', but it is convenient to keep to the name of tectum).

Thus in primates some visual information goes from the eye to the tectum, from the tectum to the thalamus and from the thalamus to further projections in the cerebral hemisphere. Exactly the same thing is true of birds, except that a larger proportion of optic nerve fibres begin this route. Again the same thing is true of fish, although the final forebrain destinations are better known in the large brains of sharks than in the smaller brains of the bony fish (Ebbesson, 1970; Réperant and Lemire, 1976).

Is this anatomically similar sequence serving the same function in primates as it is in the pigeon? Or, alternatively, has the sequence from tectum to forebrain been freed from its earlier role by the arrival of the striate region of mammalian cortex, remaining to acquire newer, more cognitive, functions? These two alternatives are clear enough, but it is surprisingly difficult to say which is true.

The first problem is that pigeons (to a greater extent other birds such as the owl or crow, and to a lesser extent all other non-mammalian vertebrates), while they may not have the striate cortex of a monkey or cat, do have a visual pathway from retina direct to the thalamus and then to the higher centres, which looks analogous to the main mammalian geniculostriate system (Nauta and Karten, 1970). Why does the pigeon need this if the larger eye-to-tectum path is already doing what the striate cortex in mammals is supposed to do instead? The second problem is that the eye-to-tectum pathway, retained in mammals, seems to have some of the properties which it has in non-mammalian vertebrates (such as sensitivity to movement) and thus there is little direct evidence of its function being radically changed.

What can be said is that, in non-mammals such as the goldfish and pigeon, it is the optic tectum which is the most obvious 'super-retina'. Each point on the retina maps on to a point on the optic tectum, which is a large and highly differentiated part of submammalian brains, with several laminated layers. In mammals such as the cat, with front-facing eyes, the projection on to the tectum is somewhat complicated, but it has a point-to-point correspondence with the visual field. However, in the cat, the new point-to-point correspondence on the striate cortex takes up much more of the available visual information.

The most convenient way to ascribe functions to these two internal mappings of the external visual scene inside the brain is to suggest that the older, tectal projection is for 'noticing' and the new and improved striate cortex projection in mammals is for 'examining' (Weiskrantz, 1972). 'Noticing' might require either vague knowledge of movement and brightness changes in a particular part of the visual field to be connected to various eye, head and body movements to bring the noticed source into better view, or to instigate reflexive attack or escape movements. 'Examining' on the other hand, might involve a much more detailed reconstitution of the optical image, with greater utilisation of previous experience to identify particular objects and object categories. Noticing would be more automatic and reflexive, with examining and identifying being more cognitive and controlled by context, as befits something especially well developed in mammals. The integrating of noticing and examining by the combination of striate and extra-striate mechanisms in primates could be thought to be reflected in, for example, the cognitive control of eye movements, and the necessity to use a great deal of fairly reflexive noticing in the periphery of the visual field in order to direct fixation of the eyes for the foveal processes not present in other mammals.

To some extent, this distinction fits well with behavioural evidence, if we are content with the assumption that non-mammals do rather a lot of reflexive noticing, and relatively little examining. The apparently abstract coding of form irregularities by goldfish, for instance, could be a consequence of the vagueness of perception resulting from their retina-to-tectum projection. Possibly even the comparative generality of the two-way classifications of coloured slides by pigeons could be put down to rather global noticing capacities in their well-developed midbrain visual analysis. There is a difficulty in that the behavioural evidence as it stands does not suggest that pigeons have any great difficulty with tasks that appear to involve some examining, such as finding the 'X's in an array of 'noughts' (Blough, 1977, 1979) or selecting only the seeds which they prefer from a handful of mixed grain (in some cases eating wheat but leaving tares). The finding that they can classify together slides showing a particular human individual (Herrnstein *et al.*, 1976) as well as recognising their own mate and young in natural conditions, also argues against any general lack of detailed form vision in pigeons.

Birds especially, among the non-mammalian classes, have a reasonable analogy to the mammalian striate cortex system, as well as massive projections from their midbrain tectal mapping to the thalamus, with further back-and-forth exchange of information between thalamus and higher centres roughly comparable anatomically to the extra-striate cortex circuits in primates (see Karten, 1979). Thus it is not necessary to assume that birds are no good at examining, in order to keep the noticing/examining distinction. There is good reason then to believe that vertebrate brain mechanisms of vision display 'conservation of function' rather than 'take-over of function' (see Chapter 5). All vertebrates have a midbrain mapping of the visual field, a mapping which is sensitive to the movement and retinal position of simple light patterns, but also all vertebrates transmit visual information directly from the eye to the thalamus in the forebrain, where modes of perception which are more cognitive than the reflexes of the midbrain may be initiated. Using this division we should expect that vision in species where a high proportion of the optic nerve is devoted to the midbrain (tectal) projections should be largely a matter of instinctive motor responses to visual stimuli which fit inbuilt feature detectors, but since all species have some forebrain involvement, perceptual learning via this forebrain pathway can never be ruled out. Also, some of the interesting achievements in vision, such as the categorisation of optical images independently of their size and position on the retina, occur in vertebrates which apparently rely mainly on the midbrain projection.

In mammals, where the projection from eye-to-thalamus-to-striate cortex takes a higher proportion of the optic nerve, we should expect visual perception to take on a distinctly more cognitive, and less reflexive, character. It is quite possible, however, that the striate cortex projection in mammals is in some ways equivalent to the optic tectum projection in birds, even though they happen to be in different locations. Székély (1973, p. 20) points out that 'The general arrangement of neurons in the tectum, especially their interconnections, strongly resembles that of the cortex of the higher vertebrates.' The layering of the surface of the tectum, especially in birds, is extremely reminiscent of the layering of the visual cortex on the surface of the cerebrum, and the 'tectal columns' of neurons connected through the layers may serve the same function as the more celebrated cortical columns of mammals. My own view is that while this may be true in terms of local coding of the visual array, what is important for the cognitive aspects of visual perception is the interchange of successive transformations of the information originally coded in relatively faithful mappings of the retinal image. In mammals, and particularly in primates, facilities for the progressive separation and re-assembly of features derived from the retinal images are anatomically obvious in the physical adjacencies of the striate cortex, the areas immediately surrounding it, and the further reachings of visually receptive mappings into the temporal and parietal lobes to make contact with transformations of the auditory and tactile projections. The projections of the visual field to the striate cortex, the body surface to sensory motor cortex, and the basilar membrane of the ear to the temporal lobe, are found spread out over the surface of the cerebral hemispheres only in mammals. It is reasonable to expect, therefore, that the type of perceptual organisation which arises from these highly interconnected representations of sensory data on the cortex of mammals should be lacking in other vertebrate classes. But some of the differences in anatomical layout, especially those between birds and mammals, may be partly due to historical accidents. In birds, and to a lesser extent in lower vertebrates as well, sensory information from all available modalities reaches the forebrain, but only after considerable filtering and adjustment along the way. As the distinctive thing about the forebrain is that it should treat sensory data in a more abstract, flexible and selective way than is possible in lower centres, closer to the sense organs themselves, this is understandable. The mammalian forebrain is peculiar in having the maximum possible remoteness from immediate sensory input, along with pathways that seem designed to bring sensory images to it very directly. Perhaps it is this combination which brings about the controlled and detached assessment of the perceivable world which characterises human subjective experience.

If this is the case, then limitations of the perceptual pathways in the brains of non-mammalian vertebrates may be in confining selectivity and flexibility to more abstract and less detailed sensory content. This brings us back to the 'noticing' and 'examining' division of modes of perception, with the corollary that non-mammals may be able to notice, and to react to such details as are provided by their sense organs, and also examine relatively abstract features, in the sense that they may learn to pay attention to modalities, irregularities within modalities or such complex combinations of features as are required for recognition of classes of objects. The advantages of the mammalian perceptual systems ought then to lie in the cognitive treatment of exact sensory representations. Mammals ought to be able to switch in and out analysers for many features of sensory information less amenable to optional separation in non-mammals. If the detachment of perception from immediate response is one of the advantages of forebrain mechanisms, mammals ought to be able selectively to retain small parts of sensory experiences for future use : mammals should remember more details than non-mammals. Unfortunately there is very little evidence from behavioural testing which convincingly demonstrates superior mammalian capacities along these lines, but the separation of memory of perceived events from fine sensory discriminations which may be 'noticed' only in terms of reflexive response is a step in the right direction.

The comparative anatomy of vision—conclusions

Human sight requires the receipt of an optical image by the eye and the transmission of this image, coded as the electrical firing of nerve cells, to the striate cortex of the brain, which is designed to break the code, and reconstitute the optical image in a form in which the firing of neurons indicates brightness changes, angles and movements in particular places in the scene presented to the eyes. The conscious experience of seeing requires the integrity of both the image on the retina, and the coded image in the striate cortex of the brain—damage to local regions of the retina or of the striate cortex makes people unaware of the presence of lights or objects in corresponding places in the visual field.

Other mammals utilise a similar anatomical system, with similar neural codes, and other primates, such as the rhesus monkey and chimpanzee, have relationships between eye and brain which are to all intents and purposes identical to those in man. For mammals, and especially primates, the physical apparatus available for visual perception is not radically different from that available to humans. To the extent that the subjective and cognitive aspects of human visual perception reflect the activities of eye and brain, it can therefore be argued that we share them with other mammals.

However, the striate cortex is not the only part of the brain involved in vision. If it is damaged, even in man or monkey, visual perception is radically impaired, but residual capacities to detect visual cues remain. The phenomenon of 'blind-sight' (Weiskrantz, 1977, 1980) demonstrates that people with lesions can correctly guess at the angle of a line which they are unable to describe in the normal way. Monkeys with extensive damage to the striate cortex can, with retraining, use information from the eyes to detect and manipulate objects (Humphrey, 1974). Other mammals are if anything even more resistant to the effects of striate cortex loss. One of the reasons for this is that output from the eye is sent in mammals not only to striate cortex, but also to a second mapping of the visual array, in the midbrain. This midbrain centre is the main mapping apparent in birds and lower vertebrates.

An apparently reasonable conclusion is that the especially human aspects of visual perception, the detailed examination and conscious experience of what is seen, are based on the workings of striate cortex, non-mammals making do with reflexive and instinctive reactions even to the very detailed and accurate distinctions available to their excellent eyes. Of all the vertebrates only the species closely related to ourselves, the monkeys and apes, have both an eye equipped for detailed, concentrated colour vision (at the fovea of the retina) and the striate cortex brain receiving apparatus like our own. Thus one might suspect that only these primates have human-like capacities for acquiring sophisticated knowledge of the nature of objects and the relationships between them through visual perception.

Though it is reasonable, there are objections to this conclusion. The visual projection to the striate cortex has its limitations, since it could not by itself be of much help in recognising images of differing sizes, or at different positions in the visual field. And it is just this sort of abstraction which we would expect to be necessary even in lower vertebrates, such as reptiles. I have quoted evidence from behavioural experiments which suggests that species without the advantages of a visual cortex—as it happens, domesticated animals such as the goldfish and pigeon—have very considerable capacities for abstraction beyond exact retinal images and for selective combination of visual features into object categories. Therefore, although only the primates may have visual perception precisely like our own, the behavioural capacities of other kinds of vertebrate support the theory that feature analysis and combination, and the interpretation of visual patterns in terms of complex inner descriptions, are rather general characteristics of vertebrate visual systems.

A closer look at the paths travelled by visual information in non-mammalian brains suggests that the complexity of non-mammalian brain anatomy is quite sufficient for the complexity of this theory. Even if the visual projection to the more primitive midbrain centres is regarded as always more reflexive, the presence of, for instance, eleven distinct forebrain regions receiving optic nerve fibres in some species of bony fish (Réperant and Lemire, 1976), six distinct thalamic nuclei in the visual pathways of a lizard (Butler and Northcutt, 1978), and the clear post-thalamic projections of the visual pathways in birds (Nauta and Karten, 1970; Karten, 1979), show that the difference between mammals and non-mammals in the involvement of the cerebral hemispheres in the visual pathways is a matter of degree. There may well be advantages in having a complete topographic mapping of the visual field present in the hemispheres, as well as in the midbrain, and birds at least have an area in the hemispheres where the cells respond to retinal stimulation like the cells in the striate cortex (Revzin, 1969,

Karten, 1979). But projections which are *not* faithful repetitions of retinal patterns, but responsive rather to features of the patterns in a conditional way, depending on the experience and motivation of the animal, would be of more help in accounting for the behavioural data. Thus the extra-striate regions in mammals, and the analogous regions in birds and lower vertebrates, which interpret and direct the flow of information from the more immediate visual projections that are closer to the optical image, have considerable theoretical interest.

Modes of perception—conclusions

The theoretical analysis of perception implies that seeing a tree as a tree is a remarkable cognitive achievement. It is difficult to separate our own perceptions of this kind from verbal relationships in language, but if a bird sees a tree as something which can be flown around and possibly landed on and nested in, the argument is that this requires a perceptual schema of some complexity, which may be closer to an expressible verbal concept than to a succession of instinctive responses to exactly preprogrammed sensations. It is possible that much of the perception of animals is in fact composed of reflexive reactions to simple forms of stimulation, but experimental evidence of the flexibility of discriminations made under laboratory conditions implies that some of the mechanisms available to many humble creatures are of the sort which we would expect to find if sensations are taken to signify objects and arouse processes of categorisation.

Even if, in this sense, animals perceive objects, it is of course a rather limited form of cognition. But attempts to construct machines which analyse inputs from television cameras so as to recognise objects, and spatial relationships between them, emphasise that object recognition is not something which should be taken for granted (Sutherland, 1973).

Perceiving facts and discriminating stimuli

If we see a tree, and a squirrel climbing it, we do not merely activate inner descriptions of trees and squirrels. We can say afterwards that the squirrel was climbing the tree, that the squirrel was red and the tree was green, and that the squirrel climbed very fast, if that was the case.

We perceive not only the prerequisites for nouns but also those for verbs and adjectives, and everything else we can put into words, and we retain this knowledge, if not indefinitely, for a few minutes at the very least. Since animals lack language, it is extremely difficult to know if they perceive facts, other than the presence or absence of various objects or object categories. But there are at least two ways in which it is obvious that the perceptions of animals are more long lasting than merely momentary detections and categorisations. The first is imitation, or mimicry. Locke suggested that the efforts of parrots to reproduce heard sounds indicates the retention of the sound perceived, as a form of memory. The instigation of action which corresponds to the initial perception demonstrates that a description or schema of the perceptual input is retained, and that it is retained in such a form that it can be translated into appropriate movements. The fact that self-observation is relatively straightforward for vocal production means that birds might simply modify their own output until it matched their auditory memory, with little need for such translation. One can perceive one's own vocal output in more or less the same way as one perceives someone else's. But, in the absence of video-recordings, we cannot watch ourselves doing something in the same way that we watch someone else doing it. Therefore the characteristic visually based imitation of apes implies a great deal about the conceptual organisation behind their immediate perception. A chimpanzee which puts a man's hat on its own head may know little of the function and social significance of hats, but has perceived visually that the objects which are hats are put on the parts of the body that are heads. After watching a man put a hat on, the retinal images have to be translated into an abstract code, so that a chimp puts a hat on its own head (which it cannot see) in response to the events which it saw previously.

Animals other than apes and talking parrots do not so obviously imitate human behaviours, and when an animal imitates a member of its own species (as parrots and apes do in the absence of humans) it is less easy to distinguish imitation based on perceived facts from simpler triggering of natural behaviours. Chickens will eat if others do so, but it is not clear whether a chicken perceives 'eating' as an activity which either other chickens, or itself, might perform, or whether the presence of other birds moving about serves as a 'releasing stimulus', reflexively producing the motor responses which we call eating. Many social species of animal co-ordinate their individual activities, but there is no doubt that special purpose instincts are one of the mechanisms used.

Lorenz (1952), for instance, suggests that the sight of a conspecific flying overhead may reflexively elicit following responses in social birds. True copying of seen arbitrary body movements or co-ordinated actions may be confined to apes and man. But whenever it occurs, it demonstrates a high degree of conceptual organisation.

Apart from imitation, perceptual knowledge over and above the categorisation and recognition of sensory patterns can be demonstrated by extrapolation and inference based on perception. A dog retrieving a thrown stick is an example which should not be discounted because of its familiarity: chasers of moving prey need to be able to cut corners and run to where the quarry is going to be when they get there, not towards where moving prey happens to be when it is first perceived. More generally, the function of perception is to direct actions, and actions may need to be determined not only by present sensations but also by prior perceptual experience and inferences based on it. The paradigm of reflexive perception is a fixed motor response to an unvarying input to the sense organs, but in human perception information is detected, stored, and made available for use in the future. The theme of this chapter has been that animal perception is not always reflexive; the internal analysis of current activity in the sensory nerves is usually flexible and conditional, showing selective attention, and may be entered into in brain networks which function as inner descriptions of objects or perceptual categories. The existence of perceptual categories may be manifested by the immediate response to current forms of sensation. Whether or not representations of perceived events are retained or reinstated for future use is a rather different question, one asked in more detail in the next chapter.

8 Memory — sustained and revived perceptions

Human memory is inextricably bound up with verbal reports and commentaries. It is rare to think that one remembers something without being able to say anything at all about it, and the experimental study of human memory can almost be defined as the measurement of verbal or quasi-verbal responses. (Someone can be asked to press a button instead of saying 'yes, I remember seeing that picture before', but if they could have said the phrase, the button-push is more than just a motor reaction.) Because of this, it may cause confusion to discuss the retention of sense impressions in animal nervous systems in the same terms as we apply to linguistically expressed recollections and judgments. But on balance, I would rather risk misunderstandings of this kind than to adopt the artificial alternative of applying new labels to all cases where past experience achieves memory-like status in unspeaking creatures.

I ought to make it clear, though, that I do not intend to attribute all effects of past experience on future behaviour to 'memories'. Relatively clear exceptions are learned perceptual-motor skills and automatic habits. Our skill, or lack of it, at tying our shoes, getting dressed, or washing up, to say nothing of playing musical instruments, may demonstrably depend on accumulated previous practice without our necessarily being able to remember anything specific about important episodes of previous experience. There are plenty of cases of co-ordination of muscles, as important components of skilled movements, which we not only cannot remember, but do not know are taking place at the time. Similarly, there are components of perceptual skills, such as reading, or recognising speech, which are learned through experience, but are never available to introspection. And a dogma common to many forms of psychotherapy is that emotional adjustment, or lack of it, is a consequence of prior experiences that are not available as memories in the normal way. It is always necessary to take account of the possibility that animal behaviour which reflects past experience is doing so by similar unconscious processes, or by even more rudimentary mechanisms that ought to be distinguished from those requiring more interesting forms of the internalisation of knowledge.

Rudimentary mechanisms which would manifest learning by experience in the absence of anything we should wish to call memory have been discussed in Chapter 3 as 'stimulus-response' devices. We can imagine a very simple animal that withdraws into its shell as a reflex response to the detection of vibration, and detects flashing lights without normally withdrawing in response to them. If such an animal were to be lightly jiggled once every minute, it would, if it were anything like a real snail, withdraw to begin with, but gradually cease to do so, after repeated jigglings. This in itself is a form of profiting from experience and retention of information, but the waning of a response to a repeated stimulus (known as 'habituation') can be interpreted as a temporary modification of a simple neural connection between sensory input and response output. As an extreme case, one may assume that a single sensory neuron, which functions as a jiggle-detector, synapses with a single motor neuron, which activates withdrawal (cf. Horn, 1967; discussed in Hinde, 1970; and Gray, 1975; also Kandel, 1974, for experimental work on the isolated ganglions and withdrawal reflexes in the sea-slug *Aplysia*). If this circuit becomes less sensitive as a function of use, the phenomenon of habituation would be mimicked. It could be said that the neural changes involved coded past experience, but the representation is confined to the stimulus-response circuit, and is not available when this circuit itself is not being used.

It would be consistent with what usually happens in real animals if our imaginary creature always withdrew into its shell in response to a very vigorous jiggle. Now suppose that it gets a spaced-out sequence of these very vigorous vibrations in which every jiggle is preceded by flashing lights; and, although it does not normally withdraw in response to flashing lights, we now find that it does so. This looks like a Pavlovian conditioned reflex, and some would say that our creature possessed a 'capacity for associative learning', in common with Pavlov's dogs. But provided that a neuron from a light detector reaches the single synapse in the hypothetical jiggle-withdraw circuit, one could put forward the theory that conjunction of activity at the end of the light detector neuron with transmission across the synapse due to a jiggle has somehow welded the light detector into the circuit, so that the light detector can operate the withdrawal neuron by itself. In this case one would hardly want to claim that the animal had any independent memory of the light-jiggle pairing, or was subject to jiggle expectancies when exposed to flashing lights.

To make life more complicated for this simple animal we might poke small pieces of food under its shell, but only when it had just withdrawn there after faint jiggles which would usually be ignored. If it now began to withdraw very promptly in response to mild jiggles, when it had been for some time without any food, we could argue that we had demonstrated instrumental learning and would have to construct a slightly more elaborate theory about its nervous system. Following Thorndike and Hull (see Chapter 3) we could suppose that our animal was equipped with a food detector, and that this reached back to the jiggle-withdraw synapse in such a way that the activation of the food detector just after the synapse had fired 'stamped in' the jiggle-withdraw connection. To explain any decline in responsiveness when the animal was full of food, or when we stopped giving it food for withdrawing, we should have to add in extra inhibitory mechanisms, but clearly we could account for the changes in the creature's behaviour, caused by its encounters with food, in terms of reflex-like response tendencies, without anything corresponding to a memory, or to an internal description of past experience.

I concluded in Chapter 3 that explanations in terms of altering strengths of behavioural responses, without recourse to inner memories and expectations, are distinctly implausible over the range of learned activities exhibited by the rats, cats and dogs which are the source of such explanations. However, it would obviously be useful if experiments could be designed which reduced ambiguities about the characteristics of internal representations which can be directly inferred from behavioural data. There is a fair amount of data from such experiments which I shall briefly review before returning to theoretical issues. For convenience the evidence can be put under the headings of: response to recent perceptions; comparison of current and recent perceptions; and extrapolation from remembered experience.

Response to recent perceptions

The question of whether sensory images persist for relatively short periods of time after their instigation by outside events is rather different from that of whether representations of external stimuli can be revived or retrieved long after brain activities induced by the initial receipt of the stimuli have died away. Even without special-purpose design for retention of sensory information, the successive stages in, for instance, the visual pathways, would each allow for persistence of patterns of neural activity induced by external events. Then, given the number of loops in the visual pathways (from thalamus to cortex and back again, for instance; see E. G. Jones, 1974 and Gross, *et al.*, 1974), it is easy to imagine that some visual information can be shunted around the loops for seconds or minutes after a given retinal input has ended. It is harder to imagine how activity in the visual pathways characteristic of a given retinal image could be reinstated at will, with the eyes closed: retrieval of information long gone is more likely to be partial and abstract, and the physical brain mechanisms by which inner descriptions and representations can be quietly put away and stored, to be brought back to life at a later date, are completely obscure still, although biological retention of information in the genetic code on the one hand, and the workings of computers on the other, provide appealing metaphors.

In terms of subjective analysis, and of behavioural experiments, it is also possible to distinguish between 'short-term' sustaining of immediate perceptions, and the retrieval of information which has lain dormant in 'long-term' memory. Remembering what we were doing ten minutes ago, or what has just happened in a game of football, is automatic and effortless, and still has the character of perceptions of present events: remembering the same sorts of things after time intervals of days of weeks is more arduous and uncertain, except for very rare and vivid experiences. Sometimes, it is difficult to draw any line between active remembering, and automatic knowing. We do not have to remember how to get from the kitchen to the bathroom in our own house, in the sense that we can do this without pausing for thought, but our knowledge of spatial relationships which allows us to do this is certainly based on past experience, and the storing of information. It is only in someone else's house, which we may have visited once, months or years before, that our knowledge of where the bathroom is becomes sufficiently uncertain to require headscratching, and attempts at mental reconstructions.

In behavioural experiments with animals, it is only possible to guess at mental processes which may parallel such introspections. But especially for 'short-term memory' or the retention of recent perceptions, fairly direct evidence can be obtained as to whether any sensory information at all persisted in the brain of the animal, and if so for how long. In experiments on 'long-term' spatial knowledge, such as that exhibited by maze-running or 'homing', it is clear that animals benefit from previous experience, but less clear that independent perceptual memories can be distinguished from habitual body orientation and hierarchies of response.

Delayed response methods

The paradigm for experimental demonstration of reference to recently perceived events is the 'delayed response' method pioneered by Hunter (1913). Animals can be easily trained to run to one of, say, four doors to find food, if the correct door is indicated by a consistent signal such as a light. If the animal is prevented from making its choice until a minute or so after the signal has been removed, but continues to respond correctly, then some information must have been retained over the span of the delay period. It is uncertain, though, whether what is retained is a perceptual representation—for instance, activity in the visual pathways which corresponds to the presence of a light over one of the doors—or a motor instruction, such as a tendency to move to the extreme left, or to the middle right door. It is usually stressed that the persistence of a motor instruction could take the form of 'pointing' at the correct location by bodily orientation (e.g. Ruggiero and Flagg, 1976) which would not require any internal kind of memory. This possibility makes the interpretation of results from some delayed response experiments difficult. Hunter (1913) himself concluded that rats and dogs in his experiments could only manage to respond correctly with the help of pointing postures, since preventing pointing by moving the animals, or moving the visual displays, induced mistakes. But racoons, as well as children, responded accurately despite these types of disruption. There is little doubt that animals frequently resort to postures, pointing of the eyes, and similar strategies to solve delayed-response problems they are set, since such strategies are successful. But this does not mean that the same animals might not use more interesting internal forms of memory if postures were not so much part and parcel of the procedure (Weiskrantz, 1968).

In tasks requiring the use of perceptual comparisons, discussed in the next section, postures do not help, and therefore this problem of interpretation is eliminated.

But there are many results obtained using simple forms of delayed response that also provide evidence for memory processes going beyond maintained body postures. Even if rats move about a good deal during delay periods of up to an hour or more they can select locations where food has been signalled prior to the delay (Maier and Schneirla, 1935; Ladieu, 1944; Sinnamon *et al.*, 1978), whether the movements during the delay were spontaneous (Maier and Schneirla, 1935) or because the animal has been carried about by the experimenter (Sinnamon *et al.*, 1978). Similarly, although monkeys are sometimes confused if they are distracted during the delay between observing a visual cue in a certain position and manually searching for food in that position (Ruggiero and Flagg, 1976), they often appear to retain information about individual position cues over long intervals, while they are running about and looking at other things (e.g. Yerkes and Yerkes, 1928; Weiskrantz, 1968; Medin and Davis, 1974).

A systematic and substantial body of work on animal memory, which includes the use of delayed response methods, has been presented by Beritoff (1965, 1971). He was a student at St Petersburg in Pavlov's day, and worked initially with conditioned reflex techniques. The story goes that he first began to search for more elaborate explanatory concepts after observing that a dog who saw a piece of meat thrown out of a second floor laboratory window reacted by running downstairs. In any event, Beritoff and his colleagues in Georgia, where he worked for many decades after 1919, used tests of the kind where a dog in a cage would be shown a piece of food, which was then hidden behind one of several screens and the dog let out of its cage several minutes later. If the animal then went directly to the hidden food, Beritoff (1971) attributed this to 'image-memory'. It is not always clear from Beritoff's accounts that postural pointing or the use of the sense of smell has been ruled out, but taken as a whole, this sort of experimental evidence suggests very strongly that some kind of inner memory of where food is, a memory which appears to dissipate with time, is present in dogs. The fact that an experienced dog would sometimes go to sleep during a memory-interval of thirty minutes, and then perform correctly when its cage was opened, shows that sustained pointing is not always necessary, and the finding that even the best animals made random choices if periods of more than one or two hours had passed since they saw where the food was put demonstrates that the smell of food by itself was not a sufficient cue for correct choices under these conditions.

Beritoff (1971) attempts the difficult task of comparing the effectiveness of this 'image-memory' in a variety of vertebrate species including goldfish, frogs, turtles, lizards and pigeons. Only a very limited form of image memory could be demonstrated in goldfish. They were adapted to a large aquarium divided into three sections at one end where they were fed, and then netted and transferred back to the other end, from which they could swim back into one of the sections to be fed again. Although the fish were initially frightened by this procedure, Beritoff reports that they eventually came to 'follow the net of their own accord' (Beritoff, 1971, p. 92), a surprising result in itself. However, the main point was that if they were allowed to swim back to the feeding sections within 10 seconds of being placed back at the starting end of the aquarium they swam directly to the place where they had just been fed, whereas if they were held back in the starting end for more than 10 seconds, they usually swam down the middle of the aquarium, whether or not they had just been fed in the middle section. This may mean that in goldfish there is only a very brief persistence of internal brain activities sufficient to direct movements towards particular locations in space, but isolated results like this obviously need to be interpreted with caution.

It is rare for frogs and other amphibians to reveal even the most rudimentary effects of conditioning procedures, let alone 'image-memory'. Beritoff reports that frogs learned to go to a feeding tray in response to a light only after scores of feedings in which a worm was put in the tray 10 seconds after the lamp was turned on. Frogs also swam away from electrodes which delivered painful shocks, and selectively refrained from eating strips of meat after tasting one that had been dosed with oil of cloves. Such 'conditioned aversions' are probably the most reliable way of demonstrating responsiveness to past experience, but can be interpreted as special-purpose instincts for modifications of food selection (see Garcia *et al.*, 1977).

For lizards and turtles, however, the behavioural evidence for 'image-memory' was similar in kind to that obtained from dogs. These reptiles were confined to a certain part of their living quarters, shown a piece of food being hidden within their sight, and then released to see if they could retrieve it. This they could do successfully if they were released within 2 or 3 minutes of seeing the food hidden, but not after longer intervals. If some obstruction were deliberately placed in the most direct path to the hidden food, the animals climbed over it or detoured around it. These and other results indicating a considerable degree of flexibility of reptile behaviour in response to prior experience are reviewed by Burghardt (1977). There is far less experimental work on memory and learning in reptiles than there is on birds and mammals, and negative results are often obtained because many species feed infrequently and require high ambient temperatures for free movement, but it would be unwise to conclude because of this that the control of reptile behaviour is entirely a matter of simple reflexes and instincts.

According to Beritoff's data, the time intervals over which pigeons and chickens can be restrained after being shown food being hidden, while still being able to locate the food when released, are roughly the same as those for the reptiles, that is 2 or 3 minutes. However, if the birds were allowed to eat part of the hidden food, carried back to their cage, and then released again, this second release could be delayed up to 10 minutes with the birds successfully returning to the partly eaten bait. This effect did not occur with the turtles and lizards, which could only return to partially eaten food after the same interval of 2 or 3 minutes after an initial visual sighting of where food was hidden. In terms of the time intervals used in the visual sighting test, the birds seemed only marginally better than the reptiles. In all mammals tested, including rabbits, cats, and baboons, Beritoff says that appreciably longer intervals could be used, but, especially in the case of the rabbits, prolonged training with gradually increasing delay periods was necessary to establish this superiority, so the assertion should be treated with caution. It would be churlish to deny, however, that the image-memory of the baboons was remarkably robust, and appeared to survive longer time intervals and greater distraction than that in any other of the species tested by Beritoff. It took 2 or 3 months to acclimatise the baboons to living in a cage in the experimental room, and to moving around quietly outside the cage, with or without a collar and leash. When this had been done, they could be tested in the conventional way, by being shown a piece of apple in a basin, before the basin was placed behind one of six screens a few yards distant. They could be relied on to go directly to the hidden basin if they were released from their cage up to 30 minutes later. It is not clear that there is a large quantitative difference between the baboons and the dogs and cats in the length of this interval, but Beritoff's conclusion that the baboons' memory was 'better developed' may be based on slightly different tests given to the primates. For instance, if a baboon's cage was covered after it had seen food being hidden, it might shake the cage and make prolonged vocal protestations, but still go directly to the hidden food when the cage was uncovered and it was let out. Or, if a baboon was taken out of its cage on a collar and leash and led about the room without being let near hidden food, but being given something else to eat instead before it was shut up again, it could still go to the previously hidden bait if it was now let out without a leash. This certainly rules out body orientation or pointing as the memory mechanism, and one presumes that olfactory cues were discounted by sometimes removing food after it had been hidden. (The deterioration of food finding after delays of more than 30 minutes is also evidence against the importance of olfactory cues.)

In the baboons, but in the dogs and cats as well, it was possible to demonstrate memories lasting weeks or months, it they were carried into a new room which they had not seen before, given food in a particular place, and then released at the door of this room days or weeks later. Going directly to sniff or search in the place where they had once been fed—under a table or behind a chair—was, very reasonably, taken as evidence for the long-term retention of information picked up at the previous feeding. The comparisons between species may be misleading, since it is difficult, if not impossible, to be sure that one can equate across species factors such as motivation—how interested particular species are in the rewards selected for them, at the levels of hunger used—and the degree to which a species is adapted to the conditions of testing, either in terms of its natural capacities or in terms of the amount of experience of the testing conditions. In the case of memory for food locations in new environments over long periods, Beritoff suggests that pigeons and chickens can manage only 5 days, by comparison with the several weeks observed in the larger mammals, but the quantitative difference is perhaps less important than the fact that in both birds and mammals it is possible to demonstrate retention over periods measured in days rather than minutes.

One can say, however, that the most elaborate memory for observed food locations reported in animals has been that found by Menzel (1973) in chimpanzees. In this case, a group of six wild-born chimps had lived in a one-acre field in which tests were conducted for over a year before the tests began. Just before an experiment, all six animals were locked in a cage just outside the field. Then someone carried one of the chimps from the cage and around the field, accompanied by another person who, while the chimpanzee watched, placed 18 pieces of fruit in different hiding places. This took about 10 minutes, and then the animal was put back in the outside cage for 2 minutes before being released with the other five to look for the fruit. The main outcome of the experiment was that a chimp who had just seen the 18 pieces of fruit hidden (four animals were given four tests each) managed, on average, to find 12 of them. Other chimps in the field at the same time, who had no prior knowledge of the whereabouts of the hidden items, occasionally came across them, but on average the five uninformed animals only discovered one piece of fruit between them during each trial when the informed chimp was picking up 12.

There is thus no doubt at all that the animals who watched the pieces of fruit being hidden retained information derived from this experience, in a form which allowed them to run in direct lines to the various food locations. Other aspects of their behaviour suggest that their memory could be described as a spatially organised description of what was hidden where. For instance, they did not pick up the fruit in the order in which it had been hidden, rather, they started with a piece fairly close to the position at which they were released into the field, then went to the hiding place closest to their current position, and so on. There was some variation in this, but they organised their search route more or less according to a principle of 'least-distance' between successive stopping places. Some of the variation may have been due to preferences for individual hidden items: in further tests 9 pieces of fruit and 9 pieces of vegetable were dispersed over the field, with the result that the chimps (who preferred fruit to vegetables) modified the 'least-distance' principle in order to pick up fruit rather than vegetables first. They thus remembered not only that something was hidden in the various hiding places, but also, to some extent, knew what it was that was available at each location.

It should not be thought that the only form which animal memory can take is one which elicits movement towards food. Most of the tests discussed so far could be interpreted in this way, but spatial memory must include other landmarks besides food locations, and there are other large parts of the behavioural repertoire, in particular social interactions, which involve much more than spatial position. Even with food searches it needs to be pointed out that the chimpanzees in Menzel's experiment had to remember not only the original locations of hidden food, but also whether or not they had already harvested these locations during their current search. A simple rule of 'move to where food has recently been experienced' would lead to many wasteful returns to empty holes in the ground and unproductive tree stumps. It may be noted that Thorndike's 'stamping-in' principle and other theories in which rewards are supposed to automatically strengthen preceding responses would predict much wasted effort in these circumstances.

A rule of not returning to places recently emptied of food seems to be readily adopted by rats as well as chimpanzees according to experiments reported by Olton and Samuelson (1976) Olton *et al.* (1977) and Olton (1978). These experiments make use of an apparatus known as a 'radial maze', in which a number of arms (usually 8) project out from a horizontal platform like the spokes of a cartwheel lying on its side. There is no outer perimeter, so the only way for rats to move about the maze is back and forth to and from the central platform and the end of any one of the projecting arms. The procedure is straighforward. If the spoke pattern is composed of alleyways on a floor, rats will explore every part of it spontaneously, and if elevated pathways raised a few feet above the floor are used, a little preliminary encouragement, in the form of bits of food visible on the arms, is all that is necessary. The experimental test is to place one food pellet, out of sight, in a hole drilled at the end of each arm. The most efficient thing for a rat to do in these circumstances is to traverse each arm in turn, picking up the food pellet, but never returning down any arm for a second time. In fact, rats do not always select arms in any systematic order, but if there are 8 arms, they almost never visit the same place twice during the first 8 choices (Olton and Samuelson, 1976). In other words, they seem to possess what Olton (1978) calls a 'working memory' of the previous choices they have made, plus a strategy of not repeating the same choice. If a similar maze was made more difficult, by including 17 arms radiating from a central platform rather than 8, then errors were made, but trained rats chose an average of about 15 different arms in their first 17 choices (Olton *et al.*, 1977). This is somewhat less dramatic than it may seem, since choosing entirely at random would lead to traversing 11 different arms in the 17 attempts (e.g. going down 6 of these 11 twice). However, if there were no tendency to avoid previously chosen arms, making 15 or more different choices in the 17 attempts would be statistically extremely unlikely ($p < .002$) and so it is almost certain that there was some form of retention of what previous choices had been made. Additional experimental procedures (e.g. confining the animals in the central platform to prevent systematic turning into a new alley as the animal emerges from one just traversed) suggest that neither body orientation nor the use of odour is necessary, and that previous choices are remembered by rats in terms of the directions they have gone in before (Olton, 1978).

Remembered perceptions directing delayed responses

The work of Hunter (1913), Beritoff (1965, 1971) and others suggests that what is perceived at one moment may be used by animals to direct responses a few minutes later, and in some cases hours or days later. The nature of the information perceived and retained is a matter of inference and theory, but in most experiments its content has something to do with the location of food. This is partly a matter of experimental convenience—hungry animals will reveal their inner memories by external actions directed at getting food. But it also points to the utility of memory. Purely instinctive reactions which take no account of recent experience of food distribution may serve some species well, but being able to adjust foraging strategies according to circumstances might confer profound advantages on species equipped with brains which allow this (see Krebs and Davies, 1978).

It should be acknowledged that although it makes sense to assume that many vertebrate species have evolved mechanisms which enable them to incorporate both remote and recent experience into searches for food and other patterns of behaviour, and that delayed response methods provide clear experimental evidence for such abilities, parallels between animal memory in this form and human memory, as it is subjectively known or experimentally tested, are still rather speculative. Current availability of items of information recently received is usually attributed to a particular theoretical component of human memory such as 'primary memory' (James, 1891), 'short-term memory' or 'working memory' (Gregg, 1975; Baddeley, 1976). A subvocal or 'phonological' method of temporary retention, such as an 'articulatory loop' is usually emphasised in these discussions, and clearly the 'image-memory', inferred by Beritoff from his delayed-response experiments on animals, does not correspond to a speech-related process of this kind. On the other hand, it seems possible that Beritoff's 'image-memory' has something in common with the 'visual short-term memory' proposed by Baddeley (1976) on the basis of experiments with people.

Retrieval of spatial information from a longer-lasting store is suggested by the ability of Beritoff's baboons to find hidden food after an interval of some minutes during which they had been distracted by eating other bits of food, as well as by their ability to go back to a room after a week's absence and search in the exact place where they had seen food before. Menzel (1978) reports that his chimpanzees, after finding and eating 10 or so of the 18 pieces of fruit secreted in various parts of the field they lived in, would often lie down and rest, and appear to doze off. Then, suddenly, they would rise to their feet and run 10 or 20 yards to collect another bit of fruit that had been concealed (in their sight) close by. It is hard to resist the conclusion that, after a period of rest and digestion, they had just remembered another convenient food location, after it had been temporarily forgotten about, in much the same way that a human subject might remember things when participating in a similar exercise.

What may be true of the chimpanzee, whose brain and digestive system are very like ours, may not be true of other mammals, and almost certainly has even less in common with what is true of other classes of vertebrates, represented perhaps by the goldfish and pigeon, with brains more than a hundred times smaller than the ape's. Additional behavioural evidence concerning relations between current actions and previous perceptions would be helpful, as well as data which might tell us something about how mechanisms inferred from behaviours are in practice accomplished by brain processes. But before going on to these further issues it is worth looking at some work by Krushinsky (1962, 1965) on what he terms 'extrapolation reflexes', which can be used as examples of the functional utility of remembering visual information about food location in order to direct food-seeking activities.

Extrapolation from remembered perceptions

In all the delayed response problems discussed so far, the solution required some form of memory of the locations of stationary food objects. For many animals, food objects are commonly not stationary, but moving. Predators who chase their prey may be observed to head off moving prey, and respond as if sophisticated calculations are made about the likely intersections of their own and the prey's movements. We can thus ask whether, if a dog is given a brief glance of a moving rabbit, and released a couple of minutes later, it will run to where it saw the rabbit, or to a point off in the direction in which the rabbit was running. Such an experiment would be difficult to set up and interpret, and Krushinsky, after having worked with dogs in the Pavlovian tradition, at Moscow, chose to use simple laboratory apparatus to investigate questions of this type.

One form of test which may involve very recent memory is the 'Umweg' or barrier problem (see Kohler, 1925) in which an animal can see food on the other side of a short screen, and must go around the screen to reach it. Possibly a dog which loses sight of the goal as it runs around a barrier for the first time retains an expectation that something will still be there when it arrives, and the fact that mammals seem to react more intelligently to such detour problems than, for instance, reptiles (Burghardt, 1977) is often taken to imply greater cognition in the sense that mammals can react more effectively than reptiles to objects not immediately present.

Krushinsky modified the barrier problem in the following way. An opaque screen roughly two meters wide had a slit down the middle through which animals of various species were allowed to poke their heads to eat from a bowl on the other side. There were in fact two bowls, to the left and right of the gap in the screen, one containing food and the other not. The important test was when, for the first time in the experience of an individual animal, both bowls began to move out of reach, away from the gap, and along the screen which separated the animal from the bowls. If this was done with pigeons, they usually withdrew their heads from the gap and walked a few steps in the direction in which the food bowl had moved, making poking movements at their side of the screen. By contrast, dogs, given the same test, but of course allowed a larger gap to get their heads through in the first place, reacted to the withdrawal of the bowls by running round the screen to the side where the food had been (Krushinsky, 1965). Out of 27 pigeons, only 2 ran around the screen; while out of 18 dogs tested, 14 ran around to the food side and 2 ran round the other side.

This could be taken as an expression of a natural aptitude for the tracking of moving objects in dogs, which is absent in pigeons, but also indicates an effective short-term retention of perceived events which is more marked in the dogs. Krushinsky's detour test does not, however, cleanly separate the abilities of birds from those of mammals. Birds of the crow family (crows, magpies and rooks) did just as well as dogs, about three-quarters of those tested immediately running around the screen on the correct side as soon as the bowls moved out of reach. A few (6 out of 42 tested) ran around on the wrong side, in the direction of the empty bowl, and a couple of crows quite sensibly flew over the barrier to the point where the food bowl had moved to (Krushinsky, 1965). Over a hundred chickens were given the same test, and about half of them went around the screen when the bowls were moved, but, of these, as many went to the empty side as to the food side. This is rather better performance, in so far as such judgments can be made, than was obtained with rabbits, since only a minority of the rabbits used detoured around the screen, some to one side and some to the other. Cats, like the dogs and crows, could usually be relied on to go around the screen, but almost as many cats went in the direction of the empty bowls as detoured on the side of the full one.

All these results refer to the proportion of animals detouring around a barrier for the first time: this is important since it means the actions were directed by what had just been perceived, and were not stamped in by special training. With prolonged trial-and-error learning, Krushinsky found that pigeons would run around the screen, but in the same direction each time, while some of the chickens and rabbits learned to run in the direction of the food, which changed randomly from trial to trial. It was always easier, however, to train chickens and rabbits to run in a particular direction—going round to the left each time for instance—than to train them to run in the direction where the food was. It looks very much as though, for these species, it is easier to remember that there is food on the other side of the screen, than it is to remember whether the food is to the left or to the right on any particular occasion.

Various other food-finding tests were used by Krushinsky, all of which supported the idea that what he calls 'extrapolation' is easier for some species than for others, where the extrapolation is from very recent to current experience. It is worth mentioning one of his more unusual tests, which required a special apparatus rather like a toy railway set. A food bowl could be run down a straight track, at 8 cm per second, for a metre and a half in the open, then into a 3 metre tunnel, emerging again at the other end. The measure of an animal's recent memory could be taken as how long it searched for food after it disappeared down the tunnel, and the distance it ran down alongside the tunnel. Pigeons, which followed the moving bowl and fed from it, simply turned round and walked back along the track as soon as the bowl entered the tunnel. Chickens and rabbits stayed at the entrance of the tunnel (which was covered with a flap) for a few seconds or sometimes half a minute, while crows and magpies walked up and down outside the tunnel for about a minute. Even the crows did not initially walk all the way to the end of the tunnel but in a couple of cases where the tunnel was cut in the middle so that the birds could see the bowl going past, Krushinsky reports that the crows went all the way to the end and stayed until the food bowl emerged. This is not very much to go on, and the test was not tried with cats and dogs, but this kind of set-up reminds us again that even for a chicken scratching for insects, it might be extremely useful to be able to go on scratching in a place where an insect had just been seen, and, for many predators, being able to remember where a moving prey item has just disappeared to ought to have high priority as a psychological function.

Comparison of current and recent perceptions

Although the relatively straightforward methods of delayed response testing may correspond to the natural uses of retained perceptions in animals, it is often hard to decide whether responses to recent stimuli are controlled by the retention of sensory information as opposed to the persistence of motor reactions. The sight of an insect may elicit scratching reflexes in a chicken, and such reflexive behaviour, once begun, may continue for some seconds in the absence of any internal representation in the brain of the bird which could be considered to be a visual memory of the eliciting image. In many experiments the length of the interval for which responses are delayed, and variation in motor activities observed during this interval, may argue against such simple mechanisms of response persistence, but it is helpful if ways can be found to get clearer evidence for the retention of information in the form in which it is initially perceived. Experimental procedures which require animals to make comparisons between recent and current events appear to do this.

Delayed matching to sample

A technique which has been used for some time with primates (French, 1965; D'Amato, 1973) and occasionally with pigeons (Blough, 1959; Smith, 1967; Roberts and Grant, 1976) assesses knowledge of recent stimuli by choice among two or more current comparison items. Typically there is a row of three panels, on which visual stimuli such a coloured lights can be displayed. A 'sample' image is first put on the centre panel—let us suppose that it is a horizontal line. Usually the animal has to touch the sample stimulus in some way to go any further. When it does, the sample goes out, and a fixed time later (say 20 seconds) the two outer panels are lit, one with a horizontal line, and one with a vertical line. In most experiments the procedure is such that the animal is given food reward if it touches whichever outer panel is the same as the centre panel was a few seconds previously; and usually there are only two possible stimuli to choose between. Even so, it would seem to be necessary for an animal to retain some perceptual knowledge of which of the two stimuli had just been presented in order to respond correctly at the end of the delay interval.

The experiment reported by Smith (1967) can be used as an example. In this case pigeons pecked at a centre display which was either a horizontal or a vertical line. A few seconds after the centre display had disappeared left and right displays came on, one with a horizontal line and the other with a vertical line. The crucial point about this type of experiment is that sometimes the horizontal line is on the left and the vertical line on the right, and sometimes vice versa, in a completely unpredictable way; and the rule is that whichever display is the same as the preceding centre sample must be pecked by the bird in order briefly to operate a food dispenser. In Smith's experiment, each individual pigeon had a daily session of 120 trials, one after the other. After some weeks of training, the birds responded correctly on more than 90 per cent of these trials if there was a minimal memory problem, that is, if the side choices came on just as soon as the centre sample went off. But there was a steady decline in accuracy, on days when there was a delay between the sample and the choice stimuli, as the delay increased from 1 to 51 seconds. With a 5-second delay, the three pigeons tested were only correct on about 60 per cent of the trials, which is not sufficiently different from the 50 per cent that would be achieved by chance to say that anything very much was being remembered. With only 1 or 2 seconds delay, performance at better than 70 per cent correct indicated that choices were being influenced in some way by the character of the preceding sample display.

Extensive research using similar experimental procedures, but with colours as the visual stimuli, has been summarised by Roberts and Grant (1976: see also Grant, 1976; Roberts and Grant, 1978). When the sample colour has been seen for only one or two seconds, it is not usually possible to detect any influence of the sample on choices made more than 20 seconds later, and accuracy always drops off rapidly when the sample has to be remembered for more than 2 or 3 seconds. However, if each sample is seen for 10 seconds or more, the effects of the sample last for up to a minute. In other words if a pigeon sees red on a centre panel for 10 seconds, and then has to wait for a minute before the side panels are lit up red and green, it is still statistically more likely to choose the red panel, whichever side it is on (Grant, 1975, 1976).

Fairly similar experiments with New World monkeys have been reviewed by D'Amato (1973). On the face of it, the initial performance of these primates is not all that different from that of pigeons, since they appear to retain a memory of the sample sufficient to have a statistically significant effect on subsequent choices only for delays from 10 to 20 seconds. However the usual emphasis (D'Amato and Cox, 1976) is that after years of training these monkeys are very different from pigeons because they can remember the colour of a sample for 3 or 4 minutes. One monkey in particular was reported to perform at chance levels with delays of more than 10 seconds with less than 5,000 trials of training, but to have improved, after 30,000 trials spread over 6 years, so that the colour of the sample influenced choices made 9 minutes later. This is interesting, but one can argue that it shows that over a few weeks of training both pigeons and monkeys display 'short-term memories' which last roughly 10 seconds, which is a value in the range quoted for experimental studies of human capacities for things like remembering a telephone number after seeing it for the first time (see e.g. Gregg, 1975; Baddeley, 1976). The fact that monkeys get much better after years of specialised practice is difficult to compare with standard human experimental data, but people with specialised interests in remembering quickly presented information such as telephone numbers or the orders of restaurant customers should not have any difficulty in surpassing textbook figures, and remembering things seen or heard only once for 10 minutes or more.

It is likely that there are differences between species in the time intervals and richness of content possible in this sort of memory for recent events, and also that there are differences between sensory modalities. But there is little evidence available from experiments using modalities other than vision, and even for vision one is limited to experiments on pigeons and a handful of species of monkey. Herman and Gordon (1974), using three localised sounds in a procedure like the one described above using three visual displays, found that bottlenose dolphins could select a sound which matched a sample heard 2 or 3 minutes earlier, and the experiments reported by Pavlov (1927: discussed in Chapter 3), in which dogs were trained to salivate only to certain sequences of musical tones, imply retention of auditory information for periods of seconds at least. Especially using sounds it would be an advantage to test memory for the location of a stimulus separately from memory for other auditory characteristics, but there is little evidence on memory for sound location as such, although Beritoff (1971), as part of the work on delayed food-seeking described above, included experiments in which blindfolded dogs and cats heard a food basin being banged in a particular location, and were able to go directly to it if released within 5 minutes.

A technique for avoiding the spatial aspect of choosing stimulus locations had been suggested by Polish researchers (see Konorski, 1967, and Wasserman, 1976). Two sounds are presented one after the other, with a short intervening interval. If they are the same, the animal is trained to make a response; if they are different it is trained not to. To the extent that this training is successful, over a wide enough range of sounds, one can infer that information about the first sound is being retained long enough for a comparison to be made with the second. The results quoted by Wasserman (1976) indicate that dogs can learn to move a paw when two low tones occur in sequence, or two high tones, but not to move their paw if there is a high-low, or low-high, succession. A similar task provided no difficulties for Old World monkeys tested by Stepien *et al.* (1960). One would assume, perhaps, that dogs or monkeys hearing the barks or shrieks of conspecifics do not lose all the information contained in these noises immediately the sounds cease. But memory for sequences of stimuli is not confined to hearing in mammals. It has been shown, for instance, that pigeons are influenced by the order of recent visual stimuli; they can be trained to respond to a vertical line which follows a sequence in which a green light preceded an orange light, but to respond instead to a horizontal line if the previous sequence included orange before green (Weisman, *et al.*, 1980).

Recognition memory in monkey and man

On the grounds of phylogeny and brain anatomy, we should certainly expect that the characteristics of memory in monkeys and other primates approximate our own much more closely than those of the pigeon ever could. The perennial question is whether the verbal coding of information by man radically alters capacities that may be measured by non-verbal methods. In the case of memory, it might be said that the predominant characteristic of human performance is the verbal description of past events—in particular the 'recall' or reproduction of words previously heard or seen. As species other than ourselves do not give verbal descriptions of anything at all, let alone descriptions of previous events, we could conclude that memory as we know it is, by definition, completely impossible in animals.

But some aspects of human memory are less bound up with linguistic description than others. We may remember a face, whether or not we can put a name to it, and perhaps it is not stretching the imagination too far to suggest that we might be able to point to what we had for breakfast yesterday, as a means of getting it again today, even if we were deprived of all the powers of language. Discriminating between the familiar and the unfamiliar, and perceiving objects and events as belonging to certain categories, are often referred to as 'recognition memory' in man. It is a matter of considerable dispute as to whether 'recognition' and 'recall' of verbal material are different manifestations of the same underlying capacity for memory, or require alternative kinds of theoretical explanation, in experiments on human subjects (e.g. Brown, 1976). Whatever the merits of these arguments, it is clear that something akin to recognition is relatively easy to assess in monkeys, even though the existence of anything remotely like verbal recall in apes is extremely dubious (see Chapter 9).

Detecting familiarity or novelty in visual images is subjectively one of the easiest ways to demonstrate the retention of previous experience. A self-administered test suggested by Davis and Fitts (1976) is to leaf through a well-illustrated magazine, idly looking at the pictures. Half an hour later, turn the pages over systematically one at a time, trying to decide for each illustration whether it was one you had looked at before or not. A test such as this may indicate a memory of a kind for hundreds or thousands of separate visual displays, even though, after the first thumbing through, one might not be able to give verbal descriptions of more than half a dozen (Standing, Conezio and Haber, 1970). Regular readers of illustrated magazines would expect to make a reasonable guess not only at whether a given photograph had appeared in the last year, but whether they had seen it in the last week or much longer ago. Inference about content would of course prevent this from being a fair estimate of visual memory alone, but few would dispute that an enormous amount of information that is not normally available to our faculties of verbal recall can be revealed by tests of visual recognition.

Hints that a large capacity for recognition of visual images exists in monkeys are contained in experiments reported by Gaffan (1977a) and Davis and Fitts (1976). Gaffan (1977a) trained monkeys to watch a screen on which 25 different coloured slides were each presented twice during a testing session. The 25 were made up of 9 snapshots (for example, a beach, or a view from the Eiffel Tower) and 16 reproductions of figurative paintings (including landscapes and nudes). The point was that the slides were presented in a random sequence, and the animals had to notice whether a given slide was being presented for the first or second time during the test session. If they repeatedly pressed a response button during the second presentation of a slide, they were given a sugar pellet (via an automatic delivery device). But if they pressed this button during the first presentation of a slide, the effort was wasted, since nothing happened.

After a course of training, the two young rhesus monkeys used were able to distinguish with an accuracy of over 90 per cent between first and second showings of the 25 slides, when an average of 9 other slides and up to 18 others might intervene between the first and second showings. (Obviously, in the sequence of 50 presentations, the beginning ones had to be mostly first showings, and the last half-dozen or so had to be second showings, and correct performance here would not necessarily indicate visual recognition of individual pictures, but only the middle part of the test-sessions was used to assess the monkey's accuracy.) All the pictures must by this time have been familiar to the animals, although this was not explicitly confirmed in the experiment. What the animals were doing was therefore not closely analogous to the illustrated magazine example just discussed, but more like remembering what cards have been played during a particular game of gin-rummy. Considerable training was required before the monkeys could perform the task accurately and they were no longer able to do much simpler forms of this recognition test after a brain operation (see below).

Davis and Fitts (1976) cut large numbers of illustrations out of magazines and pasted them on small boards which could be presented to monkeys as covers over wells in which titbits could be found—a standard way of testing the perceptual capacities of monkeys (a version of the Wisconsin General Test Apparatus or WGTA; Harlow, 1959).

The experimenters were not interested in finding out if their animals (rhesus and pigtailed macaques) could remember whether or not they had seen a particular picture before, but in testing the monkeys' capacity for selecting a picture seen only once before according to whether that picture had been rewarded or not.

Their suggestion was that this ought to be much more difficult than responding according to familiarity, partly on the basis of the illustrated magazine analogy. Remembering whether individual pictures have been rewarded or not is a two-way classification, such as one may attempt to make by going through a series of pictures in a magazine and noting whether each one is on an odd or an even page. This is certainly much more difficult than just recognising recently seen illustrations as recently seen, but peanut versus no peanut is presumably a rather more vivid dichotomy for the monkey than odd versus even is for us. In any event the difference between familiarity, and remembered associations with rewards, was not actually assessed. The importance of Davis and Fitt's results is that they provide separate evidence for remembered associations of particular pictures with reward, which, although it is not especially surprising, provides an experimental demonstration that emotional associations of recent events are retained, as well as the recent events themselves.

The procedure used by Davis and Fitts was to provide a monkey with one 'sample' picture, which the animal pushed away from a food well, thus discovering whether the sample was rewarded or not. Then, as quickly as possible (about one second later) or after a short delay, two pictures were presented at once, one of them the sample and the other a completely new one. The animal revealed its knowledge of the sample by choosing it, if it had been rewarded, but choosing the alternative, if the sample had previously covered an empty food well. (In two-picture choices, rewards were distributed according to this rule: that is, a rewarded sample was rewarded again, but the alternative choice to a previously disappointing sample covered the peanut.) The fact that the monkeys were able to do this at all is a considerable achievement, since each picture was seen only once (if it was an alternative) or twice (if it was a sample). This means that their visual memory functions reasonably well with unfamiliar material. In more stringent assessments of memory the monkeys were presented with 'lists' of two, four or sixteen sample pictures in succession, some covering bits of food and some not, before tests in which each sample was paired with an alternative picture. As might be expected by extrapolation from human capacities, remembering whether individual items in these lists had been rewarded or not proved quite difficult, and there was a very marked decline in the accuracy of the animals' choices according to the length of the list in which a sample had appeared. Again in line with what happens when human subjects are shown lists of words, position in the list made a difference. The main effect with lists of 2 or 4 pictures was that the most recently seen samples at the end of the lists were much better remembered than those at the beginning of the list. With a list of 16, the monkeys did not remember very much anyway, choices being only 60 per cent accurate on average, and so it was difficult to make reliable comparisons between the various positions, but it looked as though accuracy was still better with the more recent samples, with the first few items on the list being remembered a little better than those in the middle. These variations seem rather trivial aspects of the procedure, but are of interest because enormous amounts of effort have been expended on measuring the recognition of words which have appeared in different positions on lists used in laboratory experiments on human memory.

The crucial aspect of the procedure was whether or not a given sample picture was rewarded. If only one picture had been seen before a choice test, one can imagine that whether it had been seen before, and whether or not the monkey had just eaten a peanut, ought both to be easily remembered. But if two samples had been given before a test, one rewarded and the other not, then the monkey had to remember which was which. Davis and Fitts's data show that this was much more difficult. By examining in detail the choices made after lists of two samples each, it was possible to see that if both samples had been rewarded, or both unrewarded, so that the animals did not have to worry about the distinction between them, choices were very accurate indeed, but if one was rewarded and one not, many mistakes were made. A curious aspect of these results was that the poor performance after the mixed samples was most obvious if the animals were tested within 5 seconds of seeing the samples—if the tests were delayed for just a little longer (20 seconds) choices after mixed samples actually became more accurate. Perhaps a little time to think was beneficial.

In these experiments (Davis and Fitts, 1976), what had to be remembered, over a few seconds, was whether novel visual patterns had covered full or empty food wells. What exactly it was about individual pictures that was remembered—colour, texture, or details of shape, is impossible to tell. The rule which needed to be followed was to choose again a novel display which had just been rewarded, but avoid visual patterns recently seen without reward. Gaffan (1977b) used a technique in which colour, or spatial location, was definitely the visual cue which had to be retained, and monkeys had to respond according to whether or not a certain colour, or location, had just appeared in a short list.

Automatic apparatus was used to light up display panels, detect responses, and deliver sugar pellets to rhesus monkeys inside a special cage. For lists of colours, there was one display panel which could be illuminated with six different hues (red, green, yellow, magenta, blue and greenish-blue) and a response panel lit with plain white light. After some preliminary training with simpler versions of the task, individual animals were given test-sessions of the following sort. The display panel was lit with the first colour in a list of three (say red),—and the monkey had to touch the panel to make this colour go off. One second later another colour appeared (say blue), was touched, and after another second a third (yellow, perhaps) completed the sequence. Now there was a loud buzz, and a test colour appeared on the display panel, with the response panel plainly illuminated at the same time. This was the moment of choice. In order to get a sugar pellet, the monkey had to press the *display* panel if the test colour was one of the ones in the preceding list (in this example, red, blue or yellow), but needed to press the *response* panel if the test colour was one of the others (in this case, green, magenta, or greenish-blue). Assessed over several daily sessions each containing almost 200 lists, allowing for all the different permutations of the colours, the animals performed very creditably at this recognition task. Not surprisingly, they were rather better at correctly touching the test colour if it had just been seen as the last one in the list, than if it had been given first or second, and overall they made correct decisions after more than 70 per cent of the lists. This was not as good as the 90 per cent they achieved when only one sample colour was shown before each choice, but given the longer time intervals between the recognition tests and the earlier samples in the lists of three, and the possibilities for confusions between lists (it would be counted as an error if they touched a test colour that was in the last-but-one list instead of the most recent list) it would be very peculiar if they had not made a good many mistakes.

After this measurement of recognition of recently seen colours, the same monkeys were run through an identical procedure to assess memory for the spatial location of illuminated panels. In this case three separate display panels from an array of six were illuminated (in orange light) in succession, the monkey touching each one in turn. Then after the buzzer signal, just one of the six panels, and the response panel, was lit up at the same time, and the animals had to choose as before: touching the display panel if it was one of those seen in the previous list of three but selecting the response panel instead if the display was not one of the previous three. Again, they did very well, making few mistakes if the test display was the same as the last one on the previous list, and making about 75 per cent correct choices over all.

These experiments, and others like them (Overman and Doty, 1980; Sands *et al.*, 1984; Wright *et al.*, 1984) leave very little doubt that current visual perceptions of monkeys can in some way be matched against the animals' recent experiences. What mental processes enable this to take place is a different matter. It seems possible that with very short memory intervals, of one or two seconds, a record of visual experience might persist automatically. But for successful performance at longer intervals, some special attention to the to-be-remembered cue, and a specific mental comparison of the choice stimuli with what is retained from recent experience, would surely be helpful. In other words, one tends to assume that monkeys exposed to these procedures adopted mental strategies which they might not employ otherwise.

Recognising exact repetitions of visual displays, especially if simple features such as colour or location are all that is needed, may be a particularly easy strategy to adopt, being to some extent built into perception as a means of establishing familiarity (see Sokolov, 1963, 1975). There are indications that monkeys may have more difficulty in utilising visual memories to make quite arbitrary connections between past and present perceptions. D'Amato and Worsham (1974) presented cebus monkeys with a sample display which was either a red disc or a vertical line. Some seconds later the monkeys were required to make a choice between a triangle and a white dot, according to the rule that the triangle should be selected if they had just seen the red disc, but the dot should be selected if the preceding sample was the vertical line. They eventually managed to follow this rule, but months of daily training with the choice following the sample immediately was required. This is not very systematic evidence, but in the absence of anything better, we must assume that detecting the presence or absence of stimuli which match recent experience may be much easier than this kind of delayed and arbitrary association.

It should be emphasised that matching current with recent images is not the only thing that animals can do which implies a form of memory. The monkeys which took a long time to adopt the rule of touching a triangle after a red disc but a dot after a line had no difficulty in stretching the 'after' intervals to a minute or more, once this very peculiar convention had been established (D'Amato and Worsham, 1974). It is interesting to speculate as to whether the monkeys did this by remembering, at the end of the minute, if the sample had been a red disc, or by remembering that they should be selecting the triangle (or by remembering both these things). Rather subtle experiments would be needed to distinguish between these possibilities. With a different sort of arbitrary association to be remembered, Gaffan (1977c) was able to design an experiment where the results suggested that it was the end product of the association, rather than the initial cue, which was remembered. This makes sense if one assumes that animals will tend to remember whatever it is that is going to be connected with their getting their reward, since in these kinds of experiment the rewards are the only reason the animals are paying any attention in the first place.

In this experiment (Gaffan, 1977c) monkeys saw briefly one of three sample colours (red, orange or blue). Ten seconds later, they had to press one of three plainly lit panels, depending on what the colour had been. (If it had been red, they should press bottom right; if blue, top right; if orange, top left.) The catch was that only one of these panels was lit, and sometimes it was the wrong one—in these cases the alternative choice of a specially marked 'No' panel was necessary. In itself, this is a revealing variation of the delayed-response problem, but the arbitrary connection between individual sample colours and the required response allows two possible strategies. The animals could retain knowledge of the colour of the sample, and work out after a panel was illuminated, if it was the correct one. Or rather more directly, they could select a panel as soon as the sample was seen, and retain this selection, switching to the 'No' response if it did not come up. Gaffan argues that this direct method of 'response coding' is what took place, because there were many more mistakes that looked like confusions between adjacent panels (presses on the lower right panel after a blue sample which would have required a press on the panel just above) than mistakes that looked like confusions between similar colours (lower right 'red' choices after an orange sample that would have prepared the animals to point upper left). These data are hardly conclusive, but there is certainly no reason to doubt that animals can remember response orientations or spatial locations just as well, if not better, than discriminations of colour or shape (cf. data for pigeons in Smith, 1967). The least intellectually demanding strategy for the monkeys in this case would have been to hold their hand poised over the appropriate panel during the 10-second memory interval. Sitting still, even for such short periods, is not however a very popular activity for young monkeys, and Gaffan (1977c) reports that they jumped around the cage during the memory interval. Therefore he suggests that there must have been internal representations, corresponding to 'it should be upper left this time', held, or recovered, over the 10-second intervals.

Memory tests and memory functions

Experimental tests of capacities for memory in animals require information previously obtained to be brought to bear on choices made during laboratory procedures in which animals behave in unnaturally repetitive and arbitrary ways to obtain food rewards. Such tests are performed because they establish the presence of psychological processes which are not always obvious in the natural behaviours of the animals involved, or in other laboratory procedures. To some extent, it is obvious that details of the remembering that takes place are brought about by extensive and specialised training, and the character of the tests themselves. But equally, if special purpose tests demonstrate capacities for various forms of memory we ought to ask, first, how such capacities evolved in the context of a species's natural life and, second, whether similar forms of memory might be utilised during tests of animal learning and perception which are not deliberately designed to involve remembering, but which do not necessarily exclude it. (Shettleworth and Krebs, 1982; Kamil and Balda, 1985).

No certain answers can be given to questions about the evolution of mental capacities, but it is reassuring that abilities shown in many delayed response tests would clearly be helpful in natural patterns of food-seeking, and in some cases would be logically necessary for animals to accomplish the strategies of foraging that actually occur in nature (Pyke *et al.*, 1977; Krebs and Davies, 1978). It is less clear how the abilities to compare recent and current perceptions, that are manifested in tests of the 'delayed matching to sample' type, might help animals cope with their usual conditions of life. Being able to tell whether a projection screen is illuminated with the same colour that it was 10 seconds ago or not seems at first sight far removed from any naturally occurring behaviour. It may be, however, that a general capacity for recognition of short-term continuities is part and parcel of perception. If animal perception is a method of constructing internal representations of reality rather than merely picking up isolated sensations, as I argued in the previous chapter, there needs to be some correspondence between continuities or discontinuities in time in the outside world and the inner representations. The dating of perceptions in time sounds a complicated and mysterious matter, but if we suppose that a monkey surveying its surroundings identifies landmarks, and other monkeys, we should surely assume that as it glances from side to side it retains, if only briefly, the information detected in each glance, for incorporation into its assessment of where it is, where other individual monkeys are, and what is generally going on. Detecting external regularities over time may therefore be a rather fundamental aspect of brain processes serving perception. It is perhaps surprising that anything so fundamental should be revealed in tests in which animals are motivated by the delivery of food rewards, but the combination of persistence and ingenuity on the part of experimenters and greed on the part of laboratory animals should never be underestimated.

Discrimination learning sets

The switching in of information about recent events, as a function of experience, is one explanation for a phenomenon in animal learning known as '*learning set*' (Harlow, 1949; Mackintosh, 1974, pp. 610–14; R. C. Miles, 1965). This occurs most strongly in Old World monkeys (such as the rhesus) and anthropoid apes. If a monkey is repeatedly presented with a matchbox and a dry-cell battery lying on a tray in different positions, with a raisin always under the matchbox but never under the battery, it will gradually learn to always pick up the matchbox rather than the battery. But this takes time—even after choosing the matchbox and getting the raisin three times, and picking the battery and getting no raisin two or three times, the odds on the monkey choosing correctly next time would only be about 7 to 3. If it is now given a different pair of objects, say a ball of wool and a tobacco tin, with the raisin always under the tin, very much the same thing happens: after half a dozen trials there will be some evidence of a preference for the tin, but no certain solution to the problem. In order to observe the learning set phenomenon, one has to keep on giving the same animal pair after pair of objects, presenting each pair six or more times before moving on to a new pair, for upwards of one hundred different pairs. The eventual outcome, after monkeys have experienced 250 successive pairs of objects, is rather different from the original tentative preferences (Harlow, 1949). If an animal is now given an entirely new pair of things to choose between—let us say a plastic bottle and an ashtray—it needs only one choice to establish a virtually certain solution. On once finding a raisin under the bottle, or not under the ashtray, there will be a chance of less than one in ten that the monkey will make a mistake on following tests with the same pair. This can be quantified by looking at the choices made for the second time with all the pairs from, for instance, the 250th to the 300th: it is a reliable result that more than 45 of these 50 should be correct (Miles, 1965).

Without going into details, there are grounds for believing that the accurate choices made at the end of learning-set experiments occur because the animal is then using its memory of preceding trials as a successful basis for choosing. This must involve what is referred to as a 'Win-stay/Lose-shift' strategy (Mackintosh, 1983), since if the animal remembers that the raisin was under the bottle, it must choose the bottle again, whereas if it remembers that there was *no* raisin under the ashtray, it must leave the ashtray alone. Animals (even rats) are perfectly willing to adopt other strategies if they pay off (e.g. Olton, 1978): what interests us here is that no such strategy can work unless information is available at the time of choice which reflects which of the current objects was selected last time, and whether this selection resulted in a 'win' or a 'loss' (that is whether the animal ate a raisin or not). The availability of this information can be related to more direct experiments on memory because the normal procedure is for the animals to make successive choices within a few seconds. If the monkey successfully chooses the bottle but then has to wait half a minute or more before the next choice, it is much more liable to make a mistake (Bessemer and Stollnitz, 1971). What is not certain is whether, during the long training which results in more accurate choices, the animals are coming to terms with the 'Win-stay/Lose-shift' strategy in the light of already available memories, or whether the training is in some sense improving their memories, or encouraging the strategy of paying attention to what they can remember about what they had just done. Probably a number of factors like this are important.

It is appropriate to acknowledge here that utilising recent memories is not the only mechanism which governs systematic choices made by animals. Innate preferences may influence choices made under experimental conditions as well as in natural environments. The standard explanation for choices of experimental stimuli which are brought about by experience of reward and punishment is of course automatic habits, in the form of strengths of reactions elicited by given sensations (Spence, 1936; see Chapter 3). The point is that one can have a tendency to make a certain choice without remembering the details of the previous experience responsible for that tendency. In human behaviour this is usually only obvious in the case of highly practised skills such as driving a car or playing tennis, where conscious control via remembered verbal instructions may have been crucial in the early development of habits, but in the case of animals the most parsimonious theories assume that certain classes of stimulus input acquire properties of eliciting response output, as a function of reward and punishment, and without the intervention of any mental processes outside individual stimulus-response circuits.

If a pigeon pecks at a green card which covers a hole containing grain, thereby displacing the card, and thus eats soon after the act of pecking something green, and is also allowed to peck at red cards which cover empty holes, it will very soon peck at green cards but not at red ones. One can construct several kinds of metaphorical mental processes which could account for this outer behaviour. Most simply, green cards merely could elicit an inner instruction 'peck at that', the subsequent uncovering of food coming as a pleasant surprise each time, or perhaps merely eliciting another instruction, 'eat that'. Allowing for a slightly greater degree of cognition, we might suppose that either before or after pecking at green cards, the bird possesses some kind of expectation that eating is imminent, without any inner representation of previous events. Assuming, for the sake of argument, quite unrealistic mental capacities, then the sight of a green card might give rise to a train of thought along the lines of 'I distinctly remember that I ate food from the hole underneath a green card like that a minute ago, and there has always been food underneath green cards on previous occasions'. The view I expressed in Chapter 3 was that a theory somewhere in the middle of this range is needed to cover most of the effects of previous experience on animal behaviour, but it must be common to all theoretical positions that, especially after long training, previous experience is accumulated into automatic response tendencies, without any necessary access to individual episodes from the past (Dickinson, 1985).

The purpose of the elaborate experiments on delayed responses and delayed perceptual comparisons is precisely to ensure that automatic tendencies, of the type 'always peck at green' would *not* be sufficient to account for the data, because another rule has to be followed, such as 'peck at green if green was present a minute ago, but not otherwise' (Grant, 1976). The success of these experiments does not mean that animals never make automatic, reflex-like responses — they frequently do — but it adds weight to the view that automatic habits may be modified, and in some cases formed and broken, by the persistence over time of what has been previously perceived.

Memory and brain processes

If it is true that past experience can influence future behaviour in many different ways, including the formation of automatic habits and the revival of perceived features of previous events, there is reason to hope that we may be able to distinguish between types of brain, or between different parts of particular types of brain, which provide the physical mechanisms for accomplishing these psychological processes. For over a century there has been an almost political division between a party of localisers, who believe that psychologically defined mental processes can be assigned to distinct regions of the brain, and a party of unified action, which asserts that such theoretical divisions between brain activities are illusory. The party of localisers has slightly disreputable roots in the early nineteenth-century phrenology of Gall and Spurzheim, which held that protrusions of parts of the brain concerned with such faculties as Hope and Time could be detected as bumps on the skull, but became more firmly established later in the century with the medical and experimental evidence of Broca and Ferrier.

Set against the localisers are those who are convinced that the physiological apparatus required for any particular psychological functions cannot be pinpointed at particular places in the brain because the brain acts as a whole, and that any identifiable working parts are diffused and spread about rather than neatly collected in anatomical units. In the first half of the last century, the most influential protagonist of these views was Flourens (see Chapter 5) whose slogans referred to the 'communal action' and 'unity of function' of the various parts of the brain. His counterpart in this century is Lashley, who worked in the 1930s and 1940s, but who is still quoted as an authority on 'mass action' of the brain and the 'equipotentiality' of its different parts for accomplishing individual functions (see Boring, 1950). We should say first that this unity and indivisibility of function, for Lashley, and to a lesser extent perhaps Flourens as well, applies mainly to the cerebral hemispheres. Flourens himself was responsible for ascribing the higher aspects of perception and intention to the hemispheres, but the co-ordination of muscle movements to the cerebellum and basic maintenance of life to the medulla.

Even the most extreme diffusionists might tolerate, for instance, the proposition that memory in the form of detailed sequencing of muscle movements is located primarily in the cerebellum. There are modern theories (Bloomfield and Marr, 1970; Eccles, 1973) about how the neuronal structure of the cerebellum may be adapted for this sort of flexible motor-programming. It would probably also have been possible to persuade Flourens and Lashley that the midbrain and the medulla retain previous experience in the form of altered reflexes, while the cerebral hemispheres are able to do something over and above this.

Even such rudimentary distinctions between ways of storing information in the gross divisions of the vertebrate brain would, of course, be a novelty in the context of standard treatments of animal learning, but it would be powerful support for the separate consideration of automatic habits and independent perceptual memories if there were conclusive evidence that these hypothetical mechanisms are characteristic of different anatomical levels of brain action.

Neither Lashley, nor Flourens, nor anyone else, would dispute that, if other mammals possess anything remotely like human memory for past events, it will be located in the cerebral hemispheres rather than at lower brain levels. The arguments start if we ask whether the physical changes that allow for memories (what Semon, 1921, and Lashley, 1950, called the 'engrams') are diffused throughout the hemispheres, or collected in particular forebrain structures. However, the empirical evidence, if not the political momentum, is now very much with the localisers. Since Lashley's time, the physiological mapping out of sensory areas of cortex has become very firmly established. The traditional doctrine of the localisers was that 'association areas' (more or less every expanse of cerebral cortex that was not known to have specific sensory or motor functions) played an important role in memory (Diamond and Hall, 1969). There is still something to be said for this idea, although the trend has been to tie particular association areas more and more closely with adjacent sensory and motor projections (Diamond, 1979).

The most extreme plank of the localisers' platform contends that, although long-term storage of mental associations can be attributed to neural connections within and between the various projection areas of cerebral cortex, a particular brain structure has something special to do with setting up such associations. This structure is the hippocampus, 'old' cortex characteristic of all mammals, and distinguishable as a forebrain region in even the most primitive vertebrates (Faucette, 1969; Isaacson, 1974). The initial suggestion that the hippocampus is a special organ of memory came from studies of human patients with loss of memory. The questions of whether, how and why human memory depends on this particular brain structure have implications for the theory of animal memory, since, once it has been claimed that any particular brain part serves memory in man, we can then ask 'What is this structure doing in the brains of other animals?' (Weiskrantz and Warrington, 1975; Weiskrantz, 1977).

The function of the hippocampus in the brains of monkeys and man

It is worth beginning with the issue of loss of memory due to brain damage in man and monkey before setting out to consider brain mechanisms and the retention of past experience more generally, since it illustrates most vividly the difference between remembered perceptions and retained habits. The study of human amnesia also illustrates the great variety of things which might go under the name of human remembered perceptions. The simplest distinction between forms of memory loss in human patients is between loss of previous memories (retrograde amnesia) and loss of the ability to form new ones (anterograde amnesia). Case-histories of the first kind, when for instance someone walks into a hospital unable to say who they are or what their address is, are very dramatic, but not very helpful for present purposes. Any brain trauma, such as a blow on the head, or electro-convulsive shock, is likely to blank out memory for events a few hours preceding the trauma, and it is possible to observe similar effects in animals (Miller and Springer, 1973). The second kind of 'amnesic syndrome' in which people become permanently unable to report on the events of a few minutes past, is the one in which the hippocampus is implicated.

The most common cause of severe memory loss is alcoholism, or sustained heavy drinking. This may have a number of unfortunate consequences, one of which is the 'Korsakoff syndrome', which includes as a rule total amnesia for events during several years prior to its onset, and difficulties in retaining new information, as well as emotional disorders (Victor, Adams and Collins, 1971). The precise nature of the brain pathology underlying these deficits is uncertain. There are some individuals, however, in whom amnesia for current events has been apparently produced by misguided surgical intervention of a relatively circumscribed kind. These are people of normal intelligence, who suffered from epileptic attacks severe enough to persuade neurosurgeons in the 1950s that radical brain operations were worth trying. In a small number of patients, Scoville in Montreal deliberately removed the hippocampus from both cerebral hemispheres. The number was small because, although removing damaged tissue reduced the frequency of epileptic seizures, it was soon discovered that removal of the hippocampus also destroyed certain kinds of memory ability. One cannot be entirely sure about this, especially as rather a large proportion of what is said about the effects of the operation is based on a single patient, 'H. M.' (Scoville and Milner, 1957; Milner *et al.*, 1968). But the evidence is fairly strong that interference with the inside surface of the temporal lobe, where the hippocampus is found in man and other primates, is likely to have very severe, and very bad, consequences for everyday memory capacities (Warrington and Weiskrantz, 1973).

The nature of H. M.'s memory after surgical removal of the hippocampus was as follows. He could report normally on his life before the operation (when he was 27) except for vagueness about the year or so immediately prior to it. He could perform previously acquired skills, such as reading, writing and his trade of motor-winding, and could recognise already known persons, including Scoville, who had done the operation. But he appeared to have difficulty in laying down any new memories, being unable to remember how to find the lavatory in the hospital where he convalesced, or to find a lawnmower he used regularly at the house he lived in afterwards (but whose address he never learned). In two important ways, however, it was apparent that new information could be retained. First, short-term memory, or the persistence of immediate perceptions over a period of seconds and minutes, was normal. H. M. could carry on a conversation of sorts about his earlier life, and understand spoken instructions and questions, so that he could repeat back short strings of numbers and perform mental arithmetic. He could remember what he was looking for long enough to do jigsaw puzzles, even though he could remember little about a puzzle done the day before. Second, H. M. could show gradual improvement at simple learning tasks, such as tracing short finger mazes, or pencilling round shapes seen only as a reflection in a mirror. Given certain hints and cues about words or pictures in lists normally used to demonstrate the presence of long-term remembering, H. M., and similar patients, can remember about as much as normal subjects prompted in the same way (Weiskrantz and Warrington, 1975; Weiskrantz, 1977; Milner, 1970). One patient with an operation like H. M.'s happened to have played the piano, and could learn new pieces, and perform them later if given the opening bars, even though professing no recollection of the music, the time he had played it before, or the person he had then played it to (Starr and Phillips, 1970).

In these amnesic patients, then, previous experience can be incorporated into automatic routines and habits, without episodes of previous experience being accessible to conscious, verbally reportable, awareness. At its simplest, this amounts to retention of responses, and short-term persistence of perception, without any facility for reviving or retrieving recent perceptions. Also, mental skills, such as reading words written backwards, may improve in amnesic patients, even if they cannot remember having practised them (Cohen and Squire, 1980).

Is it possible to compare this syndrome with the behaviour of animals given experimental lesions of the hippocampal region? It was initially thought not, since one of the excuses for removing the hippocampus in human patients was that animals did not seem to suffer any ill effects after analogous operations. This is true only for the most cursory examination of the animal subjects, using the extremely ingenuous and naive assumption that if behaviour was modified in any way by experience, memory must have been all right. It is now the case that many parallels can be drawn between the behaviour of mammals with experimental lesions of the hippocampus and the clinical reports and systematic assessments of the abilities of amnesic patients (Weiskrantz and Warrington, 1975; Weiskrantz, 1977; Gaffan, 1976).

For some time it has been known that, although animals with hippocampal damage can be trained to perform simple habits to obtain food rewards, they differ from normal animals in persisting with the same habits long after the rewards have been discontinued (e.g. Douglas, 1967). This could have the interesting implication that memory of the recent absence of reward is one reason why the normal animals cease to perform previously rewarded habits, but alternative formulations, in terms of the automatic inhibition of responses, have been preferred (Kimble, 1968).

More direct evidence of the involvement of the hippocampus in the memories of animals can be obtained by the delayed-response and delayed-perceptual-comparison methods discussed earlier in this chapter (as I hope normal readers will remember). Sinnamon *et al.* (1978), for instance, tried a relatively straightforward delayed-response procedure with hippocampally damaged rats. Each day, the animals were allowed to find water behind one of four doors, which were recognisable by their position and surface appearance. Some time later, they were released to make a choice, water being given behind the same door on any given day. Rats that were normal in the sense of having had lesions to superficial cortical areas managed to make consistently correct choices at intervals of over two hours after initial discovery of the water location. But rats with certain kinds of interference to the hippocampus appeared unable to remember where the water was after delay intervals of 15 seconds or longer. O'Keefe and Nadel (1978) have published a monumental review of evidence suggesting that in rats the hippocampus functions as a repository for memories about places (*The Hippocampus as a Cognitive Map*). As places are the only things which rats usually can be demonstrated to have memories about, this is an adequate summary for that species. Where other sorts of memory can be shown, these too seem to depend on an intact hippocampus. The most powerful indications that this is so come from the procedures developed by Gaffan (1977a, 1977b) which I described earlier.

One of these procedures allowed a fairly close parallel to be drawn between tests given to human amnesics (Warrington, 1974; Huppert and Piercy, 1976) and the assessment of memory function in monkeys, since in both cases what was required was the classification of snapshots according to whether or not they had been seen before. Gaffan (1977a) succeeded in training rhesus monkeys to observe a sequence of coloured slides, and indicate when a given picture occurred for the second time in the sequence (see pp. 307–11 above). Following this training, the animals were given a brain operation to eliminate output from the hippocampus. After the operation they were put through the same sequence of training as before. Like human amnesics such as H. M., they appeared to have satisfactory immediate recognition of what they had just seen, over very short intervals. If a view from the Eiffel Tower was shown twice in succession, or with only one intervening slide in between, the operated monkeys held back the first time, but pushed a panel to get their sugar pellet when it came up again, in the same way that they did before the operation. But, again like human amnesics, the brain-damaged monkeys seemed to have difficulties in identifying repeated slides when more than one other picture came between the initial showing and the repetition. Before the operation they had performed with few mistakes (misclassifications were less than 10 per cent) even when several other pictures might have been seen since the first showing of a repeated slide. Afterwards, in tests of only moderate difficulty in terms of the length of these intervening lists, errors reached about 20 per cent (the animals sometimes responded to the initial showing of a picture, when they should have kept still, and sometimes missed rewards by failing to respond to second showings).

In an alternative assessment of the retention of perceptions over short intervals, using the simpler stimuli of colours, very much the same thing was found with monkeys given the operation designed to disturb the functioning of the hippocampus (Gaffan, 1977b). In this case monkeys looked at a 'list' of one, two or three particular colours shown in succession, and then, when a test colour was presented a few seconds later, had to respond according to whether the test colour had been given in the previous list (see pp. 310–13 above). With only a single colour to remember, operated monkeys did just as well as normals, making few mistakes, but with lists of two or three, which were more difficult, the operated animals were distinctly worse than the others, especially at correctly identifying a colour which had been seen at the beginning of a previous list of three. (Overall, about half the mistakes took the form of responding as if a test colour had been on the last list, when it hadn't, and in the other half colours which had been present were missed—this precludes simple response biases.) Exactly the same results were obtained when the spatial location of illuminated panels had to be recognised, rather than colours: monkeys whose hippocampus had been interfered with could remember which was the last panel that they had seen lit up, and the last but one, but did much worse than the control animals when they had to remember the last but two.

These findings clearly suggest that the brain-operated monkeys had difficulties in detecting whether current perceptions matched or did not match those of the recent past, even though they were perfectly competent at detecting similarities between current perceptions and those immediately preceding them. A peculiarity is that the same sort of surgical intervention did not seem to have as much effect on a task which required monkeys to select objects on the basis of whether or not the objects had recently covered a desirable food object (a piece of sugared wheat; Gaffan, 1974). If 5 household objects had just been pushed away to uncover bits of sugared wheat, then monkeys with the brain operation were unable correctly to choose these 5 in preference to 5 others, when offered pairs composed of one of each, although unoperated control animals made very few errors. This would be expected if the operated monkeys had difficulties with recent memory. When 10 objects in succession were manipulated by monkeys, but 5 objects covered sugared wheat while the other 5 did not, this contrast in the availability of the food incentive meant that the 5 rewarded objects were more likely to be manipulated than the non-rewarded ones, when they were presented again singly. This preference was not very strong, but the peculiarity is that the operated animals had just as much of a preference as others.

One interpretation of the various abilities and disabilities seen in these 'amnesic' monkeys (Gaffan, 1974, 1976) is that they are bad at anything which requires a differentiation of the familiar from the unfamiliar that cannot be done on the basis of very recent, 'short-term' memories. This is a more limited deficit than one would expect on the basis of the human amnesic patients, but I must reveal now that, apart from the obvious problems of comparing human verbal memory with the choices of animals, all of the 'amnesic' monkeys discussed in this section had much more limited brain damage than that brought about in attempts to relieve epilepsy. In the monkeys, a small tract of nerve fibres that is one of the main connections between the hippocampus and other parts of the brain, the fornix, was cleanly transected. In H. M. and similar patients, the hippocampus itself was removed from both hemispheres, and it is likely that nearby parts of the inside of the temporal lobes were damaged as well. Especially given the prior history of tissue damage connected with epilepsy in the first place, it is probable that anatomical abnormalities are more extensive in the human amnesic patients than in the experimental animals.

Problems of equating the extent of brain damage need not obscure the important fact that anatomical interference with hippocampal function has little or no effect on some behaviour, but produces a profound impairment of performance on certain tests. In animals, procedures which very explicitly involve moderately recent memory, memory for places, or assessments of the familiarity of visual displays, are sensitive to the effects of hippocampal damage. But response habits, and stimulus discriminations, trained up by selective reward and punishment, can be readily acquired by animals suffering from the same anatomical deficiencies. The implication is that sensory-motor skills and routines can develop in the absence of memory for previous perceptions, detection of familiarity, or whatever it is that the hippocampus usually does. In the human amnesic also, motor skills can be acquired, and with sufficient prompting it is evident that something about previous lists of words is retained (Weiskrantz, 1977), but the gaps in subjective memory are painfully obvious.

All this is useful in emphasising that memory is different from reflex-like habits. What we refer to as memory in man is usually subjective availability of mental content which we can, if we wish, comment on. The ubiquity of our verbal comments on our subjective states, and the absence of any such thing in experimental animals might be taken as an indication that animals possess *only* reflex-like habits, and have nothing which might correspond to our memories of previous events. But anatomical disturbances which cause subjective memory loss in man disrupt the ability of rats and monkeys to perform tasks designed to require some forms of memory. This strengthens the case that mammalian brains contain facilities for the retention of perceived information, which work in roughly the same way as the facilities which we ourselves may put to more elaborate uses. The practice of testing animal learning abilities by repeated and invariant routines, though perhaps convenient for other purposes, turns out to be singularly inappropriate for the study of memory, since it encourages automatic habits. These may form a substantial part of the mechanisms by which animals cope with experienced regularities in their natural environment, but the special tests developed to assess memory should not be regarded as necessarily unnatural. No one has tried it, but one would not be optimistic about the chances of a chimpanzee getting along in its natural environment after being given the brain surgery which produces human amnesia. Certainly one would not expect such a chimpanzee to demonstrate memory for the locations of previously hidden food in experimental tests.

Even if we accept that there appear to be parts of the brain, of which the hippocampus is one, that seem to have something to do with memory in both monkeys and men, this does not take us very far towards specifying exactly what the hippocampus does. It has been suggested that it receives a version of events coded by the perceptual system, and serves mainly to distinguish between old and new perceptions (Sokolov, 1975; Gaffan, 1976). Individual hippocampal cells respond to novel, but not repeated stimuli (Vinogradova, 1975) so there may be something in this, although it is hardly an adequate explanation for the range of phenomena found in human amnesia (Weiskrantz and Warrington, 1975). However, a device for clocking in perceptions as they occur, tagging them for recency over minutes and hours, would in theory be useful in a number of ways, and if one considers the absence of any subjective sense of temporal order in the remembered events of the day, one can well imagine that other confusions would arise. It remains to be seen, however, whether Weiskrantz (1977) was correct in looking forward to the day when the same theory of brain function (and of hippocampal function in particular) can be applied to both man and monkey. There is considerable evidence that the hippocampus of rats, as well as that of primates, is used as a temporary or 'working' memory store, over intermediate time intervals (Rawlins and Tsaltas, 1983; Meck *et al.*, 1984).

Phylogenetic development of memory and forebrain

The hippocampus is part of the limbic system of the forebrain, which is usually characterised as primitive, originally devoted to the sense of smell, and the seat of the baser emotions of man. The traditional story (Sherrington, 1906; Romer, 1949) is that the forebrain began as a centre of smell, acquired the dominant role of directing and organising the actions of early vertebrates because smell was the most important sense, and then attracted to itself the other sensory modalities, ultimately having to invent the cerebral neocortex, and grossly expand its physical proportions until, as in the human cerebral hemispheres, it enveloped and dwarfed all other parts. This story may have a happy ending, but the beginning and middle are suspect (see Chapter 5). It is a fact that olfactory tracts go into the brain at the front, while sensory nerves for taste, touch and hearing go in at the back, and the output from the eyes goes to the middle. Originally this may have been a matter of anatomical convenience, given the layout of the respective sense organs. But in the lower vertebrates we know about (present-day sharks, other fish, amphibians and reptiles) it is not true that smell is the *only* input to the forebrain. Although sharks do indeed have an acute sense of smell, and large forebrains, only a small part of their forebrain appears to receive direct or indirect olfactory input (Ebbesson and Heimer, 1970; Graebner, 1980) — about the same proportion as in the rat (Ebbesson, 1980). And at least one other sensory modality, vision, takes up some of the remaining space. The visual inputs to the forebrain telencephalon are less direct than the olfactory inputs, but we no longer need to localise brain function simply in terms of the point of entry of the sensory nerves.

The story of the telencephalon should thus be that once upon a time it received direct smell input and only indirect input from other senses. When it grew bigger and bigger in reptiles and birds, this plan stayed the same. And when it grew even bigger, in mammals and especially in man, the plan still stayed the same, but the indirect input of other sensory projections to the surface of the forebrain became just as good as the direct input to the smell centres (see Chapter 5, pp. 179–81).

Why then, did the forebrain grow at all, if it was not changing from a smell centre to a general purpose perceiver, having been general purpose all along? A nice story to finish this chapter with would be that the forebrain was always the best of all the parts of the brain at forming and storing memories, and so the forebrain grew bigger and better, as memories of what had happened before in the life of individual animals became more important than inherited instincts or modified reflexes.

Perhaps the forebrain was good at memories in the first place because of something about smells. Smells in the air (or water) tend to hang about, and do not usually change over time as rapidly as sights and sounds. One would think, on these grounds, that there would be less need for internal retention of olfactory sensations, though the slower pace of external changes might be matched in the receiving apparatus. Sherrington's argument was that immediate smells may arise from objects at some distance in time and space, whereas for early vertebrates, living he supposes in muddy waters, vision, as well as touch, was only for the here and now. Smells needed to be used to direct actions towards their remote sources, and the receiving station for smells was thus required to be a mechanism for retention and emotion rather than for reflex motor reactions. Such speculations take place in very muddy theoretical waters. My own preferred shot in the dark is that the cerebral hemispheres became important because they are *not* the first reception areas for other sensory modalities as much as because they *are* the point of entry for olfaction.

Just as, in perception, internal selection and organisation of sensory input can only take place beyond the sense organs themselves, so, for any kind of selective retention of sensory information over time, each extra stage of sensory processing has an advantage over the last. It is hard to imagine a monkey encoding a list of three colours in its retina, if the retina is designed to capture current visual images. Each new retinal image must wipe out the last—there has to be a later stage at which successive bits of visual information can be, metaphorically, 'filed away'. Similarly the retina itself cannot retain the spatial location of an insect that has just disappeared out of sight, if at the same time it is registering a visual array in which there is an absence of insects. Something just beyond the retina might maintain orientation to a departed food object. But in general a memory store should be far removed from the immediate arrival of sensory messages, if the past is to be made independent of the present. Therefore there are theoretical grounds for assuming that the expansion of the cerebral hemispheres of the forebrain in birds and mammals should bring with it a greater capacity for storing perceptual descriptions and representations, in modalities other than olfaction. There is no doubt that in many mammals, and probably in the earliest ones, there are facilities for the storing of olfactory information as well, in the form of a sequence of olfactory processing within the hemispheres. But in birds the clear views of daytime flying, and the absence of restrictions imposed by nocturnal prowling, meant that the avian forebrain expanded while vision, rather than olfaction, became the dominant sense.

Whichever myth about the origins of forebrain powers one chooses to believe in, it is undeniable that our forebrain is very large, and we have supposedly unlimited, if fallible, memories, while an animal such as a toad has a very small forebrain, and shows few signs of being influenced at all by its previous experience. This in itself might initiate the idea that forebrains go with memory. It should be noted that there is no such thing as a large vertebrate brain with extremely small cerebral hemispheres (see Chapter 2). But we need behavioural evidence, and it would be best if we could show that measured capacities for memory increased across species with forebrain size, and that these capacities can be selectively reduced by experimental interference with forebrain function.

Forebrain components and unity of function

I have already described, a few pages ago, evidence which suggests that in man, and probably in other primates, a small part of the cerebral hemisphere, the hippocampus, plays a special role in some kinds of remembering. Structures in the interior of the forebrain, which together with the hippocampus are identified as the limbic system, are usually thought to be primarily concerned with emotional drives and the regulation of bodily needs. (In a way, emotions function as a form of memory for provoking stimuli.) The surface cortex of mammalian hemispheres is largely taken up by areas devoted to specific sensory modalities, and subsequent perceptual analysis, as I emphasised when discussing perception (Chapter 4). Especially in primates, other regions of the cerebrum appear to be specialised for the planning and execution of motor acts, and this by no means exhausts the list of duties which the forebrain may be supposed to discharge.

Concentrating on the relation between forebrain function as a whole and memory is thus a considerable oversimplification, especially since memory in this context is vague and undefined. The practical reason for being so vague is that some of the experimental evidence concerns such things as the effect of wholesale removals of most or all of the forebrain on the behavioural capacities of a given species. The theoretical reason for examining general as well as specific aspects of forebrain mechanisms is that distinctions between such things as perception, memory and emotion are to some extent artificial abstractions. One experimenter will lesion a part of the limbic system of rats and discuss the effects of this on subsequent aggressive behaviour, without otherwise assessing adaptation to familiar surroundings, while another will make systematic tests of delayed-response abilities in animals with similar forebrain damage, only mentioning in passing that the rats struggled and bit when handled. Animals do not have special parts of their forebrain designed for performance on experimental tests of memory and perception; abilities to perceive and remember, if they are present, exist because they are useful in the course of fighting, fleeing, feeding and philandering. The assertion to be judged is that the integration of experience and action over time by the retention of perceptual information is a characteristic of forebrain function. This is hardly the only thing one would want to know about the brain, or about memory, but it seems to me to be a reasonable claim to examine, even if the complexities of both anatomy and behaviour might appear to rule out anything so simple-minded.

Beritoff's review of memory for food locations

A very clear claim was made by Beritoff (1971, p. 116): 'image memory is a function of the forebrain'. I described some of the findings on which this claim is based earlier on in this chapter—the time intervals over which animals appear to remember the location of food appear to lengthen in accordance with a crude phylogenetic scale of forebrain development. Goldfish swim back to a place where they have just been eating for only up to 10 seconds after they have been removed from it, whereas baboons who watch a piece of apple being hidden outside their cage may go directly to fetch it if they are released up to an hour later. The details of comparisons between species may be dubious, and the exact time values should not be taken too seriously, but these tests provide some sort of support for the theory that memory is useful and species with large forebrains can make more use of it than others.

This is less likely to be a spurious connection if damaging the forebrain prevents all the animals remembering food locations in the usual way. Beritoff (1971) says that this is in fact the case, and quotes experiments in which goldfish with their forebrains removed, though eating and swimming normally, no longer swam back to a place where they had just been fed. Turtles, lizards and chickens with substantial forebrain ablations could find food a few seconds after it had been shown to them, but not after the delays of two or three minutes which could be negotiated successfully by normal animals of these species. In cats and dogs 'image memory is exclusively a function of the neocortex'—total removal of all sensory and motor areas of cerebral cortex stops the animals spontaneously running to a particular feeding place permanently, and lesions to secondary projection areas in a particular modality temporarily prevents the direction of movement toward previously experienced spatial cues in that modality.

This evidence is rather limited in scope. Beritoff, of course, goes into more detail than I have here, and discusses experiments on the avoidance of places where animals have recently been given electric shocks, in which the results correspond roughly to those obtained with the food locations method, as well as various other behavioural tests of the conditioned-reflex type, whose results are more difficult to interpret. Many of the experiments are open to technical criticisms: for instance there does not generally seem to be any account taken of the possibility that changes in behaviour after forebrain damage could be due to impairments of olfaction. But there appears to me to be some sense in his overall conclusions: vertebrate memory takes various forms; 'image memory' depends on the forebrain; this and other kinds of memory vary from species to species and develop phylogenetically so that memory is better in monkeys than in fish.

Forebrain functions in non-mammals

Few would deny that human forms of memory depend on the integrity of the human cerebral hemispheres, and there is a considerable measure of agreement that particular parts of the human forebrain have particular functions that have to do with memory in one way or another. Awareness of even momentary visual experience is eliminated by damage to the visual cortex, satisfactory recall of recent visual experience is disrupted by interference with the hippocampus, and so on. Working backwards to other primates, it is reasonable to claim that there is some correspondence between human and monkey forebrain components (Weiskrantz, 1977). Although there is less experimental evidence to support detailed analysis of the function of individual forebrain components in other mammals, most current theories of the role of the neocortex of the mammalian hemispheres make little sense unless one assumes that some of the information collected and analysed by the cortex is stored for later use.

There is even less evidence, apart from Beritoff's work, which is appropriate for applying to the hypothesis that the forebrain in other vertebrates functions so as to retain perceived information. For birds, the investigations of short-term memory in the pigeon, and the apparent use of strategies requiring detailed knowledge of previous events in the formation of learning sets by mynah birds and jays (Kamil and Hunter, 1970; Kamil *et al.*, 1977) imply that significant perceptual retention takes place. There are experiments on the effects of forebrain lesions on forms of learning in birds (Stettner, 1974; Zeier, 1974; Macphail, 1975) but none that I know of that directly examine which, if any, structures in the hemispheres of birds are necessary for such tasks as delayed perceptual comparisons (Roberts and Grant, 1975).

Even Beritoff reports no experiments on the effects of forebrain lesions in amphibia—there is very little sign of any form of behavioural modifications due to experimental experience in normal frogs anyway. There are, however, large numbers of papers on the effects of forebrain lesions in fish (see Chapter 5, pp. 185–8 and Savage, 1980) and a rather smaller number of similar investigations with reptiles (Peterson, 1980) none of which permit any strong theoretical conclusion. Generally speaking behavioural effects of forebrain lesions in lower vertebrates are notable by their absence, in standard tests of loco-motion, feeding and simple forms of conditioning and learning. More complex natural behaviours, such as nest-building, courtship and aggressive social interactions, are more likely to be affected. But it is worth mentioning a few isolated results which suggest comparisons with mammalian forebrain function.

Forebrain lesions in reptiles
Lesions of the temporal lobe in mammals which involve the amydala, a subcortical limbic structure associated with the hippocampus, pro-duce placidity, lack of aggression and sexual and feeding activity involving inappropriate objects (Kluver and Bucy, 1937, 1939; Rosvold *et al.*, 1954; Plotnik, 1968). Roughly similar results are obtained by damage to the putative analogue to the amydala in mallard ducks (Phillips, 1964). Keating *et al.* (1970) and Tarr (1977) have extended the series to reptiles (Caimans and iguanid lizards). Caimans with amydaloid lesions did not show the usual attack or retreat reactions to the human experimenters except under extreme provocation (Keating *et al.*, 1970). The lizards were studied in groups in small enclosures, in which they normally established dominance hierarchies ('pecking orders') maintained by aggressive encounters and displays and the adoption of restricted territories by individuals. After suffering lesions in the forebrain amydaloid areas, a lizard would become socially indifferent, not making aggressive displays itself and ignoring those of others (Tarr, 1977). This perhaps ought to be interpreted as a disturbance of aggressive instincts, although I would prefer to put it down to a failure of social perception. Greenberg (1977) found that a slightly different type of forebrain lesion also stopped adult male lizards from issuing the normal challenge display to other adult males intruding into their personal territory, and deduced from

elaborations of the experiment that the lesions produced a failure to register the social cue rather than interference with the execution of display movements. These findings, among others, imply that the forebrain in vertebrates generally is an organising centre for inherited forms of perception and emotion.

In so far as personal territories are recognised by individual reptiles one could argue that the forebrain is the repository for cognitive maps, but it is a rare thing to find any direct indication that reptile hemispheres mediate any form of individually acquired knowledge. However, Peterson (1980), in the course of a review of all work on reptile hemispheric function since 1916, revealed that she had performed an experiment which suggested that certain forebrain lesions prevent maze learning in desert iguanas. (Burghardt, 1977, could quote only four reports of any experiments showing the learning of turns in mazes by lizards, so the lack of previous evidence of forebrain involvement in this task does not indicate negative results.) A large part of all methods of directing behaviour in lizards is devoted to temperature control: this Peterson turned to the advantage of psychological investigation by using a hot plate (at 40 degrees centigrade) as the goal for the desert iguanas. With this method, it had been shown that desert iguanas could rather laboriously learn simple mazes of the Hampton Court type (Julian and Richardson, 1968). If, after having done this, such animals had operations to destroy the dorsal cortex on the top surface of the forebrain hemispheres, they could no longer find their way around the maze they had previously learned, nor did they show any signs of recovering this ability in long training after the operation. But, operated animals could learn perfectly well to perform a simpler task of moving into a white rather than a black compartment, for the same reward of lying on a hot plate (Peterson, 1980). This may not be much to go on, but it provides a welcome chink in an otherwise blank wall. The dorsal cortex of reptiles has on anatomical grounds been thought to represent an early version of the mammalian cerebral cortex, and it would be encouraging if a reptilian dorsal cortex is necessary for some kinds of spatial learning, especially if it is required to direct movement toward relatively remote goals.

Forebrain lesions in fish
It is something of an embarrassment for any theory which proposes a gradual phylogenetic development of psychological abilities that

common aquarium fish are easy to train and perform well on most of the tests of learning capacity designed for mammals (e.g. Bitterman, 1965; Bitterman and Woodward, 1976). The ease of training fish has meant that (despite the ticklish nature of the surgery) there is a large amount of data concerning the effect of forebrain lesions on behaviours acquired as a result of individual experience. Savage (1980) suggests that no theoretical conclusions can be reached, but much of the data is consistent with the proposition that retention of recent perceptions is impaired by forebrain lesions (Savage, 1968; Flood and Overmeir, 1971; Flood *et al.*, 1976). Fish with much of their forebrains (the telencephalon) removed have difficulty in learning mazes (Hale, 1956; Warren, 1961). In many experiments where there are delays within episodes of experience (after a choice, before the reward) or between these episodes (delays between successive runs in a maze, or between trials when fish are trained to swim away from a signal to avoid electric shock), forebrain-damaged fish are more affected by the delays than others. As a rule, fish with forebrain lesions are compared with others with intact brains, but disabled olfactory organs, to ensure that impairments are not due to lack of the sense of smell. In one such case, where the procedure used comes close to a direct test of memory, goldfish first received electric shocks preceded by a signal light (Farr and Savage, 1978). Normal and forebrain-ablated animals show Pavlovian conditioning in these circumstances, as measured for instance by heart-rate changes or swimming activity in response to the light (e.g. Overmeier and Curnow, 1969). Now, however, the fish were allowed to swim in a 'T' maze, the signal light being placed at one side of the 'T', but with no shocks or any other motivating events applied. Fish without forebrain removal learned to turn towards the side of the maze away from the light but those with forebrain ablations did not. It thus seems that the successful goldfish retained what had been learned from the association between the light and pain in a form that was capable of influencing subsequent choices, whereas forebrain lesions prevented this happening. There are many ways of putting this, and it can certainly be labelled as an aspect of conditioning ('secondary reinforcement'; Flood *et al.*, 1976). But it is inescapable that some information was retained from the time of the initial light shock pairings, until the time of the 'T' maze tests. The dispute is whether it is retained in the form of a response habit, an emotional connection or as a representation of events as they occurred. This may not be resolvable, but it appears that something can be retained with a forebrain that cannot be retained without it. Since simple response-habits appear to be formed and retained in the absence of the forebrain, it is arguable that, even in the goldfish, the cerebral hemispheres make possible the retention of something more complicated.

The retention of perceived information and the modification of habits

It is time to look again at the distinction between knowledge and habit. I have mentioned this several times already, and at the beginning of this chapter I especially invented a hypothetical animal that could alter its behaviour in various ways as an adjustment to life experiences, using only very rudimentary neural mechanisms of habit formation. With a circuit of only two or three neurons, it could habituate to repeated stimuli, develop Pavlovian conditioned reflexes, and react selectively on the basis of previous reward and punishment. That is, it could do these things under certain very restricted circumstances. I bring up this fairy-tale creature again now, in order to emphasise that these elementary categories of adjustment to past experience by themselves are of very limited value in examining psychological capacities. An elaborate central nervous system is not necessary for accomplishing the bare essentials of adaptation to repeated stimulation and stimulus-response associative learning. The waning of fixed instinctive actions as a consequence of repeated elicitation is found throughout the animal kingdom (Hinde, 1970). Changes describable as Pavlovian or Skinnerian conditioning occur in various worms and in the amputated legs of cockroaches (Fantino and Logan, 1979; Horridge, 1962; Eisenstein and Colton, 1965; Distenhoff *et al.*, 1971).

It should not come as any surprise, then, that, as well as vertebrates created with very little forebrain, others, who have a lack of forebrain tissue thrust upon them by experimental surgery, are capable of demonstrating conditioned reflexes and limited motor habits stamped in by reward and punishment. Oakley (1979a) has given a most helpful account of his own and others' findings of this kind with mammals. Some claim that the isolated spinal cord can 'learn'. Mild electric shock to the thigh of a human paraplegic elicited urination after Pavlovian pairings with a current delivered to the abdomen strong enough to do this reliably (Ince *et al.*, 1978). Spinal rats appear to learn to flex a leg if stretching the leg causes shock (Chopin and

Buerger, 1975). Cats with the entire forebrain removed learn to blink their eyes at the sound of a high-pitched tone, if the high tone, but not a low tone, signals an electric shock to the cheek. Rabbits with the neocortex of the cerebral hemispheres removed (leaving the hippocampus, thalamus and basal ganglia) readily and flexibly form conditioned eye-blinking reflexes to tone or light signals paired with electric shocks to the cheek (Oakley and Russell, 1977). With sufficiently arduous or specialised training programmes, rabbits with this radical forebrain operation press a treadle many times for each food pellet received in a Skinner box (Oakley, 1979b; Oakley and Russell, 1978). Walking, climbing, swimming, grooming, and eating (including picking up food in the paws) are only slightly disturbed in rats with both neocortex and the hippocampal formation destroyed (Vanderwolf *et al.*, 1978).

All of this shows that in mammals the forebrain, or a major part of it, is not absolutely essential for certain types of behavioural phenomena. It does not show what, if anything, the forebrain in mammals *is* absolutely essential for. Unfortunately, much more effort has been spent on showing what animals can do in the absence of forebrain structures than on what they cannot do. It is a fairly safe bet however that mammals deprived of cerebral cortex could not cope with anything approaching natural conditions. In decorticated rats, 'food hoarding and social behaviour were essentially abolished' (Vanderwolf *et al.*, 1978). Decorticated rabbits trained to press a treadle for food fail to press the same treadle if it is moved a short distance from its original position (Oakley, 1978). Forebrain-damaged mammals are thus only capable of forming very stereotyped motor habits and exhibiting instinctive response patterns such as locomotion and grooming. Oakley (1979) suggests that, unlike normal mammals, they do not know what they are doing, and cannot form conscious images which would allow them to reason. Although he is apologetic about using these terms, it would be foolish to beg the question by quibbling about their applicability. I do not believe that a normal rabbit has a subjective life very much like mine or yours, but we have to say something about how its mental processes differ from those of a spinal cord, or those of a rabbit with no sensory projections beyond the thalamus. I prefer to say that the normal rabbit has remembered perceptions, expectancies and so on, while an animal with little or no forebrain has only habits and reflexes. This may be inadequate, false or even meaningless, but it can hardly be more misleading than the assumption that there is no psychological difference between a spinal cord and a complete brain, or between a goldfish and a chimpanzee, because all are capable of forming conditioned reflexes and habits (Fantino and Logan, 1979; Macphail, 1982).

Animal memory—conclusions

Vertebrate animals typically absorb information about the reality that surrounds them. It is possible to imagine creatures whose reactions can be exactly predicted by what they sense of the immediate present, but for real animals one would always have to know about previous events in order predict current reactions. Some sorts of predetermining conditions could clearly be important without raising the question of memory—a tired and well-fed beast is predictably different from an alert and hungry one. But if the tired animal finds its way back to a particular resting place, or the hungry one forages or hunts according to a previous pattern of success, we have to ask what psychological processes enable previous experiences of that individual to direct its behaviour.

I have drawn a crude theoretical distinction between habit and memory, habits being automatic reactions whose form may have been determined by previous practice and past successes and failures, and memory being distinguished by its independence from particular habits. In terms of experimental tests, the best distinction is that memories may be unique whereas habits are always repetitive. If an animal responds according to exactly where food had been on one particular previous occasion, it usually requires us to assume that something has been remembered about the unique occasion (although we may have had to train the animal habitually to remember food locations in order to make this demonstration). There are various other experimental methods which make it possible to prove that, in principle, animals retain particular features of perceived events in the recent past.

If the perceptual apparatus of an animal is used to construct descriptions of what is perceived, in order to detect objects and things rather than isolated sensations, then one would certainly expect continuity and discontinuity with time to be a necessary part of the descriptions. However, more complicated brains would be needed to construct such descriptions, and to store them over time, than would be needed to react to a simple stimulus, such as a bright light, and to modify reactions according to whether previous reactions to bright light had been strengthened by the ingestion of food, or such like. There is reason to believe that the cerebral hemispheres of vertebrate brains are particularly important for, among other things, the utilisation of memories as opposed to such simple habits. Behavioural evidence is distinctly patchy, but any vertebrate whose forebrain is removed is likely to be measurably less influenced by retained perceptions of previous events, although simple automatic habits may still be gradually acquired. In men certain parts of the cerebral hemispheres seem to be identified with particular aspects of memory: damage to the inner sides of the temporal lobes may leave intact information of long standing and the perceptions of the last few seconds, but prevent access to the events of previous days, hours or minutes. The same structures of the forebrain also serve memory functions in other mammals. It is probable that the memory capacity of animal species varies according to forebrain development, so that lower vertebrates such as fish and reptiles are very much less influenced by information retained from previous perceptions than are mammals and birds.

9 Knowing and meaning in monkeys and apes

Although there are many uncertainties about the course of vertebrate evolution, it is pretty obvious that monkeys and apes are physically more like us than other species are. They look a bit like us, and such details as teeth, or the biochemistry of the blood, suggest that we are rather close relatives of the great apes—the chimpanzee, the orang-utang, and the gorilla (e.g. Goodman, M., 1974; King and Wilson, 1975; Zihlman *et al.*, 1978). Most importantly for the theme I am pursuing, the brains of monkeys and apes are much more like the human brain than are those of other mammals, not to mention the brains of birds and lower vertebrates. If size of brain alone was considered, then we might expect that the functions of a brain a third or a tenth the size of ours (in a chimpanzee or a rhesus monkey) should bear more relation to the functions of the human brain than the things done by brains that are a hundred, a thousand, or ten thousand times smaller. An equally compelling reason for predicting that there should be similarities between human and primate mental characteristics is that the details of the anatomical arrangements of the human brain reflect those in other primates. Much work has been done since Huxley emphasised 100 years ago that 'every principal gyrus and sulcus of a chimpanzee brain is clearly represented in that of a man', but there is nothing which contradicts his conclusion that the differences between the human and chimpanzee brains are remarkably minor by evolutionary standards—as compared with, for instance, the difference between the brain of a chimpanzee and that of a lemur or marmoset.

Other physical features which might have a bearing on psychological development, such as sensory and motor apparatus (in particular the structure of the eyes and the hands), would lead us to expect similarities between primate and human perception and action. Social and emotional parallels between man and the primates are perhaps more debatable (see Goodall, 1965, 1979). But emotional, social and cognitive development during the life-span of individuals is certainly one of the areas where the affinities between man and other primates are clearly greater than those between man and mammals generally. Occasionally very strange things are said about the speed of human growth, and the length of human infancy, so it is worth pointing out that differences between man and the anthropoid apes in age-related physical changes are not terribly dramatic. Pregnancy is 8 months long in the chimpanzee, and gorilla gestation is a day less than the human term, in so far as one accepts available figures (Napier and Napier, 1967). All such figures are rather approximate, especially if derived from field observations, but it seems that civilised human life-span, at 70–75 years, is about twice as long as that of the apes, at 35 years plus. If this is so, then the rate of progress through the life-span, in proportion to the duration of the span, is roughly the same in man and other primates. If infancy is measured as the period of close dependency on the mother, which means in apes that the mother continues to breast-feed and carry the infant, then great-ape infancy lasts about 3 years. The comparable human figure is clearly influenced by culture and is rather arbitrary, but is often given as 6 years (Napier and Napier, 1967; Jolly, 1972). Even more arbitrary is the dividing line between sub-adult and adult life. However, it can be said fairly reliably that the apes reach sexual maturity when about 10 or 11 years old, which fits well enough with the convention that human adulthood begins at 21. Obviously one's doubts about this comparison would be because the years of human sexual activity, if not those of discretion, may begin rather earlier than at 21. The point is that the apes remain immature for about a quarter of their life span, and there is no case for saying that the proportion of the human life-span spent as a juvenile has been radically extended. The rhesus monkey, the commonest subject of psychological investigations of primate behaviour, lives to be 28 or 30 and is juvenile for the first 7 or 8 of these years—again a juvenile phase of up to a quarter of the life-span.

Cognitive development in primate infants

The time intervals involved in physical development are not in themselves particularly informative about the processes of psychological development which may or may not be occurring. But much of interest has been found in the establishment of mother-infant affectional ties, the gradual acquisition of social skills, and the progress of emotional adjustment, in the rhesus monkey and other non-human primates (Harlow, 1958; Harlow and Mears, 1979; Hinde, 1974). There is less work on the separate assessment of cognitive and intellectual development in monkeys and apes. One study may be used as an example of the sort of results which may be obtainable (Redshaw, 1978). Differentiation between linguistic and non-linguistic knowledge, as far as that is possible, is of course necessary if comparisons between human and primate intellectual development are to be made. It happens, perhaps quite fortuitously, that the theories and methods of Piaget, which provide the major body of work available on human cognitive development in childhood, concentrate on changes which are supposedly independent of verbal fluency, or the receipt of propositional knowledge expressed in language. This allows for clearer comparisons between human and non-human cognition than would be possible if one were to emphasise intellectual accomplishments known through speech or writing. I do not mean to discount the importance of human speech for human cognition—it is because human thought is so largely based on language that psychological comparisons with other species are so difficult. But this fact should make us seize all the more eagerly on opportunities to assess the non-linguistic capacities of animals in any way which allows some form of comparison with human abilities.

Perhaps the only time that this can be done with any confidence is in the period before human children make use of language, i.e. Piaget's 'sensory-motor period' during the first one-and-a-half years of the life of human infants. Redshaw examined 4 gorilla infants (hand-reared in a zoo) and 2 human infants, over a period of 18 months, using tests designed and standardised to assess changes in the cognition and perception of human babies at this stage of life (Uzigiris and Hunt, 1974). In these, there are about forty individual achievements, such as 'Finds an object hidden behind one of two screens'; 'Grasps toy when both toy and hand are in view'; 'Uses one object as a container for another'; 'Attempts to wind up a mechanical toy following a demonstration'. Each achievement is measured in terms of how many weeks old a particular infant is when it first does it. On the basis of Piagetian theory, the individual tests are rather arbitrarily grouped into four scales: 'Visual pursuit and object permanence'; 'The development of means for achieving desired ends'; 'The construction of object relations in space'; and 'The development of operational causality'. The examples given above represent one from each scale. There is a fairly reliable and predictable standard order in which human babies progress through the tasks: at 10 weeks their eyes follow moving objects, including hands, and by 50 weeks they can find objects which have been moved about behind screens, pull things up on the end of strings, detour around obstructions to retrieve toys, and wind up clockwork toys.

The findings for the gorilla babies are pretty straightforward: generally they do all the things which human babies do, and progress through the scales in the same sequence, but are a few weeks more advanced than the human babies in everything except playing with clockwork toys, where they are a few weeks behind. There are just four things none of the gorilla infants were observed to do in Redshaw's study: they did not use a stick to retrieve an out-of-reach toy; they did not make towers by putting one block on top of another; they did not point to familiar persons; and they did not give their toys back to the human adult who had handed them out. The last two tests may not be entirely fair for gorillas. Young gorillas presumably can identify familiar gorilla adults, notably their mothers, although they may not be naturally inclined to point or to hand objects back and forth. The other failures indicate that infant apes may already be falling behind on the conceptualisation of space and/or causality, although, as we shall see shortly, adult chimpanzees, if not infant gorillas, can under some conditions use sticks to retrieve objects, and pile up two or three boxes to form towers. The main point, which would not necessarily have been predictable from the normal lifestyle of adult animals, is that the infant gorillas appear to go through the same preliminary stages as human babies: following falling objects, pulling in a cloth if a toy is resting on it, but not when the toy is held just above it, and so on. This provides empirical support for Piaget's theoretical contention that the beginnings of human knowledge of the external world arise from rather basic forms of object perception (see Chapter 3, pp. 95–7).

It is likely that, even in the first year of life, the experience of interacting with reality, by playing with toys, crawling about, being fed, and so on, contributes to the internal organisation of human perception. This makes it all the more notable that the zoo-reared apes got as far as they did, lacking the degree of practice and imitation available to a human baby in a human home. They did have the benefits of the care of a human residential parent-substitute, but this is not quite the same thing.

Most of the research which I shall now go on to discuss involves environmental enrichment of one kind or another for apes at various ages. This is certainly artificial, but it is arguable that all human environments from the stone ages on are artificial too. The question of what types of mental ability are available to apes in their natural conditions of life is an important one, but if they can be persuaded to exhibit greater cognitive capacities by certain kinds of experimental intervention, this is in some senses an even better basis for comparison with the human abilities which we may regard as natural, but which we always observe in individuals who have been surrounded by artifacts from the moment of birth.

The Mentality of Apes

Material pertinent to the cognitive development of apes after the first year of life is sparse. The Hayeses (Hayes, 1951; Hayes and Nissen, 1971) and the Kelloggs (Kellogg, 1968) reported on the gradual development of problem-solving and discriminatory abilities in young chimpanzees which they reared in their homes with the hope of observing the appearance of speech. As only two or three imitative vocalisations emerged, their efforts are usually regarded as wasted, although the non-verbal abilities of the animals should have some interest. (On the basis of rigorous comparisons with human toddlers, the Hayeses concluded that their chimpanzees had at least the rudimentary stages of several human mental abilities.) The concentration on the development of gesture, or other specialised efforts at communication in more recent intensive training of chimpanzees, which I will discuss later, has meant that other indications of intelligence have tended to be ignored. We must therefore move on from the relationship between chronological age and intellectual abilities, and look simply at object perception, and object manipulation, achieved at any age. The classic study of this type is Kohler's *The Mentality of Apes* (1925). The Prussian Academy of Sciences maintained a research station on the island of Tenerife between 1912 and 1920, in which chimpanzees were kept, in fairly restricted conditions. Kohler stayed there from 1913 to 1917 observing and testing these animals, although most of the data reported in his books were collected in the comparatively short space of six months during 1914. His book is remembered for the evidence of the mental solution to problems, by 'insight', prior to the execution of problem-solving actions, but is based on phenomena which have been frequently replicated by subsequent investigators (e.g. see Menzel, 1978). The main findings were that chimpanzees would drag food towards them, through the bars of a cage, by the use of a stick; would plug one piece of cane into another to make a longer stick, when this was necessary; and would construct towers, from wooden crates, in order to reach bananas hung far out of reach above them. Considerable effort has been spent on showing that chimpanzees will not do these things in the absence of prior experience of appropriate kinds (e.g. Birch, 1945; Davenport and Rogers, 1970). This is certainly the case: a chimpanzee will not drag in out-of-reach fruit with a stick on the very first occasion it sees a stick, and preliminary play and practice in the manipulation of objects is necessary if subsequent problems are to be rapidly solved. But this does not conflict with the details of Kohler's observations, in which it is made clear that the animals needed to 'familiarise themselves' with the use of the objects concerned. It is true, however, that Kohler liked to describe his animals as 'striking on solutions' after having first scratched their heads in doubt. This did not go down well with sceptical and behaviourist readers, and perhaps Kohler went a little too far in the direction of imaginative interpretation. But stripped of the more enthusiastic Prussian anthropomorphisms (Kohler has it that some of his apes marched around in circles, one behind the other, with accentuated rhythmic stamping of the feet, feeling stateliness and pride and heightened bodily consciousness—pp. 96–7), *The Mentality of Apes* still contains much of value.

A task which was one of Kohler's first tests, and which seemed to elicit a rapid perceptual solution, involved a swinging basket. The basket, containing fruit and some heavy ballast, was out of the reach of the animals when hanging still at the end of a rope, but if given a big enough push (by Kohler), would swing like a pendulum, getting close enough to scaffolding to be caught. This is an 'extrapolation' problem. Some of the chimps, on first seeing the basket swinging like this, unsuccessfully leapt up towards it, but others, in less than a minute sprang up the scaffolding and, so Kohler says, waited with arms outstretched for the basket to come to them. Solving the other problems was never so immediate, but Kohler's theory was apparently that the chimps eventually 'saw' a solution in the same way that some of them were able to extract from the movements of the swinging basket sufficient information to direct their movements up the scaffolding. I think, from reading his own accounts, that he was probably wrong in this, and that the later problems involved a greater element of habit, and the remembering of previous experience, but this is largely a matter of opinion.

Kohler himself certainly acknowledges the element of gradually acquired skills, in the case of the use of a 'jumping pole'. The problem of getting at bananas suspended high up in the air was one solved in a number of different ways. Kohler's animals had a succession of problems of this type, which meant that they had general experience of manoeuvres aimed at suspended objects, and if there are any inherited mental abilities in chimpanzees, then these should be exhibited in getting at bananas, if in nothing else. Sultan, a fully grown male with a history of using smaller sticks, is credited with the invention of jumping with the aid of a pole or board, but most of the animals did this at some time or another, and a young female, Chica, became particularly skilful. According to Kohler, the jumping was primarily a matter of play, which could be put to practical uses if the opportunity arose. The technique was not like human pole vaulting—one end of the pole was planted in the ground without any preliminary run, and the chimp then gained upward momentum by climbing straight up the stick and pushing off, before it fell over. Chica, after showing promise with short sticks and boards, and a pole two metres long, was given a bamboo pole of four metres, with which she was able to make five-metre vaults, being one metre tall herself. It is this instance that Kohler uses as an example of acquired skills of muscular co-ordination and balance. Jumping for Chica was evidently an end in itself, and the bamboo pole a valued possession. Deprived of food and the pole, and then returned to the enclosure with access to the pole, and to food placed on the ground, she would alternate between eating and jumping.

Sticks of one sort of another were used in a variety of ways by Kohler's animals, but usually to get food. The only common use of this kind of tool observed in natural conditions is the collections of termites on small twigs (Goodall, 1965). Kohler saw something very similar—the pushing of sticks and straws through wire netting to collect ants on the other side. Sticks were also used for general poking, and in particular for surprisingly vicious treatment of chickens kept on the other side of a wire-netting fence. Some of the chimps appeared to

Kohler to be charitable, throwing pieces of bread (which the chimps themselves did not like very much) over the netting, and watching the chickens eat. Others were less kind, since they habitually held pieces of bread against the wire netting until a hen came to peck at it, and then pulled it away and ate it themselves. A perverse variant of this was to attract the chickens with bread, and then repel them by poking with sticks or wires. Stronger sticks were used in digging for roots. Digging with the hands is seen in the wild in chimpanzees and gorillas (Schaller, 1963), but not the use of tools, which apparently requires human encouragement. One specific form of encouragement used by Kohler was to bury fruit underground, within sight of the animals. This can be a test of memory, but clearly provides a reason for digging that is not present in nature.

It is in general quite impossible to tell, from Kohler's account, how far the chimpanzees were being trained in certain particular techniques, as opposed to arriving at them by their own insights. This is not always crucial, but in the 'building' experiments, in which the chimpanzees made a tower of two or three boxes, it is obvious that the final behaviour depended on the accumulation of previous experience at simpler versions of the task, and not the spontaneous idea that a tower of three boxes is needed to climb to a particular suspended banana. The animals first had to be trained to pull one box underneath suspended fruit—by leaving them in a room with a box which was just the right size. After this, they were left with the fruit hanging much higher, and two available boxes. They always first tried bringing just one box under the fruit, and only after some time brought the second one. After an attempt of this kind, Kohler records that he himself placed the second box firmly on top of the first one, and held it in position while the chimpanzee involved, Grande, climbed up to fetch the reward (Kohler, 1925, p. 141). This animal 'progressed with time' eventually building towers from three or four boxes. Such an ability to manipulate objects in space demonstrates many capacities including patience and a certain amount of spatial imagination needed for positioning the boxes on top of one another. But the building technique as such was clearly more a matter of memory than of inspiration.

Menzel (1972, 1973, 1978) observed the apparently spontaneous acquisition of the technique of using large stripped branches as ladders or bridges in a group of chimpanzees living in a one-acre field, but argues that such behaviours arise from 'specific motivational factors and perceptual-motor coordinations' which are heavily influenced by social facilitation and early social experience (Menzel, 1978, p. 386). The one-acre field was enclosed from surrounding woodland by concrete and barbed wire fences, and trees inside the enclosure had live electric wires wrapped round the base of their trunks to prevent climbing. Photographic evidence is supplied to support the observation that the animals leant tree branches against the walls and against the wired-up trees in such a way that they were able to escape over the walls, and bypass the wired bases of the trees. It is also claimed that on some occasions one animal held the bottom of the 'ladder' while others climbed up, and that when the branches were confiscated, the chimps pulled posts out of the ground and used them in the same way. It would seem appropriate to deduce that these individuals possessed comparatively rich mental representations of the objects they manipulated and mental organisation by which the objects were systematically related to future goals. Although it took several years for the animals to develop the ability to use branches and poles in the way that they did, and social interactions during these years were necessary, this does not make the cognitive achievements negligible.

It is difficult to say what these cognitive achievements are. Clearly if chimpanzees use poles or piles of boxes as means to attain desired ends, this implies a recognition of poles and boxes as things which may be used for getting to otherwise inaccessible places, but if the manipulations become accustomed routines it can be claimed that the object perceptions and associated motor skills are not held together by any abstract inner knowledge. Pavlov repeated Kohler's experiments with apes kept in his own laboratory and managed to get his chimpanzee, Raphael, to pile up six boxes to reach suspended fruit. Raphael was also trained to turn on a water tap which was positioned over flames which guarded a box with fruit in it, 'and when the tap ran dry he took a bottle with water in and poured it on to the flame' (Pavlov, 1955, p. 594). But Pavlov firmly interpreted this as a form of association, not different in principle from what he studied by the conditioned reflex method. Since he then went on to say that human thinking is also just a form of association, his objection rather loses its force. It seems to me sensible to assume that internal associations and connections of whatever kind, that govern the learned use of tools by chimpanzees, are very much more like human thinking than are simple anticipatory reflexes which may be observed in decerebrate goldfish. Clearly this is rather vague, and better tests to distinguish higher forms of cognition in apes from simpler discriminations in other animals would be helpful. But Kohler's observations should stand as evidence for sophisticated spatial memory and object manipulation in the chimpanzee.

Estimation of quantities

In the Piagetian theory of the development of human cognition in childhood, the use of tools would be a rather primitive aspect of 'sensory-motor' intelligence, and a more advanced type of mental operation would be one involved with the perceived stability of quantity over sequences of qualitative change. This may or may not be a worthwhile distinction to make for the purposes of comparing species: it happens to be reliably correlated with age changes in human children. A child of 3 or 4 tends to be misled by superficial changes in the appearance of given quantities of liquids or solids since if orange juice in a short wide glass is poured into a tall thin one, the 3-year-old will give every appearance of believing that there is more juice in the thin glass than there was in the wide one. A 7- or 8-year-old, on the other hand, should know that there is something important about orange juice which does not change when it is poured from one glass to another—this is known as 'conservation of volume'. Similarly a round ball of clay rolled into a sausage shape does not lose or gain any volume, as far as an adult is concerned, but a very young child is likely to be more impressed by the change in shape than the constancy of substance, and is very reluctant to admit that the sausage is the same quantity as the ball (Piaget and Inhelder, 1969).

Although this is a reliable observation about the behaviour of young and old children respectively, it is not obvious that it ought to have very much theoretical importance. However, belief in the immutability of clay, or orange juice, is an abstract concept, which requires immediately perceived dimensions, such as length or height, to be ignored, in favour of memory. It is only because we remember that the sausage of clay has been formed from the ball it was before, without anything being added or subtracted, that we judge the sausage to be the same as the ball. If non-human animals can demonstrate anything like this judgment about the constancy of material over time, it may similarly indicate a triumph of recent memory over immediate perception.

Children are given conservation tests by being asked questions—'Is the orange juice the same?' or 'Is there more orange juice?'—we might ask after pouring it from one glass to another. To some extent the answers may reflect what a child thinks words refer to, and such niceties may not apply to tests designed for animals. It is possible, however, to give choices to monkeys which require non-verbal judgments of constancy and change. Pasnak (1979) conducted an elaborate investigation along these lines. A monkey was shown two balls of clay of equal size. One of these balls then had a lump detached from it. The other ball was then rolled into a sausage shape, both operations being performed in the animal's sight. The monkey then had to choose the clay which had been changed in volume rather than shape (getting a piece of apple if it chose correctly). The problem was difficult because sometimes a lump was added, rather than subtracted from the ball being changed in mass, and sometimes the changed ball, rather than the unchanged one, was rolled into a sausage. (And at other times both balls were squeezed into sausages, after one had been changed in size.) The obvious way for the monkey to solve the problem was, therefore, for it to remember which ball had been changed in size, and to use this information whether or not the objects changed in shape. Apparently the monkey (a rhesus macaque as usual) was able to do this, since it chose correctly with this example, and also with 24 others, in which clay balls were squeezed into various shapes after size alterations, or in which stacks of sponge cubes or piles of drinking straws (or various other collections of objects) underwent analogous transformations, first in size and then in shape. A second rhesus macaque went through the same series of tests, always rewarded for choosing the object or pile which had *not* been changed in quantity, whether or not it was changed in shape. A number of careful modifications to the procedures make it almost certain that the animals were not responding on the basis of the static appearance of the objects present at the moment of choice, but on the basis of whether a given object, as it appeared, had *previously* undergone addition or subtraction of some of its material. This is not precisely the same thing as a child giving the right answers on a conservation test, but Pasnak was entitled to claim that his animals had demonstrated cognitive components necessary for conservation, namely the differentiation between the adding and subtracting of material on the one hand, and changes in superficial appearance of objects on the other.

A somewhat closer approximation to the test for remembered sameness of quantities as it is administered to children was used by

Woodruff *et al.* (1978) with a 14-year-old chimpanzee, Sarah, who had had ten years of experience of interacting with human experimenters by the manipulation of bits of plastic (see below, pp. 357–64). Sarah was shown two objects, and was not required to choose between them, but rather to make a judgment about their equivalence. Food titbits were given at the end of a long testing session, whether or not the judgments were correct, so there was no direct reinforcement of particular responses.

One series of problems involved two lumps of modelling clay, but I shall quote the details of the other series, in which glass jars of three different sizes were filled with various amounts of blue water. At the beginning of a trial, two glass jars of the same size and shape were placed in front of the chimpanzee. Either they contained the same volume of blue liquid (reaching the same height in the two jars), or they contained different amounts (the heights reached in the two jars differing quite clearly—by 5 cm or more). The experimenter then took one of the original jars, and poured its contents into a glass container of different proportions. The jars were selected so that if the original jars contained water to the same height, after the pouring the new jar had a different height of water than the other; but if the original jars held different amounts of water, after the pouring the water in the new jar came up to the same height as the water in the old one. The experimenter then handed the chimpanzee a covered dish containing two pieces of plastic, one of which she was accustomed to use to indicate 'same', the other of which she had used for many years to indicate 'different'. The experimenter left the room and the chimpanzee picked one of the pieces of plastic, and put it between the two jars. Roughly 8 times out of 10, Sarah selected 'same' when the two original jars had held the same amounts, and 'different' when they had held different amounts. By itself, this might not mean very much. However, preliminary tests had shown that 'same' and 'different' were normally used appropriately for two jars of the same shape containing equal or unequal amounts of water. Also, as a check that the state of the original two jars on each trial determined the final judgment, the procedure was repeated, with the chimpanzee being allowed to see only the final stage of the sequence, that is two jars of different shapes containing either equal or unequal amounts. Judgments in this case were not accurate: there was a tendency for 'different' to be selected, whatever the amounts of liquid present, but this was not quite statistically significant. This suggests that when the chimpanzee was allowed to observe the initial state of the two jars, followed by the pouring episode, it selected the 'same' and 'different' responses on the basis of the initial state, and ignored their final appearance. This would only require remembering the initial state for a minute or two, well within the chimpanzee's range, but it means that the animal must be interested enough in the heights of liquids to remember whether the two jars were initially the same or different, and be able to discount the heights of the liquids immediately present when the judgment is given.

This may not be quite the same thing as 'conservation of liquid quantity' as it occurs in a 7-year-old child, but it shows flexibility of memory, and an independence from current vivid stimuli. Sarah was certainly capable of watching the pouring of liquids very closely; at the final stage of this experiment (Woodruff *et al.*, 1978) the two jars always started out with the same amount of water in them, but when the experimenter did the pouring from one of the original pair into the jar of a different shape, he sometimes poured a little of the water into a non-transparent cup, or used water already in this cup to add to the new jar along with all the original water. Sarah was again about 80 per cent accurate on this procedure, giving 'same' when pouring took place normally and 'different' when the cup was used for adding or subtracting. The very least this demonstrates is that the chimpanzee noticed when the experimenter was fiddling with the cup, and used this as a cue for the subsequent selection of one from two bits of plastic. Since the rhesus monkeys used by Pasnak (1979) were not fooled by the experimenter patting clay with a spatula, when adding or subtracting with the spatula was important, it seems sensible to assume that something about the liquid was being perceived. A further experiment with the chimpanzee Sarah suggests that she readily 'sees' quite abstract relationships in visual displays (Gillan *et al.*, 1981). Presented with a cut apple with a knife on one side, and a piece of paper and scissors on the other, she selected the 'same' symbol to put between them, whereas given the cut apple and knife paired with the paper and a bowl of water, she gave the symbol 'different'. On the basis of a number of tests like this the experimenters concluded that the chimpanzee was bringing to bear a process of 'analogical reasoning' in order to deduce similarities which reside in relationships between objects. 'Reasoning' is a contentious term to use, but clearly something was going on in the chimpanzee's head during these tests beyond the plain comparison of visual patterns.

What exactly was going on in the two experiments on 'conservation' of quantity by non-human primates (Pasnak, 1979; Woodruff *et al.*, 1978) is uncertain, and whatever it was probably depended on the exact conditions of training in each case. But it is not unreasonable to suggest that monkeys and apes can come to know things about objects which progress beyond the simplest sensory-motor levels of the hierarchies of cognition observable in man. In the natural environment such cognitions are presumably put to the service of eating and social adjustment. One can well imagine that it is useful to know that a large banana is large, whether it is perceived in a vertical or horizontal alignment, and to some extent this must be regarded as a form of conservation. It cannot be denied, however, that detailed comparisons between such forms of cognition in primates and corresponding human knowledge must always be qualified by the absence of verbal expression of ideas in primates other than man. It is only when a child becomes able to give a verbal explanation of why orange juice poured from one glass to another is 'the same' that we are likely to accept that his knowledge approximates that of an adult (Piaget and Inhelder, 1969). The child is eventually able to argue that a given volume of liquid must stay the same in different containers: either by explaining that sameness depends on nothing being added or subtracted; or by pointing out variations on this theme, such as the possibility of restoring the liquid to its original appearance in the original container. Few would suppose that the chimpanzee's knowledge of liquids and solids could ever be given this sort of expression. But on the basis of data such as Kohler's, which apparently demonstrates comprehension of ends and means, many have felt that these animals if no others, should be able to give verbal expression to their more concrete inner ideas, if given sufficient encouragement.

Communication by sign and symbol in the great apes

Unfortunately, captive apes display a notable lack of interest in imitating human speech. Of the great apes, the orang-utang, being largely solitary, has little use for frequent vocal signals, while gorilla social groups are fairly quiet (Schaller, 1963) and the noise produced by chest-beating in aggressive male displays is probably as important as vocally produced sounds. The chimpanzee is more vocal and more actively social than the other great apes, but gesture, posture and touch seem to have a wider application in social exchanges than vocalisation.

The natural social vocabulary of even the chimpanzee is almost certainly less extensive than that of Old World monkeys (e.g. Green, 1975; Seyfarth, *et al.*, 1980) or of the lesser apes, the gibbons (Tenaza and Marler, 1977; Tenaza and Tilson, 1977). It is often suggested that the sound-producing apparatus of apes—the resonating cavities of the throat and mouth and the adjusting mechanism of lips and tongue—is physically incapable of producing human speech sounds (e.g. Lieberman, 1975). To the naked eye physical specialisations for speech in man seem remarkably minor, but whether the difference lies in the anatomy of the tongue and throat, or in psychological inclinations to utilise the anatomy to make interesting noises, there is no doubt that apes intransigently resist any temptation to cross the Rubicon of human speech.

The evidence is mostly negative: apes kept in zoos, or in human homes, are highly imitative, form strong social attachments to people, and are prepared to adopt human habits of personal hygiene and social decorum, but have never been known to imitate speech. It is the more strongly negative, in that deliberate attempts to foster speech, by bringing up infant chimpanzees in human homes, and maximising the social and the more tangible incentives for vocalisation, have had very little success. One of the most domesticated apes was probably the gorilla John Daniel (Cunningham, 1921; quoted in Tilney, 1928) who behaved himself well in company, but died when only 6. ('His table manners were rather exceptionally good. He always sat at the table, and whenever the meal was ready would pull up his own chair to his place . . . He always took afternoon tea of which he was very fond, and then would eat a thin slice of bread with plenty of jam': Tilney, 1928, p. 635.)

Two psychologists, W. N. and L. A. Kellogg, brought up an infant chimpanzee in their own home in the 1920s (see Kellogg, 1968) and were able to draw comparisons between its social development and that of children, but saw no signs of speech-like vocalisation. This enterprise was repeated by K. J. and C. Hayes two decades later (see Hayes, 1951; Hayes and Hayes, 1951, 1952; Hayes and Nissen, 1971). They were able by dint of explicit training, to get their animal, Vicki, to make noises that sounded vaguely like human words, but only four of them (Mama, Poppa, cup and up). Vicki also made other sounds in specific contexts which were not recognisable as English words, but which were not natural chimpanzee vocalisations either. This was a considerable achievement, if the anatomical barriers to speech production in chimps are as great as is now generally supposed, but the four words themselves do not expand very much either the chimpanzee's cognition or our interpretation of it. If a chimpanzee could say 'cup' when a cup is presented at various angles and distances, this would demonstrate the perceptual capacity of object recognition, but the same inference could be drawn from observations of a thirsty chimp reaching for cups of various shapes and sizes.

Training chimpanzees to make gestures

It may be that the verdict on the numerous efforts to teach chimpanzees sign-language will be rather similar—just as the attempt to make a chimpanzee talk produced only the most minimal approximation to human speech, attempts to make chimpanzees communicate by a gestural system usable by the human deaf produce only a pale reflection of human performance (Terrace, *et al.*, 1979). There is a myth that we could converse with animals as easily as with other people, if only we did something rather special and magical, such as drinking dragon's blood. One can detect in some of the discussions of chimpanzee gesturing (Gardner and Gardner, 1975, 1978; Linden, 1976) an air of the false hope that sign-language might be the modern equivalent of dragon's blood, allowing us to communicate with apes on an equal footing. It is obvious that this dream is not going to come true. But it is equally obvious that chimpanzees' cognitions are not, as some still claim (Terrace *et al.*, 1979), as far removed from human thinking as those of a pigeon or rat. Training apes to make a large number of distinct hand movements, which correspond to objects and perceptual categories, reveals a good deal about perception and memory in the chimpanzee, even if it is a very poor substitute for dragon's blood.

Before discussing the evidence which is obtained from chimpanzees trained to make artificial gestures, I want to make a clear distinction between claims that these animals do things that are strictly comparable to the human use of language (e.g. Gardner and Gardner, 1975) and more limited inferences about perception and memory. Because claims for the conversation-like attributes of chimpanzee gesturing have been exaggerated, it is sometimes suggested that, on the contrary, their gestures have no meaning at all. It is perfectly possible, however, that something useful may be learned from experiments which fall short of demonstrating human levels of linguistic competence in apes, and I believe this is true of the projects designed to teach chimpanzees sign-language.

The first of these was begun by R. A. and B. T. Gardner, with the chimpanzee Washoe (see Gardner and Gardner, 1969, 1971). The idea was that, as chimpanzees never imitate sounds but frequently imitate actions, they should have less difficulty in learning the arm and hand movements of American Sign Language, widely used by the deaf in North America, than they do in learning speech. It is customary to describe the individual signs in this system by giving translations: it is begging the question to translate gestures made by animals directly into ordinary words, but there seems to be no realistic alternative. I shall follow the usual convention, but the reader is warned not to take translations of chimpanzee gestures as evidence that the mental states accompanying the gestures were the same as those which may accompany the verbal translations. Examples of gestures eventually performed by Washoe, and their translations, are as follows. An extended arm moved upward, with or without the index finger also extended, is interpreted as '*up*'. A beckoning motion with the whole hand or the ends of the fingers is '*Come-gimme*'; a palm patting the top of the head is '*hat*'; slapping the thigh is '*dog*'; an index finger drawn over the back of the other hand is '*tickle*' (Gardner and Gardner, 1969). Some of these, such as '*up*', are iconic or intuitive, while others such as '*dog*' are more arbitrary.

The training programme was first to make gestures of this kind a ubiquitous part of the only social life the animal experienced. Washoe was wild-caught, but after entering the Gardners' laboratory at the age of approximately 12 months, she lived in an environment of human artifacts and human companions. One or more persons were present during all Washoe's waking hours, making ASL (American Sign Language) signs directed at the chimpanzee, and between themselves. Imitation was therefore possible, but direct guidance, by putting the animal's hands in the desired position, was used as well, and deliberate reward and punishment was pervasive (for instance, tickling only when Washoe made the signs for '*tickle*' or '*more tickle*').

As a result of these efforts, Washoe exhibited a number of gestures which corresponded quite closely to standard ASL signs: 30 when she was about 2 years old, and 132 after two further years of training. It seems safe to conclude that a vocabulary of gestures is more readily acquired than a vocabulary of spoken words, but it is prodigiously difficult to determine how far the gestures are performed at random, or in immediate imitation of human companions, in the 'free-living' context of play and persuasion which is filmed or photographed to provide the most appealing record of the results of this type of experiment (see Patterson, 1978; Terrace, 1980). Close examination of some of these photographic records suggests that imitation of recent signs produced by the trainer is one of the things that happens (Terrace *et al.*, 1979; Seidenberg and Petitto, 1979). Claims by trainers that Washoe, or other apes subjected to similar procedures, 'learned sign language' thus need to be treated with some caution. Fortunately, there is sufficient evidence from carefully controlled tests to make it clear that individual gestures are reliably connected with particular contexts or referents. The disagreements are not so much about whether chimpanzees learn to associate particular gestures with particular objects, and particular actions, but about whether they achieve the higher levels of mental organisation that would be indicated by the understanding of relationships between words.

Evidence that individual gestures have individual referents (or individual meanings, to use that term loosely) can be obtained simply by recording (using films or videotapes and independent observers) that an ape uses a sign—say *'cat'* when it sees a cat—without any help from human companions. This was done with Nim Chimpsky, a male chimpanzee reared under more or less the same conditions as Washoe by another team of people (Terrace *et al.*, 1979). Alternatively the chimpanzee can be shown a random series of objects, or of pictures of objects, with an observer, who cannot see these objects, noting the gestures made (Gardner and Gardner, 1971, 1978). With both these techniques, it is apparent that particular object categories elicit appropriate signs. In the reverse direction, if the chimpanzee sees a human trainer make a gesture, it is able to identify appropriate objects. Some of the evidence for this is rather anecdotal, it is true. Terrace (1980) reports that signed instructions of the type 'give me brush' were responded to by Nim selecting whatever object was asked for from an array of possibilities, and that this animal would also leaf through the pages of a picture book to find and point to illustrations of objects referred to by gesture of the human trainer. A more systematic and elaborate test of the received meanings of sign-language gestures is reported by Fouts *et al.* (1976). The subject was a chimpanzee born in captivity, and reared in a human home hearing spoken English as well as seeing ASL gestures. The design of the experiment involved establishing to begin with reliable indications that this chimpanzee could identify 10 objects, which it did not know by gesture, by hearing *spoken* words (the 10 were spoon, foot, curtain, water, banana, shocker, raisin, nut, leaf and pillow). If the experimenter said 'spoon' the animal fetched one, but if the word spoken was 'pillow', it fetched a pillow. At the next stage the human trainer spoke the word and at the same time made the corresponding gesture, in the absence of the appropriate object. This was done with individual words, one at a time. The test was that, after sound-gesture experience, the chimpanzee was assessed by another experimenter, who was not aware of which gestures the chimpanzee was supposed to know. The assessment was to pick up each object in turn (the experiment was split up into two groups of five objects) and see if the animal could make the appropriate gesture. The result was that the 10 individual gestures were acquired by the animal, in the order in which it received instruction via speech and gesture conjunctions, in the absence of the objects referred to.

It would be unwise to place a great deal of weight on any single anecdotal or experimental report, but unless there has been widespread fraud or delusion, it seems necessary to accept that under the conditions described, chimpanzees form mental associations between perceptual schemata for manual gestures and others for object categories. This is not to say, in Romanes's phrase, that they can mean propositions, in forms such as 'all chimpanzees like bananas', although it is arguable that individual animals make gestures that bear some relation to the proposition 'I would very much like a banana now'. The relation is more interesting than that between 'I would like a banana' in human speech, and tugging at the sleeve of someone who is holding a banana, but, since it has not been convincingly demonstrated that one chimpanzee gesture modifies another, or that there is any approximation to syntax and grammar in the comprehension or expression of artificial gestures, the similarity between the use of individual signs by apes, and the use of words by people, is definitely limited.

Objects as symbols for other things

Premack (1970, 1971, 1976) developed a training system for use with chimpanzees which, according to his interpretation, allows them to comprehend and express propositions of the form 'all the biscuits are round' and 'these two objects are the same'. This interpretation is extremely suspect, since it depends on the translation of fairly simple actions into verbal terms, but Premack's evidence deserves serious consideration. Most of it was obtained from one wild-born chimpanzee, Sarah, who was kept in a laboratory cage from the time she was acquired, when she was less than a year old. Not surprisingly, her social attachments to people were not as marked as those of chimpanzees reared in homes, or with constant human companionship. All of the initial training with the Premack system took place in a two-year period between the sixth and eighth year of Sarah's life, the human experimenters entering the cage during training sessions amounting to an hour or so per day, for the first sixteen months, but remaining outside the cage, because of the chimpanzee's aggressiveness, for the last eight months.

Given the limitations of this sort of laboratory training, it is remarkable that so much data was obtained. But Sarah is the only one of four chimpanzees used by Premack (see Premack, 1976) to get very far, while the method of immersion in gestures has been successful with dozens of animals, trained by different teams of people. Vocalisation as used in human speech has a number of advantages as a means of communication. It requires very little physical energy, and self-produced signals can be monitored in the same way as sounds received from other sources. If necessary vocalisation can take place under almost all circumstances of bodily activity. Gesturing with the arm is somewhat more energetic, and can only be done if the arms are not being used for other purposes, but it does not require any artificial equipment. Premack's communication device required both artificial equipment and use of the arms, since objects and concepts were signified by the placement of metal-backed coloured plastic shapes on a magnetised board in the chimpanzee's cage. As with vocalisation, self-produced messages corresponded closely to externally presented patterns. The great advantage of the plastic symbols, if the animal pays attention to them, is that they circumvent the problem of memory. If a sequence of instructions is given to the animal, in the form of plastic symbols placed in a particular serial order, the internal retention of the sequence is not crucial, as it would be with transient gestures or sounds, since the animal can continually refer to the external record. In a sense, then, the plastic symbol system used by Premack avoids the requirement of memory for signs or sequences of informative signals, and thus makes things considerably easier for the chimpanzee.

In the early stages of training, however, the transactions between man and animal were depressingly familiar. After having a particular plastic shape always placed alongside an apple, the chimpanzee was required to place this shape on the magnetised board before she was given the apple, then she had to place in sequence several shapes, translated as '*Mary give apple Sarah*' (Mary being the human trainer). But with preliminary experience of this kind, more complicated interchanges took place. The bulk of these can be construed as questions, put to the animal by the experimenter, who placed an array of plastic shapes on the metal board, or on a shelf, the chimpanzee answering by making alterations to this array. It seems probable from the nature of these questions and answers that the plastic shapes signalled something other than themselves, as we shall see, but the most direct evidence that they carried messages, or conveyed meaning, arose when sequences of the plastic tokens implied an instruction.

The simplest instruction was the reversal of the chimpanzee's requests. Instead of the animal writing out '*Mary give apple Sarah*', the trainer wrote out '*Sarah give apple Mary*' or '*Sarah give apple Gussie*' (another chimp). Occasionally these instructions elicited refusals, in the form of tantrums or re-ordering of the symbols, but by rewarding compliance the experimenters usually obtained obedient reactions. When Sarah had acquired a larger vocabulary, via various kinds of association between symbols and events, other actions could be elicited by the use of sequences of tokens—for instance, '*Sarah apple cut*' and '*Sarah apple wash*' could be used as instructions for the chimpanzee to cut or wash an apple (Premack, 1976, p. 76). These messages would be used individually, but the most elaborate instruction which Sarah followed was a compound of two instances of the same command, '*insert*'. After considerable experience of single instances, such as '*Sarah banana pail insert*' and '*Sarah apple dish insert*' when the two objects and the two containers were available, she was able to put the correct item in the container indicated. She was then given instructions in the form '*Sarah banana dish apple pail insert*', so that two actions were required in the same command. Once the banana had been put in the dish in this example, a desire for regularity might have prompted the assignment of the remaining object to the unfilled container. But various complications of the instruction were given with two containers and several objects of various categories available. Sarah seemed to have little difficulty in complying with the command to put chocolate in both the dish and the pail, or the command to put apple and a cracker in the dish and just a cracker in the pail (*Sarah apple cracker dish cracker pail insert*: Premack 1976, pp. 325–30).

The final variation was to use two dishes of different colours, and to identify them with the colour 'words' that Sarah already knew (which were particular plastic shapes, not coloured themselves). This gave instructions like '*Sarah cracker candy yellow dish cracker blue dish insert*', which the chimpanzee complied with correctly about 8 times out of 10. This sort of performance is not as complicated as it looks, because the general practice of putting either one or two kinds of food into each container was well established. But the details of exactly which food has to be put in which dish could only be extracted by noticing the positions of symbols in the sequence (which was a vertical line of the plastic tokens, in which top-to-bottom corresponded to left-to-right: the chimpanzee appeared at first to prefer the vertical arrangement). It may be misleading to call this syntax, since it is a single case, and rather a simple one. However, the order of the symbols, and not just their presence or absence, was clearly an important component of this kind of instruction. Human patients with certain kinds of brain damage sometimes can read individual nouns, but have difficulties in understanding or expressing phrases whose meaning is determined by the order of words, and are thus diagnosed as 'agrammatic' (Goodglass and Geschwind, 1976; Goodglass, 1976). Although it would be foolish to claim that Sarah the chimpanzee demonstrated human levels of syntax or grammatical competence, it would appear that in some limited sense she was not completely 'agrammatic'.

A particular deficit in human 'agrammatic' patients is the inability to read function words, such as prepositions like 'on' or 'under', which includes some instances of failure to follow instructions involving simple interpretations of prepositions. It is interesting, therefore, that Sarah was able, albeit in the same limited conditions, to respond appropriately with a plastic token designated as 'on'.

When she was already familiar with the series of achromatic shapes which corresponded to particular colours, she was introduced to *on* by manipulations of pairs of coloured cards. The trainer wrote *Red on Green*, gave Sarah a red card, and guided her hand so that she placed it overlapping a green card already lying on the work table in front of her. After very little practice of this kind, the trainer put up instructions, with three cards lying on the table, in the same form ('*Red on Green*', '*Green on Yellow*', etc.) which the animal followed by picking up the first mentioned card and placing it over the second. The chimpanzee was also able to describe pairs of overlapping cards put in position by the trainer: the trainer, for instance, might put the yellow card on top of the red card, giving Sarah the three colour tokens and the 'on' token, with the result that the chimpanzee stuck the tokens of the board in the order '*Yellow on Red*'. A second chimpanzee, Elizabeth, who was the only one of the others tested to reach Sarah's standards, soon followed 'on' instructions when they were introduced with objects, instead of cards. Knowing all the object names, she was first instructed in '*keys on clay*', and then successfully tested with '*chow on shoe*' or '*shoe on chow*' (Premack, 1976, pp. 107–11).

As the sequences of tokens were written vertically from top to bottom, it may be that both 'on' and 'insert' succeeded as instructions because of the similarity between the format of the tokens and the required positions of the objects. Since the top-down sequence was used in many other instructions, such as give, take, push, cut and wash, I suspect Sarah would have eventually managed to respond to '*Yellow under Red*' by putting yellow and red cards in the opposite relation to their corresponding tokens on the board, but it is a great pity that this was not, apparently, attempted.

Questions and answers

The vertical sequence of tokens was abandoned for many of the tests, since these involved questions about real objects, which could not be conveniently attached to the metal board. Objects and tokens were laid out on a shelf or table instead. The simplest questions were, one presumes, perceptually very easy, since they required only that the chimpanzee detect whether two real objects were identical or not. The perceptual judgment itself was tested very directly by giving Sarah two spoons and a cup, and encouraging her to place the two spoons together and the cup to one side. The transfer to this perceptual judgment into the manipulation of tokens was accomplished by designating particular plastic shapes as *same, different, yes, no* and *question*, and establishing their usage in certain contexts. Let me first make explicit my convention here of identifying real objects by words, and plastic tokens with putative meanings by italicised words. Using this convention, the layout for a question might be like this: 'cork *question* cork' laid in line from left to right, with *same* and *different* placed in line an inch or so nearer to the animal. The answer in this case would be to remove the *question* token, and replace it with *same*. Clearly if the array was 'cork *question* scissors/*same, different*', the answer is to replace *question* with *different*. The solution to these problems seemed to be clear enough to the chimpanzee, even if the problem arrays took more complicated forms, such as: 'key *different question*/key, rubber band'; 'clothes-peg *same* clothes-peg *question*/*yes, no*': (Premack, 1971; 1976, pp. 147–52).

Linguistic functions of tokens

Reaching the final arrays of *same* between two similar objects and *different* between two different objects could be construed as merely the assignment of particular tokens to perceptions of similarity and dissimilarity which could be assessed just as well by other methods. But the correct addition of *yes* and *no* to triplets containing *same* and *different* seems to require the animal to make judgments about the meanings of the tokens rather than just about the real objects. Decisions about the relations between tokens perhaps come rather closer to the kind of abstraction achievable with speech than decisions about the relations between objects as objects. This may seem slightly obscure, but there are some fairly straightforward examples.

For instance, a particular bit of plastic was designated '*name*', and (to begin with, later they were separate) *no* was glued to *name* to make '*noname*' ('not the name of'). Sarah was then given the arrays '*apple name* apple *question*/*yes, no*', and '*banana noname* apple/*yes, no*' and modifications of these such as '*apple question* banana/*name, noname*'. This is very much like the same-different judgments, but the similarity is between object and the token for the object, rather than between two objects. One would expect the main source of confusion to be the double negative necessary in '*apple noname* apple' which requires the addition of *no*. It is hardly surprising that Sarah made more mistakes when negatives were involved, in the course of achieving the standard level of 80 per cent correct answers on a series of problems about the correct names for apricots, raisins, dishes and pails (Premack, 1976, pp. 162–4).

In a similar way, tokens about tokens, rather than tokens about objects, were introduced in the case of *colour, shape* and *size* (Premack, 1976, pp. 189–98). Of course, before this could be done, the chimpanzee had to assign tokens for individual colours, shapes and sizes to appropriate objects, for instance, *yellow* to a banana but *red* to an apple, *round* to a button but *square* to a box, and *small* to a grommet but *large* to a sponge. Then she could be given problems in the form '*Question colour* banana/*red, yellow*'; '*Question shape* ball/*round, square*'; '*Question size* sponge/*large, small*'. Such problems were answered correctly more than 8 times out of 10, except that performance on the size problems was slightly worse since Sarah tended to put *large* when the experimenters wanted *small*.

The most abstract of all the problems solved by Sarah, it seems to me, were those in which she had to identify the tokens indicating classes of properties on the basis of instances. For instance, she was given '*banana question* banana', '*yellow question* banana', '*brown question* chocolate', '*chocolate question* chocolate', with the alternatives *name* and *colour* to choose from. On one of the rare occasions when there were three answers to choose from rather than two, a series of arrays like these were given with *name, shape* and *colour* as possible choices. Thus something like '*round question* apple' was answered by replacing *question* with *shape*, while '*red question* apple' resulted in *question* being replaced by *colour*. Premack gives only a brief account of this, but if anything it appears that Sarah found it easier to choose classes than to choose individual properties since fewer errors than usual were made, and in some series such as the choices between *colour* and *shape*, no errors were made at all. Premack (1976, p. 198) suggests that the improved performance came about because by this time Sarah had had plenty of practice with tokens involved, but in any case it seems that identifying *yellow* as needing to be accompanied by *colour* rather than *shape* or *name*, that is, remembering associations between tokens rather than associations between objects and tokens, presented no particular difficulties.

The tokens indicating classes of property were also used to identify new plastic labels with new stimulus qualities and object. For instance, Sarah was given the array '*question colour chocolate*' provided only with the token *brown*, with which she replaced *question*, subsequently demonstrating the meaning of *brown* by selecting a brown card from among four others on the instruction '*Sarah take brown*' (Premack, 1976, pp. 202–3). After being introduced to the tokens for figs, peaches and other appealing food items by seeing propositional arrays in the form '*fig name* fig' she used the appropriate tokens to request whichever item she was shown (Premack, 1976, pp. 196–266). This implies that associations between particular tokens and the object classes or stimulus properties which they signified could be formed very quickly. In fact, towards the end of Sarah's training, new tokens as labels for objects could be introduced simply by the trainer holding up the token and an object together.

All these results might be taken to suggest that the plastic tokens were capable of signifying other things to the chimpanzee, and that seeing a token resulted in inner representations of qualities or objects not immediately present. Colloquially, seeing a token made the chimpanzee think of something else. Great emphasis is placed by Premack on descriptive choices elicited by tokens. If shown a real apple between the tokens *red* and *green* or between the tokens *round* and *square*, the chimpanzee promptly chose *red* and *round* as properties which went with the apple. And if shown the token for apple (which was in fact a blue triangle) in similar circumstances there was no hesitation in the similar choices of *red* and *round*, even though these qualities were not being observed at the time. The same results were obtained if cards that were actually red and green, and square and round, instead of the tokens for these qualities, had to be selected from.

On the basis of these results, the plastic tokens were very informative to the chimpanzee, and the relations between token and token, and token and object, may imply a theoretically vital degree of mental organisation possible in this species. But it is misleading, in my view, to say that the tokens had the same function as words in human speech and writing. In practical terms the tokens were only used in a very restricted set of circumstances, and in theoretical terms there is no evidence that the involvement of tokens in such things as grammar and semantic categorisation approaches the way that words are involved with these things in man. The importance of Premack's results, taken together with other work on apes, is not that the apes can be trained to do things that are equivalent to human language. Rather, apes can be trained to do things which might plausibly be equivalent to a preliminary stage in the evolution of human language, or which indicate that apes have a level of cognitive organisation which one can imagine might be sufficient to make the beginnings of speech useful

Keyboard experiments, and exchange of information between apes

There are many who suspect that both Premack's work with plastic tokens, and the Gardners' method of interpreting learned gestures, may be seriously at fault because of artifacts in the procedure, statistical unreliability, and so on (Terrace, 1979; Seidenberg and

Petitto, 1979). It is just as well that a third body of work on chimpanzee communication is available, which gets round some of the problems of human participation by training the animals to operate a computer-controlled console like a simplified typewriter. Initially this system was used so that a single animal could exchange information with the computer, eliminating the possibility of the human trainer (by subtle changes in posture, tone of voice, or facial expression), providing external cues which would allow the chimpanzee to exhibit correct responses without working them out for itself. (This is known as the 'Clever Hans' phenomenon, after a German horse of that name which stamped out answers to arithmetical problems written on a blackboard, but only because it sensed from the trainer's reactions when it should stop raising and lowering its hoof.)

But the most important development with this keyboard system has been the exchange of information between two chimpanzees. Chimpanzees in the wild respond to each others' gestures, postures, facial expressions and vocalisations, but it is usually argued that this is a case of fixed emotional reactions to social signals, rather than the communication of ideas. Anecdotal reports of chimpanzees communicating to each other in any way at all using the sign-language gestures which they have been taught by human intervention are extremely fragmentary (Linden, 1976). The artificial nature of the keyboard system makes early training rather difficult (Savage-Rumbaugh *et al.*, 1978a), but has the advantage that, once animals are familiar with visual patterns used as symbols to denote objects, relatively clear evidence of reference to absent objects can be obtained, in communications made between two animals.

The keyboard is an array of small rectangular screens. Particular visual symbols made up of lines, circles and dots against coloured backgrounds can be projected on any one of these keys, so that the visual pattern itself, rather than a given position in the array (as in a typewriter) must be attended to (Rumbaugh *et al.*, 1973). When a pattern in the array is touched, it is put up in a line of projectors above the keyboards, giving a record of the sequence of symbols pressed, going from left to right. Certain patterns are assigned by the experimenters to certain items of food and drink, which can be delivered to the animal automatically, and other patterns are required as the first and last symbols in an acceptable sequence, and as connection symbols which are given verbal translation, such as '*machine*' and '*give*'. Not surprisingly, chimpanzees have little natural tendency to connect two-dimensional patterns of lines and squiggles with other events, and it is probable that early training with these visual cues leaves them with a rather limited symbolic significance, by comparison with the manipulable plastic chips used by Premack, or the imitable gestures of the Gardners' sign-language method (Savage and Rumbaugh, 1978). Lengthy training is needed, in which the chimpanzees press keys in the sequence '*Start give banana stop*' to get a banana, '*Start pour coke stop*' to activate an automatic drink dispenser, and so on. The original chimpanzee which learned this system, Lana, could make a wide variety of requests via the keyboard, including '*Start trainer tickle Lana stop*', if the trainer was in the room, and '*Start machine make window open stop*' (Rumbaugh and von Glaserfeld, 1973; Rumbaugh, 1977). Social relationships with human beings, and interaction with people via pointing and gesturing on their part, and some imitation by the animals, appears to be necessary with this method of training, as it is with the others, but after training has taken place, the trainers can absent themselves, leaving the animal alone with the computer, to provide the crucial tests of the animal's abilities (Savage-Rumbaugh *et al.*, 1978b).

Intensive individual training of the female Lana established that a chimpanzee could use the keyboard system to make a wide range of requests for desired objects and events, and that the chimpanzee could be induced to select patterns designated as the names of things such as sticks and keys if these were present (Rumbaugh, 1977). More specialised and limited training given to two young males, Austin and Sherman, resulted in their gradually acquiring the theoretically valuable ability to communicate with each other. In the first instance of this the identity of a hidden item of food was transmitted from one animal, who had seen the food hidden, to the other, who had not (Savage-Rumbaugh *et al.*, 1978b) and in the second, one chimpanzee requested and received from the other an object which could be used as a tool to obtain food (Savage-Rumbaugh *et al.*, 1978a). A preliminary step was to test the ability of each animal to press the appropriate key when a particular kind of food was visible. Eleven types of comestible were used altogether: beancake, banana, chow, milk, orange drink, juice, cola, pieces of orange, sweet potato, bread and candy. The chimpanzees were also given practice at repeating, by pressing a key, the symbol for one of the foods included in a series of symbols displayed on the projector line above the keyboard. In tasks like this some practice is needed on the symbols which correspond to foods the animals do not actually like to eat such as beancake and the commercially produced chow. The first version of the communication experiment went as follows. One of the animals (either Austin or Sherman—they alternated as sender and receiver) was led out of the room with the keyboard to another room, where it watched the experimenter place a single item from the eleven possibilities in a container, which was then sealed. This 'sender' animal was then taken back, with the container, to the keyboard, and given signals on the projector line which served as an instruction to name the food present in the container, and elicited the pressing of a key. The receiving chimpanzee then had to repeat the same interaction with the keyboard. If both the 'sender' (who had seen the food hidden) and the receiver (who had not) selected the appropriate symbol, they were allowed to share the food in the container. If either of them was wrong, they were both allowed to look at what had been hidden, but not to eat it.

In fact, they were very rarely wrong, since both responded correctly on more than 90 per cent of the trials in the initial procedure, and throughout a number of variations designed to eliminate unwanted explanations of the results. In these it was established that a 'Clever Hans' effect, of utilising the knowledge of the human experimenter, was not occurring, since the experimenters present at the keyboard did not know the answer, not having seen which of the eleven foods had been hidden. The second animal was not simply copying the movements of the first, since he could do just as well by only being allowed to see the results of the first one's movements in the symbols on the projector line. And the second animal was not just copying the visual symbol, although that would have been sufficient for success, since after seeing the symbol he could select a photograph of the correct food on that trial, out of a choice of three alternatives (Savage-Rumbaugh *et al.*, 1978b). Apparently the arbitrary visual patterns had come to elicit a mental image, or inner representation, of the foods they signified.

A further variation was to put Austin and Sherman in adjacent compartments, with a window between them, each with his own keyboard which the other could see. This arrangement was used for the transmission of the symbol for the food in the sealed container experiment, and also for a different test of communication. In this, one chimpanzee was given a tray containing a variety of foods, but the other was given none. Without any prompting from the experimenters, the have-not animal used his keyboard to request food. With encouragement from the experimenters, the animal with food passed what was asked for through a gap in the window. After some alternation of roles between giving and receiving, compliance with requests from the other animal became fairly routine, especially for non-preferred items.

The passing of things through the window, by one animal to the other, was examined more systematically when the things which had to be passed were tools rather than items of food (Savage-Rumbaugh *et al.*, 1978a). In this case the chimpanzees were first taught to use six objects to gain access to food, by imitating demonstrations made by the experimenter. These tools were: (1) a key, used to unlock padlocks on boxes and doors; (2) a wrench, used to unscrew bolted doors; (3) washers, used like coins to operate vending devices; (4) a stick, used either to dip into a yoghurt or puddings in containers not accessible in other ways, or to push a piece of fruit out of a horizontal tube; (5) a long straw, used to obtain liquids when this could be done by pushing the straw through a small hole in the tops of containers; (6) a sponge on a string, used by dropping it down a tall vertical container, as well as to soak up liquids from flat surfaces. Investigation of tool-using as such was not the purpose of this experiment, and it became highly practised, but it is worth noting that each chimpanzee had to master a variety of unnatural manipulative skills. The important point was that the chimpanzees should associate a particular tool with a particular visual pattern used on the keyboard. This took a certain amount of training, but both animals were eventually able to select the appropriate key with 100 per cent accuracy if the experimenter held up one of the tools, and they were almost as good at picking out the correct object in response to instructions in the form of symbols appearing on the projector line above the keyboard, and in punching the appropriate key if they saw that a particular tool was needed—for instance if they watched the human experimenter put some fruit in a box and padlock the box they were accustomed to press the symbol for '*key*' rather than any of the others.

The test for co-operation between the two chimpanzees came when they were placed in adjacent rooms, one being shown food or drink that was obtainable only with a particular tool, and the other being given the complete set of six tools. The room in which food was concealed contained a complete set of vending devices, horizontal and vertical tubes, padlocked boxes and so on, and the window between the two rooms was covered while the tool-requesting animal (in turn, either Austin or Sherman) was shown one of these places being baited. When the window was opened, neither chimpanzee could see the hidden food, and thus only the tool-requester knew which tool was needed. On the first day of this testing, the requester animal readily used the keyboard to select the symbols *give straw* (or whatever tool was necessary) but directed his attention to the experimenter, who was present, and who had previously functioned as a donator of tools. The experimenter encouraged co-operation between the animals by pointing and gesturing to draw their attention to each other's presence. After this the requesting animal began pointing out the symbols he had produced on the projectors to the other chimpanzee with the tools. By the end of the second day co-operative behaviour was well established —the chimpanzee with the tools quickly looked to see what the other chimpanzee had produced on the projector display, and handed over a tool, and the tool-using animal (again after encouragement from the experimenter) occasionally handed back through the window some of the food he had obtained with the aid of the tool. Errors were made quite often at this stage, although the level of accuracy (correct tool both requested and provided) was well above chance at 76 per cent. By the fifth day, however, without any intervention from the experimenter, 55 out of 60 (92 per cent) correct tool transfers were recorded (Savage-Rumbaugh *et al.*, 1978a). The day after this, the requester's keyboard was turned off to see if the animals could get anywhere by gesturing, but the donor chimpanzee under these circumstances offered the same wrong implement re-peatedly, or offered all the tools in turn.

There can be little doubt, in the case of this experiment, that the visual patterns used in the keyboard system had mental associations with objects, and that the chimpanzee who punched a particular key did this in the expectation that the other animal would hand him a particular tool. It depends, of course, on what one means by 'intention', but this seems to be a reasonable approximation to intentional communication. It may be that the intentionality of this use of symbols by the chimpanzees Austin and Sherman contributed to their later development of capacities for comprehension of the meaning of symbols which go beyond those demonstrated in any other individual animals. When they were trained with arbitrary symbols assigned to the two object categories 'foods' and 'tools' Austin and Sherman successfully selected the appropriate category, when shown arbitrary symbols which were the names for particular foods or tools (Savage-Rumbaugh *et al.*, 1980). That is, they were able to label labels, rather than merely label objects: for instance if shown the arbitrary pattern indicating '*banana*' they responded by pressing the key meaning '*food*', but if shown the symbol for '*wrench*' they pressed the '*tool*' key.

Intentional communication and deception by pointing

Before assessing the implications of the various more elaborate artificial methods of communication used by specially trained chimpanzees, it is worth looking at a study of one of the simplest means of intentional exchange of information—pointing by limb extension and gaze direction. Woodruff and Premack (1979) devised yet another variation of the 'hidden food' problem, in which a chimpanzee indicated the location of hidden food to a human partner, or vice versa. A small room contained a cage area partitioned off with wire mesh. In the first phase of the investigation, which lasted for 5 months, a chimpanzee sitting in the cage was shown that a piece of food was concealed in one of two containers (a box and a cup) placed in the room outside. After some to-ing and fro-ing, a human partner, who did not know where the food was, came into the room, and the chimpanzee was returned to the cage (the only access to the room was apparently through the cage and so the chimpanzee had to be removed while the human partner went through it). The task of the human participant was to guess, from the posture of the chimpanzee, where the food was. A peculiarity of the experiment was that the human participants were of two types. 'Co-operative' participants wore standard green laboratory clothing and were instructed to behave in a generally friendly and soothing manner. 'Competitive' participants wore black boots, a white coat and hat, and dark sunglasses, and were instructed to speak gruffly. Whether these features of dress and mannerism as such made any difference to chimpanzees is uncertain, but the two types ought to have been readily distinguishable. What presumably did make a difference was that the 'co-operative participants', if they found food at their first attempt, gave some of it to their animal partners, whereas the competitive participants kept it. But if the competitive partner failed to find food, the chimpanzee was released to retrieve it for itself. Four chimpanzees were used, with a number of human partners, and the animals differed considerably in their behaviour. However, it is claimed that all the chimpanzees conveyed more information to the co-operative human participants, and that two of the chimpanzees deliberately misled the competitive humans by pointing to the object that did not contain the food. One of the chimpanzees, Sadie, quite unambiguously stuck a leg under the wire caging in the direction of one of the containers, and stared at it—pointing to the location of food in the case of a co-operative participant, but to the wrong container in the case of competitive participants.

In later stages of the experiment, lasting more than a year and starting 10 months after the first stage, the human participant remained inside the cage, knowing the location of food, while the chimpanzees had to guess where the food was, with the aid of the postures of the humans. The co-operative human participants attempted to mimic what had been observed in the chimpanzees, by sitting on the floor of the cage facing the correct container, extending an arm or a leg in that direction. The competitive humans did the same thing, but pointed towards the wrong container. With the co-operative humans, three of the chimpanzees were able to choose the correct container from the start, and another one gradually learned to do so. With the competitive human partner, all the animals were initially misled, and chose the empty container pointed at. One of them continued to do this, but the other three gradually learned to avoid picking up the container pointed at by a competitive partner, and chose the alternative one instead, being allowed to keep the food they thus acquired.

In many ways this is a rather messy experiment, but it provides support for the contention that postures and gestures may be given varying interpretations by chimpanzees depending on the human individual in whom they are observed, which is perhaps not surprising. More important, it is arguable that the chimpanzee's own postures in this experiment were modified by their communicative intent. If they hoped that their human partner would succeed in finding food (because they would get some themselves) their posture was helpful, but if it was to the advantage of the chimpanzee that their human partner fail, it was not.

The relation between human speech and the use of artificial systems of communication by apes

It has often been argued that a chimpanzee (Gardner and Gardner, 1969) or a gorilla (Patterson, 1978) that makes a certain number of gestures which approximate those of American Sign Language can be said to have 'acquired language', thus bridging an important gap between ape and man. Premack (1976) has made similar claims on the basis of chimpanzees' manipulation of plastic tokens and, although Savage-Rumbaugh *et al.* (1978a, 1980) have been more cautious in interpreting the results they obtained with the keyboard system, they argue that the two animals in their experiment were 'able to comprehend the symbolic and communicative function of the symbols'.

I should like first to emphasise that analogies between the demonstrated abilities of chimpanzees and the human use of speech are extremely shaky. There has of course been no shortage of sceptics, ready to point out the limitations of communicative abilities demonstrated by apes (see the collection of articles collected by Sebeok and Umriker-Sebeok, 1980: especially Chomsky, 1979; Bronowski and Bellugi, 1970; Mounin, 1976; Terrace, 1979; also Petitto and Seidenberg, 1979; Seidenberg and Petitto, 1979; Terrace *et al.*, 1979). The most serious criticism of all is the assertion that the results obtained in communication experiments with apes are bogus, and not what they seem, because of surreptitious sensing by the apes of cues other than the ostensible causes of their communicative acts—the 'Clever Hans' problem. I shall argue that this criticism could apply to some, but not all, of the data. What remains, as achievements of the animals rather than interpretations by their trainers, can easily be distinguished from human speech on a number of grounds, among them modality of expression, syntactic complexity, disengagement from context, separation from emotions and goals, and internalisation. The problem is not so much to show that human speech is different from anything done by other species, but to say exactly how and why it is different.

Surreptitious use of human directions

Osker Pfungst (1911) was able to debunk the performances of Clever Hans, the horse that stamped out answers to sums chalked on a blackboard, by presenting the horse with questions which the horse's trainer could not see. Evidently the horse started and stopped stamping its hoof according to cues of very slight changes in posture and facial expression given—unwittingly—by the human intermediary.

Umiker-Sebeok and Sebeok (1980) have put forward a blanket

condemnation of all work with apes of the type discussed in this chapter, on the grounds that similar social cues could enable the animals to make the observed responses even in 'double-blind' tests, in which the person accompanying the animal supposedly does not himself know enough to be of any help. In my view a certain amount of doubt of this kind must be attached to most of the work with the plastic token system discussed by Premack (1976), since many of the responses of the chimpanzees required the selection of one token from a choice of two—something easily influenced by the trainer glancing at the correct one. When a trainer was used who did not himself know the correct answers, the chimpanzee was considerably less accurate, although she performed well enough to rule out the possibility that dependence on cues from the trainer was total (Premack, 1976, pp. 32–6). In some of the later experiments, the chimpanzee became accustomed to making choices after the trainer had left the room, which provides much stronger evidence (Woodruff *et al.*, 1978; Gillan *et al.*, 1981).

When two chimpanzees exchanged information between themselves, using the computer-controlled keyboard system, with experimenters not in the same room (Savage-Rumbaugh *et al.*, 1978b), the evidence seems relatively robust. In this case, the animals had to choose one from six possibilities (and in the first test of communication between the same two animals, one from eleven different symbols for food objects: Savage-Rumbaugh *et al.*, 1978b), and this sort of choice could not so easily be influenced by extraneous cues. All in all, with the computer-controlled keyboards, and with the carefully controlled tests of naming with the gesture-sign method (Fouts, 1973; Gardner and Gardner, 1978) the explanations in terms of social cuing appear to me to be much more far-fetched than the assumption that the animals pay attention to the ostensible objects and signals.

The most important type of unwitting human direction of behaviour which has been interpreted as the product of the mental organisation of the apes themselves is in the 'prompting' of sequences of gestures in animals trained with the American Sign Language method. Terrace *et al.* (1979), by detailed examination of film and videotape records, have shown that sequences of gestures such as *me hug cat* are usually interspersed with gestures from a human companion, such as *you*, just before *me* and *who* just before *cat*. Since, in this instance, the trainer was holding a cat (in one arm, while signing with the other), at the beginning of the sequences, and the chimpanzee was allowed to hold the cat after gesturing for it, one might reasonably assume that the separate gesture-sign, *cat*, was elicited by the sight of the cat. But the order in which the signs were given was very clearly open to the influence of the trainer. As practically all instances of sequences or combinations of gestures by chimpanzees or gorillas are made in the context of interactions with a human companion, there is virtually no evidence of this kind which is not vulnerable to the charge that the human contact determined the sequence of combinations observed.

Syntactic complexity

It is especially unfortunate that one must discard evidence concerning regularities in the serial combination of signs of chimpanzees and gorillas, because these would bear on the question of whether any grammatical rules whatsoever can be observed within this kind of use of symbols. If it was the case that internal organisation, rather than external cues, led to such regularities, the use of *more* before rather than after signs for such things as banana, drink and tickle (e.g. Patterson, 1978) might be the starting point for arguments about whether this should count as a primitive form of syntax. However, even with the benefit of human prompting, the serial combination of gesture-signs by apes is limited in the extreme. Nim Chimsky, the chimpanzee studied by Terrace *et al.* (1979) recorded '*banana Nim eat*' occasionally, but '*banana eat Nim*' occurred almost as often. What are listed as 'Four-sign combinations' turn out to be such things as '*eat drink eat drink*' and '*banana Nim banana Nim*'. It may be that *banana* has a rather high priority, for obvious reasons, and tends to come first if it is going to be signed at all, but this would be only a marginal form of syntax. Thus, even accepting such gesture sequences as have been reported as genuine products of ordering by the animals, and taking a gesture as equivalent to a spoken word, variety and regularities in gestures that appear to be strung together by the trained apes bear comparison only with the speech of children who use two- and three-word utterances for a few months after they have begun to talk, and this comparison itself is very superficial.

Although the order of words in a sentence or phrase is not as significant a feature of syntax in other languages as it is in English, it is often emphasised that hierarchical recombination of elements is a pervasive characteristic of human language. In speech, phonetic elements such as the positions of the tongue and lips, voicing and aspiration are combined into phonemes (e.g., roughly, the English vowels and consonants); these are combined into units of meaning (morphemes) such as words and parts of words in English; and morphemes are combined according to grammatical rules to make phrases. The artificial systems of communication used with apes to all intents and purposes circumvent the need for hierarchical permutations and combinations of elements by providing the animals with a ready-made fixed correspondence between a set of referents (mostly objects and simple actions) and a set of symbols which are all individually recognisable. Does this mean that apes can label individual objects with individual gestures, or other symbols, but lack the ability to associate qualities and features of objects and perceived events with detachable components of gestures or symbols? Is the facility for syntax and grammar, which allows rules for the recombination of linguistic elements, the crucial achievement of human intelligence, entirely absent in other primates (e.g. Chomsky, 1979)? In effect, this is what the data suggest. However, there are a number of other limitations in the communicative performance of apes. Take for example the lack of disengagement of communication from context (Bronowski and Belugi, 1970; see below). Is the lack of disengagement from context due to the absence of syntactical rules, or could the difficulties with syntax arise from the lack of disengagement from context?

Disengagement from context and separation from goals: ends and means

Children may use the early stages of speech for the expression of wants and needs, and more generally, as a means to the end of social attention. But words typically become ends in themselves if they form questions and answers between child and parent, and exchanges of narrative, even if only in the utilitarian social contexts of the child saying 'Daddy gone', or the parent telling a bedtime story. Comment on the external world, rather than a change in the world, seems to become a primary motivation for speech very early on (Clark and Clark, 1977). By comparison, the use of artificial systems of symbols by apes appears to be very closely tied to the achievement of immediate tangible goals. It is not true that the animals have to get a banana, or be tickled, every time they gesture or manipulate a symbol, but the frequency of external rewards, and the frequency of deliberate social instigation of symbols used by human experimenters, is very high. It seems necessary to conclude that communicative acts by apes remain very closely tied to specific external goals, and the exchange of information does not become an end in itself (Mounin, 1976). Proposing an innate tendency for social communication confined to the human species is rather unwieldy, but for whatever reason, the actual quantity of communication induced in apes is small, and it is possible to characterise it as goal-directed problem solving (Terrace, 1979) as opposed to an independent means of information exchange.

Internalisation and inner speech: communication and thought

In English, grammatical irregularities, especially of plural nouns and the past tense, make it apparent that 3- and 4-year-old children do not merely mimic everything that is said to them, they deduce rules, and are thus led into errors such as 'mans' and 'mouses' and 'falled' and 'comed'. For this and more obscure reasons, children are said to create their own internal system of grammar. Whether this results from an inherited linguistic blueprint, or a more general tendency to extend perceived regularities, is still a moot point. Of course it would be expected that apes should lack anything as specific as innate devices to deal with linguistic problems *per se*, whereas they ought to possess a good measure of any tendency to generalise perceived regularities. But if the interest that apes have in the symbolic communication systems presented to them is largely confined to the achievement of particular tangible goals, this in itself might prevent the emergence of internal grammatical regularities. In any event, the incorporation of external communication skills, such as they are, into an internal syntactical system is not a reliable consequence of the training schemes so far devised. This is one aspect of internal mental organisation which is bound up with the human use of language and which apes appear to resist.

A more intuitively obvious question about the internalisation of communication concerns the use of language for inner speech—self-instruction, imaginary conversations, verbal thought, and the organisation of conscious experience. In the child, the use of speech for self-instruction can sometimes be observed because the child's instructions to himself are spoken out loud, and overheard conversations with dolls or reports of discussions held with imaginary friends leave little doubt that the internal use of speech goes far beyond the more overt behavioural manifestations. The most coherent and widely accepted theory of the relation between speech and thought in childhood (Vygotsky, 1962) suggests that verbal and non-verbal mental processes are initially independent, and gradually intertwine. But adults, and especially academic adults, are often reluctant to accept that their own conscious thought is possible without the internal use of language. Some still argue that visual imagery is theoretically indistinguishable from verbal propositions (e.g. Anderson, 1978, 1979).

Although chimpanzees such as the Gardners' Washoe, who have been taught sign-language gestures, use signs to label objects seen in picture books, and in association with actions in play, the communicative abilities of these and other apes provide little evidence that the associations of symbols and objects give rise to anything analogous to inner speech. In most cases, the assumption should be that the animals think in terms of perceptual schemata (of bananas, sticks, being tickled and so on) and apply labels to their inner perceptions in order to achieve a current goal, or as a result of prior training. The main exceptions are those when the chimpanzee Sarah (Premack, 1976; see pp. 357–64 above) apparently identified symbols in terms of other symbols: as when a plastic token designated *name* was placed beside tokens that designated objects but a token called *colour* was placed next to those which referred to particular hues. If it is genuine, this result is extremely significant since it implies a form of mental organisation in which artificial labels are related to each other rather than only directly related to internal representations of external events. But the test is suspect (a) on the grounds of social cueing from the trainer; and (b) the correct token was selected from only two alternatives—this kind of 'forced-choice' is not particularly convincing. It may very well be possible for apes to make some distinctions between categories of symbols which they have been taught, but even so, this would be a far cry from the propositions which are characteristic of human speech and thought.

Labels imply mental representations

Apes trained to employ artificial systems of symbolic communication ought not, therefore, to be said to have acquired a language, in the sense that people acquire a language. Human language is unique to humans, and although some of the distinctive features of human speech, such as the mimicking of sounds, may be observed in other species, the resemblance between, for instance, the trained gesturing of a chimpanzee and communication via sign-language among the human deaf is in some senses no greater than the resemblance between the speech of a parrot and that of its owner. This being clear, what may be deduced from the study of the mental capacities of non-human primates? I suggest that the experiments on symbolic communication support work such as that of Kohler (1925) on problem-solving and that of Menzel (1978) on spatial memory: we should conclude that apes are capable of organised mental knowledge about objects and actions.

Experimental evidence of problem-solving and memory might by itself be sufficient to make this case, but doubts about whether even chimpanzees can categorise objects are surely resolved if symbolic labels can be attached to their perceptions. I have suggested that perceptual categorisation and the retention of inner descriptions of objects are intrinsic characteristics of brain function in many other animals apart from the anthropoid apes. The additional capacity which appears to be demonstrated by training apes with artificial methods of communication is the generation of mental associations between inner descriptions and representations for one set of perceptual categories which deal with a world of food items, physical space and social relationships, and another set of categories within the system of gestures or visual patterns imposed by specialised training. In so far as it can be demonstrated that the apes establish a collection of associations between signs and objects, then the results of their training extend further than any previously observed form of animal learning, but it is not clear that they need a substantially different kind of ability to make these associations from that which may be used by other mammals to respond to smaller sets of signals. A dog which usually hears a buzzer before being given a piece of liver may be said to form an association between the arbitrary sign of the buzzer and the object category of 'liver': is this any different from the mental linkage between a banana and the human gesture which precedes bananas, established in the training of chimpanzees? One difference is in the sheer quantity of associations—over 100 distinct signals are often claimed to be understood by a chimpanzee thoroughly exposed to the gesture-sign method, whereas experimental techniques used with other species rarely provide evidence that an animal can give distinct responses to more than one or two arbitrary signals. This may be partly a restriction in the method rather than in the animals—sheepdogs, working horses and working elephants may respond to more than just one or two commands, although it seems likely that the number would be far less than 100.

The distinctive behavioural fact about the chimpanzee experiments is of course that the animals themselves produce or select signs rather than only reacting to external commands. This in itself may be helpful in establishing connections between signs and references but it is difficult to say whether the productive use of signs is a result of a superior kind of mental organisation or of the greater physical opportunities provided. It is theoretically important that the production of signs is accompanied by communicative intent. This is not something which can be quantitatively assessed, but there is general agreement that a social context to the production of any form of signing is essential. Even when a computer-controlled keyboard is used, so that tests can be made in the absence of a human presence, social interactions between human trainers and the animal being trained are apparently necessary if the animal is to show any interest in using the keyboard (Rumbaugh, 1977; Savage-Rumbaugh *et al.*, 1985).

Names and labels and words and things

One way of describing the outcome of the experiments in which apes learn gesture-signs or other symbols is to say that these animals can be taught to use names, 'in a way which strongly resembles the child's early learning of words' (Bronowski and Bellugi, 1970). Apes do not get very much further, at least with the training methods now used. Therefore it may be misleading to talk about the 'ability to name', since the use of names by human adults is certainly not the same as the use of names by young children (Clark, 1973), and may reflect syntactic and other internal complexities which the apes lack. However, as long as naming is opposed to other kinds of linguistic competence it may be useful to emphasise that the use of symbols by apes is more like naming than anything else. In so far as they string gestures together we might call this 'serial naming', a phrase used by Luria (1970) to describe agrammatic speech in human aphasia due to left-hemisphere brain damage. But a word used as a name in normal human speech may carry with it many more implications than a symbolic label apparently serving a roughly similar purpose in the rudimentary signing of an ape. We may assume that a person who says or reads the word 'canary' has access to a network of knowledge expressible in propositions such as 'a canary is a bird' and 'a canary has wings' (Collins and Quillian, 1969; Collins and Loftus, 1975). We cannot assume that an ape which makes a gesture designated as the name of its human companion has access to similar propositions by which that individual is identified as a mammal, with a list of mammalian characteristics therefore attached. Names in human speech, even if used singly, are potentially insertable into purely verbal propositions, whereas in most cases signs used as names by apes are not.

Any theory of why this should be so must be largely a matter of speculation, but in order to defend the contention that there are significant continuities between the functions of the human brain, and those of other vertebrates, some account needs to be taken of the evident discontinuities. The first step must surely be to acknowledge that the utilisation of speech as we know it amplifies the cognitive capacities of the primate brain almost, but not quite, beyond recognition. Some try to avoid this step by exaggerating the similarities between natural human speech and the linguistic competence of apes (Premack, 1976; Gardner and Gardner, 1978); others, once they have taken the step, simply assert that the human species is biologically different from any other, to such an extent that any comparison with other species is futile (Chomsky, 1976, 1980; Lenneberg, 1967).

In between these positions, theories of how human language may have evolved are legion (Hewes, 1975). What I would like to suggest is that, whatever the sources and stages in the evolution of human language, there remain sufficient similarities between human and animal brain function to allow for comparisons. The similarities, which I have discussed in previous chapters, depend on the assumption that animal brains are devices for selecting and organising perceived information, and that the neural systems which accomplish perception and memory exhibit evolutionary continuity. Behavioural data from tests of perception and memory support the contention that mental organisation exists in animals, in particular in non-human primates, as a necessary part of the perception of objects and their localisation and interrelationships in space and time. It does not seem unreasonable to suppose, therefore, that the development of the distinctively human capacity for language took place via the deployment of the same forms of mental organisation for new purposes. Gregory (1970), for instance, suggested that human language capacity makes use of the existence of a 'grammar' of rules which the brain uses to interpret patterns of light impinging on the retina in terms of objects. O'Keefe and Nadel (1978) imagine that the brain organisation necessary for cognitive maps in strictly spatial co-ordinates becomes used in man for verbal relationships. We have Chomsky's imprimatur to continue such speculation, provided proper caution is observed (Chomsky, 1979, p. 132).

It does not seem necessary to add further speculative details, except perhaps to observe that hearing seems to have been neglected and that linking the identity and location of objects to *sounds* ought to be one of the prerequisites for human speech. But generally, work I have reviewed in previous chapters supports the assumption that animals perceive and remember things in terms of inner descriptions and cognitive schemata. We can say then that the human and non-human species may in the first place perceive and remember, without the assistance of language, in a roughly similar way. In addition we humans may perceive, remember and reproduce words, instead of things. It is important that words can serve as labels for things, but perhaps even more important that words become alternatives to things, so that we perceive and remember relationships between words, as if the words were themselves things. According to this view the human brain is able to accommodate mental organisation in the form of relationships between words because the brains from which it evolved were already accommodating mental organisation in the form of relations between and within perceptual schemata. Language can be internalised in the human brain because the vertebrate brain in general and the mammalian brain in particular serves to construct internal representations as a means of adapting to external realities.

Although this is vague, the assumption that advanced vertebrate brains construct models, images or schemata with which to interpret the outside world is not unusual (e.g. Piaget, 1971; Craik, 1943). It would certainly be very mysterious if adapting this system to treat vocalisations as objects allowed for human language and all that flows from it, but it would be even more mysterious if the functions of the human brain bore no relation whatever to the functions of brains which are physically rather similar.

10 Animal thought and human thought—conclusions

Thought is a word, rather than a thing, and we can use the word as we choose. If we use it to refer to psychological processes which cannot take place in the absence of human linguistic abilities, then animal thought is a conjunction of words that has no real meaning. But if we take it that some thinking can be done without words, and that a thought may be a mental disposition, an image, intention or anticipation, then the question of whether this sort of thought can be said to occur in animals other than ourselves becomes genuine. Moreover, if mental states of all kinds are believed to refer to brain activities, there is a prima facie case for asking whether the activities of the human brain, which subserve our own mental processes, are in any way related to the activities of the brains of animals. I have argued in the previous chapters that perception, as the analysis of information received by the sense organs, and memory, as the retention or revival, or reconstruction of perceptions, are functions which are performed in the human brain in a way which is understandable in terms of the physical evolution of the vertebrate brain, and that, extrapolating across species, it makes sense to discuss animal perception and memory in the same breath as their human equivalents. Behavioural evidence as to the abilities of birds and mammals to recognise visual patterns, and to remember, for instance, recent locations of food, implies that the brains of these animals do in fact accomplish things which suggest a certain degree of mental organisation.

Behaviour such as the imitation of human actions, which suggests mental organisation more like our own than that of less closely related species, is found in the chimpanzee. But attempts to induce these animals to exhibit linguistic skills have as yet demonstrated little beyond extremely rudimentary forms of symbolic labelling. The gulf

382

between all other living species of animals and ourselves thus remains large, despite these attempts artificially to close it, which is why animal thought is a very different topic from human thought. Nevertheless, the relation between animal cognitive capacities and those of man is still very much an open issue, rather than one that is permanently closed because of the obvious differences.

A number of other themes which I have either emphasised or neglected are far from resolution. To recapitulate and extend what I have said earlier I will now return to some of these.

Consciousness

This is a word I have tended to avoid because it is used in several distinctly different ways. If we use 'conscious' to refer to being awake, then it is relatively easy to answer the question 'Are animals conscious?' by describing cycles of sleeping and waking in, for instance, the cat. At the other extreme, if we are concerned with subjective verbal analysis of visual perception, things get much more difficult, since the attribution of consciousness may have more to do with the verbal analysis than with events in the eye or in the parts of the brain that react directly to visual stimulation. In order to answer questions about whether animals have conscious perceptions, or conscious intentions to act, I believe it would first be necessary to disentangle overt or potential verbal descriptions and beliefs from other mental states. Weiskrantz (1977) has pointed out that much experimental investigation of human memory and perception is in effect the investigation of people's verbal commentary on their own mental processes, which in most cases cannot be helped, but which inevitably makes comparison with research on animals hazardous. It is perfectly reasonable to say that animals do not comment on their own mental states, and in this sense lack consciousness, but this begs certain other questions. For instance we may be subjectively aware of pain, or of other intense emotional experiences, without being able to comment on this at the time, and without wishing publicly or privately to recount the event at a later date. The subjective intensity of the conscious experience in such cases does not seem to be related to the possibility of linguistic description. Should we therefore follow Popper (Popper and Eccles, 1977, p. 127) and entertain the theoretical possibility that dumb animals have a proto-awareness of emotionally significant perceptions, anticipations and expectancies? There does not seem to be any easy solution to this problem beyond stressing that we typically try to define our own subjective experiences in verbal terms, which is why we doubt their existence in other species in the first place.

A second matter of definition is that if we ascribe to the view that all our own mental states require the existence of certain forms of brain activity, then we ought to accept that there are physical limitations to the possible similarities between human and animal conscious experience. According to this view, we would be entitled to expect some degree of common ground between our own immediate awareness and that of the chimpanzee, but relatively little similarity between our own subjective experiences, however construed, and those of vertebrates in other orders and classes.

A final consideration is whether anything under the heading of consciousness can be said to have a utilitarian function, other than in providing topics for verbal discussion. Shallice (1972) has provided one of the few theories which identify consciousness with a distinct behaviour-controlling function in addition to functions related to speech: the selection of actions. In general it is possible to link awareness with priorities either of action or attention. We may not always devote our conscious thoughts to objectively important subjects, but it is arguable that human awareness serves to select perceptions and direct actions, and that only when we are neither perceiving nor acting are relatively frivolous trains of thought and streams of consciousness permitted to engage our attention. When consciousness refers to brain-states which direct and select perception, memory and action, even in the absence of verbal processes, there is no compelling reason to believe that it is uniquely human.

Encephalisation and the cerebral cortex

Conscious experience, linguistic expression, and all other forms of human cognition are attributed to the cerebral hemispheres and in particular to their surface covering, the neocortex. It is appealing to suppose that a progressive evolution of cognitive capacities paralleled the increase in the relative size of the cerebral hemispheres, in comparison with the rest of the brain, that can be observed over the time course of vertebrate evolution, roughly matching the increase in the size of the brain as a whole in relation to the rest of the body. I have argued that an important general feature of the vertebrate forebrain hemispheres is that they contain sensory projections which are remote from the untransformed output of the sense organs, and that the possibility of perceptual descriptions and representations which are relatively remote from immediate sense data supplies a functional advantage to forebrain evolutionary development. The more traditional view of encephalisation is that the forebrain expanded as, for unspecified reasons, it made successful take-over bids for the businesses of lower brain centres. It is certainly true that the most thoroughly analysed area of the forebrain, the primary visual cortex of the cat and the monkey (which is assumed to closely approximate, in anatomy and physiology, the corresponding part of the human brain) includes relatively direct transformations of visual patterns impinging on the retina of the eye. And in primates especially there are facilities for some fairly direct output from the cortex to muscle movements. But it may still be the case that the distinctive advantage of forebrain development lies in the independence of some of its activities from direct input-output connections—it has always been agreed that the mammalian cortex at any rate subserves flexible and integrated perception and action, allowing for choice, integration and shifting priorities, to a greater extent than the more automatic reactions of other parts of the brain. Recent anatomical evidence suggests that the cerebral hemispheres of birds and lower vertebrates can be seen as alternative forms of the same general plan.

Hand in hand with the traditional account of progressive brain evolution and the difference between mammals and other vertebrate classes went the belief that the brains of lower vertebrates were entirely preprogrammed with reflexes and instinctive formulae for patterns of reaction to stimuli, whereas the cortex of mammals allowed for perception and action that was not so innately predetermined, man being dominated by the cortex to such an extent that there were no innate determinants of human thought and cognition. There is clearly something in this, but it is ironic that the emphasis of current theories of cortical function is on predetermined organisation rather than the possibility of adaptation within the lifetime of the individual. There are two particular cases: visual perception and language. In the brain areas concerned with vision, the layout of individual neurons, as well as of interrelated topographic mappings, is consistent from individual to individual, and can be said to conform to innate plans, though naturally maturation and use are of some importance. The outstanding property of the human brain, the capacity for language, can at the same time be localised in broadly confined regions of cortex (usually in only the left hemisphere) and for linguistic reasons is supposed to require absolutely crucial forms of innate organisation in the brain. Thus any innate capacities required for language should be embodied in the neocortex rather than anywhere else.

Even the notion that man and other primates possess large areas of 'association cortex' which is without specific genetically assigned functions, and left as free as Locke's *tabula rasa* to record ideas acquired in the life of the individual, can be questioned on anatomical grounds. What was called association cortex, because it had no apparent specific sensory or motor properties, has predictable connections within the brain and can equally well be classified as a variety of secondary sensory areas. The cerebral cortex is thus not characterised by the lack of innate functional organisation, rather, it is innately organised in ways which allow for certain kinds of learning and the acquisition of knowledge by individuals. This is all part of the argument between nativists and empiricists, which is unlikely to cease. It is apparent, though, that it would be difficult now to claim that all animal behaviour is a matter of innate predetermination, while all human behaviour is not, on the basis that human abilities have come to depend on the cerebral cortex. As an alternative, one could say that all species have biologically determined innate propensities, and that human innate propensities include the faculties of language and reason, determined by brain organisation which is characteristic of our species.

Continuities and discontinuities

The contrast between human history and civilisation and the re-latively fixed and constant adjustment of other species to natural environments is a complete and unassailable discontinuity. For many purposes, the place of man in nature and possible continuities between human and animal psychology can be wisely ignored. Theorists from Hume to Skinner who have sought to apply strictly identical explanations to human and animal cognition must always be regarded with suspicion. The problem remains that man and other vertebrates patently share innumerable similarities of body and brain, and since Darwin it is impossible to give a complete and convincing account of the origin of human abilities without addressing the question of comparisons between man and other species. It appears to me that, oddly enough, a general fault which arises from considering human psychology in isolation is the assumption that civilised and artificial abilities, such as may be found in undergraduates participating in laboratory experiments, are attributable to mechanisms especially evolved for these purposes. To take an only partly hypothetical example, the recognition of individual typewritten letters may be studied as an example of human perception or cognition, but it is quite inconceivable that there should be a peculiarly human 'letter recognition mechanism'. The human visual system was around for a long time before letters were thought of, and most critical aspects of the system, such as the presence of binocular foveal vision, are a consequence of our membership of the order Primates. The primate eye and brain are not as they are so that we can identify letters, rather we are able to identify letters because of the nature of the primate eye and brain. Clearly there may be many psychological processes which are specific to the human species—speech-recognition mechanisms, or language-acquisition devices are more plausible candidates—but it is probable that even these grew out of capacities present in other animals.

Of all the discontinuities between man and animals that could be quoted, including the exclusively human faculties for abstraction, reason, morality, culture and technology, and the division of labour (see Chapters 1 and 2) the evergreen candidate for the fundamental discontinuity, which might qualify all others, is language. It is unlikely that a community of naked human beings, lacking all art and artifacts, but possessing language, ever existed, but it is usual to suppose that primitive levels of technology may exist along with a language that is in principle as complex as it is possible for speech to be. In a state of nature we expect humans to talk, and by comparison, the most unrelenting efforts to induce our closest living relatives to reveal hidden linguistic potential have left the discontinuity of speech bloodied, but unbowed.

It is therefore still reasonable to say that animals do not think as we do, when we think in words, and that in so far as we are only conscious when we think in words, they lack conscious awareness. Arguably perception, memory, reason, abstraction and feeling as processes of human thought are at the mercy of the faculty for speech. But tacit mental organisation is evident not only in ourselves but in many other species. The brain, as an organ of thought, is available for our use only because it was formed and developed before our time.

Our organ of thought may be superior, and we may play it better, but it is surely vain to believe that other possessors of similar instruments leave them quite untouched.

Bibliography

With few exceptions, items in the bibliography have been referred to in the text, and the page numbers for these references are given at the end of the listings here.

Adamo, N. J. (1967), 'Connections of efferent fibres from hyperstriatal areas in chicken, raven and African lovebird', *Journal of Comparative Neurology*, vol. 131, pp. 337–56. *187*

Adrian, E. D. (1941), 'Afferent discharges to the cerebral cortex from peripheral sense organs', *Journal of Physiology*, vol. 100, pp. 159–91. *177*

Agranoff, B. W. (1972), 'Further studies on memory formation in the goldfish', in J. L. McGaugh (ed.), *The Chemistry of Mood, Motivation and Memory*, New York: Plenum Press, pp. 175–85. *128*

Allison, T. (1972), 'Comparative and evolutionary aspects of sleep', in M. H. Chase (ed.), *The Sleeping Brain*, Los Angeles: Brain Research Institute Brain Information Service, pp. 1–57. *232–3*

Allison, T. (1976), 'Sleep in mammals: ecological and constitutional correlates', *Science*, vol. 194, pp. 723–34. *230*

Allison, T. and Van Twyver, H. (1970), 'Sleep in the moles, *Scalopus acquaticus* and *Condylura cristata*', *Experimental Neurology*, vol. 27, pp. 564–79. *229*

Allison, T., Van Twyver, H. and Goff, W. R. (1972), 'Electrophysiological studies of the echidna. *Tachyglossus aculeatus*. I. Waking and sleep', *Archives Italiennes de Biologie*, vol. 110, pp. 145–84.

Anderson, J. R. (1978), 'Arguments concerning representations for mental imagery', *Psychological Review*, vol. 85, pp. 249–77. *377*

Anderson, J. R. (1979), 'Further arguments concerning representations for mental imagery: a response to Hayes-Roth and Pylyshyn', *Psychological Review*, vol. 86, pp. 395–406. *377*

Andrew, R. H. (1967), 'Intracranial self-stimulation in the chick', *Nature*, vol. 213, pp. 847–8. *224*

Andrew, R. J. (1976), 'Attentional processes and animal behaviour', in P. P. G. Bateson and R. A. Hinde (eds), *Growing Points in Ethology*, Cambridge University Press, pp. 95–133. *189*

Aquinas, St Thomas (1951), *Philosophical Texts*, Oxford University Press. *3–4*

Armstrong, D. M. (1968), *A Materialist Theory of the Mind*, London: Routledge & Kegan Paul. *17–20, 106*

Armstrong, D. M. (1973), *Belief, Truth and Knowledge*, Cambridge University Press.

Aronson, L. R. (1970), 'Functional evolution of the forebrain in lower vertebrates'. in L. R. Aronson (ed.), *Development and Evolution of Behaviour*, San Francisco: W. H. Freeman, pp. 75–107. *186, 191, 200*

Aronson, L. R. and Kaplan, H. (1968), 'Function of the teleostean forebrain', in D. Ingle (ed.), *The Central Nervous System and Fish Behaviour*, University of Chicago Press, pp. 107–25. *141*

Ayer, A. J. (1980), *Hume*, Oxford University Press. *51*

Baddeley, A. D. (1976), *The Psychology of Memory*, New York: Basic Books. *22, 190*

Baillarger, J. (1845), 'De l'étendue de la surface du cerveau et de ses rapports avec le développement de l'intelligence', *Gazette des Hôpitaux*, Paris, vol. 18, pp. 179–194. *156*

Barlow, H. B. (1972), 'Single units and sensation: a neuron doctrine for perceptual psychology?', *Perception*, vol. 1, pp. 371–94. *100*

Barrington, E. J. W. (1964), *Hormones and Evolution*, London: English Universities Press.

Bastian, H. C. (1880), *The Brain as an Organ of the Mind*, London: Kegan Paul. *145–6, 178*

Beach, F. A. (1942), 'Analysis of the stimuli adequate to elicit mating behaviour in the sexually inexperienced male rat', *Journal of Comparative Psychology*, vol. 33, pp. 227–47. *188*

Beach, F. A. (1947), 'Evolutionary changes in the physiological control of mating behaviour in mammals', *Psychological Review*, vol. 54, pp. 297–315. *152, 188*

Bennett, J. (1976), *Linguistic Behaviour*, Cambridge University Press. *111*

Benninger, R. J., Bellisle, F. and Milner, P. M. (1977), 'Schedule control of behavior reinforced by electrical stimulation of the brain', *Science*, vol. 196, pp. 547–9. *129, 224*

Benowitz, L. I. and Karten, H. J. (1976), 'Organization of the tectofugal visual pathway in the pigeon: a retrograde transport study', *Journal of Comparative Neurology*, vol. 167, pp. 503–20. *128*

Bentley, P. J. (1976), *Comparative Vertebrate Endocrinology*, Cambridge University Press *152*

Berger, R. J. (1969), 'Oculomotor control: a possible function of REM sleep', *Psychological Review*, vol. 76, pp. 144–64. *229*

Berger, R. J. and Walker, J. M. (1972), 'Sleep in the burrowing owl (*Speotyto cunicularia hypugaea*)', *Behavioural Biology*, vol. 7, pp. 183–94. *232*

Beritoff, J. S. (1965), *Neural Mechanisms of Higher Vertebrate Behaviour*, trans. W. T. Liberson, London: J. and A. Churchill. *292, 298*

Beritoff, J. S. (1971), *Vertebrate Memory*, trans. J. S. Barlow, New York: Plenum Press. *292–5, 298, 305, 330*

Berkeley, G. (1965), *Philosophical Writings*, ed. D. M. Armstrong, London: Collier-Macmillan. *26*

Berkley, M. (1979), 'Vision: geniculocortical system', in R. B. Masterton (ed.), *Handbook of Behavioural Neurobiology*, vol. 1, *Sensory Integration*, New York: Plenum Press, pp. 165–208. *272*

Bernstein, J. S. (1961), 'The utilization of visual cues in dimension-abstracted oddity by primates', *Journal of Comparative and Physiological Psychology*, vol. 54, pp. 243–7. *261*

Bertram, B. C. R. (1970), 'The vocal behaviour of the Indian hill mynah, *Gracula religiosa*', *Animal Behaviour Monographs*, vol. 3, pp. 79–192. *217*

Bessemer, D. W. and Stollnitz, F. (1971), 'Retention of discrimination and an analysis of learning set', in A. M. Schries and F. Stollnitz (eds) *Behaviour of Nonhuman Primates*, vol. 4, New York: Academic Press, pp. 1–58. *315*

Bindra, D. (1976), *A Theory of Intelligent Behaviour*, London: John Wiley. *81, 99–102, 254*

Birch, H. G. (1945), 'The relation of previous experience to insightful problem-solving', *Journal of Comparative Psychology*, vol. 38, pp. 367–83. *344*

Bitterman, M. E. (1965), 'Phyletic differences in learning', *American Psychologist*, vol. 20, pp. 396–410. *334*

Bitterman, M. E. (1969), 'Thorndike and the problem of animal intelligence', *American Psychologist*, vol. 24, pp. 444–53. *62*

Bitterman, M. E. and Woodward, W. T. (1976), 'Vertebrate learning: common processes', in R. B. Masterton, M. E. Bitterman, G. B. G. Campbell and N. Holton (eds), *Evolution of Brain and Behaviour in Vertebrates*, Hillsdale: Laurence Erlbaum, pp. 169–89. *179, 334*

Blakemore, C. (1975), 'Central visual processing', in M. S. Gazzaniga and C. Blakemore (eds), *Handbook of Psychobiology*, New York: Academic Press, pp. 241–68. *272*

Blodgett, H. C. (1929), 'The effect of the introduction of reward upon the maze performance of rats', *University of California Publications in Psychology*, vol. 4, pp. 113–34. *80*

Bloomfield, S. and Marr, D. (1970), 'How the cerebellum may be used', *Nature*, vol. 227, pp. 1224–8. *318*

Blough, D. S. (1959), 'Delayed matching in the pigeon', *Journal of the Experimental Analysis of Behaviour*, vol. 2, pp. 151–60. *302*

Blough, D. S. (1979), 'Effects of number and form of stimuli on visual search in the pigeon', *Journal of Experimental Psychology: Animal Behaviour Process*, vol. 5, pp. 211–33. *279*

Blough, D. S. (1984), 'Form recognition in pigeons', in H. L. Roitblat, T. G. Bever and H. S. Terrace (eds), *Animal Cognition*, Hillsdale, Erlbaum, pp. 277–89 *256, 279.*

Boden, M. A. (1979), *Piaget*, London: Fontana. *95*

Bok, S. T. (1959), *Histonomy of the Cerebral Cortex*, Princeton: Van Nostrand Reinhold. *139*

Bolles, R. C. (1972), 'Reinforcement, expectancy, and learning', *Psychological Review*, vol. 79, pp. 394–409. *81, 223*

Boring, E. G. (1950), *A History of Experimental Psychology*, New York: Appleton-Century-Crofts. *31–2, 49, 57, 187, 318*

Bowman, R. S. and Sutherland, N. S. (1970), 'Shape discrimination by goldfish: coding of irregularities', *Journal of Comparative and Physiological Psychology*, vol. 72, pp. 90–7. *265–6*

Boyd, E. S. and Gardner, L. C. (1962), 'Positive and negative reinforcement from intracranial stimulation of a teleost', *Science*, vol. 136, pp. 648–9. *224*

Braitenberg, V. and Kemali, M. (1970), 'Exceptions to bilateral symmetry in the epithalamus of lower vertebrates', *Journal of Comparative Neurology*, vol. 138, pp. 137–46. *167*

Breder, C. M. Jr. and Rosen, D. E. (1966), *Modes of Reproduction in Fishes*, Jersey City: T. F. H. Publications. *209–11*

Broad, C. D. (1937), *The Mind and its Place in Nature*, London: Kegan Paul, Trench & Trubner. *17*

Brodmann, K. (1909), *Vergeichende lokalisationslehre der Grosshirnrinde*, Leipzig: Barth. *155*

Bronowski, J. and Bellugi, U. (1970), 'Language, name and concept', *Science*, vol. 168, pp. 669–73. *372, 375, 379*

Brown, J. (ed.) (1976), *Recall and Recognition*, London: Wiley. *190, 306*

Brown, J. J., Chan-Palay, V. and Palay, S. L. (1977), 'A study of afferent input to the inferior olivary complex in the rat by retrograde axonal transport of horseradish peridoxase', *Journal of Comparative Neurology*, vol. 176, pp. 1–22. *128*

Burghardt, G. M. (1977), 'Learning processes in reptiles', in C. Gans and D. W. Tinkle (eds), *Biology of the Reptilia*, vol. 7, New York: Academic Press, pp. 555–681. *158, 195, 294, 300*

Butler, A. B. and Northcutt, R. G. (1978), 'New thalamic visual nuclei in lizards', *Brain Research*, vol. 149, pp. 469–76. *283*

Bykov, K. M. (1957), *The Cerebral Cortex and the Internal Organs*, trans. W. H. Grant, New York: Chemical Publishing. *67*

Cain, D. P. and Wada, J. A. (1979), 'An anatomical asymmetry in the baboon brain', *Brain Behaviour and Evolution*, vol. 16, pp. 222–6'. *173*

Cajal Ramón y, S. (1911), *Histologie du système nerveux de l'homme de des vertebres*, reprinted 1955, Madrid: C.S.I.C. *126*

Campbell, A. W. (1905), *Histological Studies on the Localization of Cerebral Function*, Cambridge University Press. *155*

Campbell, C. B. G. (1966), 'Taxonomic status of tree shrews', *Science*, vol. 153, p. 436. *218*

Carlsson, A. (1978), 'Does dopamine have a role in schizophrenia?', *Biological Psychiatry*, vol. 13, pp. 3–21. *128*

Carr, A. and Coleman, P. J. (1974), 'Sea floor spreading and the odyssey of the green turtle', *Nature*, vol. 249, pp. 128–30. *198*

Castelluchi, V., Pinsker, H., Kupkerman, N. and Kandel, E. R. (1970), 'Neuronal mechanisms of habituation and dishabituation of the gill-withdrawal reflex in *Aphysia*', *Science*, vol. 167, pp. 1745–8.

Catania, A. C. and Reynolds, G. S. (1968), 'A quantitative analysis of responding maintained by interval schedules of reinforcement', *Journal of the Experimental Analysis of Behaviour*, vol. 11, pp. 327–83. *93*

Cerella, J. (1977), 'Absence of perspective processing in the pigeon', *Pattern Recognition*, vol. 9, pp. 65–8. *259*

Cerella, J. (1979), 'Visual classes and natural categories in the pigeon', *Journal of Experimental Psychology: Human Perception and Performance*, vol. 5, pp. 68–77. *257–8*

Chadwick, A. (1977), 'Comparison of milk-like secretions found in non-mammals', *Symposia of the Zoological Society of London*, vol. 41, pp. 341–58. *153*

Chomsky, N. (1976), *Reflections on Language*, London: Fontana. *380*

Chomsky, N. (1979), 'Human language and other semiotic systems', *Semiotica*, vol. 25, pp. 31–44. *372, 375, 381*

Chomsky, N. (1980), *Rules and Representations*, New York: Columbia University Press. *380*

Chopin, S. F. and Buerger, A. H. (1975), 'Graded acquisition of an instrumental avoidance response by the spinal rat', *Physiology and Behaviour*, vol. 15, pp. 155–8. *335*

Clark, E. V. (1973), 'What's in a word? On the child's acquisition of semantics in his first language', in T. E. Moore (ed.), *Cognitive Development and the Acquisition of Language*, New York: Academic Press, pp. 55–110. *379*

Clark, H. H. and Clark, E. V. (1977), *Psychology and Language*, New York: Harcourt Brace. *375*

Cohen, N. J. and Squire, L. R. (1980), 'Preserved learning and retention of pattern analysing in amnesia: dissociation of knowing how and knowing that', *Science*, vol. 210, pp. 207–10. *321*

Collins, A. M. and Quillian, M. R. (1969), 'Retrieval time from semantic memory', *Journal of Verbal Learning and Verbal Behaviour*, vol. 8, pp. 240–8. *380*

Collins, A. M. and Loftus, E. F. (1975), 'A spreading activation theory of semantic processing', *Psychological Review*, vol. 82, pp. 407–28. *380*

Collins, R. L. (1977), 'Towards an admissible genetic model for the inheritance of the degree and direction of asymmetry', in S. Harnad, R. W. Doty, L. Goldstein, J. Jaynes and G. Krauthaner (eds), *Lateralisation in the Nervous System*, London: Academic Press, pp. 137–50. *168*

Cook, S. B. and Cook, C. B. (1975), 'Directionality in the trail following Response of the pulmonate limpet *Siphonaria alternata*', *Marine Behaviour and Physiology*, vol. 3, pp. 147–55. *199*

Corballis, M. C. and Beale, I. L. (1976), *The Psychology of Left and Right*, Hillsdale: Lawrence Erlbaum. *161, 164*

Cowan, W. M., Gottleib, D. I., Hendrickson, A., Price, J. L. and Woolsey, T. A. (1972), 'The autoradiographic demonstration of axonal connections in the central nervous system', *Brain Research*, vol. 37, pp. 21–51. *127*

Cowey, A. (1979), 'Cortical maps and visual perception', *Quarterly Journal of Experimental Psychology*, vol. 31, pp. 1–17. *275–6*

Craik, K. J. W. (1943), *The Nature of Explanation*, Cambridge University Press. *109, 113, 253, 260, 381*

Croze, H. J. (1970), 'Searching images in carrion crows', *Zeitschrift für Tierpsychologie*, vol. 5, pp. 1–85. *250*

Cuenod, M. (1974), 'Commissural pathways in interhemispheric transfer of visual information in the pigeon', in F. O. Schmidt and F. G. Worden (eds), *The Neurosciences: Third Study Program*. Cambridge, Mass.: MIT Press, pp. 21–9. *163, 166*

Cunningham, A. (1921), 'A gorilla's life in civilization', *Bulletin of the Zoological Societies*, New York, vol. 24, pp. 118. *353*

Cunningham, D. F. (1892), *Contribution to the Surface Anatomy of the Cerebral Hemispheres*, Dublin: Royal Irish Academy. *167, 173*

D'Amato, M. R. (1973), 'Delayed matching and short-term memory in monkeys', in G. H. Bower (ed.), *The Psychology of Learning and*

394   *Bibliography*

Motivation: Advances in Research and Theory, vol. 7, New York: Academic Press, pp. 227–69. *302, 304*

D'Amato, M. R. and Cox, J. K. (1976), 'Delay of consequences and short-term memory in monkeys', in D. L. Medin, W. A. Roberts and R. T. Davis (eds), *Processes of Animal Memory*, Hillsdale: Lawrence Erlbaum, pp. 49–78. *304*

D'Amato, M. R. and Worsham, R. W. (1974), 'Retrieval cues and short-term memory in capuchin monkeys', *Journal of Comparative Physiological Psychology*, vol. 86, pp. 274–82. *311–12*

Dareste, M. C. (1862), 'Sur les rapports de la masse encéphalique avec le développement de l'intelligence', *Bulletin et mémoires de la Societé d'Anthropologie de Paris*, vol. 3, p. 26. *156*

Darwin, C. (1901), *The Descent of Man and Selection in Relation to Sex*, London: John Murray. *39, 47, 53–4*

Darwin, C. (1965), *The Expression of the Emotions in Man and Animals*, University of Chicago Press. *44*

Darwin, C. (1968), *The Origin of Species*, Harmondsworth: Penguin Books. *39–46*

Davenport, R. K., and Rogers, C. M. (1970), 'Differential rearing of the chimpanzee', in G. Bourne (ed.), *The Chimpanzee*, vol. 3, Basel: Karger, pp. 337–60. *334*

Davis, R. E., Kassel, J. and Schwagmeyer, P. (1976), 'Telencephalic lesions in the teleost, *Macropodus Operoularis*: reproduction, startle reaction and operant behaviour in the male', *Behavioural Biology*, vol. 18, pp. 165–77.

Davis, R. T. and Fitts, S. S. (1976), 'Memory and coding processes in discrimination learning', in D. L. Medin, W. A. Roberts and R. T. Davis (eds), *Processes of Animal Memory*, Hillsdale: Lawrence Erlbaum, pp. 117–80. *306–9*

Dawkins, R. (1976a), 'Hierarchical organization: a candidate principle for ethology', in P. P. G. Bateson and R. A. Hinde (eds), *Growing Points in Ethology*, Cambridge University Press, pp. 7–54. *99, 126*

Dawkins, R. (1976b), *The Selfish Gene*, Oxford University Press. *210, 221*

Dean, P. (1980), 'Recapitulation of a theme by Lashley? Comment on Wood's simulated lesion experiment', *Psychological Review*, vol. 87, pp. 470–3.

Delius, J. D. and Habers, G. (1978), 'Symmetry: can pigeons conceptualize it?', *Behavioural Biology*, vol. 22, pp. 336–42. *264*

Delius, J. D., Williams, A. S. and Wootton, R. J. (1976), 'Motivation dependence of brain self-stimulation in the pigeon', *Behavioural Processes*, vol. 1, pp. 15–27. *224*

Dement, W. (1960), 'Effect of dream deprivation', *Science*, vol. 131, pp. 1705–7. *225*

De Monasterio, F. M. and Gouras, P. (1975), 'Functional properties of ganglion cells of the rhesus monkey retina', *Journal of Physiology*, London, vol. 251, pp. 167–95. *268*

Denenberg, V. H. (1981), 'Hemispheric laterality in animals and the effects of early experience', *Behavioural and Brain Sciences*, vol. 4, pp. 1–49. *168, 173*

Descartes, R. (1952), *Descartes' Philosophical Writings*, trans. N. Kemp-Smith, London: Macmillan. *5–17*

Descartes, R. (1970), *Philosophical Writings* (Anscombe, E. and Geach, P. T., eds), Sunbury-on-Thames: Nelson University Paperbacks. *5–17*

Descartes, R. (1978a), *A Discourse on Method, Meditations on the First Philosophy, Principles of Philosophy*, London: J. M. Dent & Sons. *5–17*

Descartes, R. (1978b), *Descartes: his Moral Philosophy and Psychology*, trans. J. J. Blom, Hassocks, Sussex: Harvester Press. *5–17*

Deutsch, J. A. and Clarkson, J. K. (1959), 'Reasoning in the hooded rat', *Quarterly Journal of Experimental Psychology*, vol. 11, pp. 150–4. *78*

Dewson, J. H. (1977), 'Preliminary evidence of hemispheric asymmetry of auditory function in monkeys', in S. Harnad, R. W. Doty, J. Jaynes, C. Goldstein, and K. Krauthamer (eds), *Laterlization in the Nervous System*, New York: Academic Press, pp. 63–71. *173*

Diamond, I. T. (1979), 'The subdivisions of neocortex: a proposal to revise the traditional view of sensory, motor and association areas', in J. M. Sprague and A. N. Epstein (eds), *Progress in Psychobiology and Psychological Psychology*, vol. 8, New York: Academic Press, pp. 2–44. *319*

Diamond, I. T. and Hall, W. C. (1969), 'Evolution of neocortex', *Science*, vol. 164, pp. 251–62. *122, 153, 179, 184, 319*

Dickinson, A. (1985), 'Actions and habits: the development of behavioral autonomy', *Philosophical Transactions of the Royal Society B*, vol. 308, pp. 67–78. *111, 317*

Diderot, D. (1916), *Diderot's Early Philosophical Works*, trans. M. Jourdain, Chicago and London: Open Court Series of Classics of Science and Philosophy. *31*

Dimond, S. J. (1972), *The Double Brain*, Edinburgh: Churchill. *161*

Distenhoff, J. F., Haggerty, R. and Corning, V. C. (1971), 'An analysis of leg position learning in the cockroach yoked control', *Physiology and Behaviour*, vol. 7, pp. 359–62. *335*

Dorst, J. (1962), *The Migrations of Birds*, London: Heinemann. *198*

Douglas, R. J. (1967), 'The hippocampus and behaviour', *Psychological Bulletin*, vol. 67, pp. 416–22. *322*

Ebbesson, S. O. E. (1970), 'On the organization of central visual pathways in vertebrates', *Brain, Behaviour and Evolution*, vol. 3, pp. 178–94. *166, 176, 277*

Ebbesson, S. O. E. (1980), 'On the organization of the telencephalon in elasmobranchs', in S. O. E. Ebbesson (ed.), *Comparative Neurology of the Telencephalon*, New York: Plenum Press, pp. 1–6. *181, 327*

Ebbesson, S. O. E. and Heimer, L. (1970), 'Projections of the olfactory tract fibres in the nurse shark (*Ginglymostoma cirratum*)', *Brain Research*, vol. 17, pp. 47–55. *187, 327*

Ebbesson, S. O. E. and Northcutt, R. G. (1976), 'Neurology of anamniotic vertebrates', in R. B. Masterton, M. E. Bitterman, C. B. G. Campbell and N. Hotton (eds), *Evolution of Brain and Behaviour in Vertebrates*, Hillsdale: Lawrence Erlbaum, pp. 115–46. *122, 159, 187, 202*

Ebner, F. F. (1976), 'The forebrain of reptiles and mammals', in R. B. Masterton, M. E. Bitterman, C. B. G. Campbell and N. Hotton (eds),

Evolution of Brain and Behaviour in Vertebrates, Hillsdale: Lawrence
Erlbaum, pp. 147–67. *186–7, 202*

Eccles, J. C. (1965), *The Brain and the Unity of Conscious Experience*,
Cambridge University Press. *11, 16, 17*

Eccles, J. C. (1973), 'The cerebellum as a computer: patterns in space and
time', *Journal of Physiology*, vol. 229, pp. 1–32. *318*

Eccles, J. C., Ito, M. and Szentágothai, J. (1967), *The Cerebellum as a
Neuronal Machine*, Berlin: Springer-Verlag.

Eccles, J. C., Taborikova, H. and Tsukahara, N. (1970), 'Responses of the
Purkinje cells of a selachian cerebellum (*Mustelis canis*)', *Brain Research*,
vol. 17, pp. 57–86. *143*

Eibl-Eibesfeldt, I. (1970), *Ethology: the Biology of Behaviour*, New York: Holt,
Rinehart & Winston. *126, 213, 220*

Eisenstein, G. M. and Colton, M. J. (1965), 'Learning in an isolated
prothoracic insect ganglion', *Animal Behaviour*, vol. 13, pp. 104–8. *335*

Elias, H. and Schwartz, D. (1969), 'Surface areas of the cerebral cortex of
mammals determined by stereological methods', *Science*, vol. 166,
pp. 111–13. *156*

Elliot, H. C. (1963), *Textbook of Neuroanatomy*, Philadelphia: J. B.
Lippincott. *153*

Ewer, R. F. (1973), *The Carnivores*, London: Weidenfeld & Nicolson. *205*

Fantino, E. and Logan, L. (1979), *The Experimental Analysis of Behaviour: A
Biological Perspective*, San Francisco: W. H. Freeman. *335, 337*

Farr, E. J. and Savage, G. E. (1978), 'First- and second-order
conditioning in the goldfish and their relation to the telencephalon',
Behavioural Biology, vol. 22, pp. 50–9. *186, 334*

Faucette, J. R. (1969), 'The olfactory bulb and medial hemisphere wall of
the rat-fish, *Chimaera*', *Journal of Comparative Neurology*, vol. 137,
pp. 377–406. *319*

Ferster, C. B. and Skinner, B. F. (1957), *Schedules of Reinforcement*, New
York: Appleton-Century-Crofts. *89–94*

Finger, F. E. (1980), 'Nonolfactory sensory pathway to the telencephalon
in a teleost fish', *Science*, vol. 210, pp. 671–2.

Fink, R. P. and Heimer, L. (1967), 'Two methods for selective silver
impregnation of degenerating axons and their synaptic endings in the
central nervous system', *Brain Research*, vol. 4, pp. 369–71. *127*

Fiskin, R. A., Garey, L. J. and Powell, T. P. S. (1973), 'Patterns of
degeneration after intrinsic lesions of the visual cortex (area 17) of the
monkey', *Brain Research*, vol. 53, pp. 208–13. *274*

Flanigan, W. F. (1973), 'Sleep and wakefulness in iguanid lizards,
Ctenosaura pectinata and *Iguana iguana*', *Brain, Behaviour and Evolution*, vol.
8, pp. 401–36. *233–4*

Flanigan, W. F., Knight, C. P., Hartse, K. M. and Rechtschaften, A.
(1974), 'Sleep and wakefulness in chelonian reptiles. I. The box turtle,
Terrapene Carolina', *Archives Italiennes de Biologie*, vol. 112, pp. 227–52. *232*

Flood, N. C. and Overmeier, J. B. (1971), 'Effects of telencephalic and
olfactory lesions on appetitive learning in goldfish', *Physiology and
Behaviour*, vol. 6, pp. 35–40. *334*

Flood, N. C., Overmeier, J. B. and Savage, G. (1976), 'Teleost telencephalon and learning: an interpretive review of data and hypotheses', *Physiology and Behaviour*, vol. 16, pp. 783–98. *334*

Flourens, P. (1960), 'Investigations of the properties and functions of the various parts which comprise the cerebral mass', in G. von Bonin (ed.), *The Cerebral Cortex*, Springfield: C. C. Thomas, pp. 3–21. *185*

Foster, R. E. and Hall, W. C. (1978), 'The organization of central auditory pathways in a reptile, *Iguana iguana*', *Journal of Comparative Neurology*, vol. 178, pp. 783–831. *183*

Fouts, R. (1973), 'Acquisition and testing of gestural signs in four young chimpanzees', *Science*, vol. 180, pp. 978–80. *373*

Fouts, R. S., Chown, B. and Goodin, L. (1976), 'Transfer of signed responses in American Sign Language from vocal English to physical object stimuli by a chimpanzee *(pan)*', *Learning and Motivation*, vol. 7, pp. 458–75. *356*

Fox, M. W. (ed.) (1975), *The Wild Canids*, New York: Van Nostrand Reinhold. *218*

Fox, R., Lehmkuhle, S. W. and Bush, R. L. (1977), 'Stereopsis in the falcon', *Science*, vol. 197, pp. 79–81.

French, G. M. (1965), 'Association problems', in A. M. Schrier, H. F. Harlow and F. Stollnitz (eds), *Behaviour of Nonhuman Primates*, vol. 1, New York: Academic Press pp. 167–209. *302*

Frisby, J. P. (1979), *Seeing*, Oxford University Press. *251, 272–4*

Gaffan, D. (1974), 'Recognition impaired and association intact in the memory of monkeys after transection of the fornix', *Journal of Comparative and Physiological Psychology*, vol. 86, pp. 1100–9. *324*

Gaffan, D. (1976), 'Recognition memory in animals', in J. Brown (ed.), *Recognition and Recall*, London: Wiley, pp. 229–42. *321, 324, 326*

Gaffan, D. (1977a), 'Monkey's recognition of complex pictures and the effects of fornix transection', *Quarterly Journal of Experimental Psychology*, vol. 29, pp. 505–14. *307, 322*

Gaffan, D. (1977b), 'Recognition memory after short retention intervals in fornix transected monkeys', *Quarterly Journal of Experimental Psychology*, vol. 29, pp. 577–88. *310, 322–3*

Gaffan, D. (1977c), 'Response coding in recall of colours by monkeys', *Quarterly Journal of Experimental Psychology*, vol. 29, pp. 597–605. *312–3*

Gallup, G. G. (1974), 'Animal hypnosis: factual status of a fictional concept', *Psychological Bulletin*, vol. 81, pp. 836–53.

Garcia, J., Rusiniak, K. W. and Brett, L. P. (1977), 'Conditioning food-illness aversions in wild animals: *Caveat Canonict*', in H. Davis and H. M. B. Hurwitz (eds), *Operant-Pavlovian Interactions*, Hillsdale: Lawrence Erlbaum, pp. 273–311. *182, 293*

Gardner, B. T. and Gardner, R. A. (1971), 'Two-way communication with an infant chimpanzee', in A. M. Schrier and F. Stollnitz (eds), *Behaviour of Nonhuman Primates*, vol. 4, New York: Academic Press, pp. 117–83. *355*

Gardner, R. A. and Gardner, B. T. (1969), 'Teaching sign language to a chimpanzee', *Science*, vol. 165, pp. 664–72. *335–6, 371*

Gardner, R. A. and Gardner, B. T. (1975), 'Early signs of language in child and chimpanzee', *Science*, vol. 187, pp. 752–3. *354*

Gardner, R. A. and Gardner, B. T. (1978), 'Comparative psychology and language acquisition', *Annals of the New York Academy of Science*, vol. 309, pp. 37–76. *354, 373, 380*

Gazzaniga, M. S. (1975), 'Brain mechanisms and behaviour', in M. S. Gazzaniga (ed.), *Handbook of Psychobiology*, New York: Academic Press, pp. 565–90. *161, 168*

Gazzaniga, M. S. and Young, E. D. (1967), 'Effects of commissurotomy on the processing of visual information', *Experimental Brain Research*, vol. 3, pp. 368–71.

Geschwind, N. (1965), 'Disconnexion syndromes in animals and man', *Brain*, vol. 88, pp. 237–94. *109, 189*

Geschwind, N. (1970), 'Intermodal equivalence of stimuli in apes', *Science*, vol. 168, p. 1249.

Geschwind, N. and Levitsky, W. (1968), 'Human brain: left-right asymmetries in temporal speech region', *Science*, vol. 161, pp. 186–7. *167*

Gilbert, P. (1975), 'How the cerebellum could memorise movements', *Nature*, vol. 254, pp. 688–9.

Gillan, D., Premack, D. and Woodruff, G. (1981), 'Reasoning in the chimpanzee: I. Analogical reasoning', *Journal of Experimental Psychology: Animal Behaviour Processes*, vol. 7, pp. 1–17. *373*

Glickman, S. E. and Schiff, B. (1967), 'A biological theory of reinforcement', *Psychological Review*, vol. 74, pp. 81–109. *224*

Goldstein, K. (1948), *Language and Language Disturbances*, New York: Grune & Stratton. *173*

Goodall, J. (1965), 'Chimpanzees of the Gombe Stream Reserve', in I. DeVore (ed.), *Primate Behaviour: Field Studies of Monkeys and Apes*, New York: Holt, Rinehart & Winston, pp. 425–73. *340, 345*

Goodall, J. (1979), 'Life and death at Gombe', *National Geographic*, May, pp. 592–621. *340*

Goodglass, H. (1976), 'Aggramatism', in H. Whitaker and H. A. Whitaker (eds), *Studies in Neurolinguistics*, vol. 1, London: Academic Press, pp. 237–60.

Goodglass, A. and Geschwind, N. (1976), 'Language disorders (aphasia)', in E. C. Carterette and M. P. Friedman (eds), *Handbook of Perception*, vol. vii, *Language and Speech*, London: Academic Press, pp. 389–428. *360*

Goodman, I. J. (1974), 'The study of sleep in birds', in I. J. Goodman and M. W. Schein (eds), *Birds: Brain and Behaviour*, New York: Academic Press. *231*

Goodman, M. (1974), 'Biochemical evidence on hominid phylogeny', *Annual Review of Anthropology*, vol. 3, pp. 203–28. *339*

Gould, S. J. (1976), 'Grades and clades revisited', in R. B. Masterton, W. Hodos and H. Jerison (eds), *Evolution, Brain and Behavior: Persistent Problems*, Hillsdale: Lawrence Erlbaum, pp. 115–22. *121, 123*

Graebner, R. C. (1980), 'Telencephalic function in elasmobranchs', in S. O. E. Ebbeson (ed.), *Comparative Neurology of the Telencephalon,*, New York: Plenum Press, pp. 17–39. *176, 327*

Graebner, R. C., Schroeder, D. M., Jane, J. A. and Ebbesson, S. O. E. (1978), 'Visual discrimination following partial telencephalic ablation in nurse sharks *(Ginglymostoma cirratum)*', *Journal of Comparative Neurology*, vol. 180, pp. 325–44. *186*

Grant, D. S. (1976), 'Effect of sample presentation time on long-delay matching in the pigeon', *Learning and Motivation*, vol. 7, pp. 580–90. *303–4, 317*

Gray, H. (1967), *Gray's Anatomy*, D. V. Davies and R. E. Coupland (eds), 34th edn, London: Longman. *146*

Gray, J. A. (1975), *Elements of Two-Process Theory of Learning*, London: Academic Press. *222, 288*

Gray, J. A. (1979), *Pavlov*, London: Fontana. *72*

Green, S. (1975), 'Variation of vocal pattern with social situation in the Japanese monkey *(Macaca fuscata)*', in L. A. Rosenblum (ed.), *Primate Behaviour*, vol. 4, New York: Academic Press, pp. 1–102. *353*

Greenberg, N. (1977), 'A neuroethological study of display behaviour in the lizard *Anolis carolinensis*', *American Zoologist*, vol. 17, pp. 191–201. *333*

Gregg, V. (1975), *Human Memory*, London: Methuen. *22, 298, 304*

Gregory, R. (1970), 'The grammar of vision', the *Listener*, Feb. 19, pp. 242–4. *381*

Griffin, D. R. (1976), *The Question of Animal Awareness*, New York: Rockerfeller University Press. *98–9*

Griffiths, M. (1978), *The Biology of the Monotremes*, New York: Academic Press. *120*

Gross, C. G. (1973), 'Inferotemporal cortex and vision', in E. Stellar and J. M. Sprague (eds), *Progress in Physiological Psychology*, vol. 5, New York: Academic Press, pp. 77–123. *276*

Gross, C. G., Rocha-Miranda, C. E. and Bender, D. B. (1972), 'Visual properties of neurons in the infero-temporal cortex of the macaque', *Journal of Neurophysiology*, vol. 35, pp. 96–111. *276*

Gross, C. G., Bender, D. B. and Rocha-Miranda, C. E. (1974), 'Inferotemporal cortex and vision: a single-unit analysis' in F. O. Schmidt and F. G. Wordon (eds), *The Neurosciences: Third Study Program*, London: MIT Press, pp. 229–38. *276, 290*

Gross, C. G. and Mishkin, M. (1977), 'The neural basis of stimulus equivalence across retinal translation', in S. Harnad, L. Goldstein, J. Jaynes and G. Krauthamer (eds), *Lateralization of the Nervous System*, London: Academic Press, pp. 109–22. *277*

Grossman, S. P. (1967), *A Textbook of Physiological Psychology*, New York: Wiley. *191*

Groves, P. M. and Thompson, R. F. (1970), 'Habituation: a dual process theory', *Psychological Review*, vol. 77, pp. 419–50. *147*

Gruber, H. E., Girgus, J. S. and Banuazzi, A. (1971), 'The development of object permanence in the cat', *Developmental Psychology*, vol. 4, pp. 9–15. *97*

Guthrie, E. R. (1930), 'Conditioning as a principle of learning', *Psychological Review*, vol. 35, pp. 412–28. *67*

Hale, E. B. (1956), 'Social facilitation and forebrain function in maze performance of green sunfish *(Lepomis cyanellus)*', *Physiological Zoology*, vol. 29, pp. 93–106. *334*

Hall, W. C. (1972), 'Visual pathways to the telencephalon in reptiles and mammals', *Brain, Behaviour and Evolution*, vol. 5, pp. 95–113.

Hall, W. C. and Ebner, F. F. (1970), 'Parallels in the visual afferent projections of the thalamus in the hedgehog *(Paraechinus hypomelus)* and the turtle *(Pseudemys scripta)*', *Brain, Behaviour and Evolution*, vol. 3, pp. 135–54. *122, 153*

Hamilton, W. D. (1964), 'The genetical theory of social behaviour' (I and II), *Journal of Theoretical Biology*, vol. 7, pp. 1 – 16 and pp. 17–32. *210, 221*

Hamlyn, D. W. (1980), *Schopenhauer*, London: Routledge & Kegan Paul.

Hardyck, C. (1977), 'A model of individual differences in hemisphere functioning', in H. Whitaker and H. A. Whitaker (eds), *Studies in Neurolinguistics*, vol. 3, New York: Academic Press, pp. 223–55. *170–1*

Hardyck, C. and Petrinovich, L. F. (1977), 'Left-handedness', *Psychological Bulletin*, vol. 84, pp. 385–404. *168*

Harlow, H. F. (1949), 'The formation of learning sets', *Psychological Review*, vol. 56, pp. 51–65. *314–5*

Harlow, H. F. (1958), 'The nature of love', *American Psychologist*, vol. 13, pp. 673–85. *341*

Harlow, H. F. (1959), 'Learning set and error factor theory', in S. Koch (ed.), *Psychology: A Study of a Science*, vol. 2, New York: McGraw-Hill, pp. 492–537.

Harlow, H. F. and Mears, C. (1979), *The Human Model: Primate Perspectives*, Washington: V. A. Winston. *341*

Hart, B. L. (1967), 'Sexual reflexes and mating behaviour in the male dog', *Journal of Comparative and Physiological Psychology*, vol. 64, pp. 388–99. *147*

Hart, B. L. (1974), 'Medial pre-optic-anterior hypothalamic area and socio-sexual behaviour in dogs: a comparative neuropsychological analysis', *Journal of Comparative and Physiological Psychology*, vol. 86, pp. 328–49. *200*

Hartse, K. M. and Rechtschaffen, A. (1974), 'Effect of atropine sulphate and sleep-related EEG spike activity of the tortoise *(Geochelone carbonaria)*', *Brain, Behaviour and Evolution*, vol. 9, pp. 81–94. *234*

Hayes, C. H. (1951), *The Ape in Our House*, New York: Harper & Row. *343*

Hayes, K. J. and Hayes, C. (1951), 'The intellectual development of a home raised chimpanzee', *Proceedings of the American Philosophical Society*, vol. 95, pp. 105–9. *343, 353*

Hayes, K. J. and Hayes, C. (1952), 'Imitation in a home raised chimpanzee', *Journal of Comparative and Physiological Psychology*, vol. 46, pp. 470–74. *353*

Hayes, K. J. and Nissen, C. H. (1971), 'Higher mental functions of a home raised chimpanzee', in A. M. Schrier and F. Stollnitz (eds), *Behaviour of Nonhuman Primates*, vol. 4, New York: Academic Press, pp. 59–115. *343, 353*

Hebb, D. O. (1949), *The Organization of Behavior*, New York: Wiley. *99–100*

Hebb, D. O. (1966). *A Textbook of Psychology*, 2nd edn, Philadelphia:
W. B. Saunders. *7*
Hebb, D. O. (1968), 'Concerning imagery', *Psychological Review*, vol. 75,
pp. 466–77. *100*
Heffner, R. and Masterton, B. (1975), 'Variations in the form of the
pyramidal trait and its relation to digital dexterity', *Brain, Behaviour and
Evolution*, vol. 12, pp. 161–204. *203*
Hegel, G. W. F. (1949), *The Phenomenology of Mind*, 2nd edn, London:
Allen & Unwin. *34*
Hegel, G. W. F. (1977), *Phenomenology of Spirit*, trans. A. V. Miller,
Oxford: Clarendon Press. *33*
Heier, P. (1948), 'Fundamental principles in the structure of the brain: a
study of the brain of *Petromyzon fluviatilis*', *Acta Anatomica*, vol. 5, (suppl.
8), pp. 1–213. *145*
Herman, L. M. and Gordon, J. A. (1974), 'Auditory delayed matching in
the bottenose dolphin', *Journal of the Experimental Analysis of Behaviour*,
vol. 21, pp. 19–26. *304*
Herrnstein, R. J. (1979), 'Acquisition, generalization and discrimination:
reversal of a natural concept', *Journal of Experimental Psychology: Animal
Behaviour Processes*, vol. 5, pp. 116–25. *258–9*
Herrnstein, R. J. (1985), 'Riddles of natural categorization', *Philosophical
Transactions of the Royal Society, B*, vol. 308, pp. 129–43. *258*
Herrnstein, R. J. and Loveland, D. H. (1964), 'Complex visual concept in
the pigeon', *Science*, vol. 146, pp. 549–51. *256*
Herrnstein, R. J., Loveland, D. H. and Cable, C. (1976), 'Natural
concepts in pigeons', *Journal of Experimental Psychology: Animal Behaviour
Processes*, vol. 2, pp. 285–302. *257–9, 279*
Hess, E. H. (1959), 'Imprinting', *Science*, vol. 130, pp. 130–41. *212*
Hewes, G. (1975), *Language Origins: A Bibliography*, The Hague: Mouton.
380
Hilgard, E. R. and Bower, G. H. (1975), *Theory of Learning*, 4th edn,
New York: Appleton-Century-Crofts. *32, 222*
Himmelfarb, G. (1959), *Darwin and the Darwinian Revolution*, London:
Chatto & Windus. *39–40*
Hinde, R. A. (1959), 'Unitary drives', *Animal Behaviour*, vol. 7, pp. 130–41.
223
Hinde, R. A. (1970), *Animal Behaviour*, 2nd edn, New York: McGraw-
Hill. *58, 190, 212, 288*
Hinde, R. A. (1974), *Biological Bases of Human Social Behaviour*, New York:
McGraw-Hill. *341*
Hinde, R. A. and Stevenson-Hinde, J. (eds) (1973), *Constraints on Learning*,
New York: Academic Press. *27, 223*
Hodos, W. (1976), 'Vision and the visual system: a bird's eye view', in
J. M. Sprague and A. N. Epstein (eds), *Progress in Psychobiology and
Physiological Psychology*, vol. 6, New York: Academic Press, pp. 29–62. *158*
Hodos, W. and Campbell, C. B. G. (1969), '*Scala Naturae*: why there is no
theory of comparative psychology', *Psychological Review*, vol. 76,
pp. 337–50. *116–25, 179*

Hodos, W. and Karten, H. J. (1970), 'Visual intensity and pattern discrimination deficits after lesions of the ectostriatum in pigeons', *Journal of Comparative Neurology*, vol. 140, pp. 53–68. *126*

Hodos, W. and Yolen, N. M. (1976), 'Behavioural correlates of "tectal compression" in goldfish. II Visual acuity', *Brain, Behaviour and Evolution*, vol. 13, pp. 468–74. *142*

Holden, C. (1977), 'Carl Rogers: giving people permission to be themselves', *Science*, vol. 198, pp. 31–5. *9*

Honzik, C. H. (1936), 'The sensory basis of maze learning in rats', *Comparative Psychology Monographs*, vol. 13, pp. 1–113. *188*

Horn, G. (1967), 'Neuronal mechanisms of habituation', *Nature* (London), vol. 215, pp. 707–11. *288*

Horridge, G. A. (1962), 'Learning of leg position by the ventral nerve cord in headless insects', *Proceedings of the Royal Society, Series B*, vol. 157, pp. 33–52. *335*

Hubel, D. A. and Wiesel, T. N. (1962), 'Receptive fields, binocular interaction and functional architecture in the cat's visual cortex', *Journal of Physiology* (London), vol. 160, pp. 106–54. *129, 272*

Hubel, D. H. and Wiesel, T. N. (1965), 'Receptive fields and functional architecture in two non-striate visual areas (18 and 19) of the cat', *Journal of Neurophysiology*, vol. 28, pp. 229–89.

Hubel, D. H. and Wiesel, T. N. (1974), 'Uniformity of monkey striate cortex: A parallel relationship between field size, scatter, and magnification factor', *Journal of Comparative Neurology*, vol. 158, pp. 295–306. *272*

Hubel, D. H. and Wiesel, T. N. (1977), 'Functional architecture of macaque monkey visual cortex', *Proceedings of the Royal Society, Series B*, vol. 198, pp. 1–59. *272–3*

Hubel, D. H., Wiesel, T. N. and Stryker, M. P. (1978), 'Anatomical demonstration of orientation columns in macaque monkey', *Journal of Comparative Neurology*, vol. 177, pp. 361–80. *128*

Hull, C. L. (1929), 'A functional interpretation of the conditioned reflex', *Psychological Review*, vol. 36, pp. 498–511. *67, 74*

Hull, C. L. (1934), 'The concept of the habit-family hierarchy and maze learning', *Psychological Review*, vol. 41, pp. 33–54. *77*

Hull, C. L. (1937), 'Mind, mechanism, and adaptive behaviour', *Psychological Review*, vol. 44, pp. 1–32. *67, 75, 77*

Hull, C. L. (1938), 'The goal gradient hypothesis applied to some "field force" problems in the behaviour of young children', *Psychological Review*, vol. 45, pp. 271–99. *75*

Hull, C. L. (1939), 'Modern behaviourism and psychoanalysis', *Transactions of the New York Academy of Sciences*, Series 11, vol. 1, pp. 78–82. *75*

Hull, C. L. (1943), *Principles of Behavior*, New York: Appleton-Century-Crofts. *67, 74, 223*

Hull, C. L. (1952), *A Behavior System*, New Haven: Yale University Press. *77–8*

Hull, C. L. and Kruger, R. C. (1931), 'An electro-chemical parallel to the conditioned reflex', *Journal of General Psychology*, vol. 5, 262–9. *75*

Hume, D. (1888), *Treatise on Human Nature*, (L. A. Selby-Bigge, ed.), Oxford: Clarendon Press. *26–31*

Hume, D. (1902), *Enquiries Concerning the Human Understanding and Concerning the Principles of Morals* (L. A. Selby-Bigge, ed.), Oxford: Clarendon Press. *26–31*

Hume, D. (1906), *Essays*, London: George Routledge & Sons. *26–31*

Humphrey, N. K. (1974), 'Vision in a monkey without a striate cortex: a case study', *Perception*, vol. 3, pp. 241–55. *183, 282*

Humphrey, N. K. (1976), 'The social functions of intellect', in P. P. G. Bateson and R. A. Hinde (eds), *Growing Points in Ethology*, Cambridge University Press, pp. 303–21. *191, 219*

Humphrey, N. K. and Weiskrantz, L. (1967), 'Vision in monkeys after removal of the striate cortex', *Nature* (London), vol. 215, pp. 595–7.

Hunter, W. S. (1913), 'The delayed reaction in animals and children', *Behaviour Monographs*, vol. 2, vol. 1, pp. 1–86. *291*

Hunter, W. S. (1940), 'A kinaesthetically controlled maze habit in the rat', *Science*, vol. 91, pp. 267–9. *188*

Huppert, F. A. and Piercy, M. (1976), 'Recognition memory in amnesic patients: effect of temporal context and familiarity of material', *Cortex*, vol. 12, pp. 3–20. *322*

Huxley, T. H. (1893), *Methods and Results*, London: Macmillan. *51*

Huxley, T. H. (1897), *Hume: with Helps to the Study of Berkeley*, London: Macmillan. *51*

Huxley, T. H. (1906), *Man's Place in Nature and other Essays*, London: J. M. Dent. *53*

Immelmann, K. (1969), 'Song development in the zebra finch and other estrildid finches', in R. A. Hinde (ed.), *Bird Vocalizations*, Cambridge University Press, pp. 61–74. *217*

Ince, L. P., Brucker, B. S. and Alba, A. (1978), 'Reflex conditioning in a spinal man', *Journal of Comparative and Physiological Psychology*, vol. 92, pp. 796–802. *67, 335*

Ingle, D. and Campbell, A. (1977), 'Interocular transfer of visual discriminations in goldfish after selected commissure lesions', *Journal of Comparative and Physiological Psychology*, vol. 91, pp. 327–35. *164*

Isaacson, R. L. (1974), *The Limbic System*, New York: Plenum Press. *159, 181, 184, 319*

Jacobson, S. and Trotanowski, J. Q. (1975), 'Corticothalamic neurons and thalamocortical terminal fields: an investigation in rat using Horseradish peridoxase and autoradiography', *Brain Research*, vol. 85, pp. 385–401. *128*

James, W. (1891), *The Principles of Psychology*, London: Macmillan. *64, 298*

Jenkins, H. M. and Harrison, R. H. (1960), 'Effect of discrimination training on auditory generalization', *Journal of Experimental Psychology*, vol. 59, pp. 246–53. *249*

Jerison, H. (1973), *Evolution of the Brain and Intelligence*, New York: Academic Press. *121, 127, 131–8, 146, 160, 180, 206*

Jerison, H. (1976), 'Principles of the evolution of brain and behaviour', in

R. B. Masterton, W. Hodos and H. Jerison (eds), *Evolution, Brain and Behaviour: Persistent Problems*, Hillsdale: Lawrence Erlbaum, pp. 23–45. *119*

Jolly, A. (1972), *The Evolution of Primate Behaviour*, New York: Macmillan. *205, 208, 218, 340*

Joncich, G. (1968), *The Sane Positivist: A Biography of Edward L. Thorndike*, Middletown, Connecticut: Wesleyan University Press. *65*

Jones, E. G. (1974), 'The anatomy of extrageniculostriate visual mechanisms', in F. O. Schmidt and F. G. Worden (eds), *The Neurosciences: Third Study Program*, London: MIT Press, pp. 215–28. *290*

Jones, R. M. (1978), *The New Psychology of Dreaming*, Harmondsworth: Penguin Books.

Jouvet, M. (1967), 'Neurophysiology of the states of sleep', *Physiological Reviews*, vol. 47, pp. 117–77. *225–9*

Jouvet, M. (1975), 'The function of dreaming: a neurophysiologist's point of view', in M. S. Gazzaniga (ed.), *Handbook of Psychobiology*, New York: Academic Press, pp. 499–527. *225–9*

Julian, B. and Richardson, A. M. (1968), 'Maze learning in the lizard *Dipsosaurus dorsalis*', *Journal of Biological Psychology*, vol. 10, pp. 4–9. *333*

Juorio, A. V. and Vogt, A. (1967), 'Monoamines and their metabolites in avian brain', *Journal of Physiology*, vol. 189, pp. 489–518. *128*

Kalmus, H. (1955), 'The discrimination by the nose of the dog of individual human odours and in particular the odours of twins', *British Journal of Animal Behaviour*, vol. 5, pp. 25–31. *246*

Kamil, A.C. and Balda, R.P. (1985), 'Cache recovery and spatial memory in Clark's nutcrackers (*Nucifraga columbiana*)', *Journal of Experimental Psychology: Animal Behavior Processes*, vol. 11, pp. 95–111. *313*

Kamil, A. C., Jones, T. B., Pietrewicz, A. and Mauldin, J. E. (1977), 'Positive transfer from successive reversal training to learning set in Blue Jays (*Cyanocitta cristata*)', *Journal of Comparative and Physiological Psychology*, vol. 91, pp. 79–86. *331*

Kandel, E. R. (1974), 'An invertebrate system for the cellular analyses of simple behaviours and their modifications', in F. O. Schmidt and F. G. Worden (eds), *The Neurosciences: Third Study Program*, London: MIT Press, pp. 347–70. *288*

Kant, I. (1914), *Kant's Critique of Judgement* trans. J. H. Bernard, 2nd revised edn, London: Macmillan. *31–4*

Kant, I. (1930), *Lectures on Ethics*, London: Methuen. *32*

Kappers, C. U. A. (1947), *Anatomie comparée du système nerveux*, Paris: Masson. *140*

Kappers, C. U. A., Huber, G. C. and Crosby, E. C. (1936), *The Comparative Anatomy of the Nervous System of Vertebrates, including Man*, New York: Macmillan. *126, 142, 146, 155–6, 160, 162–3, 182, 233*

Karten, H. J. (1979), 'Visual lemniscal pathways in birds', in A. M. Granda and J. H. Maxwell (eds), *Neural Mechanisms of Behaviour in the Pigeon*, New York: Plenum. *153, 158, 279, 283*

Keating, E. G., Kormann, L. A. and Horel, T. A. (1970), 'The behavioural effects of stimulating and ablating the reptilian amygdala (*Caiman Sklerops*)', *Physiology and Behaviour*, vol. 5, pp. 55–9. *332*

Kellogg, W. N. (1968), 'Communication and language in the home-raised chimpanzee', *Science*, vol. 162, pp. 423–7. *343, 353*

Kennedy. M. C. and Rubinson, K. (1977), 'Retinal projections in larval, transforming and adult sea lamprey, *Petromyzon marinus*', *Journal of Comparative Neurology*, vol. 171, pp. 465–80. *166*

Kimble, D. P. (1968), 'Hippocampus and internal inhibition', *Psychological Bulletin*, vol. 70, pp. 285–95. *322*

King, M. and Wilson, A. C. (1975), 'Evolution at two levels in humans and chimpanzees', *Science*, vol. 188, pp. 107–16. *339*

Kingsley, C. (1886), *The Water Babies*, London: Macmillan. *107*

Klein, M., Mitchel, F. and Jouvet, M. (1964), 'Etude polygraphique du sommeil des oiseaux', *Comptes Rendus des Séances de la Société de Biologie*, vol. 158, pp. 99–103. *231*

Kleitman, M. (1939), *Sleep and Wakefullness as Alternating Phases in the Cycle of Existence*, University of Chicago Press. *227*

Klinghammer, E. (1967), 'Factors influencing the choice of mate in altricial birds', in H. W. Stevenson, E. H. Hess and H. L. Rheingold (eds), *Early Behaviour: Comparative and Developmental Approaches*, New York: Wiley, pp. 5–42. *220*

Kluver, H. and Bucy, P. C. (1937), '"Psychic blindness" and other symptoms following bilateral temporal lobectomy in rhesus monkeys', *American Journal of Physiology*, vol. 119, pp. 352–3. *191, 332*

Kluver, H. and Bucy, P. C. (1939), 'Preliminary analysis of functions of the temporal lobe in monkeys', *Archives of Neurology and Psychiatry*, vol. 42, pp. 979–1000. *332*

Koffka, K. (1935), *Principles of Gestalt Psychology*, New York: Harcourt, Brace & World. *32*

Kohler, W. (1925), *The Mentality of Apes*, London: Kegan Paul, Trench & Trubner. *300, 343–6, 378*

Kohler, W. (1929), *Gestalt Psychology*, New York: Liveright. *32*

Konishi, M. (1963), 'The role of auditory feedback in the vocal behaviour of the domestic fowl', *Zeitschrift für Tierpsychologie*, vol. 20, pp. 349–67. *214*

Konishi, M. (1965), 'The role of auditory feedback in the control of vocalization in the white-crowned sparrow', *Zeitschrift für Tierpsychologie*, vol. 22, pp. 770–83. *214*

Konishi, M. and Nottehohm, F. (1969), 'Experimental studies in the ontogeny of avian vocalizations', in R. A. Hinde (ed.), *Bird Vocalizations*, Cambridge University Press, pp. 29–48. *215*

Konorski, J. (1967), *Integrative Activity of the Brain*, University of Chicago Press. *99–100, 305*

Kornhuber, H. H. (1974), 'Cerebral cortex, cerebellum and basal ganglia: an introduction', in F. O. Schmidt and F. G. Worden (eds), *The Neurosciences: Third Study Program*, London: MIT Press, pp. 267–80. *181*

Krebs, J. R. and Davies, N. B. (eds) (1978), *Behavioural Econoly: an Evolutionary Approach*, Oxford: Blackwell Scientific Publications. *250, 298, 313*

Kristensson, K. and Olsson, Y. (1974), 'Retrograde transport of horseradish peridoxase in transected axons. I. Time relations between transport and induction of chromatolysis', *Brain Research*, vol. 79, pp. 101–9. *128*

Kruger, L. and Stein, B. E. (1973), 'Primordial sense organs and the evolution of sensory systems', in E. C. Carterette and M. P. Friedman (eds), *Handbook of Perception*, vol. 3, New York and London: Academic Press, pp. 63–87. *267*

Krushinsky, L. V. (1962), *Animal Behaviour*, trans. B. Haigh, New York: Consultants Bureau Enterprises. *299–302*

Krushinsky, L. V. (1965), 'Solution of elementary logical problems by animals on the basis of extrapolation', in N. Wiener and J. P. Shade (eds), *Progress in Brain Research*, vol. 17, pp. 280–308. *299–302*

Kuffler, S. W. (1953), 'Discharge patterns and functional organisation of mammalian retina', *Journal of Neurophysiology*, vol. 16, pp. 37–68. *129, 268*

Kuhlenbeck, H. (1967), *The Central Nervous System of Vertebrates*, vol. 2, *Invertebrates and the Origin of Vertebrates*, Basel: Karger. *142–4*

Kuhlenbeck, H. (1970), *The Central Nervous System of Vertebrates*, vol. 3, Part I, *Structural Elements: Biology of Nervous Tissue*, Basel: Karger. *142*

Kummer, H. and Goodall, J. (1985), 'Conditions of innovative behaviour in primates', *Philosophical Transactions of the Royal Society*, B, vol. 308, pp. 203–14. *208*

Lack, D. (1947), *Darwin's Finches*, Cambridge University Press. *124*

Ladieu, G. (1944), 'The effect of length of the delay interval upon delayed alternation in the albino rat', *Journal of Comparative Psychology*, vol. 37, pp. 273–86. *292*

Lamendella, J. (1977), 'The limbic system in human communication', in H. Whitaker and H. A. Whitaker (eds), *Studies in Neurolinguistics*, vol. 3, New York: Academic Press, pp. 157–222. *159*

Lang, J. W. (1976), 'Amphibious behaviour of *Alligator mississippiensis*: roles of a circadian rhythm and light', *science*, vol. 191, pp. 575–7. *232*

Lashley, K. S. (1929), *Brain Mechanisms and Intelligence*, University of Chicago Press. *100*

Lashley, K. S. (1950), 'In search of the engram', in *Symposia of the Society of Experimental Biology* (no. IV), Cambridge University Press, pp. 454–82. *100, 318*

Lavail, J. H. and Lavail, M. M. (1972), 'Retrograde axonal transport in the central nervous system, *Science*, vol. 176, pp. 1416–17. *128*

Lawrence, D. H. (1949), 'Acquired distinctiveness of cues: I. Transfer between discriminations on the basis of familiarity with the stimulus', *Journal of Experimental Psychology*, vol. 39, pp. 770–84. *247*

Lawrence, D. H. (1950), 'Acquired distinctiveness of cues: II. Selective association in a constant stimulus situation', *Journal of Experimental Psychology*, vol. 40, pp. 175–88. *247*

Leakey, L. S. B., Tobias, P. V. and Napier, J. R. (1964), 'A new species of homo from Olduvai Gorge', *Nature*, vol. 202, pp. 7–9. *137*

Leakey, R. E. F. (1973), 'Australopithacines and Hominines: a summary of the evidence from the early Pleistocene of Eastern Africa', *Symposium of the Zoological Society of London*, vol. 33, pp. 53–69. *137*

Ledoux, J. E., Wilson, D. H. and Gazzaniga, M. W. (1977), 'Manipulospatial aspects of cerebral lateralization: clues for the origin of lateralization', *Neuropsychologia*, vol. 15, pp. 743–50.

Lehman, R. A. W. (1978), 'The handedness of Rhesus monkeys: I', *Neuropsychologia*, vol. 16, pp. 33–42. *168*

Leibniz, G. W. (1896), *New Essays Concerning Human Understanding*, London: Macmillan. *24–5*

Lemay, M. (1976), 'Morphological cerebral asymmetries of modern man, fossil man, and non-human primates', *Annals of the New York Academy of Sciences*, vol. 280, pp. 349–66. *171*

Lemay, M. and Geschwind, N. (1975), 'Hemispheric differences in the brains of Great Apes', *Brain, Behaviour and Evolution*, vol. 11, pp. 48–52.

Lenneberg, E. H. (1967), *Biological Foundations of Language*, New York: Wiley. *214, 380*

Lennie, P. (1980), 'Parallel visual pathways: a review', *Vision Research*, vol. 20, pp. 561–94. *268*

Leonard, R. B., Coggeshall, R. E. and Willis, W. D. (1978), 'A documentation of an age related increase in neuronal and axonal numbers in the stingray', *Journal of Comparative Neurology*, vol. 179, pp. 13–22. *141*

Levin, M. E. (1979), *Metaphysics and the Mind-Body Problem*, Oxford: Clarendon Press. *18*

Levine, B. A. (1974), 'Effects of drive and incentive magnitude on serial discrimination reversal learning in pigeons and chickens', *Journal of Comparative and Physiological Psychology*, vol. 86, pp. 730–5. *248*

Lévi-Strauss, C. (1962), *The Savage Mind*, London: Weidenfeld & Nicholson. *207*

Levy, J. (1969), 'Possible basis for the evolution lateral specialization of the human brain', *Nature*, vol. 224, 614–15. *161, 170–1*

Levy, J. (1977), 'The mammalian brain and the adaptive advantage of cerebral asymmetry', *Annals of the New York Academy of Sciences*, vol. 299, pp. 264–72. *161*

Lieberman, P. (1975), *On the Origins of Language*, New York: Macmillan.

Linden, E. (1976), *Apes, Men and Language*, Harmondsworth: Penguin Books. *354, 365*

Llinás, R. (1970), 'Neuronal operations in cerebellar transactions', in F. O. Schmitt (ed.), *The Neurosciences: Second Study Program*, New York: Rockefeller University Press, pp. 409–26. *183*

Locke, J. (1959), *An Essay Concerning Human Understanding*, vols I and II, New York: Dover. *20–5*

Long, D. M., Bodenheimer, T. S., Hartmann, J. F. and Klatzo, I. (1968), 'Ultrastructural features of the shark brain', *American Journal of Anatomy*, vol. 118, pp. 375–90. *144*

Lorenz, K. (1952), *King Solomon's Ring*, trans. M. K. Wilson, London: Methuen. *286*

Lorenz, K. (1966), *On Aggression*, trans. M. K. Wilson, London: Methuen. *32, 99, 219–21*

Lubbock, J. (1884), 'Teaching animals to converse', *Nature*, pp. 547–8. *50*

Lubow, R. E. (1974), 'Higher-order concept formation in the pigeon', *Journal of the Experimental Analysis of Behaviour*, vol. 21, pp. 475–83. *259*

Luria, A. R. (1970), *Traumatic Aphasia: Its Syndromes, Psychology and Treatment*, The Hague: Mouton. *379*

McFarland, D. J. (1976), 'Form and function in the temporal organization of behaviour', in P. P. G. Bateson and R. A. Hinde (eds), *Growing Points in Ethology*, Cambridge University Press, pp. 55–93. *190*

MacFarlane, D. A. (1930), 'The role of kinesis in maze learning', *University of California Publications in Psychology*, vol. 4, pp. 277–305. *77*

Mackay, D. A. and Underwood, A. J. (1977), 'Experimental studies on homing in the intertidal patellid limpet *Cellana tramoserica* (Sowerby)', *Oecologia*, vol. 30, pp. 215–37. *199*

Mackintosh, N. J. (1974), *The Psychology of Animal Learning*, London: Academic Press. *72, 81, 86–7, 102–4, 247–9, 259, 314*

Mackintosh, N. J. (1983), *Conditioning and Association Learning*, Oxford, Clarendon Press. *112, 222, 315*

Mackintosh, N. J., Wilson, B. and Boakes, R. A. (1985), 'Differences in mechanisms of intelligence among vertebrates', *Philosophical Transactions of the Royal Society, B*, vol. 308, pp. 53–63. *216*

Macphail, E. M. (1966), 'Self-stimulation in pigeons: the problem of priming', *Psychonomic Science*, vol. 5, pp. 7–8. *224*

Macphail, E. M. (1975), 'The role of the avian hyperstriatal complex in learning', in P. Wright, P. G. Caryl, and D. M. Vowles (eds), *Neural and Endocrine Aspects of Behaviour in Birds*, Amsterdam: Elsevier, pp. 139–62. *158, 186, 331*

Macphail, E. M. (1982), *Brain and Intelligence in Vertebrates*, Oxford, Clarendon Press. *126, 337*

Maier, N. R. F. and Schneirla, J. C. (1935), *Principles of Animal Psychology*, New York: McGraw-Hill. *292*

Marler, P. (1970), 'A comparative approach to vocal learning: song development in white-crowned sparrows', *Journal of Comparative and Physiological Psychology Monograph*, vol. 71, no. 2, part 2, pp. 1–25. *215–6*

Marr, D. (1970), 'A theory for cerebral neocortex', *Proceedings of the Royal Society*, Series B, vol. 176, pp. 161–234.

Marr, D. (1976), 'Early processing of visual information', *Philosophical Transactions of the Royal Society of London*, Series B, vol. 275. pp. 483–524. *274–5*

Marr, D. (1982), *Vision*, San Francisco, W. S. Freeman. *274*

Marshall, J. J. Jr. and Marshall, E. R. (1976), 'Gibbons and their territorial songs', *Science*, vol. 193, pp. 235–7.

Martin, R. D. (1973), 'Comparative anatomy and primate systematics', *Symposia of the Zoological Society of London*, no. 33, pp. 301–37. *123*

Marx, K. (1971), *Marx: Early Texts*, Oxford: Basil Blackwell. *54*

Marx, K. and Engels, F. (1968), *Selected Works*, Moscow: Progress

Publishers. *54*

Maser, J. D. and Gallup, G. G. Jr. (1977), 'Tonic immobility and related phenomena: a partially annotated, tricentennial bibliography', *Psychological Record*, vol. 27, pp. 177–217. *234*

Masterton, R. B. and Glendenning, K. K. (1979), 'Phylogeny of the vertebrate sensory systems', in R. B. Masterton (ed.), *Handbook of Behavioural Neurology*, vol. I, *Sensory Integration*, New York: Plenum Press, pp. 1–38. *267–9*

Mathews, G. V. T. (1955), *Bird Navigation*, Cambridge University Press. *198*

Maturana, H. R. and Frenck, S. (1963), 'Directional movement and horizontal edge detectors in the pigeon retina', *Science*, vol. 142, pp. 977–9. *273*

Mechner, F. (1958), 'Probability relations within response sequences under ratio reinforcement', *Journal of the Experimental Analysis of Behaviour*, vol. 1, pp. 109–21. *90*

Meck, W. H., Church, R. M. and Olton, D. S. (1984), 'Hippocampus, time, and memory', *Behavioural Neuroscience*, vol. 98, pp. 3–22. *326*

Medin, D. L. and Davis, R. T. (1974), 'Memory', in A. M. Schrier and F. Stollnitz (eds), *Behavior of Nonhuman Primates: Modern Research Trends*, vol. 5, pp. 1–47.

Medin, D. L., Roberts, W. A. and Davis, R. T. (1976), *Processes of Animal Memory*, Hillsdale: Lawrence Erlbaum. *190, 292*

Meddis, R. (1975), 'On the function of sleep', *Animal Behaviour*, vol. 23, pp. 676–91. *225, 231*

Menzel, E. W. (1972), 'Spontaneous invention of ladders in a group of young chimpanzees', *Folia Primatologica*, vol. 17, pp. 87–106. *346*

Menzel, E. W. (1973), 'Chimpanzee spatial memory organization', *Science*, vol. 182, pp. 943–5. *295, 346*

Menzel, E. W. (1978), 'Cognitive mapping in chimpanzees', in S. H. Hulse, H. Fowler and W. K. Honig (eds), *Cognitive Processes in Animal Behaviour*, Hillsdale: Lawrence Erlbaum, pp. 375–422. *299, 344–7, 378*

Miceli, D., Peyrichoux, J. and Repérant, J. (1975), 'The retino-thalamo-hyperstriatal pathway in the pigeon (*Columbia livia*)', *Brain Research*, vol. 100, pp. 125–31.

Midgley, M. (1980), *Beast and Man*, London: Methuen. *32*

Miles, F. A. (1970), 'Centrigual effects in the avian retina', *Science*, vol. 170, pp. 992–5. *268*

Miles, R. C. (1965), 'Discrimination-learning sets', in A. M. Schrier, H. F. Harlow and F. Stollnitz (eds), *Behaviour of Nonhuman Primates*, vol. 1, pp. 51–95. *314–15*

Miller, B. F. and Lund, R. D. (1975), 'The pattern of retinotectal connections in albino rats can be modified by fetal surgery', *Brain Research*, Vol. 91, pp. 119–25. *142*

Miller, R. R. and Springer, A. D. (1973), 'Amnesia, consolidation and retrieval', *Psychological Review*, vol. 80, pp. 69–79. *319*

Mills, W. (1899), 'The nature of animal intelligence and the methods of investigating it', *Psychological Review*, vol. 6, pp. 262–74. *61–2*

Milner, B. (1970), 'Memory and the medial temporal regions of the brain', in K. H. Pribram and D. E. Broadbent (eds), *Biology of Memory*, New York: Academic Press, pp. 29–50. *321*

Milner, B., Corkin, S. and Teuber, H.-L. (1968), 'Further analysis of the hippocampal amnesic syndrome: 14 year follow-up study of H. M.', *Neuropsychologia*, vol. 6, pp. 215–34. *320*

Mishkin, M. and Delacour, J. (1975), 'An analysis of short-term visual memory in the monkey', *Journal of Experimental Psychology: Animal Behavior Processes*, vol. 1, pp. 326–34. *311*

Mitchell, G. D. (1969), 'Paternalistic behaviour in primates', *Psychological Bulletin*, vol. 71, pp. 399–417. *218*

Monod, J. (1972), *Chance and Necessity*, London: Collins. *121*

Morgan, C. L. (1894), *An Introduction to Comparative Psychology*, London: Walter Scott. *48, 56*

Morgan, C. L. (1896), *Habit and Instinct*, London: Edward Arnold. *59–60*

Morgan, M. J., Fitch, M. D., Holman, J. G. and Lea, S. E. G. (1976), 'Pigeons learn the concept of an "A"', *Perception*, vol. 5, pp. 57–66. *254*

Mounin, G. (1976), 'Language, communication and chimpanzees', *Current Anthropology*, vol. 17, pp. 1–7. *372, 376*

Mrosovsky, N. (1971), *Hibernation and the Hypothalamus*, New York: Appleton-Century-Crofts. *234*

Mulligan, T. A. (1966), 'Singing behaviour and its development in the song sparrow, *Melospiza melodia*', *University of California Publications in Zoology*, vol. 81, pp. 1–76. *214*

Murton, R. K. (1971), 'The significance of a specific search image in the feeding behaviour of the wood pigeon', *Behaviour*, vol. 40, pp. 10–42. *250*

Napier, J. R. (1960), 'Studies of the hands of living primates', *Proceedings of the Zoological Society of London*, vol. 134, pp. 647–57. *203*

Napier, J. R. and Napier, P. H. (1967), *A Handbook of Living Primates*, London: Academic Press. *340*

Nauta, W. J. H. and Gygax, P. A. (1954), 'Silver impregnation of degenerating axons in the central nervous system: a modified technique', *Brain Technology*, vol. 29, pp. 91–3. *127*

Nauta, W. J. H. and Karten, H. J. (1970), 'A general profile of the vertebrate brain with sidelights on the ancestry of cerebral cortex', in F. O. Schmidt (ed.), *The Neurosciences: Second Study Program*, New York: Rockefeller University Press, pp. 7–26. *153, 158, 175–6, 181, 188, 278, 283*

Nebes, R. D. (1974), 'Hemispheric specialization in commmissurotomized man', *Psychological Bulletin*, vol. 81, pp. 1–14.

Neisser, U. (1967), *Cognitive Psychology*, New York: Appleton-Century-Crofts. *189, 251*

Neisser, U. (1976), *Cognition and Reality*, San Francisco: W. H. Freeman. *189, 244*

Nicolai, J. (1959), 'Familientradion in der Gesangsentwicklung des Gimpels (*Pyrrhula pyrrhula* L.)', *Journal für Ornithologie*, vol. 100, pp. 39–46. *216*

Noble, G. K. (1931), *The Biology of the Amphibia*, New York: McGraw-Hill. *211*

Norberg, R. A. (1977), 'Occurrence and independent evolution of bilateral ear asymmetry in owls and implications on owl taxonomy', *Philosophical Transactions of the Royal Society of London*, Series B, vol. 280. pp. 375–408. *173*

Northcutt, R. G. and Butler, A. B. (1976), 'Retinofugal pathways in the Longnose Gar, Lepisosteus ossais *(Linnaeus)*', *Journal of Comparative Neurology*, vol. 166, pp. 1–16. *166*

Norton-Griffiths, M. (1969), 'The organization, control and development of parental feeding in the oyster catcher', *Behaviour*, vol. 34, pp. 55–114. *204*

Nottebohm, F. (1971), 'Neural lateralization of vocal control in a passerine bird. I. Song', *Journal of Experimental Zoology*, vol. 177, pp. 229–62. *172*

Nottebohm, F. (1976), 'Phonation in the orange-winged amazon parrot, *Amazona amazonica*', *Journal of Comparative Physiology*, Series A, vol. 108, pp. 157–70. *172*

Nottebohm, F. (1977), 'Asymmetries in neural control of vocalization in the canary', in S. Harnad, R. W. Doty, L. Goldstein, T. Jaynes and G. Krauthamer (eds), *Lateralization in the Nervous System*, London: Academic Press, pp. 23–44. *172–3, 214*

Nottebohm, F. (1979), 'Origins and mechanisms in the establishment of cerebral dominance', in M. S. Gazzaniga (ed.), *Handbook of Behavioural Neurology*, vol. 2, *Neuropsychology*, New York: Plenum, pp. 295–344. *172*

Nottebohm, F. and Nottebohm, M. E. (1976), 'Left hypoglossal dominance in the control of canary and white-crowned sparrow song', *Journal of Comparative Physiology*, vol. 108, pp. 171–92.

Nottebohm, F., Stokes, M. M. Q., Leonard, C. M. (1976), 'Central control of song in the canary *Serinus canaria*', *Journal of Comparative Neurology*, vol. 165, pp. 456–86. *172*

Notterman, J. M. and Mintz, D. E. (1965), *Dynamics of Response*, New York: Wiley. *88*

Oakley, D. A. (1979a), 'Cerebral cortex and adaptive behaviour', in D. A. Oakley and H. C. Plotkin (eds), *Brain, Behaviour and Evolution*, London: Methuen, pp. 154–88. *335*

Oakley, D. A. (1979b), 'Instrumental reversal learning and subsequent Fixed Ratio performance on simple and GO-NO GO schedules in neodecorticate rabbits', *Physiological Psychology*, vol. 7, pp. 29–42. *336.*

Oakley, D. A. and Russell, I. S. (1977), 'Subcortical storage of Pavlovian conditioning in the rabbit', *Physiology and Behaviour*, vol. 18, pp. 931–7. *336*

Oakley, D. A. and Russell, I. S. (1978), 'Performance of neodecorticated rabbits in a free-operant situation', *Physiology and Behaviour*, vol. 20, pp. 157–70. *336*

Oakley, K. P. (1972), *Man the Toolmaker*, London: Trustees of the British Museum (Natural History). *137*

O'Donald, P. (1980), *Genetic Models of Sexual Selection*, Cambridge University Press. *44*

O'Keefe, J. and Nadel, L. (1978), *The Hippocampus as a Cognitive Map*, Oxford: Clarendon Press. *199, 322, 326, 381*

Olds, J. and Milner, P. (1954), 'Positive reinforcement produced by electrical stimulation of septal area and other regions of rat brain', *Journal of Comparative and Physiological Psychology*, vol. 47, pp. 419–27. *129, 224*

Olds, M. E. and Olds, J. (1963), 'Approach-avoidance analysis of the rat diencephalon', *Journal of Comparative Neurology*, vol. 120, pp. 259–95. *129, 224*

Olton, D. S. (1978), 'Characteristics of spatial memory', in S. H. Hulse, H. Fowler and W. H. Honig (eds), *Cognitive Processes in Animal Behaviour*, Hillsdale: Lawrence Erlbaum, pp. 341–73. *78, 297–8, 315*

Olton, D. S. (1979), 'Mazes, maps and memory', *American Psychologist*, vol. 34, pp. 583–96. *78*

Olton, D. S. and Samuelson, R. J. (1976), 'Remembrance of places passed: Spatial memory in rats', *Journal of Experimental Psychology: Animal Behaviour Processes*, vol. 2, pp. 97–116. *297*

Olton, D. S. and Schlosberg, P. (1978), 'Food-searching strategies in young rats: win-shift predominates over win-stay', *Journal of Comparative Physiological Psychology*, vol. 92, pp. 609–18.

Olton, D. S., Becker, J. T. and Handelman, G. F. (1979), 'Hippocampus, space and memory', *Behavioural and Brain Sciences*, vol. 2, pp. 313–65.

Olton, D. S., Collison, C. and Werz, W. A. (1977), 'Spatial memory and radial arm maze performance by rats', *Learning and Motivation*, vol. 8, pp. 289–314. *297*

Opdam, P., Kemali, M. and Nieuwenhuys, R. (1976), 'Topological analysis of the brain stem of the frogs *Rana esculenta* and *Rana catesbeiana*', *Journal of Comparative Neurology*, vol. 165, pp. 307–32. *233*

Oppenheim, R. W. (1968), 'Color preferences in the pecking response of newly hatched ducks (*Anas Platyrhynchos*)', *Journal of Comparative and Physiological Psychology Monograph Supplement*, vol. 66, no. 3, part 2, pp. 1–17. *213*

Oswald, I. (1962), *'Sleeping and Waking: Physiology and Psychology'*, Amsterdam: Elsevier. *225–31*

Overman, W. H. and Doty, R. W. (1980), 'Prolonged visual memory in macaques and man', *Neuroscience*, vol. 5, pp. 1825–31. *311*

Overmeier, J. B. and Curnow, P. F. (1969), 'Classical conditioning, pseudoconditioning and sensitization in "normal" and forebrainless goldfish', *Journal of Comparative and Physiological Psychology*, vol. 68, pp. 193–8. *334*

Paradis, M. (1977), 'Bilingualism and aphasia', in H. Whitaker and H. A. Whitaker (eds), *Studies in Neurolinguistics*, vol. 3, New York: Academic Press, pp. 65–121. *173*

Pasnak, R. (1979), 'Acquisition of prerequisites to conservation by macaques', *Journal of Experimental Psychology: Animal Behaviour Processes*, vol. 5, pp. 194–210. *349–51*

Passingham, R. E. (1975), 'The brain and intelligence', *Brain, Behaviour and Evolution*, vol. 11, pp. 1–15. *126*

Pastore, N. (1954), 'Discrimination learning in the canary', *Journal of*

Comparative and Physiological Psychology, vol. 47, pp. 389–90. *261*

Patterson, F. G. (1978), 'The gestures of a gorilla: language acquisition in another pongid', *Brain and Language*, vol. 5, pp. 72–99. *206, 356, 371, 374*

Pavlov, I. P. (1927), *Conditioned Reflexes*, New York: Dover. *65–73, 305*

Pavlov, I. P. (1955), *Selected Works*, Moscow: Foreign Languages Publishing House. *65–73, 347*

Pearlman, A. L. and Hughes, C. P. (1976), 'Functional role of efferents to the avian retina', *Journal of Comparative Neurology*, vol. 166, pp. 111–22.

Pearson, R. (1972), *The Avian Brain*, London: Academic Press. *140, 163, 174, 199*

Pearson, R. and Pearson, L. (1976), *The Vertebrate Brain*, London: Academic Press. *128, 144, 154, 163*

Penfield, W. (1966), 'Speech, perception and the uncommitted cortex', in J. C. Eccles (ed.), *Brain and Conscious Experience*, New York: Springer-Verlag, pp. 217–37. *189*

Penfield, W. and Rasmussen, T. (1952), *The Cerebral Cortex of Man*, New York: Macmillan. *107*

Penfield, W. and Roberts, L. (1959), *Speech and Brain Mechanisms*, Princeton University Press. *107, 129*

Petersen, M. R., Beecher, M. D., Zoloth, S. R., Moody, D. and Stebbins, W. L. (1978), 'Neural lateralization of species-specific vocalizations by Japanese Macaques (Macaca fuscata)', *Science*, vol. 202, pp. 324–7. *173*

Peterson, E. (1980), 'Behavioural studies of telencephalic function in reptiles', in S. O. E. Ebbesson (ed.), *Comparative Neurology of the Telencephalon*, New York: Plenum Press, pp. 343–88. *333*

Peterson, G. M. (1934), 'Mechanisms of handedness in the rat', *Comparative Psychology Monographs*, vol. 9, pp. 1–67. *168*

Petitto, L. A. and Seidenberg, M. S. (1979), 'On the evidence for linguistic abilities in signing apes', *Brain and Language*, vol. 8, pp. 162–83. *372*

Pettigrew, T. D. and Konishi, M. (1976), 'Neurons selective for orientation and binocular disparity in the visual Wulst of the barn owl (*Tyto Alba*)', *Science*, vol. 193, pp. 675–8. *124, 158, 166*

Pfungst, O. (1911), *Clever Hans, The Horse of Mr von Osten*, New York: Holt (republished in 1965 by Holt, Rinehart & Winston). *372*

Phillips, R. E. (1964), '"Wildness" in the mallard duck: effects of brain lesions and stimulation on "escape behaviour" and reproduction', *Journal of Comparative Neurology*, vol. 122, pp. 139–55. *191, 332*

Piaget, J. (1971), *Biology and Knowledge*, Edinburgh University Press. *95–7, 381*

Piaget, J. and Inhelder, B. (1969), *The Psychology of the Child*, London: Routledge & Kegan Paul. *348, 352*

Pilbeam, P. (1972), *The Ascent of Man*, London: Macmillan. *126, 134, 205*

Place, U. T. (1956), 'Is consciousness a brain process?', *British Journal of Psychology*, vol. 47, pp. 44–51.

Plotnik, R. (1968), 'Changes in social behaviour of squirrel monkeys after anterior temporal lobectomy', *Journal of Comparative and Physiological Psychology*, vol. 66, pp. 369–77. *332*

Poliakov, G. I. (1964), 'Development and complication of the cortical part of the coupling mechanism in the evolution of vertebrates', *Journal für Hirnforschung*, vol. 7, pp. 253–73. *155*

Poole, J. and Lander, D. G. (1971), 'The pigeon's concept of pigeon', *Psychonomic Science*, vol. 25, pp. 157–8. *257*

Pooley, A. C. (1977), 'Nest opening response of the Nile crocodile *Crocodylus niloticus*', *Journal of Zoology*, London, vol. 182, pp. 17–26. *211*

Popper, K. R. (1959), *The Logic of Scientific Discovery*, London: Hutchinson. *27*

Popper, K. R. and Eccles, J. C. (1977), *The Self and Its Brain*, Berlin: Springer International. *11, 16–19, 143, 383*

Portmann, A. and Stingelin, W. (1961), 'The central nervous system', in A. J. Marshall (ed.), *The Biology and Comparative Physiology of Birds*, vol. 2, London: Academic Press, pp. 1–36. *126*

Premack, D. (1970), 'A functional analysis of language', *Journal of the Experimental Analysis of Behaviour*, vol. 14, pp. 107–25. *357*

Premack, D. (1971), 'Language in chimpanzee?', *Science*, vol. 172, pp. 808–22. *357*

Premack, D. (1976), *Intelligence in Ape and Man*, Hillsdale: Lawrence Erlbaum. *357–64, 372–3, 380*

Putnam, S. J., Megirian, D. and Manning, J. W. (1968), 'Marsupial interhemispheric relation', *Journal of Comparative Neurology*, vol. 132, pp. 227–34. *163*

Pyke, G. H., Pulliam, H. R. and Charnov, E. L. (1977), 'Optimal foraging. A selective review of theory and tests', *Quarterly Review of Biology*, vol. 52, pp. 137–54. *313*

Quinton, A. (1973), *The Nature of Things*, London: Routledge & Kegan Paul. *18*

Quiring, D. P. (1950), *The Functional Anatomy of the Vertebrates*, New York: McGraw-Hill. *138*

Radinsky, L. B. (1976), 'Later mammal radiations', in R. B. Hasterton, M. E. Bittesman, C. B. G. Campbell and N. Hotton (eds), *Evolution of Brain and Behaviour in Vertebrates*, Hillsdale, N. J.: Lawrence Erlbaum, pp. 227–43. *121*

Ramon-Moliner, E. and Nauta, W. J. H. (1966), 'The iso-dendritic core of the brain-stem', *Journal of Comparative Neurology*, vol. 126, pp. 311–35. *148*

Ramsay, A. O. and Hess, E. H. (1954), 'A laboratory approach to the study of imprinting', *Wilson Bulletin*, vol. 66, pp. 196–206. *212*

Rawlins, J. N. P. and Tsaltas, E. (1983), 'The hippocampus, time and working memory', *Behavioural Brain Research*, vol. 10, pp. 233–62. *326*

Rayner, K. and Bertera, J. A. (1979), 'Reading without a fovea', *Science*, vol. 206, pp. 468–9. *270*

Razran, G. (1971), *Mind in Evolution: An East-West Synthesis*, Boston: Houghton-Mifflin. *145*

Redshaw, M. (1978), 'Cognitive development in human and gorilla infants', *Journal of Human Evolution*, vol. 7, pp. 133–41. *97, 206, 341*

Rensch, B. (1959), *Evolution above the Species Level*, London: Methuen. *121, 132–40, 195–7*

Réperant, J. and Lemire, M. (1976), 'Retinal projections in Cyprinid fishes: a degeneration and autoradiographic study', *Brain, Behaviour and Evolution*, vol. 13, pp. 34–57. *277, 283*

Rescorla, R. A. (1979), 'Aspects of the reinforcer learned in second-order Pavlovian conditioning', *Journal of Experimental Psychology: Animal Behaviour Processes*, vol. 5, pp. 79–95. *72, 103, 252*

Rescorla, R. A. (1980), *Pavlovian Second-Order Conditioning*, Hillsdale: Lawrence Erlbaum. *103, 252*

Revzin, A. M. (1969), 'A specific visual projection area in the hyperstriatum of the pigeon', *Brain Research*, vol. 15, pp. 246–49. *158, 283*

Reynolds, G. S. (1961), 'Attention in the pigeon', *Journal of the Experimental Analysis of Behaviour*, vol. 4, pp. 203–8. *249*

Riss, W. (1968a), 'Overview of the design of the central nervous system and the problem of natural units of behaviour', *Brain, Behaviour and Evolution*, vol. 1, pp. 124–31. *122, 174, 179*

Riss, W. (1968b), 'Overview of the design of the central nervous system and the problem of natural units of behaviour. III The basic dichotomous reflex organization', *Brain, Behaviour and Evolution*, vol. 1, pp. 293–304. *222–3*

Riss, W., Pedersen, R. A., Jakeway, J. S. and Ware, C. B. (1972), 'Levels of function in the vertebrate thalamus', *Brain, Behaviour and Evolution*, vol. 6, pp. 26–41. *154, 172*

Roberts, S. and Church, R. M. (1978), 'Control of an internal clock', *Journal of Experimental Psychology: Animal Behaviour Processes*, vol. 4, pp. 318–37. *91*

Roberts, W. A. and Grant, D. S. (1976), 'Studies of short-term memory in the pigeon using the delayed matching to sample procedure', in D. L. Medin, W. A. Roberts and R. T. Davis (eds), *Processes of Animal Memory*, Hillsdale: Lawrence Erlbaum, pp. 79–112. *302–3, 332*

Roberts, W. A. and Grant, D. S. (1978), 'Interaction of sample and comparison stimuli in delayed matching to sample with the pigeon', *Journal of Experimental Psychology: Animal Behaviour Processes*, vol. 4, pp. 68–82. *303*

Roberts, W. W. and Berquist, E. H. (1968), 'Attack elicited by hypothalamic stimulation of cats reared in social isolation', *Journal of Comparative and Physiological Psychology*, vol. 66, pp. 590–5. *205*

Rodiek, R. W. (1973), *The Vertebrate Retina*, San Francisco: W. H. Freeman. *267–8*

Roitblat, A. L., Bever, T. G. and Terrace, H. S. (eds) (1984), *Animal Cognition*, Hillsdale, N. J. Lawrence Erlbaum. *81*

Rojas-Ramirez, J. and Tauber, E. S. (1970), 'Paradoxical sleep in two species of avian predator (*Falconiformes*)', *Science*, vol. 167, pp. 1754–5. *231*

Romanes, G. J. (1883), *Mental Evolution in Animals*, London: Kegan Paul, Trench. *48–51*

Romanes, G. J. (1886), *Animal Intelligence* 4th edn, London: Kegan Paul, Trench. *48–51*

Romanes, G. J. (1888), *Mental Evolution in Man*, London: Kegan Paul, Trench. *49–51*

Romer, A. S. (1949), *The Vertebrate Body*, Philadelphia: Saunders. *145, 200, 326*

Romer, A. S. (1962), *The Vertebrate Body*, 3rd edn, Philadelphia: Saunders. *149, 152–3*

Romer, A. S. and Parsons, T. S. (1977), *The Vertebrate Body*, 5th edn, Philadelphia: Saunders. *145*

Rose, S. (1976), *The Conscious Brain*, revised edn, Harmondsworth: Penguin Books. *55, 152–3*

Rosvold, H. E., Mirsky, A. F. and Pribram, K. H. (1954), 'Influence of amydalectomy on social behaviour in monkeys', *Journal of Comparative and Physiological Psychology*, vol. 47, pp. 173–9. *191, 332*

Ruggiero, F. T. and Flagg, S. F. (1976), 'Do animals have memory?', in D. L. Medin, W. A. Roberts and R. T. Davis (eds), *Processes of Animal Memory*, Hillsdale: Lawrence Erlbaum, pp. 1–20. *291–2*

Rumbaugh, D. (ed.) (1977), *Language Learning by a Chimpanzee: The LANA Project*, New York: Academic Press. *366, 379*

Rumbaugh, D. M. and von Glaserfeld, E. (1973), 'Reading and sentence completion by a chimpanzee', *Science*, vol. 182, pp. 731–3. *366*

Russell, B. (1946), *The History of Western Philosophy*, London: Allen & Unwin. *56*

Russell, B. (1959), *My Philosophical Development*, London: Allen & Unwin. *18*

Russell, I. S. (1971), 'Neurological basis of complex learning', *British Medical Bulletin*, vol. 27, pp. 278–87. *67*

Ryle, G. (1949), *The Concept of Mind*, London: Hutchinson. *12*

Sands, S. F., Urcuioli, P. J., Wright, A. A. and Santiago, H. C. (1984), 'Serial position effects and rehearsal in primate visual memory', in H. L. Roitblat, T. G. Bever and H. S. Terrace (eds), *Animal Cognition*, Hillsdale, Erlbaum, pp. 375–88. *311*

Sarnat, H. B. and Netsky, M. G. (1974), *Evolution of the Nervous System*, New York: Oxford University Press. *142, 162*

Savage, G. E. (1968), 'Function of the forebrain in the memory system of fish', in D. J. Ingle (ed.), *The Central Nervous System and Fish Behaviour*, University of Chicago Press, pp. 127–38. *334*

Savage, G. E. (1971), 'Behavioural effects of electrical stimulation of the telencephalon of the goldfish, *Carassium auratus*', *Animal Behaviour*, vol. 19, pp. 661–8.

Savage, G. E. (1980), 'The fish telencephalon and its relation to learning', in S. O. E. Ebbesson (ed.), *Comparative Neurology of the Telencephalon*, New York: Plenum Press, pp. 129–74. *334*

Savage-Rumbaugh, E. S. and Rumbaugh, D. M. (1978), 'Symbolization, language and chimpanzees: A theoretical reevaluation based on initial language acquisition processes in four young *Pan troglodytes*', *Brain and Language*, vol. 6, pp. 265–300. *366*

Savage-Rumbaugh, E. S., Rumbaugh, D. M. and Boysen, S. (1978a), 'Linguistically mediated tool use and exchange by chimpanzees (*Pan troglodytes)*', *Behavioural and Brain Sciences*, vol. 1, pp. 539–54. *365–6, 368–9, 372–3*

Savage-Rumbaugh, E. S., Rumbaugh, D. M. and Boysen, S. (1978b), 'Symbolic communication between two chimpanzees', *Science*, vol. 201, pp. 641–4. *366–7, 373*

Savage-Rumbaugh, E. S., Rumbaugh, D. M., Smith, S. T. and Lawson, J. (1980), 'Reference: the linguistic essential', *Science*, vol. 210, pp. 922–4. *369, 372*

Savage-Rumbaugh, E. S., Sevik, R. A., Rumbaugh, D. M. and Rubert, E. (1985), 'The capacity of animals to acquire language: do species differences have anything to say to us', *Philosophical Transactions of the Royal Society, B*, vol. 308, pp. 177–85. *379*

Scalia, F. and Ebbesson, S. O. E. (1971), 'The central projections of the olfactory bulb in a teleost *(Gymnothrax funebris)*', *Brain, Behaviour and Evolution*, vol. 4, pp. 376–99. *187*

Schaller, G. B. (1963), *The Mountain Gorilla: Ecology and Behaviour*, University of Chicago Press. *206–7, 346, 352*

Scharrer, E. (1928), 'Die Lichtempfindlichkeit blinder Erlitzen', *Zeitschrift für Vergleichende Physiologie*, vol. 7, pp. 1–38. *152*

Schmidt, J. T., Cicerone, C. M. and Easter, S. S. (1978), 'Expansion of the half-retinal projection to the tectum of the goldfish: an electro-physiological and anatomical study', *Journal of Comparative Neurology*, vol. 177, pp. 257–78. *142*

Schmidt-Koenig, K. and Keeton, W. T. (eds) (1978), *Animal Migration, Navigation and Homing*, Berlin: Springer-Verlag. *198*

Schopenhauer, A. (1883), *The World as Will and Idea*, vols I and II, trans. R. B. Haldane and I. Kemp, London: Kegan Paul, Trench, Trubner. *34–8*

Schopenhauer, A. (1915), *On the Fourfold Root of the Principle of Sufficient Reason and On the Will in Nature*, London: G. Bell. *34–8*

Schopenhauer, A. (1974), *Parerga and Paralipomena*, Oxford: Clarendon Press. *34–8*

Scott, J. P. (1962), 'Critical periods in behavioural development', *Science*, vol. 138, pp. 949–58. *220*

Scoville, W. B. and Milner, B. (1957), 'Loss of recent memory after bilateral hippocampal lesions', *Journal of Neurology, Neruosurgery and Psychiatry*, vol. 20, pp. 11-21. *320*

Sebeok, T. A. and Umiker-Sebeok, J. (1980), *Speaking of Apes: A Critical Anthology of Two-Way Communication with Man*, London: Plenum Press. *372*

Segaar, J. (1965), 'Behavioural aspects of degeneration and regeneration in fish brains: a comparison with higher vertebrates', *Progress in Brain Research*, vol. 14, pp. 143–231. *141*

Seidenberg, M. S. and Petitto, L. A. (1979), 'Signing behaviour in apes: a critical review', *Cognition*, vol. 7, pp. 177–215. *356, 364, 372*

Selfridge, O. G. (1959), 'Pandemonium: a paradigm for learning', in *The Mechanization of Thought Processes*, London: HMSO, pp. 511–27 (reprinted in P. C. Dodwell (ed.), *Perceptual Learning and Adaptation*, Harmondsworth: Penguin Books, 1970). *251*

Seligman, M. E. P. (1970), 'On the generality of the laws of learning', *Psychological Review*, vol. 77, pp. 406–18. *223*

Semmes, J. (1968), 'Hemispheric specialization: A possible clue to mechanism', *Neuropsychologia*, vol. 6, pp. 11–26. *171*

Semon, R. (1921), *The Mneme*, London: Allen & Unwin. *318*

Servit, Z. and Strejckova, A. (1970), 'An electrographic epileptic focus in the fish forebrain: conditions and pathways of propagation of focal and paroxysmal activity', *Brain Research*, vol. 17, pp. 103–13.

Seward, J. P. (1949), 'An experimental analysis of latent learning', *Journal of Experimental Psychology*, vol. 39, pp. 177–86. *81*

Seyfarth, R. M., Cheney, D. L. and Marler, P. (1980), 'Monkey responses to three different alarm calls: evidence of predator classification and semantic communication', *Science*, vol. 210, pp. 801–3. *353*

Shallice, T. (1972), 'Dual functions of consciousness', *Psychological Review*, vol. 79, pp. 383–99. *83, 384*

Shapiro, C. M. and Hepburn, H. R. (1976), 'Sleep in a schooling fish, *Tilapia Mossambica*', *Physiology and Behaviour*, vol. 16, pp. 613–15. *232*

Sharma, S. C. (1972), 'Reformation of retinotectal projections after various tectal ablations in adult goldfish', *Experimental Neurology*, vol. 34, pp. 171–82. *142*

Sherrington, C. S. (1906), *The Integrative Action of the Nervous System*, New Haven: Yale University Press (reprinted 1961). *147, 326–7*

Sherrington, C. S. (1940), *Man on his Nature*. Cambridge University Press. *11, 17*

Shettleworth, S.J. and Krebs, J.R. (1982), 'How marsh tits find their hoards: the roles of site preferance and spatial memory', *Journal of Experimental Psychology: Animal Behavior Processes*, vol. 8, pp. 354–75. *313*

Simpson, G. G. (1953), *The Major Features of Evolution*, New York: Columbia University Press. *123, 134–5, 146, 195, 207*

Sinnamon, H. M., Freniere, S. and Kootz, J. (1978), 'Rat hippocampus and memory for places of changing significance', *Journal of Comparative and Physiological Psychology*, vol. 92, pp. 142–55. *292, 322*

Skinner, B. F. (1938), *The Behaviour of Organisms*, New York: Appleton-Century-Crofts. *83–94*

Skinner, B. F. (1950), 'Are theories of learning necessary?', *Psychological Review*, vol. 57, pp. 193–216. *85, 94*

Skinner, B. F. (1975), 'The shaping of phylogenetic behaviour', *Journal of the Experimental Analysis of Behaviour*, vol. 24, pp. 117–20.

Skinner, B. F. (1977), 'Herrnstein and the evolution of behaviourism', *American Psychologist*, vol. 32, pp. 1006–12. *85*

Skinner, B. F. (1979), *The Shaping of a Behaviourist*, New York: Knopf.

Sluckin, W. (1964), *Imprinting and Early Learning*, London: Methuen. *212*

Smart, J. J. C. (1963), *Philosophy and Scientific Realism*, London: Routledge & Kegan Paul.

Smeets, W. J. A. J. and Nieuwenhuys, R. (1976), 'Topological analysis of the brainstem of the sharks *Squalus acanthias* and *Scyliorhinus canicula*', *Journal of Comparative Neurology*, vol. 165, pp. 333–68. *233*

Smith, G. Elliot (1910), 'Some problems relating to the evolution of the brain', *Lancet*, vol. 88, pp. 1–16. *126*

Smith, J. M. (1974), 'The theory of games and the evolution of animal conflict', *Journal of Theoretical Biology*, vol. 47, pp. 209–21.

Smith, L. (1967), 'Delayed discrimination and delayed matching in pigeons', *Journal of the Experimental Analysis of Behaviour*, vol. 10, pp. 529–33. *302–3, 313*

Snyder, F. (1966), 'Toward an evolutionary theory of dreaming', *American Journal of Psychiatry*, vol. 123, pp. 121–36. *231*

Sokolov, E. N. (1963), *Perception and the Conditioned Reflex*, Oxford: Pergamon Press. *311*

Sokolov, E. N. (1975), 'The neuronal mechanisms of the orienting reflex', in E. N. Sokolov and O. S. Vinogradova (eds), *Neuronal Mechanisms of the Orienting Reflex*, Hillsdale: Lawrence Erlbaum, pp. 217–35. *311, 326*

Sokoloff, L. (1975), 'Influence of functional activity on local cerebral glucose utilization', in D. H. Ingvar and N. A. Lassen (eds), *Brain Work: The Coupling of Function, Metabolism and Blood Flow in the Brain*, New York: Academic Press, pp. 385–8. *128*

Sommeroff, G. (1974), *Logic of the Living Brain*, London: Wiley. *143*

Spear, P. D. (1979), 'Behavioural and neurophysiological consequences of visual cortex damage: mechanisms of recovery', in J. M. Sprague and A. N. Epstein (eds), *Progress in Psychobiology and Physiological Psychology*, vol. 8, New York: Academic Press, pp. 45–90.

Spence, K. W. (1936), 'The nature of discrimination learning in animals', *Psychological Review*, vol. 43, pp. 427–49. *246, 316*

Spence, K. W. (1952), 'Clark Leonard Hull: 1884–1952', *American Journal of Psychology*, vol. 65, pp. 639–46. *74*

Spence, K. W. and Lippit, R. (1946), 'An experimental test of the sign-Gestalt theory of trial-and-error learning', *Journal of Experimental Psychology*, vol. 36, pp. 491–502. *81*

Standing, L., Conezio, J. and Haber, R. N. (1970), 'Perception and memory for pictures: single trial learning of 2500 visual stimuli', *Psychonomic Science*, vol. 19, pp. 73–4. *306*

Starr, A. and Phillips, L. (1970), 'Visual and motor memory in the Mnestic syndrome', *Neuropsychologia*, vol. 8, pp. 75–88. *321*

Stebbins, G. L. (1969), *The Basis of Progressive Evolution*, Chapel Hill: University of North Carolina Press. *119, 180*

Stepien, L. S., Cordeau, J. P. and Rasmussen, T. (1960), 'The effect of temporal lobe and hippocampal lesions on auditory and visual recent memory in monkeys', *Brain*, vol. 83, pp. 470–89. *305*

Stettner, L. J. (1974), 'The neural basis of avian discrimination and reversal learning', in I. J. Goodman and M. W. Schein (eds), *Birds: Brain and Behaviour*, New York: Academic Press, pp. 165–201. *158, 186, 331*

Stevenson, J., Hutchison, R. E., Hutchison, J., Bertram, B. L. R. and Thorpe, W. H. (1970), 'Individual recognition by auditory cues in the Common Tern (*Sterna hirundo*)', *Nature*, London, vol. 226, pp. 562–3. *214–6*

Strong, P. N. and Hedges, M. (1966), 'Comparative studies of simple oddity learning: I. Cats, raccoons, monkeys, and chimpanzees', *Psychonomic Science*, vol. 5, pp. 13–14. *261*

Sutherland, N. S. (1959), 'Stimulus analysing mechanisms', in *Proceedings of a Symposium on the Mechanisation of Thought Processes*', vol. 2, London: HMSO, pp. 575–609. *251*

Sutherland, N. S. (1968), 'Outlines of a theory of pattern recognition in animals and man', *Proceedings of the Royal Society*, Series B, vol. 171, pp. 297–317. *251*

Sutherland, N. S. (1973), 'Object recognition', in E. C. Carterette and M. P. Friedman (eds), *Handbook of Perception*, vol. 3, New York and London: Academic Press, pp. 157–85. *284*

Sutherland, N. S. and Mackintosh, N. J. (1971), *Mechanisms of Animal Discrimination Learning*, London: Academic Press. *189, 247*

Sutherland, N. S. and Williams, L. (1969), 'Discrimination of checkerboard patterns by rats', *Quarterly Journal of Experimental Psychology*, vol. 21, pp. 77–84. *263–4*

Székely, G. (1973), 'Anatomy and synaptology of the optic tectum', in R. Jung (ed.), *Central Processing of Visual Information, Handbook of Sensory Physiology*, vol. 7, part 3, B, Berlin: Springer-Verlag, pp. 1–26. *280*

Tarr, R. S. (1977), 'Role of the amygdala in the intraspecies aggressive behaviour of the iguanid lizard, *Scleroporus occidentalis*', *Physiology and Behaviour*, vol. 18, pp. 1153–8. *191, 332*

Tauber, E. S. and Weitzman, E. D. (1969), 'Eye movements during behavioural inactivity in certain Bermuda Reef fish', *Communications in Behavioural Biology*, vol. 3, pp. 131–5. *232*

Tauber, E. S., Roffwarg, H. P. and Weitzmann, E. P. (1966), 'Eye movements and electroencephalogram activity during sleep in diurnal lizards', *Nature* (London), vol. 212, pp. 1612–13. *233*

Tauber, E. S., Rojas-Ramirez, J. and Hernandez-Peon, R. (1968), 'Electro-physiological and behavioural correlates of sleep and wakefullness in the lizard *tenosaura pectinata*', *Electroencephalography and Clinical Neurophysiology*, vol. 24, pp. 424–33. *233*

Tenaza, R. and Marler, P. (1977), 'Signaling behaviour of apes with special reference to vocalization', in T. A. Seboek (ed.), *How Animals Communicate*, Bloomington: Indiana University Press, pp. 965–1033. *45, 353*

Tenaza, R. R. and Tilson, R. L. (1977), 'Evolution of long-distance alarm-call in Kloss's gibbon', *Nature*, vol. 268, pp. 233–5. *45, 353*

Terrace, H. S. (1963), 'Errorless transfer of a discrimination across two continua', *Journal of the Experimental Analysis of Behaviour*, vol. 6, pp. 223–32. *259*

Terrace, H. S. (1979), 'Is problem solving language?', *Journal of the Experimental Analysis of Behaviour*, vol. 31, pp. 161–75. *364, 372, 376*

Terrace, H. S. (1980), *Nim*, London: Eyre Methuen. *356*

Terrace, H. S., Petitto, L. A., Sanders, R. J., and Bever, T. G. (1979), 'Can an ape create a sentence', *Science*, vol. 206, pp. 891–902. *354–6, 372–4*

Thomson, R. K. R. and Herman, L. M. (1977), 'Memory for lists of sounds by bottle-nose dolphins: convergence of memory processes with humans?', *Science*, vol. 195, pp. 501–3.

Thorndike, E. L. (1898), 'Animal intelligence: An experimental study of the associative processes in animals', *Psychological Review, Monograph Supplements*, vol. 2, no. 8, pp. 1–109. *48, 64*

Thorndike, E. L. (1905), *The Elements of Psychology*, New York: A. G. Seller. *65*

Thorndike, E. L. (1913), *Educational Psychology*, New York: Teachers College. *65*

Thorpe, W. H. (1961), *Bird Song*, Cambridge University Press. *214*

Thorpe, W. H. (1966), 'Ritualization in the individual development of bird song', *Philosophical Transactions of the Royal Society*, Series B, vol. 251, pp. 351–50. *216*

Thorpe, W. H. (1972), 'Dueting and antiphonal song in birds: its extent and significance', *Behaviour: Monograph Supplement*, no. 18, pp. 1–197. *216-7*

Thorpe, W. H. (1974), *Animal Nature and Human Nature*, London: Methuen. *216*

Tilney, F. (1928), *The Brain from Ape to Man*, vol. 2, London: H. K. Lewis. *353*

Tinbergen, N. (1951), *A Study of Instinct*, Oxford University Press. *32, 200, 213*

Tinbergen, N. (1953), *The Herring Gull's World*, London: Collins. *201, 214*

Tinbergen, N. and Kuenen, D. J. (1957), 'Feeding behaviour in young thrushes', in C. H. Schiller (ed. and trans.), *Instinctive Behaviour: Development of a Modern Concept*, London: Methuen, pp. 209–36. *213, 216*

Tinbergen, N. and Perdeck, A. C. (1950), 'On the stimulus situation releasing the begging response in the newly-hatched herring gull chick (*Larus argentatus argentatus Pont*)', *Behaviour*, vol. 3, pp. 1–39.

Tolman, E. C. (1922), 'A new formula for behaviourism', *Psychological Review*, vol. 29, pp. 44–53. *79*

Tolman, E. C., (1925), 'Purpose and cognition: the determiners of animal learning', *Psychological Review*, vol. 32, pp. 285–97. *79, 81*

Tolman, E. C. (1926), 'A behaviouristic theory of ideas', *Psychological Review*, vol. 33, pp. 352–69. *79*

Tolman, E. C. (1927), 'A behaviourist's definition of consciousness', *Psychological Review*, vol. 34, pp. 433–9. *81, 83*

Tolman, E. C. (1932), *Purposive Behaviour in Animals and Men*, New York: Century. *75, 82, 111, 190*

Tolman, E. C. (1933), 'Sign-Gestalt or conditioned reflex?', *Psychological Review*, vol. 40, pp. 246–55. *82*

Tolman, E. C. (1937), 'The acquisition of string-pulling by rats—conditioned reflex or sign gestalt?', *Psychological Review*, vol. 44, pp. 195–211. *85-6*

Tolman, E. C. (1942), *Drives toward War*, New York: Appleton-Century. *80*

Tolman, E. C. (1948), 'Cognitive maps in rats and men', *Psychological Review*, vol. 55, pp. 189–208. *75*

Tolman, E. C. (1949), 'There is more than one kind of learning',

Psychological Review, vol. 56, pp. 144–55. *75, 190*

Tolman, E. C. (1959), 'Principles of purposive behaviour', in S. Koch (ed.), *Psychology: A Study of a Science*, vol. 2, New York: McGraw-Hill, pp. 92–157. *81*

Tolman, E. C. and Gleitman, H. (1949), 'Studies of learning and motivation: I. Equal reinforcements in both end-boxes, followed by shock in one end box', *Journal of Experimental Psychology*, vol. 39, pp. 810–19. *81*

Tolman, E. C. and Honzik, C. H. (1930a), '"Insight" in rats', *University of California Publications in Psychology*, vol. 4, pp. 215–32. *77–8*

Tolman, E. C. and Honzik, C. H. (1930b), 'Introduction and removal of reward, and maze learning in rats', *University of California Publications in Psychology*, vol. 4, pp. 257–75. *80*

Tolman, E. C., Ritchie, B. F. and Kalish, D. (1946), 'Studies in spatial learning II: Place learning versus response learning', *Journal of Experimental Psychology*, vol. 36, pp. 221–9. *76*

Tower, D. B. (1954), 'Structural and functional organization of mammalian cerebral cortex: the correlation of neuron density and brain size', *Journal of Comparative Neurology*, vol. 101, pp. 19–51. *139*

Tower, D. B. and Young, O. M. (1973), 'The activities of butyrylcholinesterase and carbon anhydrase, the rate of anaerobic glycolysis, and the question of a constant density of glial cells in cerebral cortices of mammalian species from mouse to whale', *Journal of Neurochemistry*, vol. 20, pp. 269–78. *139*

Tradardi, V. (1966), 'Sleep in the pigeon', *Archives Italiennes de Biologie*, vol. 104, pp. 516–21. *231*

Trapold, M. A. (1970), 'Are expectancies based upon different positive reinforcing events discriminably different?', *Learning and Motivation*, vol. 1, pp. 129–40. *103*

Turing, A. M. (1950), 'Computing machinery and intelligence', *Mind*, vol. 59, pp. 433–60. *9*

Twitmeyer, E. B. (1902), *A Study of the Knee-Jerk*, Philadelphia: Winston. *67*

Ullman, M. (1959), 'The adaptive significance of the dream', *Journal of Nervous and Mental Disorders*, vol. 129, pp. 144–9.

Umiker, Sebeok, J. and Sebeok, T. A. (1980), 'Introduction: questioning apes', in T. A. Sebeok and J. Umiker-Sebeok (eds), *Speaking of Apes: A Critical Anthology of Two-way Communication with Man*, London: Plenum Press, pp. 1–59. *372*

Urcuioli, P. J. (1977), 'Transfer of oddity from sample performance in pigeons', *Journal of the Experimental Analysis of Behaviour*, vol. 27, pp. 195–202. *261*

Urcuioli, P. J. and Nevin, J. A. (1975), 'Transfer of hue matching in pigeons', *Journal of the Experimental Analysis of Behavior*, vol. 24, pp. 149–55.

Uzigiris, I. C. and Hunt, J. McV. (1974), *Towards Ordinal Scales of Psychological Development in Infancy*, University of Illinois Press. *341*

Valenstein, E. S., Cox, V. C. and Kakalewski, J. W. (1970), 'Reexamination of the role of the hypothalamus in motivation', *Psychological Review*, vol. 77, pp. 16–31. *129, 224*

Vanderwolf, C. H., Kolls, B. and Cooley, R. K. (1978), 'Behaviour of the rat after the removal of the neocortex and hippocampal formation', *Journal of Comparative and Physiological Psychology*, vol. 92, pp. 156–75. *336*

Van Essen, D. C. and Zeki, S. M. (1978), 'The topographic organization of prestriate cortex', *Journal of Physiology* (London), vol. 277, pp. 193–266.

Van Iersel, J. J. A., (1953), 'An analysis of the parental behaviour of the male three-spined stickleback (*Gasterosteus aculeatus* L.)', *Behaviour Supplements*, vol. 3, pp. 1–159. *200*

Van Twyver, H. and Allison, T. (1970), 'Sleep in the oppossum *Didelphis marsupialis*', *Electroencephalography and Clinical Neurology*, vol. 29, pp. 181–9. *229*

Vaughter, R. M., Smotherman, W. and Ordy, J. M. (1972), 'Development of object permanence in the squirrel monkey', *Developmental Psychology*, vol. 7, pp. 34–8. *97*

Vesselkin, N. P., Agayan, A. L. and Nomokonova, L. M. (1971), 'A study of thalamo-telencephalic afferent systems in frogs', *Brain Behaviour and Evolution*, vol. 4, pp. 295–306. *187*

Victor, M., Adams, R. and Collins, G. H. (1971), *The Wernicke-Korsakoff Syndrome*, Philadelphia: F. A. Davis Co. *320*

Vinogradova, O. S. (1975), 'The hippocampus and the orienting reflex', in E. N. Sokolov and O. S. Vinogradova (eds), *Neuronal Mechanisms of the Orienting Reflex*, Hillsdale: Lawrence Erlbaum, pp. 128–54. *326*

Von Neumann, J. (1951), 'The general and logical theory of automata', in L. A. Jeffries (ed.), *Cerebral Mechanisms in Behaviour*, New York: Wiley, pp. 1–41. *130, 139*

Vygotsky, L. S. (1962), *Thought and Language*, Cambridge, Mass.: MIT Press. *377*

Walker, J. M. and Berger, R. J. (1973), 'A polygraphic study of the tortoise (*Testudo denticulata*): absence of electrophysiological signs of sleep', *Brain, Behaviour and Evolution*, vol. 8, 453–67. *232-3*

Walker, S. F. (1975), *Learning and Reinforcement*, London: Methuen. *89*

Walker, S. F. (1980), 'Lateralization of functions in the vertebrate brain: a review', *British Journal of Psychology*, vol. 71, pp. 329–67. *168, 173*

Walker, S. F. (1981), 'Necessary asymmetries in bilaterally symmetrical brains', *Speculations in Science and Technology*, vol. 10, pp. 575–8. *165*

Walls, G. L. (1942), *The Vertebrate Eye*, Broomfield Hills: Cranbrook Institute of Science. *160, 267*

Walther, F. R. (1972), 'Social grouping of Grant's gazelle (*Gazella grant* 1872) in the Serengetti National Park', *Zeitschrift für Tierpsychologie*, vol. 31, pp. 348–403. *218*

Warburton, D. (1975), *Brain, Behaviour and Drugs: Introduction to the Neurochemistry of Behaviour*, London: Wiley. *128*

Warren, J. M. (1961), 'The effect of telencephalic injuries on learning by Paradise fish, *Macrapodus opercularis*', *Journal of Comparative and Physiological Psychology*, vol. 54, pp. 130–2.

Warren, J. M. (1974), 'Learning in vertebrates', in D. A. Dewsbury and D. Rethlingshlaffer (eds), *Comparative Psychology: A Modern Survey*, New York: McGraw-Hill, pp. 471–509. *179*

Warren, J. M. (1977), 'Handedness and cerebral dominance in monkeys', in S. Harnad, R. W. Doty, L. Goldstein, J. Jaynes and G. Krauthamek (eds), *Lateralization in the Nervous System*, London: Academic Press, pp. 151–72.

Warrington, E. (1974), 'Deficient recognition memory in organic amnesia', *Cortex*, vol. 10, pp. 289–91. *322*

Warrington, E. K. and Pratt, R. T. (1973), 'Language laterality in lefthanders assessed by unilateral E.C.T.', *Neuropsychologia*, vol. 11, pp. 423–8. *168*

Warrington, E. K. and Weiskrantz, L. (1973), 'An analysis of short-term and long-term memory defects in man', in J. A. Deutsch (ed.), *The Physiological Basis of Memory*, New York: Academic Press, pp. 365–95. *320*

Waser, M. S. and Marler, P. (1977), 'Song learning in canaries', *Journal of Comparative and Physiological Psychology*, vol. 91, pp. 1–7 *215*

Wasserman, E. A. (1976), 'Successive matching-to-sample in the pigeon: variation on a theme by Konorski', *Behaviour Research Methods and Instrumentation*, vol. 8, pp. 278–82. *305*

Watkins, J. W. N. (1973), *Hobbes's System of Ideas*, 2nd edn, London: Hutchinson. *13*

Webster, K. E. (1973), 'Thalamus and basal ganglia in reptiles and birds', *Symposia of the Zoological Society of London*, no. 33, pp. 169–203. *153–4, 158*

Webster, W. G. (1977), 'Hemispheric asymmetry in cats', in S. Harnad, R. W. Doty, L. Goldstein, J. Jaynes and G. Kranthamer (eds), *Lateralization in the Nervous System*, New York: Academic Press, pp. 471–80.

Weidmann, U. (1961), 'The stimuli eliciting begging in gulls and terns', *Animal Behaviour*, vol. 9, pp. 115–16. *212*

Weiner, J. S. (1971), *Man's Natural History*, London: Weidenfeld & Nicolson. *196*

Weiskrantz, L. (1961), 'Encephalization and the scomata', in W. H. Thorpe and O. L. Zangwill (eds), *Current Problems in Animal Behaviour*, Cambridge University Press, pp. 30–58. *146–9, 178*

Weiskrantz, L. (1968), 'Memory', in L. Weiskrantz (ed.), *Analysis of Behavioural Change*, New York: Harper & Row, pp. 158–88. *291–2*

Weiskrantz, L. (1972), 'Behavioural analysis of the monkey's visual system', *Proceedings of the Royal Society of London*, Series B, vol. 182, pp. 427–55. *278*

Weiskrantz, L. (1974), 'The interaction between occipital and temporal cortex in vision: an overview', in F. O. Schmitt and F. G. Worden (eds), *The Neurosciences: Third Study Program*, London: MIT Press, pp. 189–204. *277*

Weiskrantz, L. (1977), 'Trying to bridge some neuropsychological gaps between monkey and man', *British Journal of Psychology*, vol. 68, pp. 431–45. *110, 183, 189, 282, 319, 321, 325–6, 331, 383*

Weiskrantz, L. (1980), 'Varieties of residual experience', *Quarterly Journal of Experimental Psychology*, vol. 33, pp. 365–86. *282*

Weiskrantz, L. and Warrington, E. K. (1975), 'The problem of the amnesic syndrome in man and animals', in R. L. Isaacson and K. H.

pp. 411–27. *319, 321, 326*
Weisman, R. G., Wasserman, E. A., Dodd, P. W. D. (1980),
'Representation and retention of two-event sequences in pigeons',
Journal of Experimental Psychology: Animal Behaviour Processes, vol. 6,
pp. 312–25. *305*
Welker, C. (1976), 'Receptive fields of barrels in the somato-sensory
neocortex of the rat', *Journal of Comparative Neurology*, vol. 166,
pp. 173–90. *129*
Welker, W. I., Adrian, H. O., Lifschitz, W., Kaulen, R., Caviedes, E. and
Gutman, W. (1976), 'Somatic sensory, cortex of llama *(Lama glama)*',
Brain, Behaviour and Evolution, vol. 13, pp. 284–93. *203*
Wertheimer, G. and McKee, S. P. (1977), 'Perception of temporal order
in adjacent visual stimuli', *Vision Research*, vol. 17, pp. 887–92. *268*
Wilkes, K. V. (1978), *Physicalism*, London: Routledge & Kegan Paul. *18*
Williams, B. (1978), *Descartes: The Project of Pure Enquiry*, Hassocks,
Sussex: Harvester Press. *12*
Wilson, B. (1978), 'Complex learning in birds', unpublished thesis,
University of Sussex. *261*
Wilson, E. O. (1975), *Sociobiology*, Cambridge, Mass.: Harvard University
Press. *30, 99, 219*
Wilson, M. (1979), 'Visual system: Pulvinar-extrastriate cortex', in R. B.
Masterton (ed.), *Handbook of Behavioural Neurobiology*, vol. 1. *Sensory
Integration*, New York: Plenum Press, pp. 209–48. *275–7*
Wirth, F. F. and O'Leary, J. L. (1974), 'Locomotion of decerebellated
arboreal mammals—monkey and racoon', *Journal of Comparative
Neurology*, vol. 157, pp. 53–86. *202*
Wise, K. L., Wise, L. A. and Zimmerman, R. R. (1974), 'Piagetian object
permanence in the infant rhesus monkey', *Developmental Psychology*,
vol. 10, pp. 429–37.
Wittgenstein, L. (1976), *Philosophical Investigations*, Oxford: Basil Blackwell.
24
Woodruff, G., Premack, D. and Kennel, K. (1978), 'Conservation of
liquid and solid quality by the chimpanzee', *Science*, vol. 202, pp. 991–4.
350–2, 373
Woodruff, G. and Premack, D. (1979), 'Intentional communication in the
chimpanzee', *Cognition*, vol. 7, pp. 333–62. *370*
Woolsey, C. N. (1965), 'Organization of somatic sensory and motor areas
of the cerebral cortex', in H. F. Harlow and C. N. Woolsey (eds),
Biological and Biochemical Bases of Behaviour, Madison: University of
Wisconsin Press, pp. 63–81. *107, 129, 177*
Wright, A. A., Santiago, A. C. and Sands, S. F. (1984), 'Monkey memory:
Same/Different concept learning, serial probe acquisition, and probe delay
effects', *Journal of Experimental Psychology, Animal Behavior Processes*, vol. 10, pp.
513–29. *311*
Wundt, W. (1894), *Lectures on Human and Animal Psychology*, London: Swan
Sonnenschein. *59*
Yarczower, M. and Hazlett, L. (1977), 'Evolutionary scales and
anagenesis', *Psychological Bulletin*. vol. 84, pp. 1088–97. *116, 121*
Yeni-Komshian, G. and Benson, D. (1976), 'Anatomical study of cerebral

asymmetry in the temporal lobe of humans, chimpanzees and rhesus monkeys', *Science*, vol. 192, pp. 387–9. *173*

Yerkes, R. M. and Yerkes, D. N. (1928), 'Concerning memory in the chimpanzee', *Journal of Comparative Psychology*, vol. 8, pp. 237–71. *292*

Yolen, N. M., and Hodos, W. (1976), 'Behavioural correlates of "tectal compression" in goldfish: I. Instensity and pattern discrimination', *Brain, Behaviour and Evolution*, vol. 13, pp. 451–67. *142*

Yori, J. G. (1978), 'Active one-way avoidance to a heat aversion stimulus in Tegu lizards *(Tupinambus teguixen)*', *Behavioural Biology*, vol. 23, pp. 100–6. *196*

Young, J. Z. (1962), *The Life of Vertebrates*, Oxford University Press. *124, 207*

Zeier, H. (1974), 'Behavioural adaptation on operant schedules after forebrain lesions in the pigeon', in I. J. Goodman and M. W. Schein (eds), *Birds: Brain and Behaviour*, New York: Academic Press, pp. 153–64. *331*

Zeier, H. (1975), 'Interhemispheric interactions', in P. Wright, P. G. Caryl and D. M. Vowles (eds), *Neural and Endocrine Aspects of Behaviour in Birds*, Amsterdam: Elsevier, pp. 163–80.

Zeigler, H. P., Hollard, V., Wild, J. M., and Webster, D. M. (1978), 'Intracranial self-stimulation from endbrain nuclei in the pigeon *(Columba livia)*', *Physiology and Behaviour*, vol. 21, pp. 387–94. *224*

Zeki, S. M. (1978a), 'Functional specialization in the visual cortex of the rhesus monkey', *Nature*, vol. 274, pp. 423–8. *272, 276*

Zeki, S. M. (1978b), 'Uniformity and diversity of structure and function in rhesus monkey prestriate visual cortex', *Journal of Physiology*, London, vol. 277, pp. 273–90. *276*

Zentall, T. and Hogan, D. (1974), 'Abstract concept learning in the pigeon', *Journal of Experimental Psychology*, vol. 102, pp. 393–8.

Zentall, T., Hogan, D. and Holder, J. (1974), 'Comparison of two oddity tasks with pigeons', *Learning and Motivation*, vol. 5, pp. 106–17. *261*

Zentall, T. R., Hogan, D. E., Edwards, C. A. and Hearst, E. (1980), 'Oddity learning in the pigeon as a function of the number of incorrect alternatives', *Journal of Experimental Psychology: Animal Behaviour Processes*, vol. 6, pp. 278–99. *262–4*

Zepelin, H. and Rechtschaffen, A. (1974), 'Mammalian sleep, longevity and energy metabolism', *Brain, Behaviour and Evolution*, vol. 10, pp. 425–70. *234*

Zihlman, A. L., Cronin, J. E., Cramer, D. L. and Sarich, V. M. (1978), 'Pigmy chimpanzee as a possible prototype for the common ancestor of humans, chimpanzees and gorillas' *Nature*, vol. 275, pp. 744–6. *339*

Zottoli, S. J. (1978), 'Comparison of Mauthner cell size in teleosts', *Journal of Comparative Neurology*, vol. 178, pp. 741–51. *142*

Index